Archibald Manson

The Spiritual Illumination of the Gentiles,

Coeval with the Conversion of the Jews

Archibald Manson

The Spiritual Illumination of the Gentiles,
Coeval with the Conversion of the Jews

ISBN/EAN: 9783337148522

Printed in Europe, USA, Canada, Australia, Japan

Cover: Foto ©Lupo / pixelio.de

More available books at **www.hansebooks.com**

THE SPIRITUAL ILLUMINATION OF THE GENTILES, COEVAL WITH THE CONVERSION OF THE JEWS.

A SERMON,

THE SUBSTANCE OF WHICH WAS DELIVERED,

ON SEPTEMBER 13th, 1814,

BEFORE THE

COMMITTEE AND MEMBERS

OF

Wishawtown District of the Bible Association,

IN THE PARISH OF CAMBUSNETHAN,

AND

PUBLISHED AT THEIR DESIRE.

By ARCHIBALD MASON,

MINISTER OF THE CONGREGATION OF OLD DISSENTERS AT WISHAWTOWN.

"A light to lighten the Gentiles, and the glory of thy people Israel."
LUKE ii. 32.

GLASGOW:

Printed by Jack & Gallie,

FOR M. OGLE, 8, WILSON-STREET; JOHN OGLE, OLIPHANT, WAUGH AND INNES, EDINBURGH; OGLES, DUNCAN, AND COCHRANE, LONDON; G. CUTHBERTSON, PAISLEY; W. SCOTT, GREENOCK; AND R. MATHIE, KILMARNOCK.

1814.

A MINUTE OF COMMITTEE.

The Members of the Sub-committee, of Cambusnethan Bible Association, appointed for Wishawtown District, feel grateful to their Preses, the Rev. Archibald Mason, for the interesting and appropriate Sermon delivered by him, on the evening of the 13th September, at their desire; and cordially join with the Audience of that night, in requesting him to allow the Sermon to be printed, for the promotion of the cause in which we are engaged.

ARCHIBALD MORTON, Sec.

Wishawtown,
27*th Sept.* 1814.

A SERMON, &c.

ISAIAH xxx. 26.

" *Moreover, the light of the moon shall be as the light of the sun, and the light of the sun shall be sevenfold, as the light of seven days, in the day that the Lord bindeth up the breach of his people, and healeth the stroke of their wound.*"

AN exceeding great and precious promise of God to the children of men, and a description of the time when he will accomplish it to them, are contained in this text.

The promise is recorded in the beginning of the verse. " The light of the moon shall be as the light of the sun, and the light of the sun shall be sevenfold, as the light of seven days." These words may be considered either as a promise or a prediction. As a divine promise, they exhibit to us an unspeakable blessing, which the Lord has graciously engaged to bestow on the nations, at the appointed season. As a divine prediction, they foretell a glorious change, which the Lord shall produce among men, at the latter day. These expressions are metaphorical. As spiritual blessings are often represented, in Scripture, by the light of the sun, and the moon; so the natural light of this world is employed in the text, to represent the spiritual light of the gospel, which brings salvation to men. This light is promised, not to the Jews only, but to the Gentiles also. When this promise shall be accomplished, Jesus will be a light to lighten the Gentiles, as well as he will be the glory of his people Israel. This promise has a peculiar respect to the Gentiles. As the sun and the moon are the ordinance of God, for enlightening the whole world; so when Christ, the Sun of Righteousness, shall arise on men, in the glory of his gospel and grace, he will diffuse his radiant beams, over all the nations of the Gentiles. These nations are divided into two classes —the nations who are destitute of the word and gospel of Christ, and are in gross darkness; and the nations that are in possession of those precious blessings. Both of these are the objects of this promise. On the former, this light shall be bestowed, and to the latter, it shall be greatly increased. The meaning of the promise, or prediction, appears to be this. When this promise is fulfilled, there shall be as great a change produced on the religious and moral world, as there would be in the natural world. were the moon, in the season of the night, to blaze like the meridian sun, and the sun, during the day, to shine with sevenfold brightness, concentrating, into one day, the light and splendour of seven.

The time when this promise shall be fulfilled, is described in the end of the verse. " In the day that the Lord bindeth up the breach of his people, and healeth the stroke of their wound." The people whose breach the Lord binds up, and the stroke of whose wound he heals, are the people of the God of Abraham, the posterity of Jacob, who were formerly his peculiar people. This title, his people, generally signifies, in the Old Testament Scriptures, the chosen nation of Israel, in opposition to all the other nations of the world, which are usually called, *the people*, *the nations*, *the Gentiles.* For the happy time in which those things shall be fulfilled, we are not to look, either to the day when the army of Sennacherib, in the reign of Hezekiah, was, by the power of God, miraculously destroyed; or to the day when the captives of Judah were delivered from their bondage in Babylon. The expressions in the text are too grand and sublime, to have their accomplishment in these events, or in their consequences. We cannot look for the accomplishment of this prediction, even to the days of the apostles. After the resurrection of our Redeemer, who is over all God blessed for ever, such a change indeed was effected in the church, that the light of the moon was as the light of the sun, and the light of the sun was sevenfold, as the light of seven days. The gospel was preached to the Gentile nations, and multitudes embraced the faith of Jesus. The people who sat in darkness saw a great light, and to them who dwelt in the region of the shadow of death, did light spring up. At this most eventful day, however, the Lord did not bind up the breach of his people, nor heal the stroke of their wound. It was rather the day, when the Jewish nation, for their iniquity, was broken with this dreadful breach, and received the stroke which produced that wound, under which they have languished for near eighteen hundred years. We are, therefore, constrained, for the complete fulfilment of these things, to look forward to those blessed days which are promised to the church, when, to use the words of the apostle, the natural branches shall be grafted into their own olive; when, through the mercy of the Gentiles, the Jews shall obtain mercy, when the fulness of the Gentiles shall come in, and when all Israel shall be saved. The day, in which the Lord shall bind up this breach, and heal the wound of his ancient people, shall be the time, when the light of the moon shall be as the light of the sun, and the light of the sun shall be sevenfold, as the light of seven days, to the Gentile nations.

The text, therefore, unfolds to our view this interesting truth,—All the nations of the Gentiles shall be spiritually enlightened, at the conversion of the Jews.

In discussing this subject, it is proposed, I. To illustrate the nature of the spiritual change, which shall be produced on the nations, as it is represented by the metaphor that is used in the text; II. To mention some of the blessings that are contained in this promise; III. To describe the manner in which it shall be accomplished; and IV. To explain the character of that day, when this promise or prediction shall be fulfilled, in the day when the Lord bindeth up the breach of his people, and healeth the stroke of their wound.

I. It is proposed to illustrate the nature of the spiritual change which shall be produced on the Gentile nations, when the light of the moon shall be as the light of the sun, and the light of the sun shall be sevenfold, as the light of seven days.

1*st*, This metaphor represents the spiritual change, that is signified by it, to be new and unprecedented. The moon's shining as the sun, and the sun's shining with sevenfold more brightness than ordinary, would produce phenomena in nature, which would be altogether singular and extraordinary. The blessed change, in like manner, which the church shall then experience, will be unexampled, and without a parallel. The singularity of the case does not consist in the shining of the sun and the moon; for they have shone on the earth from the beginning; but it consists in the extraordinary degree of their shining. So this extraordinary change does not consist in the shining of spiritual light upon men, for this has at all times been the church's enjoyment, but it consists in the peculiar degree of spiritual light, which shall then break forth on the nations. When the blessing signified by this metaphor, shall be conferred on men, the Lord will create a new thing in the earth. The glory of that light shall transcend all former examples. As far as the light of the moon, when shining like the sun, would exceed the light she has always reflected on the earth; so far will the light of the church, at that time, excel any of her enjoyments of this kind, in former ages. As far as the light of seven days combined into one, would excel the light of an ordinary day; so far must the spiritual light of that season exceed the light of any of the past ages of the church. If it is not a change that is without a parallel in past times, there is neither propriety nor truth in the metaphor. Though the Lord will never produce such a change in the world of nature, as that which is mentioned in the text; he will certainly accomplish that alteration in the world of grace, of which he has made that natural change the similitude; and when it takes place, it will introduce the church into a situation, which shall be entirely new and extraordinary.

2*d*, This metaphor represents the change that is signified by it, to be productive of peculiar emotions in the minds of men. Were the moon to shine as the sun, and the sun with the light of seven days, men would be filled with fear, surprise, wonder, and astonishment. This spiritual change, which shall be produced upon the nations, will also fill the minds of christians with very extraordinary emotions, and lead them to special exercises of soul. This change will fill their hearts with holy fear and reverence. This they will express in their song of adoration, " Who shall not fear thee, O Lord, and glorify thy name, for thou only art holy," Rev. xv. 4. It will fill them with surprise and astonishment; they shall then cry out, " When the Lord turned again the captivity of Sion, we were like them that dream. Then was our mouth filled with laughter, and our tongue with singing." Psa. cxxvi. 1, 2. It will produce in them holy admiration, and cause them exclaim, " Who is like unto thee, O Lord, among the gods? who is like thee, glorious in holiness, fearful in praises, doing wonders?" Exod. xv. 11. On this extraordinary occasion, they will abound with the high praise of the Lord. This is ascribed to them, Rev. vii. 10. " And cried with a loud voice, saying, Salvation to our God, who sitteth on the throne, and unto the Lamb." O how vehemently will they utter such praise as that, Psa. cxxxvi. 4. " To him who alone doeth great wonders; for his mercy endureth for ever." They shall also be employed in giving thanks to God for his wonderful works. In the summary account of this change on the nations, which is contained in the eleventh chapter of the Revelations, this part of the church's employment is mentioned in verse 17th; " We give thee thanks, O Lord God Almighty, which art, and wast, and art to come; because thou hast taken to thee thy great power, and hast reigned." They will then be constrained to say, " Blessed be the Lord God of Israel, for he has visited and redeemed his people." Luke i. 68. The christians of those times will also overflow with joy and gladness. To this they are called, Rev. xviii. 20. " Rejoice over her, thou heaven, and ye holy apostles and prophets; for God hath avenged you on her." To this exercise they will invite one another. Rev. xix. 7. " Let us be glad, and rejoice, and give honour to him, for the marriage of the Lamb is come, and his wife hath made herself ready." Nor will these spiritual emotions, though carried to their highest pitch, be found existing in the souls of believers, without a sufficient cause. This change, when it shall be accomplished, will be so glorious in itself, so beneficial to men, and so conspicuous to all, that it will prove an abundant reason for the most enlarged exercises of this kind, in the members of the church. If it is a divine rule in the duty of christians, to render to the Lord, according to the benefit done unto them, and nothing can be more reasonable, the church, in those days, receiving from her God such special mercies, will be laid under obligations peculiarly strong, to bring the sacrifice of praise, and of every other religious duty, into the house of the Lord. For these exercises, the Members of the church, in her enlarged state, will be perfectly qualified; for the external change which shall be produced in the church, at the accomplishment of this promise, will be accompanied with a proportionate alteration in the inward spiritual condition of the saints, which will make them all fire, zeal, and life, in the service of the sanctuary.

3d, This metaphor represents the spiritual change that is signified by it, to be a glorious manifestation of God, as he is the God of grace. The change in nature, mentioned in the text, would brightly display God's glory, as he is the God of providence. He is the Creator of the sun and moon. "And God made two great lights, the greater light to rule the day, and the lesser light to rule the night." Gen. i. 16. "He giveth the sun," saith the prophet Jeremiah, "for a light by day, and the ordinances of the moon and of the stars for a light by night." Whatever these great lights are in themselves, whatever are their motions and revolutions, whatever beneficial effects they produce on the face of the earth, and whatever services they do to the creatures below, all these things are of Him who hath appointed the moon for seasons, and from whom the sun knoweth his going down. Were these great lights to shine as it is expressed in this metaphor, the glory of their Creator and Preserver would be brightly displayed. It must necessarily follow, therefore, that when this great spiritual change shall be accomplished on the church of Christ, which this metaphor represents, the glory of the God of grace and salvation will be manifested abundantly. At that desirable period, these words of Isaiah, xlv. 5, shall be fulfilled, "And the glory of the Lord shall be revealed, and all flesh shall see it together; for the mouth of the Lord hath spoken it." The revelation of the divine glory, consists in the display which Jehovah will make of himself and of his attributes, by his operations of grace among men; and all flesh seeing it together, signifies the church's perception and acknowledgment of this glory; both the one and the other shall, at that time, prevail in the world; for the mouth of the Lord hath spoken it. How will he display the glory of his sovereignty, in fixing the time of this happy state of the church, and in choosing the persons who shall enjoy it! How will the glory of his wisdom be seen in ordering the means, and bringing forward the instruments, of introducing and maintaining it! How brightly will divine power appear, in overcoming opposition, and in raising his church to the height of her prosperity and glory! How will the faithfulness of God shine forth, in fulfilling his promises to his people, in executing his threatenings on his enemies, and, in both, doing as he has said! And how will the divine love, grace, and mercy, be illustrated, in bestowing on the church and her members, in an extraordinary degree, and freely, for Christ's sake, all spiritual blessings in heavenly places! The glory of each divine person shall then conspicuously appear. At that time, all shall be convinced, that "grace and peace," in whatever degree they may be enjoyed, "come from him which is, and which was, and which is to come; and from the seven spirits which are before his throne; and from Jesus Christ, who is the faithful Witness, the first-begotten of the dead, and the Prince of the kings of the earth." Rev. i. 4, 5. As this glory shall be revealed, so also shall it be discerned and acknowledged; for of them it is said, "And they sung the song of Moses the servant of God, and the song of the Lamb, saying, Great and marvellous are thy works, Lord God Almighty; just and true are thy ways, thou King of saints."

4th, This metaphor represents the spiritual change which is signified by it, to be a peculiar display of Christ's glory, and a great increase of beauty and lustre to his church. Were the sun and the moon to shine as it is stated in the text, a glory would be drawn around the sun, and a lustre would be added to the moon, far superior to any thing that has been seen about them, since the beginning of the creation of God. In the Holy Scriptures, Christ is compared to the sun. " But unto you that fear my name shall the Sun of Righteousness arise, with healing in his wings." Mal. iv. 2. The church of Christ is also compared to the moon. " Who is she that looketh forth as the morning, fair as the moon?" Song vi. 10. By this metaphor, therefore, the enlarged manifestation of Christ's glory, and the increased lustre of his church, may be represented. At this season, his glory will be brightly displayed to the nations. If he manifested forth his glory, at the beginning of his miracles, in Cana of Galilee; will he not also display his glory, when all dominions shall serve and obey him? If he received from God the Father, honour and glory, when there came such a voice to him " from the excellent glory, This is my beloved son, hear ye him;" shall he not also receive from him honour and glory, when he shall give him the heathen for his inheritance, and the uttermost ends of the earth for his possession? The brightness of his glory will then appear to the nations, by means of his word and ordinances, rendered effectual through the operation of the Holy Spirit, for regenerating, justifying, and sanctifying all them who are saved. Christ will then appear in the glory of his divine person, and in the glory of his divine and human natures in his one person, as our Mediator. Opposition to this great mystery of godliness shall then be silenced. He will appear in the glory of his eternal engagements, to be the head and surety of the covenant of grace, and the Redeemer and Saviour of his people. He will be manifested in the glory of his offices, with which, by his Father's appointment, he is invested. He will then be universally known and acknowledged in his glory, as the great Prophet of the church, as the great High Priest of the christian profession, and as the alone King and Head of his church. The glory of Jesus in his mediatorial righteousness, for the justification of the ungodly—in his communicated fulness, for the supply of his people's wants—and in his everlasting salvation, which he bestows on his people on earth and in heaven, shall then be exceeding bright, and extensively known. The church shall then be enabled to utter these words, in a very peculiar manner, "We beheld his glory, as the glory of the only-begotten of the Father, full of grace and truth." In consequence of these discoveries of his glory, they will be constrained to say, with singular impressions on their spirits, "Unto him that loved us, and washed us from our sins in his own blood, and hath made us kings and priests unto God and his Father; to him be glory and dominion for ever and ever. Amen."

At the accomplishment of this promise, the church also, who is bright and glorious by the light of the Sun of Righteousness shining on her, and is comely through his comeliness put upon her, will appear with a lustre and beauty to which she has never formerly attained. In the purity of her doctrine, the spiritual simplicity of her ordinances, the scriptural form of her government and censures, the number of her members, the zeal and spirituality of her ministers, the holiness of her saints, and the feigned submission of her enemies, the church shall be a crown of glory in the hand of the Lord, and a royal diadem in the hand of her God.

II. Head of this Discourse, was to mention some of the blessings that are contained in this promise or prediction—"The light of the moon shall be as the light of the sun, and the light of the sun shall be sevenfold, as the light of seven days."

1*st*, This promise contains the blessing of a greater degree of knowledge in divine things. This is the plain import of the metaphorical language of the text. The increase of light is the metaphor, an increase of knowledge is the blessing signified by it. Though all true believers, in every age, have had a sufficient and saving knowledge of divine truths; yet there must have been a great difference in the degree of that knowledge, of which, in these different periods, the members of the church were possessed. In the days of the patriarchs, and under the Mosaic dispensation, the knowledge of divine mysteries, concerning our salvation by Jesus Christ, was comparatively small. As that dispensation advanced, and the church enjoyed the ministry of the prophets, the light of the knowledge of the way of salvation would gradually increase. When the Son of God had appeared in our world, and had finished the work which the Father had given him to do, the gospel of the kingdom was preached, the former darkness was dissipated, the Jewish ceremonies were set aside, the spiritual ordinances of the gospel were brought into operation; and he who commanded the light to shine out of darkness, shined into the hearts of many, to give them the light of the knowledge of his glory, in the face of Jesus Christ. As spiritual light increased, under the former dispensation; so we have reason to believe in its increase, during the evangelic economy. The path of the church, as well as that of every believer, shall be as the shining light, that shineth more and more unto the perfect day. The people who shall live in the church, when this prediction shall be fulfilled, will enjoy, in a very high degree, the knowledge of divine truths. They will clearly understand the prophecies of Scripture, by having the accomplishment of them before their eyes. Their knowledge of these things will greatly increase their acquaintance with both the doctrinal and practical truths of the gospel. Great activity will be exerted to propagate among men this divine knowledge; for Daniel was informed, that, " at the time of the end, many shall run to and fro, and knowledge shall be increased." Dan. xii. 4. The elaborate researches and discoveries of gospel doctrine, in former generations—the number of those who shall then be employed in biblical studies —and the happy unanimity in the faith of Jesus, which will prevail in those days—shall greatly accelerate their progress in the knowledge of divine truths. The wonderful works of grace and providence, performed by the Lord, for introducing and establishing this happy state of the church, being deeply impressed on their mind, will excite them to accomplish a diligent search into the words of eternal life, which, by the blessing of God and the working of his Spirit, will cause them attain extraordinary degrees of knowledge in the mysteries of God.

2d, This promise contains the blessing of a more extensive communication of the light of the gospel to the nations of the world. This blessed light shall be confined no more to a few of the gentile nations: but it shall spread comparatively over all the earth. The prophet Isaiah proclaims this truth, chap. xi. 9. "They shall not hurt nor destroy in all my holy mountain; for the earth shall be full of the knowledge of the Lord as the waters cover the sea." The prophet Habakkuk confirms this, chap. ii. 14. "For the earth shall be filled with the knowledge of the glory of the Lord, as the waters cover the sea." Isaiah also foretells the willing subjection of all the nations of the earth to the sceptre of Christ; chap. ii. 2. "And it shall come to pass in the last days, that the mountain of the

Lord's house shall be established in the top of the mountains, and shall be exalted above the hills; and all nations shall flow unto it." The same thing was represented to John, Rev. xi. 15. "And the seventh angel sounded; and there were great voices in heaven, saying, The kingdoms of this world are become the kingdoms of our Lord, and of his Christ; and he shall reign for ever and ever." If the knowledge of the Lord, and of the glory of the Lord, shall cover the earth, as the waters cover the sea; if all nations shall flow to Christ; and if the kingdoms of this world shall become his kingdoms, a great extension must certainly be given to the gospel of divine grace among the nations, when "the light of the moon shall be as the light of the sun, and the light of the sun shall be sevenfold, as the light of seven days." Nations the most ignorant and barbarous—nations the most remote,—and nations the most hostile to Christianity, shall then yield subjection to the Redeemer, and shall wait for his law. If barbarians and Scythians were found among the subjects of Christ's kingdom, in the apostolic age, persons and nations of that description will certainly be ranked among his followers, when this promise shall be accomplished. The great multitude which no man could number, and which were clothed in white robes, and palms in their hands, Rev. vii. 9. represented the members of the millennial church, as the sealed company symbolized professing Christians, while the church abode in the wilderness. If this great multitude comprehended persons of all nations, and kindreds, and people, and tongues, then nations the most remote, and the most hostile, will receive the gospel of Christ, stretch out their hands unto God, and stand before the throne and before the Lamb.

3d, This promise contains the blessing of a more powerful efficacy of the gospel on the souls of men. If the moon should shine as the sun, and the sun emit sevenfold more light and heat than usual, their influence on the inhabitants and productions of the earth would be greatly increased. When the religious and spiritual state of things shall be introduced which is signified by those metaphors, the efficacy of the gospel on mankind must be inconceivably enlarged. The rod of the Redeemer's strength shall then be sent out of Sion, and will make many willing to submit to him in this day of his power. The weapons of the gospel warfare, which are not carnal but spiritual, shall then, in a most wonderful degree, be mighty through God, to the pulling down of strong holds; casting down imaginations, and every high thing that exalteth itself against the knowledge of God, and bringing into captivity every thought to the obedience of Christ. The work of convincing sinners of their guilt and misery, by the precepts and threatenings of God's holy law, shall then be general and powerful among the inhabitants of the earth. The glorious work of converting sinners to Christ, shall then prevail wonderfully among men. Multitudes, in many nations, shall be turned from darkness to light, and from the power of Satan to God, that they may receive forgiveness of sins, and inheritance among them who are sanctified, by faith that is in Christ. In that day, the work of building up christians in their most holy faith shall so prosper in the church, that they shall be enabled to keep themselves in the love of God, looking for the mercy of our Lord Jesus Christ unto eternal life. When all nations shall flow unto the mountain of the Lord's house, in the last days, the Prophet represents the language they shall utter, Isaiah xi. 3. "And many people shall go and say, Come ye, and let us go up to the mountain of the Lord, to the house of the God of Jacob; and he will teach us of his ways, and we will walk in his paths." No such causes shall then exist, as now are, and have been, for the ambassadors of peace to weep bitterly, and to say, "Who hath believed our report, and to whom is the arm of the Lord revealed?" for then, the power of the Lord being present to heal, the earth shall bring forth in one day, and nations shall be born at once.

4th, A greater degree of fruitfulness among the members of the church, is another blessing which this promise contains. Were the sun and the moon to shine in the way stated in the text, accompanied with a proportionable quantity of rain, the fertility of the earth would probably be increased. Whatever may be in this, we are assured, that, when this prediction shall be fulfilled, christians shall attain extraordinary fruitfulness in every good work, and unexampled increase in the knowledge of God. The fruitfulness of believers consists in their holiness and comfort. In the former part of the 19th chapter of the Revelation, which describes the condition and employment of the church at this blessed day, their fruitfulness in these things is clearly stated. At the beginning of the chapter, John heard "a great voice of much people in heaven, saying, Alleluia; Salvation, and glory, and honour, and power, unto the Lord our God." After describing the causes of their joy, in their deliverance from their antichristian enemies, it is said, verse, 4th, "The four and twenty elders, and the four beasts fell down and worshipped God, that sat on the throne, saying, Amen; Alleluia." In the 5th verse, a voice comes out of the throne, calling them to the exercise of praise. In the 6th verse we find them saying, "Alleluia; for the Lord God omnipotent reigneth." In the 7th verse, they encourage one another in this delightful work; "Let us be glad and rejoice and give honour to him; for the marriage of the Lamb is come, and his wife hath made herself ready."

All this indicates a most joyful and comforted state of the church. In the 8th verse, the perfection of her justifying robe, and the purity of her garments of sanctification are described; "and to her was granted that she shall be arrayed in fine linen, clean and white; for the fine linen is the righteousness of saints." The 9th verse, which concludes this part of the chapter, declares the felicity of those who shall enjoy such attainments in holiness and comfort. "And he saith unto me, write, Blessed are they who are called to the marriage supper of the Lamb." The fruitfulness of the church, at this season, is described also in the Old Testament predictions. Respecting this day, Isaiah, chap. lx. verse 21st, declares, "Thy people shall be all righteous; they shall inherit the land forever, the branch of my planting, the work of my hands, that I may be glorified." In these words, extraordinary degrees of sanctification, great spiritual privileges, and much holy joy and enjoyment are foretold of the church. The same happy condition is predicted, Isaiah xxxv. 1. 2. "The wilderness and the solitary place shall be glad for them, and the desert shall rejoice, and blossom as the rose. It shall blossom abundantly, and rejoice even with joy and singing." When this season shall commence, the darkened nations, which were a wilderness, a solitary place, and a desert, being fertilized by the word, the Spirit, and the grace of God, shall bring forth fruit as Lebanon, Carmel, and Sharon; "and they shall see the glory of the Lord, and the excellency of our God." The christians of those ages shall be fruitful in their profession, and in their practice—in their profession, for Christ's Father's name shall be written on their foreheads—and in their practice, because they shall follow the Lamb whithersoever he goeth. As the church and her true members will still be in a state of imperfection, even under all these enjoyments, it is vain to suppose that the former will be freed from nominal professors and hypocrites, or that the latter shall be delivered from the operations of indwelling sin, or from those trials and sorrows which are incident to them who are yet in the body.

III. Head was to describe the way in which this promise or prediction shall be fulfilled.

1*st*, It shall be fulfilled by the grace and power of God the Father. Every spiritual blessing, that is enjoyed by the church, or by any believer, is bestowed by the grace and power of God. This great blessedness, therefore, which the church and her members shall then enjoy, must flow from the same fountain. All those who come to Christ, must be drawn by the Father, and must hear and learn of him. Those who are the children of the church are all taught of God. These operations of grace and power must be performed by the Father, on the nations, when they submit to the sceptre of the Redeemer, and on the numerous individuals in them, who believe in him to the salvation of their souls. The cause of all spiritual good to men is unchangeably the same in God, who is the Father of lights, the Author of every good gift, and every perfect gift, and with whom is no variableness, neither shadow of turning. The displays of the grace and power of God are great, in proportion to the magnitude and number of their effects. These perfections of God are manifested in every situation of the church; but when this prediction is fulfilled, they will be more brightly displayed; for when the Lord shall build up Sion, he will appear in his glory. The grace of God freely provides the blessings which he hath in store for his church; and his power, at the appointed season, effectually bestows them on her. It is by grace that the church, at that time, shall be saved. This wonderful deliverance shall not be bestowed on them, by works of righteousness that they have done; but it shall be according to his mercy that they shall be saved. The accomplishment of this promise to the nations shall be such a display of the riches, sovereignty, and freedom of divine grace, that, when the head-stone of this building of mercy for the church shall be brought forth, it shall be with shoutings, crying, Grace, Grace unto it! In the accomplishment of this prediction, the power of God will also be manifested; for at that time, "the Lord shall make bare his holy arm in the eyes of all the nations, and all the ends of the earth shall see the salvation of our God." Is. lii. 10. The obstructions to this change are so great and many, that nothing but divine power can remove them; and the blessings to be conferred are so numerous and important, that divine power alone can bestow them. As this perfection of the divine nature was exercised at the church's deliverance out of Egypt, so it shall be illustriously exerted when the prediction of the text shall be accomplished. Respecting the enemies of Israel, the Lord said, "And in very deed, for this cause have I raised thee up, for to shew in thee my power, and that my name may be declared throughout all the earth." Concerning Israel themselves, it is declared, Nevertheless, he saved them for his name's sake, that " he might make his mighty power to be known." Ex. ix. 16. Psal. cvi. 8. When the Lord delivered his people from spiritual Sodom and Egypt, from Babylon the Great, and from all her other enemies, and when he shall advance his church to the enjoyment of her promised prosperity and glory, his power will be signally displayed; for at the time of executing this purpose, the millennial church, will peculiarly celebrate his praise, as " the Lord God omnipotent, who reigneth." Rev. xix. 6. Whatever mountains of opposition, therefore, may seem to obstruct the performance of this glorious work, the faith of the saints is warranted to answer every doubt that may arise in their mind about it, as Christ replied to the Sadducees' objections to the resurrection of the dead, " Ye do greatly err, not knowing the Scriptures, nor the power of God." Matth. xxii. 29.

2*d*, This prediction shall be fulfilled by the mediatorial agency of Christ. It is he who gathers his sheep out of every fold, and draws men to himself. " Other sheep I have, which are not of this fold; them also I must bring, and they shall hear my voice." John x. 16. " And I, if I be lifted up from the earth, will draw all men unto me." John xii. 32. To John in the visions that he saw, the mediatorial agency of Christ, in this great work, was frequently represented. This was pointed out to him in the very first vision he had of Christ, when he saw him walking in the midst of the seven golden candlesticks, and holding in his hand the seven stars, Rev. i. 13, 16. This was unfolded to him also at the opening of the first seal, chapter vi. 2. " And I saw, and behold a white horse, and he that sat on him had a bow, and a crown was given to him; and he went forth conquering and to conquer." This was likewise set before his view in the vision of the harvest of the earth, which may be the symbol of the church's deliverance, as that of the vintage is, of her enemies destruction. This is recorded, chapter xiv. In the 14th verse, the Redeemer is described: " And I looked, and, behold, a white cloud, and upon the cloud one sat, like unto the Son of Man, having on his head a golden crown, and in his hand a sharp sickle." His agency is represented in verse 16. " And he that sat on the cloud thrust in his sickle on the earth; and the harvest of the earth was reaped." His agency in these things is also mentioned in the victory he obtains over his enemies, when this prediction is accomplished, Rev. xvii. 14. " These shall make war with the Lamb, and the Lamb shall overcome them; for he is Lord of lords, and King of kings; and they that are with him are called, and chosen, and faithful." We have another most magnificent exhibition of his mediatorial agency, in fulfilling the predictions which introduce and establish the church's deliverance and prosperity, in chapter xix, from the beginning of the 11th verse to the end of the chapter; which deserves the careful consideration of every Christian. To the ancient prophets also, this agency of Christ was revealed. Isaiah, when speaking of him as the Father's Servant in the work of our redemption, who shall be exalted, and extolled, and be very high, and whose visage was so marred more than any man, and his form more than the sons of men, says, "So shall he sprinkle many nations; the kings shall shut their mouths at him, for that which had not been told them shall they see, and that which they had not heard shall they consider." To the prophet Zechariah, his agency in these mighty and merciful works of God was declared, chapter vi. 12, 13. "Behold the man whose name is the Branch; and he shall grow up out of his place, and he shall build the temple of the Lord: even he shall build the temple of the Lord; and he shall bear the glory, and shall sit and rule upon his throne; and he shall be a priest upon his throne; and the counsel of peace shall be between them both." In the execution of his offices, the divine Mediator, as glorified at his Father's right hand, will exercise this agency; and those who interfere with the prerogatives of his offices shall be broken in pieces, while those who yield themselves to him shall be saved. He will at that day so manifest his glory, by his operations among the nations, as will determine them to believe his gospel and submit to his law. Since Jesus has purchased all blessings for his church and children, it must be a display of God's wisdom and righteousness, when he commits all judgement to the Son, lays the government on his shoulders, and gives him power over all flesh, that he may give eternal life to as many as he hath given him. As our Mediator is the Sun of Righteousness, the Light of the world, and the Bright and the Morning Star; it must be necessary, as well as suitable, that he have a special agency in fulfilling, to his church, such a promise as this, "The light of the moon shall be as the light of the sun, and the light of the sun shall be sevenfold, as the light of seven days."

3*d*, This prediction shall be fulfilled by the powerful operation of the Holy Spirit. It is by his personal influence, that the whole scheme of grace, in the application of eternal life to them who are saved, is carried on and perfected. At this blessed day, the Spirit shall be poured on men from on high, and the wilderness shall become a fruitful field. As a more abundant communication of the Spirit to the church is one of the peculiar characters of gospel times, so at this brightest period of that dispensation, the Spirit shall be poured out in a most extraordinary manner, and the effects produced by his influence, shall be most beneficial and extensive. The prophecy of Joel, which was so remarkably accomplished in the days of the apostles, Acts ii. 16, shall also have at this time, an eminent fulfilment. "And it shall come to pass afterward, that I will pour out my Spirit upon all flesh; and your sons and your daughters shall prophecy; your old men shall dream dreams, your young men shall see visions. And also upon the servants, and upon the handmaids, in those days, will I pour out my

Spirit." Joel ii. 28, 29. The great gift of God to men is his Holy Spirit, which he will communicate to them. The subjects of this gift are all flesh, persons of all nations. These subjects are more particularly described,—sons, daughters, old men, young men, servants, and handmaids; including persons of every age, sex, rank, and relation among men. The effects which this gift of the Spirit shall produce on them are also stated—prophesying, dreaming dreams, and seeing visions. These expressions are taken from the scriptural accounts of the way in which the Spirit formerly influenced and guided the holy men of God, who spake as they were moved by him; and they signify the Spirit's work on the souls of men, by which he will bestow on multitudes spiritual knowledge, saving grace, gospel holiness, and ministerial and christian gifts, for glorifying God and edifying the church. The personal agency of the Spirit of God in fulfilling this prediction, is also declared in the Revelation of John. In chap. 1, verse 4th, He is called " the seven Spirits, which are before his throne." In chap. iv. verse 5. it is said " and there were seven lamps of fire burning before the throne, which are the seven Spirits of God." In chap. v. verse 6, when speaking of the seven eyes of the Lamb, who is in the midst of the throne, they are said to be " the seven Spirits of God, sent forth into all the earth." The Holy Spirit, who is one in his person and office, receives the name of the seven Spirits of God, that the perfection and variety of his relations to believers, and of his influences on them, might be made known to the church. From these representations of the office and work of the Holy Spirit, we may be assured, that his operations are connected with Jehovah's throne of grace; that he acts on the souls of men like fire, purifying, enlightening, and warming their hearts; that he is intimately connected with the Mediator and his kingdom in all his work; and that he is sent to the church to take the things of Christ, and to show them to the children of men. As he came unto the apostles like a mighty rushing wind, in communicating to them extraordinary gifts, and, on various occasions, and in different nations, fell on all them that heard the word, that the gospel kingdom might be established in the earth; so he will exert a peculiar and powerful agency upon the children of men throughout the world, that the promise in the text may be fulfilled, and that these wonderful changes, in the moral and religious state of the nations, may be accomplished. If any should ask, how these grand changes shall be produced? The answer may be given in the words of Jehovah himself: "Not by might, nor by power; but by my Spirit, saith the Lord of hosts." Zech. iv. 6.

4*th*, This prediction shall be accomplished, by the instrumentality of the word and ordinances of God. No spiritual or saving blessing will be conferred on any person or people, without the use of those means. When the Lord shall heal the nations, he will send his word and heal them. When he brings sinners to the Saviour, he magnifies his word above all his name, and gives testimony to the word of his grace, by making it effectual for turning the disobedient to the wisdom of the just. When the Lord gives spiritual reviving to his people, it is by his word that he quickens them. For their spiritual illumination, the word of God must enter the nations, and either go before or accompany the preaching of the gospel. Inspired men, as in the days of the apostles, might be instrumental, before the canon of Scripture was completed, in preaching the gospel, in converting sinners, in edifying believers, and in planting churches, before the written word was put into the hands of the members of the church. But, after the canon of Scripture is finished, and useful inventions are discovered, under the direction of divine providence, facilitating greatly the communication of the words of eternal life to the nations; it seems necessary, that the preaching of uninspired men, as in our own times, should either be preceded by the word of God, or accompanied with it, that their labour may not be in vain in the Lord. The written word, the preaching of the gospel, religious conference, prayers and praises, are the principal means by which the nations of the earth shall be constrained to bow to the Redeemer's sceptre of grace. These are the weapons of the gospel warfare, which shall be mighty, through God, for making the kingdoms of this world become the kingdoms of our Lord and of his Christ. These constitute the rod of his strength, which shall be employed, when he accomplishes his promise to Christ, in the last days,—" I will give thee the heathen for thine inheritance, and the uttermost parts of the earth, for thy possession." When Isaiah predicts, in lofty strains, the flowing of all nations, in the last days, into the kingdom of Christ, he states the means by which this great work will be accomplished; chap. ii. 3. " For out of Sion shall go forth the law, and the word of the Lord from Jerusalem." Whatever has been done already, in any part of the world, or in any age of the church, for propagating the religion of Jesus in a land, and for maintaining its existence in it, has been accomplished by these, and the like means. When " the light of the moon shall be as the light of the sun, and the light of the sun shall be sevenfold, as the light of seven days," the word and ordinances of God shall be the means of producing it. When this happy time arrives, the Lord will furnish the nations with his word, and send his commissioned ambassadors to preach it to them; for this blessed promise shall be accomplished by the written word, and by the preaching of the gospel, with the Holy Ghost sent down from heaven.

IV. The last branch of this subject was to explain the character of that day, mentioned in the text, when all these things shall be fulfilled—" In the day that the Lord bindeth up the breach of his people, and healeth the stroke of their wound."

1*st*, The Lord will accomplish this prediction to the nations, in the day that he bindeth up the breach that subsists between himself and his ancient people. For the space of almost eighteen hundred years, a great breach has subsisted between God and the Jewish nation. The ground of the controversy that God has with them, is their great sin in despising Christ while he dwelt among them, in crucifying the Lord of glory, in rejecting the gospel when the apostles preached it to them, in persecuting the ambassadors of Christ and the professors of his name, and in their aggravated immoralities. With these acts of wickedness they were chargeable, both in their national and personal capacities. By this conduct, the Jewish nation committed great trespasses against the Lord, contracted much guilt in his sight, and subjected themselves to grievous punishment. For these causes, the holy and righteous Judge, according to Christ's prediction, " brought great distress into that land, and wrath upon that people; so that they fell by the edge of the sword, were led away captive into all nations, and Jerusalem was trodden down of the Gentiles." This breach between God and the Jews is so exceeding great, that all the breaches between him and them, while they dwelt in the land of promise, were but faint shadows of it.

The time of binding up that breach shall come. The binding it up is the Lord's work; for the " Lord bindeth up the breach of his people." Of himself he says, " I kill, and I make alive; I wound, and I heal." Deut. xxxii. 39. Of him we may therefore say, "He maketh sore, and bindeth up; he woundeth, and his hands make whole." Job v. 18. God shall be reconciled to them, and they shall be reconciled to God. There are several expressions of Paul, Rom. xi. chapter, which confirm to us the healing of this breach between God and his ancient people. In verse 11th, the Apostle says, "Have they," the Jews, "stumbled, that they should fall?" that is, finally and forever. To which he answers, "God forbid." This imports that they shall be recovered from their stumbling, and that their fall is but for a time. In the 12th verse, he speaks of the fall and the diminishing of the Jews, and also of their future fulness. This proves, that as they have fallen and have been diminished by their breach, and by the stroke of their wound; so they shall yet enjoy a blessed spiritual fulness, in the binding up of the one, and in the healing of the other. In the 15th verse, he mentions the casting away of the Jews, and also the receiving of them; which shows, that as they have been cast away from their church state and privileges, so certainly shall they be received in again to the enjoyment of them all. In verse 24th, the healing of this breach is also secured: "For if thou wert cut out of the olive-tree, which is wild by nature, and wert graffed, contrary to nature, in a good olive-tree, how much more shall these, which be the natural branches, be graffed into their own olive-tree?" The apostle here represents the future conversion of the Jews, to be equally certain as the calling of the gentiles, at the beginning of the gospel-dispensation; and that it is more reasonable to expect the former, than to have looked for the latter. The Apostle also expressly says, verse 26th, " And so all Israel shall be saved." The last proof to be mentioned is contained verse 31st, which is remarkable for ascertaining, both the conversion of the Jews, and the causes and means by which it shall be accomplished: " Even so have these also now not believed, that through your mercy they also may obtain mercy." The blessedness which is reserved for God's ancient people is stated in these words, " they shall obtain mercy." When Paul represents the goodness of God to him in the day of his conversion, he says, " But I obtained mercy." 1 Tim. i. 13. As the breach was made up between God and Paul, who had been before a blasphemer, and a persecutor, and injurious, when he obtained mercy; so the breach shall be bound up between God and his ancient people, who have been long in a state of rebellion against him, when they shall obtain mercy. It is through the mercy of the Gentiles that they shall obtain mercy. The holy word of God, the preaching of the gospel, and the other ordinances; a revelation of Christ, of God in Christ, and of salvation through him; the gift of the Spirit to the church, and of divine grace and spiritual blessings to her members—all these belong to the mercy of the gentiles. It will be by these causes and means, that the Lord will bind up the breach between himself and his ancient people, and cause them to obtain mercy. By these he will convince them of their sin and misery; he will humble them to the dust on account of their wickedness, and the iniquity of their fathers in rejecting the Saviour, and continuing in unbelief; he will manifest to them the Lord Jesus, as the Author of eternal salvation to all them who obey him; and he will bring them to embrace and submit to him, as their Prophet, Priest, and King. At this happy time. the promise in the text shall be fulfilled to the Gentiles.

2*d*, The Lord will accomplish this prediction to the nations, in the day that he bindeth up the breach between the kingdoms of Judah and Israel. This breach began in the days of Rehoboam, by the defection of the ten tribes from his government, and the instituted worship of God at Jerusalem. It was occasioned by the folly of the king and his juvenile counsellors, in rejecting with pride, harshness, and insult, the reasonable proposals of the people. This breach was consummated, in the choice which the congregation of Israel made of Jeroboam to be their king—in his erecting among them, for political purposes, a religious system of will-worship and idolatry—and in the subjection given by that deluded people to this erastian and wicked establishment. This breach was still continued, notwithstanding the means that were used, by the ministry of some of the prophets. and by the judgments of God upon them, to reclaim them from their rebellion and idolatry,

This breach produced the most dismal consequences:—it involved the far greater part of God's ancient people, whom he had brought out of Egypt and settled in the land of Canaan, in the great sin of total apostacy from him, by worshipping the golden calves at Dan and Bethel;—it was infinitely dishonouring to the God of Israel, provoked him to anger against them, and procured the entire ruin of that people. This breach became wide as the sea in the reigns of some of their kings, when bloody and revengeful wars were carried on between the two kingdoms: and this breach was rendered, in all human probability, irreparable, in the total captivity of the ten tribes by the king of Assyria, and in their settlement in the towns on the river Gozan, and in the cities of the Medes. From their dispersion, that people has never yet returned; and this breach has not yet been bound up.

Scattered as the posterity of the ten tribes may be, in the land of the children of the east, they shall be gathered together, converted to Christianity, embodied with their brethren the Jews, and restored to their own land, in the day that the promise of the text will be fulfilled to the nations. This recovery of Israel, as well as Judah, seems to be evident from the words of Paul, Rom. xi. 26. "And so all Israel shall be saved, as it is written, There shall come out of Sion the Deliverer, and shall turn away ungodliness from Jacob." The people who shall be delivered and saved, are called "all Israel and Jacob." The posterity of the ten tribes, as well as the Jews, are included in those names. The posterity of Judah and Benjamin are not all Israel, nor all the descendants of Jacob; this salvation, therefore, cannot be confined to them, but must be extended to the whole house of Israel, and to all the sons of Jacob. But we have a very clear prophecy concerning the Lord's binding up this breach between Israel and Judah, Ezek. xxxvii. from the 15th verse to the end of the chapter. The symbolical actions which the prophet is commanded to perform, are mentioned verses 16, 17. "Moreover, thou son of man, take thee one stick and write upon it, For Judah and the children of Israel his companions; then take another stick and write upon it, For Ephraim and for all the house of Israel his companions: And join them one to another into one stick, and they shall become one in thine hands." The meaning of these symbols is explained, verse 19th: "Say unto them, Thus saith the Lord God, Behold I will take the stick of Joseph, which is in the hand of Ephraim, and the tribes of Israel his fellows, and will put them with him, even with the stick of Judah, and make them one stick, and they shall be one in mine hands." In the following part of the chapter, the Lord condescends to amplify this explanation, to write the vision, and to make it plain upon tables, that he may run who readeth it. In those verses, the gathering the whole posterity of Jacob, the close union of the two kingdoms, their return to the land where their fathers dwelt, their subjection to him who is the Root and the Offspring of David, their covenant-relation to their God, their happiness in that condition, and their continuance in it to the end of the world, are all particularly foretold. As no dispensation of providence has taken place, for this divided people, that can be considered as an accomplishment of this most minute prediction; we may assuredly look for it at the latter day, "when the Lord will bind up the breach of his people, and heal the stroke of their wound." There is another prediction of the same event, Jer. xxxiii. 24, 26. "Considerest thou what this people have spoken, saying, The two families which the Lord hath chosen, he hath even cast them off?" In answer to this reproach cast upon his people, he assures them he will never cast off the seed of Jacob and David his servant, and expressly says, "for I will cause their captivity to return, and have mercy upon them." This promise has a respect to both the families of his ancient people; and, when it is accomplished, he will heal the breach that subsists between them, and gather the dispersed of Israel into one.

3d, This prediction shall be accomplished to the nations, in the day that the Lord bindeth up the breach which has subsisted, between the Jews and the Gentiles. This breach took place between those parties, before the coming of Christ. The gentiles, through their ignorance and idolatry, despised the peculiar people of God, and opposed their holy religion. In the times of their degeneracy, the Jews also, by an abuse of their peculiar privileges, did often treat with supercilious contempt the gentile race. The ceremonial law, that middle wall of partition between them, was the occasion, and the corruption of their hearts, which produced enmity at each other, was the cause, of this breach. Though the wall of partition was taken down and abolished by the death of Christ, and though access was administered to both Jews and gentiles, by faith in Jesus, into a state of reconciliation to God, and to one another; yet this breach, by the Jews rejecting Christ and his gospel, did mournfully continue. It was very great, in the days of the apostles. The account of it may be given in the words of Paul. In 1 Thess. ii. 15, 16, when speaking of the Jews, he says: "Who both killed the Lord Jesus, and their own prophets, and have persecuted us; and they please not God, and are contrary to all men; forbidding us to speak to the gentiles, that they might be saved, to fill up their sin alway: for the wrath is come upon them to the uttermost." This breach has remained to the present day. Though mingled with all nations, the Jews are not incorporated with any. By their stubborn attachment to the antiquated system of the Mosaic dispensation, they are contrary to all men, and are equally at variance with heathenish, Mahometan, and christianized gentiles.

But this breach shall be healed and bound up. They shall be cordially reconciled to the Gentiles, and the Gentiles shall be brought into a state of real friendship with them. The time shall come, when the same God in Christ shall be the object of the worship of them both—the same Spirit shall animate them all—the same gospel shall be believed and received—the same Saviour shall be the foundation of their confidence,—and the same salvation shall be enjoyed by them both. All these things are signified and secured by the words of the Apostle, in which he represents both Jews and gentiles as branches graffed into one and the same olive-tree. He introduces this most beautiful and significant metaphor in Rom. xi. 16. and finishes his consideration of it in verse 24th. The nature of the privilege of both Jews and Gentiles is stated in verse 17th. "And thou," speaking of the gentiles, "being a wild olive-tree, wert graffed in among them, and with them partakest of the root and fatness of the olive-tree." The way of the restoration of the Jews to their gospel-privileges is mentioned verse 23d; which is by the power of God, and their faith in Jesus. "And they also, if they abide not still in unbelief, shall be graffed in; for God is able to graff them in again." The certainty of the joint enjoyment of Christ, who is the true vine, by both Jews and Gentiles, as the good olive-tree, is asserted, in verse 24th. "For if thou wert cut out of the olive-tree, which is wild by nature, and wert graffed, contrary to nature, into a good olive-tree; how much more shall these, which be the natural branches, be graffed into their own olive-tree." Jews and Gentiles shall be branches of the same olive-tree, and shall mutually partake of its root and fatness. This expressive metaphor teaches us, that both

Jews and Gentiles shall be the property of the same husbandman, shall grow in the same fruitful soil, shall be supported by the same root, nourished by the same fatness, covered with the same leaves, shall yield the same blossoms, and shall bear the same fruit, which shall be unto holiness, and the end everlasting life. When all this shall be performed by the Lord, the breach betwixt Jews and Gentiles shall be completely bound up. Nor are the Scriptures of the Old Testament silent on this delightful theme. In Isaiah xix. 23. 24, 25, the same blessedness is foretold; and He who confirmeth the word of his servant, and performeth the counsel of his messengers, will fulfil it in his season. "In that day shall there be an highway out of Egypt to Assyria, and the Assyrian shall come into Egypt, and the Egyptian into Assyria; and the Egyptians shall serve with the Assyrians. In that day shall Israel be the third with Egypt, and with Assyria, even a blessing in the midst of the land, whom the Lord of hosts shall bless, saying, Blessed be Egypt my people, and Assyria the work of my hands, and Israel mine inheritance." This remarkable prophecy, in which Egypt and Assyria represent the gentile nations, foretells a time, in which the most delightful peace, friendship, and intercourse, shall subsist between Jews and gentiles, and among the gentiles themselves; and when all of them, having been brought to the faith and profession of the gospel, shall be the objects of the divine favour and blessing. This can be fulfilled only when the

"Lord bindeth up the breach of his people, and healeth the stroke of their wound."

4th, This prediction shall be fulfilled to the nations, in the day that the Lord healeth the stroke of the wound of his ancient people. He will not only bind up their breach, but he will also heal the stroke of their wound. God has smitten them in his holiness and justice, with a mournful stroke, of which, all the former strokes of his anger on them were imperfect representations. The wound which they have received by this stroke, has been a grievous wound indeed. The destruction of their civil polity—the subversion of their church-state in the land of promise—the desolation of their city and temple—their extermination from the land of Canaan—their total dispersion among the nations—the great sufferings which they have endured by the unjust and cruel conduct of the gentiles to them—and, above all, their exclusion from the favour, service, and enjoyment of God, through their unbelief—constitute that distressing wound which is inflicted on them for their sin, by the stroke of the Lord's anger.

The Lord will heal this wound, by restoring them to their own land, by making them a glorious church on the earth, and by enriching them with temporal and spiritual blessings. Their wound, and the healing of it, were predicted by Hosea, chap. iii. 4, 5. "For the children of Israel shall abide many days without a king, and without a prince, and without a sacrifice, and without an image, and without an ephod, and without teraphim. Afterward shall the children of Israel return, and seek the Lord their God, and David their king; and shall fear the Lord and his goodness in the latter days." We have seen the prediction in the former verse most minutely fulfilled, in their low estate under the stroke of their wound; and the blessing foretold in the latter verse shall be as distinctly accomplished, when God shall fulfil his word to them, " I am the Lord that healeth thee." The lx. chapter of Isaiah contains a prophecy concerning this day and the events of it, which are mentioned in our text. Both the wound, and the Lord's healing it, are foretold in verse 15th. " Whereas thou hast been forsaken and hated, so that no man went through thee, I will make thee an eternal excellency, a joy of many generations." As the expressions of this verse, and indeed of the whole prophecy, are too grand to receive their accomplishment in the Jews' return from Babylon, we must therefore look to the latter days for its fulfilment. The same things are predicted, in chap. lxii. 4. " Thou shalt no more be termed, Forsaken; neither shall thy land any more be termed, Desolate: But thou shalt be called, Hephzibah; and thy land, Beulah; for the Lord delighteth in thee, and thy land shall be married." This verse refers to the things of which we are now speaking; for it is their last, and most grievous desolation, unquestionably, to which the words relate. No more were they to be termed, Desolate, nor their land any more termed Forsaken, after their restoration; it must, therefore, signify their present calamitous condition. While they lay under the stroke of their wound; the name of their nation was, Forsaken; and the title of their land was, Desolate; but when they shall be healed, they shall be called by a new name, which the mouth of the Lord shall name; verse 2d. For their nation, the name shall be "Hephzibah, for the Lord delighteth in thee;" and for their land, the name shall be, "Beulah, for it shall be married." The greatness of the misery which Israel now suffers under their bleeding wound, shall be exceeded completely by their glory and prosperity, when the Lord their God shall heal the stroke of their wound.

An improvement of the subject, in some inferences, shall conclude this discourse.

1*st*, Our duty, in improving the gospel light we enjoy, is evident from this doctrine. We are possessed of the same light which has enlightened the church in former ages, and which she shall enjoy afterwards in a superior degree. It is therefore our duty to walk while we have the light, lest darkness come upon us. Jesus hath said, "I am the light of the world; he that followeth me shall not walk in darkness, but shall have the light of life." John viii. 12. Let it, therefore, be our great endeavour to embrace Christ, and to rest on him, in his obedience, and sufferings, and death; so shall we be delivered from the darkness of our natural state, from the darkness of a sinful course, and from the blackness of darkness for ever; and shall be brought to enjoy the light of eternal life, both in grace and in glory. Though the light of the moon is not like the light of the sun in our day, nor the light of the sun sevenfold; yet this gospel-light of salvation shines on us as really as ever it did shine at any former time, or ever will shine on any future period, to the end of the world. We enjoy the whole word of God, revealing law and gospel, precept and doctrine, threatening and promise. We enjoy all the instituted ordinances of divine grace, both the word and ministry of reconciliation, exhibiting to us God as on a throne of grace, willing to bless us with all spiritual blessings—Christ the one Mediator, able to save them to the uttermost who come unto God by him—the Holy Spirit ready to apply to our souls the blessings of salvation—the grace of faith, which is the mean of interesting us in Christ, and in that everlasting salvation which is in him—and the life of holiness; for those who who have believed in Jesus "must be careful to maintain good works." O, how great are our privileges! Though the time of the church in which we live is a day of small things, yet it is really a day of salvation to saints and sinners. Woe shall be unto all those who despise it; but blessed shall all those be who improve it to the Redeemer's glory and their own salvation. Endeavour, O Christians, to consider daily your responsibility to God for the use you make of your privileges—the aggravated condemnation of gospel-despisers—

and the blessedness of all those who receive Christ and walk in him—that you may walk in the light as he is in the light, may have fellowship one with another, and the blood of Jesus Christ his Son shall cleanse you from all sin.

2. The very mournful situation of the darkened nations of the earth is obvious from this subject. They have no gospel vision; and where this is wanting, Solomon informs us, the people perish. The church, by the enjoyment of divine revelation, is called "the valley of vision." Isa. xxii. 1, 5. This vison signifies a revelation of the will of God to men, by which they have an opportunity of knowing and complying with truth and duty, for their salvation. This sense of the term *vision* is evident from the words of the verse where it is found. Prov. xxix. 18. "Where there is no vision the people perish; but he that keepeth the law, happy is he." The want of vision, and the enjoyment of the revealed law, are here contrasted. The Lord Jesus is the Author of eternal salvation unto all them that obey him. To those who have heard of Christ, who have believed in him, and who have yielded, to his holy commandments, the obedience of faith, he will be the Author of eternal salvation, and to no other. The nations of the earth, that are yet in spiritual darkness, are in the same condition in which the enlightened Gentiles were, before the light of the gospel shined on them. This was mournful indeed. The best description that can be given of it is found in

the apostle's words, Eph. ii. 12. "That at that time ye were without Christ, being aliens from the commonwealth of Israel, and strangers from the covenants of promise, having no hope, and without God in the world." Alas! brethren, how miserable is their situation, who are strangers to Christ, the only Saviour of sinnners, to the blessings of eternal life which are in him, to the everlasting covenant which God hath made with his chosen for our salvation, to the exercise and comforts of faith and hope, and to God himself, who is the infinite portion of his people! But this is the present state of all the unenlightened nations. Their condition is also described, in that prayer of the church, Psa. lxxiv. 20. "Have respect unto the covenant, for the dark places of the earth are full of the habitations of cruelty." By the murderous rites of their abominable idolatry which they practised, and by the barbarous conduct which they acted to one another, the dark places of the earth were full of the habitations of cruelty. It is a fact which is confirmed by satisfactory and unimpeachable evidence, that the dark places of the earth, at this day, are as full of the habitations of cruelty, in these and other particular ways, as they were in the days of David. How ought we to pity them, to pray for their deliverance, and to use every mean, competent to us, for sending to them the word and gospel of Christ! In the days of our remote ancestors, our own land was in the same miserable state; but, in the tender mercy of our God, the day-spring from on high hath visited us. Should we not, therefore, be filled with concern, that the same mercy may be extended to them, to guide their feet into the ways of peace?

3. This subject presents to our view the low and pitiable condition of God's ancient people. They are still under the breach with which they were broken for their sin, for it is not yet bound up. They are still suffering by the wound which they have received by the stroke of the Almighty; for the time of healing is not come. That people are divided into two families; the posterity of the ten tribes, who composed the kingdom of Israel; and the descendants of Judah and Benjamin, who constituted the kingdom of Judah. The former, it is now supposed, inhabit some regions in the East; and the latter are wanderers among all nations. In their miserable lot, the Lord has raised and maintained, for his glory, and for warning men, a monument which proclaims the greatness of the sin and punishment of those who reject divine institutions, and despise divine grace. For departing from divine institutions under the former dispensation, and despising Moses' law, the offspring of Israel have existed under the judgments of the Lord two thousand five hundred years. On account of their rejection of Christ, and the revelation of divine grace in him, the Jews have suffered the displeasure of God about eighteen hundred years. O that those warnings would produce a proper effect on professed Christians!

Contemplating the peculiarity and magnitude of their former privileges, and the greatness and singularity of their present distress, our minds should be filled with compassionate concern for their restoration. Fix your attention on them, O Christians, when they triumphantly marched out of Egypt, passed through the Red Sea, traversed the wilderness by the direction of the pillar of fire and the protection of the pillar of cloud, stood before the Lord at Horeb, walked through Jordan, conquered and possessed the land of promise, enjoyed the tabernacle and the temple of the Lord in the midst of them, assembled before the Lord in their solemn feasts, were fed to the full in the land flowing with milk and honey, and were often miraculously delivered from the hand of their enemies—and say if the words of Moses were not verified in them, " Happy art thou, O Israel! Who is like unto thee, O people saved by the Lord, the Shield of thy help, and who is the Sword of thine excellency." Deut. xxxiii. 29. Consider them also in their present state, banished from their own land, wandering among the nations, despised and persecuted by many, proverbially prophane, deceitful, and avaricious, blaspheming that divine Saviour to whom all their prophets gave witness, despising that atonement which all their sacrifices typified, turning away from him whose day their religious progenitors desired to see, and existing under all that temporal and spiritual misery which is the effect of their forefathers' imprecation, when they killed the Prince of Life, " His blood be upon us, and on our children,"—and you will see the reason they have to adopt that lamentation, "Is it nothing to you, all ye that pass by? behold, and see, if there be any sorrow like unto my sorrow, which is done unto me, wherewith the Lord hath afflicted me in the day of his fierce anger." Lam. i. 12.

4. From this subject we may see, that no very remarkable revival will be bestowed on the gentile churches, nor any general diffusion of gospel light will be made to the darkened nations, till God's ancient people shall be converted to Christianity. Our text informs us, that the "light of the moon shall be as the light of the sun, and the light of the sun shall be seven-fold, as the light of seven days, in the day," at the very time, "when the Lord bindeth up the breach of his people, and healeth the stroke of their wound." From this we may conclude, that this promise will not be accomplished to the nations, till the breach of the Jews is bound up, and their wound is healed. Great exertions may be made, with encouraging success, and such are made in the present time, for edifying Christians who reside among the heathen, and for converting some of the heathen themselves; but all this will be like the morning twilight only, which will be the harbinger of the approach of this bright meridian day of gospel light. Till this happy season come, there is reason to fear, that the gentile churches may continue under the judgment of division; errors may prevail

in the doctrine of some, human inventions may be retained in their worship, unscriptural forms of government may be practised, partiality and unauthorized usages in her censures may continue, and the papal interest may preserve its existence, prevalence, and influence in many lands. But this is not all: there is also reason to believe, that there will be a time of calamities to the gentile churches, and to the nations of the earth, till that great and notable day of the Lord shall come. The prophecy contained in the seven vials, which foretells the last judgments on the church's enemies, is not completely fulfilled. It is probable, that the fourth vial, under which the sun of the papal world scorched men with fire, is now poured out. There remain three other vials of the Lord's wrath to be poured on men—the fifth, which shall be poured upon the seat of the secular or papal beast—the sixth, which shall overturn the Turkish empire—and the seventh, by which the awful scene of judgments shall be completely finished. Those persons, therefore, who now look for a very long period of undisturbed tranquillity among the nations, may perhaps have reason to say, "We looked for peace, but no good came; and for a time of health, and behold trouble!"

5. We may see from this subject, that, at the time of the conversion of the Jews, the darkened nations shall be enlightened with the gospel, and the gentile churches shall be exceedingly revived. This is evidently contained in the text. At the

time of the binding up the breach of Israel, and the healing of the stroke of their wound, the nations that have not the gospel, shall be visited with this invaluable blessing; and the nations that are possessed of it, shall be favoured with a clearer view, and a deeper experience of its saving truths. Respecting the gentile churches, the apostle declares, Rom. xi. 12. "Now if the fall of them be the riches of the world, and the diminishing of them the riches of the gentiles, how much more their fulness." From these words we see, that there was a time when the Jews fell from being a church of God, and were diminished, and the gentile nations, who had been in spiritual poverty, were then enriched with the unsearchable riches of Christ; and that there is a time to come when the Jews shall enjoy the fulness of the blessings of the gospel of Christ, which shall be the mean, much more than their fall, of increasing the spiritual riches of the gentile churches. In the 15th verse, the apostle says, "For if the casting away of them be the reconciling of the world, what shall the receiving of them be but life from the dead." As the season in which the Jews were cast away, was the time chosen of God for reconciling to himself multitudes of the gentile world; so the blessed day of his receiving them again, shall be, to the gentile churches, as life from the dead. When this day shall come, the gentile churches will be low and languishing, and will be in great need of a revival. The change which will then take place on them, will be so great and salutary, that it is compared to a resurrection, even to life from the dead. The conversion of the Jews will be both the occasion and the mean of the gentile churches' glorious revival. The spiritual illumination of the darkened part of the gentile world, at the conversion of the Jews, is also, in this chapter, revealed to the church. "For I would not, brethren, that ye should be ignorant of this mystery, least ye should be wise in your own conceits, that blindness in part has happened to Israel, until the fulness of the gentiles be come in; and so all Israel shall be saved." Verses 25, 26. The day of the conversion of the Jews, as it is the time of enriching and reviving the gentile churches, so it shall be the season of bringing in the fulness of the gentile nations, to the knowledge of the way of salvation, by the grace of God reigning through the righteousness of Christ, unto eternal life. At this happy time, the Lord will say to his ancient people, to the gentile christians, and to the darkened nations, "From this day will I bless you." Hag. ii. 19.

6. That there is a particular time fixed by the Lord, for performing this glorious work among men, is evident from this subject. The text mentions a day in which the Lord will act the part of a Physician to his ancient people, by binding up their breach, and healing their wound; and in which he will cause light to arise upon the gentile nations. Several descriptions of this day are contained in the word of God, from which

we may obtain some knowledge of it. In Dan. xii. 7. we have two of these descriptions. In verse 6th, this important question is proposed to the man clothed with linen: "How long shall it be to the end of these wonders?" And in verse 7th we have his answer: "And I heard the man clothed in linen, who was upon the waters of the river, when he held up his right hand and his left hand unto heaven, and sware by Him that liveth forever, that it shall be for a time, times, and an half; and when he shall have accomplished to scatter the power of the holy people, all these things shall be finished." A numerical statement of this day, and a characteristic sign of it, are here, by the highest authority, and in the most solemn manner, made known to the church. The person whose voice Daniel heard, was the Son of God. The description he gives of this person at the beginning of chapter x. where this vision commences, accords so exactly with that given of Christ, in Rev. chapter i, as constrains us to believe, that he was the same person who was seen in vision, both by the Prophet and the Apostle. The way in which he confirms his answer, is by a solemn oath, with his hands lifted up to heaven. The numerical statement of this day is given in those words, "it shall be for a time, and times, and an half." This refers to the same day which those of John describe, Rev. xii. 14. "A time, and times, and half a time," which fixes the duration of the season of the woman's abode in the wilderness. The same period is mentioned, Rev. xi.

2. " And the holy city shall they tread under foot forty and two months :" and verse 3d, " And they shall prophesy a thousand and two hundred and threescore days, clothed in sackcloth." These three designations of time relate to the same period. The second and third enable us, with certainty, to fix the duration of the first. The time of forty-two months, allowing thirty days to each month, agrees exactly with twelve hundred and sixty days; and each of these numbers contains precisely one year, two years, and half a year. As a day is the prophetic symbol for a year, the time of the church's sufferings, and of her enemies' prevalence in the world, will be one thousand and two hun-hundred and sixty years. The most probable and satisfactory opinion concerning the beginning and termination of this time, is that which dates its commencement in the year six hundred and six, and brings it to a conclusion in the year eighteen hundred and sixty six. Then shall the precious promises of our text, if this calculation is correct, be fulfilled to the Jews, and to the enlightened and darkened parts of the gentile world. The characteristic sign of this day, which is given in this verse, is contained in the last clause, " And when he shall have accomplished to scatter the power of the holy people, all these things shall be finished." By the holy people we must understand the posterity of Jacob. The Lord's accomplishing to scatter the power of that people, signifies his bringing his work of judgment upon them to an end, his closing up the period in which they

were dispersed among the nations, and his finishing the season in which their political and ecclees-astic power was totally suspended.—Another characteristic sign of this day is found, Dan. xii. i. " And there shall be a time of troubles, such as never was since there was a nation, even to that same time; and at that time thy people shall be delivered, every one that shall be found written in the book." This character of that day, which consists in great judgements from God, and grievous calamities on men, agrees exactly with the representation which was made to John, when the seventh angel poured out his vial. Rev. xvi. 17, 18. " And the seventh angel poured out his vial into the air, and there came a voice out of the temple of heaven, saying, It is done. And there were voices, and thunders, and lightnings; and there was a great earthquake, such as was not since men were upon the earth, so mighty an earthquake and so great." The effects of this earthquake are detailed in the three following verses, which signify great moral, political, ecclesiastic convulsions among the nations of the earth. There is another characteristic sign of this day mentioned by Christ, Luke xxi. 24. " And Jerusalem shall be trodden down of the gentiles, until the times of the gentiles shall be fulfilled." The fulfilling those times, signifies the finishing the season in which the gospel and the ordinances of it are to be the peculiar privilege of the gentiles, and in which the posterity of Japheth shall have the exclusive possession of the tents of Shem. The Lord of the church has appointed her to exist in the world, through the whole course of time, in four grand periods. The first is that time in which the true religion was revealed unto all nations, which began at the giving of the first promise, and ends at the settlement of the Israelites in the land of Canaan. The second is that period in which the true religion was confined to the posterity of Israel; which began with their enjoyment of the land of promise, and ended in the days of the apostles. The third is that season when the true religion was exclusively enjoyed by the gentiles; which began at the rejection of the Jews, and shall end when they shall turn to the Lord. The fourth period is that in which the true religion shall be the common enjoyment of all nations; which shall take its rise on the day mentioned in the text, and shall continue to the end of the world. The times of the gentiles shall be fulfilled at the end of the third period; when the gospel shall be no more the peculiar privilege of the gentiles, but all Israel shall also enjoy the word and ordinances of eternal salvation. Another characteristic sign of this very day was made known to the church as early as the days of Noah: "God shall enlarge Japheth, and he shall dwell in the tents of Shem; and Canaan shall be his servant." Gen. xix. 27. The posterity of Ham, whom Canaan seems to represent, inhabited the vast regions of Africa and some parts of Asia. The period of time mentioned in this verse, is that in which the descendants of

Japheth, or the gentiles, succeeded the posterity of Shem, or the Jews, in the enjoyment of the privileges of the church. During this time the posterity of Ham are doomed to a state of servitude to the gentiles; but when that season shall expire, they shall be delivered from this bondage. At this glorious era, they also shall be converted to Christianity; for, of two of the principal kingdoms of that race, the Scriptures foretell, that "Princes shall come out of Egypt, and Ethiopia shall soon stretch out her hands unto God." Psal. lxviii. 31. The African slave-trade is the last, the worst, the most degrading and wicked species of that bondage which that unhappy people have suffered. While its partial abolition indicates the approach of this day; its total abolition, among all nations, will be accomplished when this light shall shine.

7. This subject presents to our view the happy state into which the church shall be introduced, when this day of light to the Gentiles, and of healing to the Jews, shall come. Many Scripture prophecies have a principal respect to it, and shall obtain the highest accomplishment which they can have on the earth, at this eventful era. The last prediction concerning it is recorded, Rev. xx. 1.—6. In these verses, the following things are foretold.—*Christ's glorious victory over Satan.* He who has the keys of hell and death, shall descend from heaven, in a bright display of his justice and power, shall lay hold on Satan, bind him with his

great chain, cast him into hell, shut him up in his prison, and place his seal on the door of it.—*The restraint that shall be laid on this enemy:* "He shall deceive the nations no more." The influence he has exerted in leading the nations to false religion, tyrannical government, abominable idolatry, inhuman cruelty, gross immorality, barbarous war, and the like, shall come to an end.—*The dignity and happiness of the subjects of Christ's kingdom:* "I saw thrones, and they sat on them, and judgement was given unto them: And they lived and reigned with Christ." These words express the power which the saints shall enjoy and exercise at that blessed day. Both civil and ecclesiastic power shall be in their hand; and they shall be directed, supported, and comforted, in an uncommon degree, with the word, the Spirit, the presence, and the blessing of Christ.—*The character and principles of the subjects of Christ's kingdom:* "And I saw the souls of them that were beheaded for the witness of Jesus, and for the word of God." The Christians of that time will be the true successors of the most holy and faithful members of the church, who have lived in the preceding ages.—*The low condition of the subjects of Satan's kingdom:* "The rest of the dead lived not again." The men who are of the same principles and spirit with the wicked generations, who have lived in former times, shall be few in number, and reduced in their influence.—*The spiritual employment of believers at that time:* "They shall be priests of

God and of Christ." They shall be holy, spiritual, devoted to God, and Christ, and religion, and examplary in all things.—*The duration of this happy time*, " a thousand years." As this number is used six times in seven verses, and as no other number is mentioned to represent the continuance of this season; there is reason to believe, that its duration will be one thousand years. Such shall the time be, which the accomplishment of the promises in the text shall introduce, and establish in the earth. This clear revelation of such a joyful day should have a practical effect on us, by influencing us to the exercise of an assured faith and hope of its coming; of ardent desire, patient waiting, and diligent preparation for its approach; for in its season it will come, as the effect of every vision. Since the Lord has been pleased to foretell and promise such a day; since its coming will glorify his name, honour Christ, and bring unspeakable blessings to men; your warrant is clear, and your encouragement great, O Christians, to cry mightily to God, at his throne of grace, that he may speedily cause Babylon to fall, and the kingdoms of this world to become the kingdoms of our Lord and of his Christ. Contemplating the quickening and purifying life that shall be infused into the gentile churches, considering the glorious light that shall arise on the darkened nations, and meditating upon the wonderful deliverance and enlargement that shall be wrought for the people of the God of Abraham at that day, we may exclaim, in the words of the Psalmist, " Blessed be the Lord God, the God of Israel, who only doeth wondrous works. And blessed be his glorious name for ever; and let the whole earth be filled with his glory. Amen, and Amen."

8. From this subject we may be informed of our duty, respecting the important matters that are contained in the text; and that is, to do every thing in our power to promote their accomplishment. Bear with me a little, my Christian Brethren, while I address you on this necessary duty. God, in his holy providence, has put in motion a great work, in our day, for conveying the knowledge of his word and gospel to the uttermost parts of the earth. In the erection of the British and Foreign Bible Society at London, which is now existing in its eleventh year; and in the erection of a great number of Bible Societies and Associations, both at home and abroad, we recognise this wonderful work of God. This general combination of Christians, for propagating the word of God, presents to our view one universal Society, which is entirely new, in its constitution, object, mode of operation, and extensive range. The grand design of the radical Society, and its auxiliary branches, is to furnish a more liberal supply, to the poor and others at home, of the authorised version of the Holy Scriptures; to give pecuniary and other assistance to Societies, having the same object, in other parts of the world; and to translate the Scriptures into foreign languages, to print them in these languages, and to circulate

them among the people by whom these languages are spoken; languages which have never formerly been the vehicle of conveying to the human understanding and heart, the words of eternal life. If these exertions are continued, with the blessing of God, they may, in a few years, be the mean of bestowing the holy oracles of God, upon many nations, where they have never been known. Of the nations who may be thus privileged, we may say, with a little variation, as was said in the second chapter of the Acts, concerning the people, from different nations, who were at Jerusalem on the day of Pentecost, when they were addressed by the Apostles, after these ambassadors of Christ had received the gift of tongues; They were all amazed and marvelled because they did read in their own language, and in their own tongues wherein they were born, the wonderful works of God. As the miraculous gift of tongues was a dispensation of God, which was most suitable to the Apostolic age; so the translating and printing the Scriptures in foreign languages, are equally congenial to the present state of things. The latter, as well as the former, we hope, is a grand operation of God, which will, in due time, promote his glory, and the salvation of men.

It matters not with whom this august scheme originated, or by whom it is conducted; sufficient it is for us to know, that it is the work of Him who does what he will in the army of heaven, and among the inhabitants of the earth. God is sovereign, wise, and holy in the choice of his instruments; and, therefore, it becomes us in this, as in many other things, to be still, and know that he is God. By giving these societies their most cordial support, Christians are by no means obliged, either to relinquish any of those principles of religion, which, by divine authority, they deem themselves bound to maintain; or to approve of any of those sentiments or practices in religion, against which, by the same authority, they feel themselves bound to testify. As there can be no valid objection, so their should be no distressing scruple, to prevent them who delight in the law of the Lord from giving assistance to a scheme, which is so scriptural in its object, and which has produced already such salutary effects. The extraordinary success that has attended the exertions of the parent Society, and others, as it should encourage those who have already contributed to continue their support; so it should excite those who have not yet countenanced this work, to come forward speedily to the help of the Lord, to the help of the Lord against the mighty. As the former have put their hand to the plough, let them beware of looking back; and, as the latter are solicited to assist, let them be on their guard lest they be found caring for none of those things.

It is impossible to read the correspondence between the radical Society of London, and some of the foreign Societies, without being deeply affected and even, in some instances, shedding tears. These will be tears of mingled emotions; tears of joy and wonder at the magnitude, extent, and efficiency of the exertions; tears of praise and thanksgiving to God, for his exciting grace, and superintending providence; and tears of faith and hope of glorious results. The holy Scriptures are the mean of humanizing mankind, by making them live like rational creatures;—they are the mean of civilizing them, by making them taste the sweets of social order, and of a more improved state of things;—they are the mean of evangelizing rational creatures, by causing them understand the doctrines of the gospel, the blessings of salvation, and their own moral and religious duties; —and the sacred Scriptures are the mean of spiritualizing men, by bringing them out of their natural state, endowing them with the image of God, clothing them with the righteousness of Christ, introducing them into fellowship with God, and enabling them to live a life of faith and holiness; the consequence of which shall be, that, to multitudes an entrance shall be ministered abundantly into the everlasting kingdom of our Lord and Saviour Jesus Christ. Impressed with these considerations of the necessity, importance, and utility to men, of the holy Scriptures, who would not rush forward to devote a part of that substance which the Lord has given them, to promote this wonderful work?

We are met here this evening, my Christian friends, to unite more fully this district of the parish in an annual contribution, for supporting these Societies in this great work. This is a privilege, and an honour, bestowed upon us by God in his providence, as well as it is a duty required at our hands. Let none be discouraged from coming forward, on account of the smallness of the sum they are able to give. Such persons should remember that the lowest contribution may be as generous in itself, and as acceptable to God, as the very highest that has been made, if the willingness of the mind, and the difference in the outward possessions of the contributors, are duly considered. Let not our love of the world, on the one hand, nor our poverty on the other, prevent us from contributing, according to our ability, for this precious purpose; but let both those classes of persons remember the words of Solomon, Prov. xi. 24. " There is that scattereth, and yet increaseth; and there is that which with-holdeth more than is meet, but it tendeth to poverty."— That we may have to give to him that needeth, and to contribute, at the same time, to the important purpose of supporting Bible Societies, let us beware of every sinful extravagance, in rioting and drunkenness, in chambering and wantonness, in strife and envying. Ah! what fruit shall we have in these things? Alas! Christians, the end of these things is death. Let us, in contributing for this end, glorify God with our substance, and with the first-fruits of our increase, and consecrate part of our gain to the Lord of the whole earth. Let us accompany our contributions with the fervent prayer of faith, for the blessing of God on the whole undertaking. Let us hope and pray, that, while we are endeavouring to furnish others with the Holy Scriptures, the Spirit of God, who is their Author, may more clearly manifest, and more powerfully apply, the doctrines, promises, precepts, and consolations of that word to our own souls. Let us daily study to embrace Christ, to believe in him, and to rest on him for our eternal salvation; and, in consequence of this, denying ungodliness and worldly lusts, let us live soberly, righteously, and godly, in the present world. Let us come cheerfully forward, at the call of God, to contribute for spreading the knowledge of his holy word, both at home and abroad; so shall we be found using a most eligible mean for promoting the accomplishment, to Jews and Gentiles, of the precious promises contained in the text: "The light of the moon shall be as the light of the sun, and the light of the sun shall be sevenfold, as the light of seven days, in the day that the Lord bindeth up the breach of his people, and healeth the stroke of their wound.

N. B.—In page 25. line 5. for *delivered*, read *shall deliver*.

THE END.

Jack & Gallie, Printers,
26, Bell-Street, Glasgow.

CHRIST JESUS, THE MEDIATORIAL ANGEL, CASTING THE FIRE OF DIVINE JUDGMENTS INTO THE EARTH.

IN

TWO SERMONS

PREACHED ON A PUBLIC FAST, FEBRUARY, 13, 1800.

By ARCHIBALD MASON,

MINISTER OF THE GOSPEL AT WISHAWTOWN.

From Rev. viii. 5.

" And the angel took the censer, and filled it with fire of the altar, and cast it into the earth: and there were voices, and thunderings, and lightnings, and an earthquake."

GLASGOW,

PRINTED BY FALCONER & WILLISON.

AND SOLD BY M. OGLE, WILSON-STREET; J. OGLE, PARLIAMENT CLOSS, EDINBURGH; R. OGLE, NO 5, GREAT TURNSTILE, HOLBORN, LONDON; J. FOWLER, PAISLEY; AND BY R. NAIRNE, RENTON.

1800.

CHRIST JESUS, THE MEDIATORIAL ANGEL, CASTING THE FIRE OF DIVINE JUDGMENTS INTO THE EARTH.

SERMON I.

Rev. viii. 5. *And the angel took the cenſer, and filled it with fire of the altar, and caſt it into the earth; and there were voices, and thunderings, and lightnings, and an earthquake.*

THIS book contains a variety of prophetic viſions which John ſaw, whereby the Lord Chriſt ſhewed him the great events which ſhould take place both in the world and in the church, from the time he received theſe diſcoveries in the Iſle of Patmos, till the conſummation of all things. Theſe events are principally repreſented by the opening of ſeven ſeals, the ſounding of ſeven trumpets, and the pouring out of ſeven vials. It is generally agreed, that the period of the ſeals extends from the days of the apoſtles, through all the heathen perſecutions of the church, and ends at the time when Chriſtianity was embraced by the Roman Emperors, and was eſtabliſhed in the empire: That the period of the trumpets comprehends the time of the overthrow of the Roman Empire by dreadful and barbarous wars, and the riſe and reign of Antichriſt in the Chriſtian world: And that the period of the vials refers to that time when the Lord would pour his judgments upon Antichriſt, upon his ſupporters, and upon all the enemies of his church for their deſtruction; which ſhould be followed immediately with the proſperous period of religion in the glory of the latter day. There is, likewiſe, in theſe Revelations, a variety of detached viſions, whereby ſome of the great events under the ſeals, trumpets and vials are either more ſummarily repreſented, or more largely and circumſtantially explained. To inſtance in a few of thoſe; The viſions recorded in the eleventh chapter contain a ſhort repreſentation of the riſe, reign, continuance and ruin of Antichriſt; with the church's low condition and ſpiritual employment during that period, her deliverance from his power, and proſperity after his overthrow; which are fully defcribed under fome of the trumpets, under all the vials, and in the events which follow them.—The tranfactions, which many underftand to be pointed out under the fifth trumpet, in the rife of Antichrift, are more particularly unfolded in the thirteenth chapter.—The awful tranfactions under the fifth vial receive a large illuftration, in the feventeenth and eighteenth chapters.—The period of war which is called the battle of Armageddon, and which belongs to the fixth and feventh vials, is particularly defcribed in the latter part of the nineteenth chapter.—And the profperous ftate of the church, which is briefly reprefented in the vifion contained at the beginning of the twentieth chapter, is largely illuftrated in many parts of the two laft chapters of this book.

In the firft verfe of the chapter where our text lies, the feventh feal is opened; and in the fecond, the feven angels, who ftood before God, receive feven trumpets which they were afterwards to found. In the mean time, we have a reprefentation of the mediatorial adminiftration of Chrift Jefus, both with refpect to his church, and her enemies, which is introduced prior to the angels actually founding the trumpets. Chrift is the glorious perfon who is called in the third verfe, *another angel*. He is *another* in his perfon, office and work than all the angels of God His work concerning his church, before the coming of the days of fearful trial, is begun in the foregoing chapter, where he is reprefented as bearing the feal of the living God, and fealing his fervants therewith on their foreheads. His further employment toward them is marked in the two verfes preceding the text. As the high prieft of old ftood at the golden altar, which was near the mercy feat, to burn incenfe in behalf of Ifrael before the Lord; fo Chrift Jefus, the great high prieft of our profeffion, ftands at the golden altar before the throne, with the golden cenfer in his hand, and, having added the much incenfe of his merit and interceffion to the prayers, or all the religious duties of the faints, he caufes them to come up with acceptance before God, out of his hands. Having thus fecured his church, and prepared them for the approaching ftorm, he proceeds to a very different work, of which the words of the text give us an account, and wherein we may obferve the following particulars.

1st, The person who is employed as the great agent in this work, " the angel." He is the same glorious one who is mentioned in the two foregoing verses, the Lord Jesus Christ, the mediatorial angel. The Son of God, in his mediatory character, is frequently called by this name. Jacob calls him " the angel who redeemed him from all evil;" Isaiah gives him the name of the angel of Jehovah's presence, who saved the church; and Malachi represents him to be the angel, or messenger of the covenant.

2d, The instrument he had in his hand, he took the censer; the same golden censer which he had used in making intercession for the church in the third and fourth verses. Censers were holy vessels used by the priests under the former dispensation, in carrying fire from the altar of burnt offering for different purposes. They probably were somewhat in the form of a large bowl, with an handle, fitted for bearing live coals from one place to another. The divine appointment concerning their use is recorded, Lev. xvi. 12, 13. *And he shall take a censer full of burning coals from off the altar before the Lord, and his hands full of sweet incense beaten small, and bring it within the vail. And he shall put the incense upon the fire before the Lord, that the cloud of the incense may cover the mercy seat that is upon the testimony, that he die not.* We find an instance of the using of the censers, on a particular occasion, in Num. xvi. 16. *And Moses said unto Aaron, take a censer, and put fire therein from off the altar, and put on incense, and go quickly unto the congregation, and make an atonement for them; for wrath is gone out from the Lord; the plague is begun.*

3d, The text informs us of the use the angel made of the censer, " he filled it with fire of the altar." The fire of the altar, with which Christ's censer was filled, denotes the wrath of God, which, in his awful judgments, is inflicted on the children of men. The fire which burned continually upon the brazen altar of burnt-offering came down from heaven, both at the erection of the tabernacle, Lev. ix. 24. and at the consecration of the temple, 2 Chron. vii. 1. and was kept continually burning there, by the ministry of the priests, in all their generations. This fire, by which the sacrifices were consumed, was a type of the wrath of God which is poured out on fallen angels, which was endured by Christ in his human nature as the sacrifice for his people's fins, which fhall torment the wicked for ever in the place of mifery, and which is poured out on finners in this world, in all divine judgments on them; it is in this laft fenfe that it muft be underftood in the words of the text.

4th, We have alfo an account of the ufe the angel made of the fire wherewith his cenfer was filled, "he caft it into the earth." He poured the fire of the altar, from his cenfer into the earth, as a reprefentation of the execution of divine judgments on the inhabitants of the world.

5th, The text unfolds the effects of this act of Chrift, "and there were voices, and thunderings, and lightnings, and an earthquake." Thefe words fignify the various and diftreffing calamities, which the Lord fends upon nations, churches and individuals on account of fin. It may be obferved, that this work of Chrift in cafting the fire of the altar into the earth, which produces thefe effects among the children of men, is not to be confined unto the period of the trumpets, which is paft; but alfo extends to the time of the vials which is going on at prefent, and partly is yet to come. This will be evident if we confider that the period of the feventh feal comprehends the whole of the trumpets. As the angels receive the trumpets immediately upon the opening of that feal, all the events fignified thereby are tranfactions under this feal. The period of the founding of the feventh trumpet extends alfo over all the vials, and the profperous ftate of the church after they are poured out; becaufe the deftruction of the church's enemies, and the converfion of the nations to Chrift are marked, at the end of the eleventh chapter, as the things which take place under it. If Chrift cafts the fire of the altar into the earth, upon opening the feventh feal, which comprehends the period of the trumpets and of the vials alfo; the effects of his doing fo muft reach, not to the time of the trumpets only, but likewife to that of the vials. As a further confirmation of this it may be obferved, that the effects of the feventh vial are the fame with thofe which are mentioned in the text. *And there were voices, and thunders, and lightnings; and there was a great earthquake, fuch as was not fince men were upon the earth, fo mighty an earthquake and fo great,*" Rev. xvi. 18. The act of Chrift and its effects, which are contained in the text, refers therefore to our own time, as well as to a former period.

The text now explained furnishes us with the following observation:

Doctrine, That the Lord Jesus Christ, the Mediatorial Angel of Jehovah's presence, is the glorious person, who, in executing his mediatory office, pours on his, and on his church's enemies, the sin-avenging judgments of the living God.

Although this doctrine is abundantly confirmed from the text, yet it may also be illustrated and established from a similar vision which Ezekiel saw, and which is recorded in the ninth and tenth chapters of his book. In the ninth chapter the Lord Jesus is represented as a man clothed with linen, with a writer's inkhorn by his side, employed in marking on their foreheads, those who were truly godly in an evil time; a work similar to that of sealing the servants of God on their foreheads. He was followed by six men whom Ezekiel saw in vision, each with a destroying weapon in his hand, who were appointed to slay all the other inhabitants of Jerusalem. In the tenth chapter we have the following remarkable words, *And he spake unto the man clothed with linen, and said, Go in between the wheels, even under the cherub, and fill thine hand with coals of fire from between the cherubims, and scatter them over the city; and he went in in my sight. And one cherub stretched forth his hand from between the cherubims, unto the fire which was between the cherubims, and took thereof, and put it into the hands of the man that was clothed with linen; who took it, and went out*, verses 2,—7. In these words we have an equally clear representation of the mediatorial work of Christ, in executing the judgments of God on incorrigible sinners, as that which is contained in the words of the text; *and the angel took the censer and filled it with fire of the altar, and cast it into the earth; and there were voices, and thunderings, and lightnings, and an earthquake.* In speaking from this text and doctrine the following method is proposed.

I. To shew what kind of fire the judgments of God are, which Christ inflicts on sinful persons, nations and churches for their iniquity.

II. To state some reasons why the judgments of God are called fire of the altar.

III. To consider the import of Christ's inflicting divine judgments on the children of men.

IV. To mention ſome of the effects of Chriſt's work, which are here repreſented by voices, thunderings, lightnings, and an earthquake.

And then to ſubjoin ſome inferences, for improving the ſubject.

I. It is now to be ſhewn what kind of fire the judgments of God are, which he inflicts upon his enemies in this world for their ſin.

1ſt, Theſe judgments are a divine fire. They are the doings of the Lord. Wherever the ſcripture ſpeaks of theſe judgments coming on men, it repreſents them as the work of God. So univerſal is this, that the Prophet Micah obſerves. *Is there evil in the city and the Lord hath not done it.* The fire of divine judgments, wherever it is caſt upon the children of men, is a burning which the Lord hath kindled. Of every calamity which is brought on perſons or ſocieties, it may be ſaid, *and the breath of the Lord, like a ſtream of brimſtone, doth kindle it.* Whatever inſtrumentality of the creatures he may be pleaſed to uſe in theſe matters, yet the work is wholly his own. This neceſſarily belongs unto him, and makes a part of that glory which he will not give to another. It belongs to him as the moral governor of his creatures. The cauſes of theſe judgments are the creature's rebellion againſt him, and therefore it belongs to him alone to puniſh them for their ſin The threatnings, in which theſe judgments are revealed to men, are the threatnings of God, and therefore the execution of them muſt be his work.

2d, Divine judgments are a juſt and righteous fire. They are not inflicted on the children of men without a cauſe, or without a cauſe that is fully adequate to the miſery that they ſuffer by their execution. The ſins of nations, churches and individuals, which are an open rebellion againſt the King eternal, immortal, and inviſible, the only wiſe God, are the procuring cauſes of theſe judgments. Whatever ſlight thoughts men may have of ſin, in its nature and principles in their ſouls, or in its effects in their converſation, by the omiſſion of duty and the commiſſion of ſin, which thoughts of it are great ſins in themſelves; yet the Lord, who knows all things as they really are, has no ſuch views of it. Sin is that abominable thing which God's ſoul hates, it is exceeding ſinful in its nature, it robs God of his glory, it is a violation of his righteous commandments, and a contempt of the fearful threatnings by which they are fenced; and, therefore, in all the misery he will inflict on men for sin, either in this or in the other world, he shall be righteous when he speaketh, and clear when he judgeth. The church discerned this properly of the judgments of God which were inflicted on herself, and therefore said, *And after all that is come upon us for our evil deeds, and for our great trespass, seeing that thou our God hast punished us less than our iniquities deserve*, Ezra ix. 13. The church shall also clearly see the holiness and righteousness of God, in the unparaleled plagues which he shall bring upon Antichrist, and therefore, when these take place, she shall triumphantly sing, *Alleluia; salvation, and glory, and honour, and power unto the Lord our God; for true and righteous are his judgments; for he hath judged the great whore, which did corrupt the earth with her fornication, and hath avenged the blood of his servants at her hand*, Rev. xix. 1, 2.

3d, The judgments of God are a wrathful and vindictive fire. To all who are strangers to Christ as a Saviour, and are in heart enemies to him, they are wrathful and vindictive. The judgments of God which are inflicted on wicked men in this world, whether of a personal or of a public nature, come on them from an angry and sin-avenging God, they are poured on them as an execution of the wrathful threatning and curse of the broken law, as the first drops of the storm of eternal vengeance, and shall be succeeded and perfected by their everlasting punishment. That temporal judgments are wrathful and vindictive is evident from their being, in scripture, frequently called the anger, the wrath, and the fury of the Lord. That these judgments are of this kind, will appear from the name which the Lord gives to the objects of them; *Cut off thine hair, O Jerusalem, and cast it away, and take up a lamentation on high places; for the Lord hath rejected and forsaken the generation of his wrath*," Jer. vii. 29. This is likewise clear from the scriptural character of the season when they are executed on men, it is called a day of wrath; *For the great day of his wrath is come, and who shall be able to stand*, Rev. vi. 17. And this is further evident from what the Lord is said to do, when he executes these judgments on men; *He made a way to his anger, he spared not their soul from death, but gave their life over to the pestilence*, Psal. lxxviii. 50.

4th, Divine judgments are a destroying and consuming fire. Fire consumes all combustible matter that is cast into it; so the fire of God's judgments consumes the objects of them; *For our God*, in the execution of his judgments on the workers of iniquity, *is a consuming fire*. This fire consumes the wealth of its objects. This it will do to Antichrist; Rev. xviii. 16, 17. *Alas! alas, that great city, that was clothed in linen, and purple, and scarlet, and decked with gold, and precious stones and pearls, for in one hour so great riches is come to nought.* It consumes their armies; Isa. xxxiv. 2. *For the indignation of the Lord is upon all nations, and his fury upon all their armies; he hath utterly destroyed them, he hath delivered them to the slaughter.* It consumes their means of safety and defence; Isa. xxv. 2. *For thou hast made of a city an heap; of a defenced city a ruin; a palace of strangers to be no city, it shall never be built* It consumes their power and authority; of Old Testament Babylon it is said, *Come down and sit in the dust, O virgin daughter of Babylon, sit on the ground; there is no throne, O daughter of the Chaldeans.* Of New Testament Babylon these words shall have their complete fulfilment; *And the fifth angel poured out his vial on the seat of the beast: and his kingdom was full of darkness, and they gnawed their tongues for pain*, Rev. xvi. 10. It shall consume their pleasurable enjoyments, *And the fruits that thy soul lusteth after are departed from thee, and all things that were dainty and goodly are departed from thee, and thou shalt find them no more at all*, Rev. xviii. 14. It shall consume many of their persons. Of the execution of divine judgments in time past this has been the effect; witness the generation in the days of Noah, the inhabitants of the cities of the plain, the Israelites in the wilderness, and many others. We have reason to believe that what has been done by the execution of divine judgments in time past, will be accomplished likewise in time to come; for the divine prediction concerning them, which shall be fulfiled in its season, is delivered in the following words; *And I saw an angel standing in the sun; and he cried with a loud voice, saying to all the fowls that fly in the midst of heaven, Come and gather yourselves together unto the supper of the great God; that ye may eat the flesh of kings, and the flesh of captains, and the flesh of mighty men, and the flesh of horses, and of them that sit on them, and the flesh of all men, both free and bond, both small and great*, Rev. xix. 17, 18.

5th, The judgments of God are an increasing fire. When fewel is furnished to fire, it is spreading in its nature; so are the judgments of God. They are a spreading fire when they wax worse and worse, and bring upon men more distress and misery. When the flame, instead of abating, becomes more dreadful, and carries more destruction in its train. When it is not confined to a few of the concerns of men, or to those of the smallest importance; but when it extends its wasting influence to many of their enjoyments, and even to those of the greatest necessity and value.—Divine judgments are a spreading fire when their number is increased. When one judgment follows another, and one calamity gives birth to more. In a day of divine recompences on his enemies, it frequently happens, that while one judgment is spending its force upon them, the Lord inflicts another, and before this is well begun a third opens to their view. As the children of men have multiplied their transgression against the Lord, so he, in his righteous displeasure, increases their plagues.—They are also a spreading fire when they extend to a greater number of objects. When their hurtful influence is not restricted to a few only, or to persons occupying certain situations in life; but when it reaches many, and affects men of every degree. When the Lord's judgments are not confined to one nation, but are poured out upon many lands; so that he is punishing many nations at the same time. When the days come that he inflicts his judgments upon *them that are circumcised with the uncircumcised; Egypt, and Judah, and Edom, and the children of Ammon and Moab, and all that are in the utmost corners, that dwell in the wilderness; for all these nations are uncircumcised, and the house of Israel are uncircumcised in the heart*, Jer. ix. 25, 26.

6th, These judgments are a painful and distressing fire. The action of fire upon men gives them pain; so divine judgments occasion distress to the children of men. As the wrath of God which he will inflict upon the wicked in the place of misery, will give them everlasting pain, so the judgments, with which he visits them in this world, will bring distress on them, on their persons, relations, and enjoyments. This is evident from the inspired account of the judgments that were inflicted on Judah by means of the Chaldeans; *That day is a day of wrath, a day of trouble and diſtreſs, a day of waſtneſs and deſolation, a day of darkneſs and gloomineſs, a day of clouds and thick darkneſs. And I will bring diſtreſs upon men, and they ſhall walk like blind men, becauſe they have ſinned againſt the Lord*, Zeph. i. 15, 17. This is alſo ſtated as the effect of the wrathful diſpenſations of God, by the Redeemer himſelf; *And there ſhall be ſigns in the ſun, and in the moon, and in the ſtars; and upon the earth diſtreſs of nations with perplexity, the ſea and the waves roaring; men's hearts failing them for fear, and for looking after thoſe things which are coming on the earth; for the powers of heaven ſhall be ſhaken*, Matt. xxi. 25, 26. The ſame thing is mentioned as the conſequence of God's judgments upon the Antichriſtian world. The events under the fifth vial, which ſhall be poured on the throne of the beaſt, are repreſented in the following words; *And his kingdom was full of darkneſs, and they gnawed their tongues with pain, and blaſphemed the God of heaven, becauſe of their pains and their ſores, and repented not of their deeds*, Rev. xvi. 10, 11.

7th, The judgments of God are an unquenchable fire. That this is a quality of theſe operations of God is evident from the words of the prophet; *But if ye will not hearken unto me to hallow the Sabbath-day, and not to bear a burden, even entering in at the gates of Jeruſalem on the Sabbath-day; then will I kindle a fire in the gates thereof, and it ſhall devour the palaces of Jeruſalem, and it ſhall not be quenched*, Jer. xvii. 27. The fire of judgments is unquenchable, becauſe it is impoſſible for men to extinguiſh them. They can no more do this, than they can ſtop the ſun in his courſe, deſtroy the ballancing of the clouds, or hinder the ebbing and flowing of the ſea. It ſome times happens, that the means which creatures uſe, for removing from them the judgments of the Lord, cauſe this fire to burn with the greater violence. They are unquenchable, becauſe God himſelf will never interpoſe to remove their raging and deſtructive influence, till he has thereby accompliſhed his deſigns. Though the judgments of the Almighty ſhould ſiſt for a time, if nations, churches and individuals continue impenitent in ſin, the dying-like embers of that fire, being blown by the breath of the Lord, ſhall return upon them till they are conſumed, and driven away to that place, where the chaff ſhall be burnt with unquenchable fire.

8th, The judgments of God are a purifying and refining

fire. They are of this nature to all true believers, and they produce this effect upon the church of Christ. The same judgments, which consume and destroy the wicked, purify and refine the saints of God. The same calamities which distress and ruin the public enemies of Christ, prove highly beneficial to the church of God. To the former they come from an angry God, as an executing on them the curse of the law, from which they take occasion to sin the more, and to blaspheme the God of heaven; but to the latter they proceed from a reconciled God, attended with his remarkable blessing, whereby their holiness and spiritual exercise are increased, and on account of which operations of God they celebrate his praise. By these judgments which he brings on men for their sin, he turns his hand on his church, and purely purges away all their dross, and taketh away all their tin. By such strange works as these, shall the iniquity of Jacob be purged, and all the fruit of them is to take away their sin. In a day of sore judgments upon men, this is his work toward his people, whose fire is in Zion, and whose furnace is in Jerusalem. In the glorious issue which the judgments of God shall have upon the nations of the world, they shall prove a purifying fire even unto them. They shall be a mean of delivering them from their ignorance, idolatry and wickedness, and of bringing them under Messiah's gracious rule; for, after they are executed, not only shall that cry go through the world *Babylon is fallen*, but it shall be succeeded by that more delightful sound, *The kingdoms of this world are become the kingdoms of our Lord, and of his Christ, and he shall reign for ever and ever.*

II. The reasons why the judgments of God are called fire of the altar are now to be stated.

1st, They are so called because they proceed from him who is the God of the altar, and who is revealed to men by the gospel, as a reconciled God in Christ Jesus. The executing judgments on sinners is the work of him, who is not only the God of the spirits of all flesh, their creator, preserver and moral governor; but who is also revealing himself to sinners from the throne of grace. Not only does the law of gospel grace come from Zion, and the word of salvation from Jerusalem; but the threatning proceeds also from the same place, and the execution of it is the work of him who dwelleth there. *The Lord shall roar out of Zion, and utter his voice from Jerusalem, and the heavens and the earth shall shake*, Joel iii. 16. A similar declaration is made by the prophet Amos, chap. i. 2. The Lord's roaring and uttering his voice refer both to his giving and executing his threatning; and his doing so out of Zion and Jerusalem plainly proves, that these are his works who is the God of the altar. The church also praises the Lord, Psal. lxviii. 35. saying, *O God, thou art terrible*, in fulfilling thy threatning on the wicked, *out of thy holy places*. This truth is also clearly made known in the visions of John. Rev. xv. 6. *And the seven angels came out of the temple, having the seven plagues, clothed in pure and white linen, and having their breasts girded with golden girdles*. They came out of the temple, signifying plainly that they were standing in the presence of the God of the temple, and had received their commission from him. The same thing is further declared, chap. xvi. 1. *And I heard a great voice out of the temple, saying to the seven angels, Go your ways, and pour out the vials of the wrath of God upon the earth*. Since the great voice, by which these angels were especially authorised to pour judgments on men, proceeded from the temple; the work of judgment must be the doing of him who is the God of the altar.

2d, They are the fire of the altar, because they are inflicted on man by the special agency of Jesus Christ, the church's great high priest, who ministers before the altar. It is the work of Christ to pour the judgments of God on his enemies. To him the Father hath committed all judgment, and this he executes not only at the last day, when all mankind shall appear before his judgment seat; but also by his operations upon them in this world. From several portions of this book, this truth may be established. *These shall make war with the Lamb, and the Lamb shall overcome them*, Rev. xvii. 14. They make war with the Lamb, by opposing his interests in the world; and the Lamb shall overcome them by executing on them the judgments of the Lord. In the latter part of the xix. chapter, and at the close of the cx. Psalm, the triumphs of the mediatorial angel over his enemies are celebrated in the loftiest strains. Besides, from the words of the text, and from the vision of Ezekiël, formerly mentioned, it is unquestionably evident, that the mediator has a special agency in executing divine threatnings on the children of men. Now, it is the peculiar work of this glorious perſon to miniſter at God's altar. In the days of his incarnation, he miniſtered at the altar as an atoning high priest, when he through the eternal ſpirit offered himſelf without ſpot unto God, and put away ſin by the ſacrifice of himſelf. In his ſtate of exaltation, he ſtill miniſters before the altar, when he, as an interceeding high prieſt, appears in the preſence of God for us. His mediatorial execution of his threatning on his enemies belongs unto his adminiſtrations at the altar, and on theſe accounts the judgments, by which the threatning is executed, are fire of the altar.

3d, Thoſe judgments receive this name, becauſe they are inflicted upon men chiefly for their deſpiſing the goſpel of divine grace, or their contemning God's altar. If the principal grounds of God's controverſy with perſons, churches and nations are examined, it will be ſound that their ſins about the altar, or the goſpel and worſhip of God, are the chief cauſes thereof. The children of men are guilty of profaning the altar, deſpiſing the goſpel, and neglecting the great ſalvation. Many, both in their perſonal and collective capacities, are involved in the guilt of oppoſing Chriſt in his perſon, divinity, office, grace and ſalvation; in his prieſthood, atonement and ſacrifice; and in his royal and kingly prerogatives; and, therefore, thoſe judgments, by which theſe ſacrilegious abominations are avenged, are juſtly called the fire of the altar. Men's oppoſition to the truths of the goſpel, their holding errors contrary thereunto, and their neglecting to receive and believe the word of ſalvation are eminent cauſes of the Lord's judgments. Their corruptions of God's ſanctuary and altar, by changing the ordinances of his worſhip, altering the laws concerning the government, and cenſures of his houſe, and ſetting office bearers in his church, which have no warrant in his word, are ſtanding grounds of the Lord's controverſy with ſinful churches and nations. Since ſuch ſins as theſe, which have a ſpecial relation to God's altar, are the principal cauſes of judgments, they may be repreſented as fire proceeding from it.

4th, Divine judgments are fire of the altar, becauſe they are inflicted on men in anſwer to the prayers, and for avenging the blood of thoſe who were ſlain for the word of God, and the teſtimony they held, whoſe ſouls are under the altar.

When the fifth seal was opened, John *saw under the altar the souls of them that were slain for the word of God, and for the testimony which they held. And they cried with a loud voice, saying, how long, O Lord, holy and true, dost thou not judge and avenge our blood, on them that dwell on the earth*, Rev. vi. 9, 10. These words assure us, that when the Lord executes his judgments on them that dwell on the earth, it is in answer to the prayers of those whose souls are under the altar; and therefore it is fire of the altar by which they are devoured. The prayers of the church of Christ, which are like incense on the golden altar, cause fire to proceed from the brazen altar, to consume their enemies. It is also evident from these words, that by the judgment of the living God, the blood of his saints, which has been shed for his names' sake, is fully avenged. Of antient Babylon the church says, *The violence done to me and to my flesh be upon Babylon, shall the inhabitants of Sion say; and my blood upon the inhabitants of Chaldea, shall Jerusalem say*, Jer. li, 35. In answer to which it is declared, ver. 49. *As Babylon has caused the slain of Israel to fall; so at Babylon shall fall the slain of all the earth.* New Testament Babylon shall not escape similar retribution. The song of the angel of the waters confirms it, *Thou art righteous, O Lord, which art, and wast, and shalt be, because thou hast judged thus; for they have shed the blood of saints and prophets, and thou hast given them blood to drink for they are worthy*, Rev. xvi. 5, 6. In the eighteenth chap. of this book we find a very detailed account of the unexampled calamities that shall be inflicted on the Antichristian state, and the last verse mentions one of the principal causes thereof; *And in her was found the blood of prophets, and of saints, and of all that were slain upon the earth.* As the persecutors of the church have cruelly shed the blood of the saints of God, and as these precious sons of Zion have not loved their lives unto the death, but have offered their blood, so to say, on God's altar, for the glory of his name, and as a testimony to his cause; so the Lord will make the fire of his jealousy, issuing from the altar, to devour the wasters of his heritage, either in their own persons or their seed, who continue to oppose the cause for which the blood of the saints was shed, or support that interest for which persecution was carried on.

5th, The judgments of God are fire of the altar, becaufe they often begin to be executed on thofe who are, either by profeffion or in reality, ftanding before the altar. The perfons who profefs to be ftanding before the altar, but are the chief corrupters of it; and thofe who fay they are apoftles and are not, but are deceitful workers, are often firft deftroyed by the fire of divine judgments. We have an affecting inftance of this, Ezek. ix. 6, 7. *Slay utterly old and young, both maids, and little children, and women; but come not near any upon whom is the mark; and begin at my fanctuary, Then they began at the antient men which were before the houfe; and he faid unto them, Defile the houfe, and fill the courts with the flain, and go ye forth; and they went forth and flew in the city.* In this vifion, by which the Lord reprefented to the prophet the execution of his judgments on Jerufalem, the leaders of the people, who were chief in the trefpafs, perifhed firft in the day of calamity. So fhall it be done in every land. When the days of Jehovah's retribution come, he will, in the operations of his providence by which his judgments are executed, mark out his victims, and caufe the leaders of a nation in apoftacy, fuperftion, idolatry and wickednefs, feel the firft and heavieft ftrokes of his vengeance. It alfo happens, that even thofe, who are in reality before the altar, may firft experience divine judgments. Of this difpenfation of an holy God, we have an account, 1 Pet. iv. 17. *For the time is come that judgment muft begin at the houfe of God: and if it firft begin at us, what fhall the end be of them that obey not the gofpel of God?* On account of the manifold and aggravated provocations of fons and daughters, the Lord brings judgments upon his church in various ways, which often are the forerunners of days of awful calamities, on thofe who corrupt and defpife the gofpel of Chrift.

6th, The Lord's judgments are called fire of the altar, becaufe he has a facrifice to confume thereby upon the earth. Fire was taken from the antient altar for the purpofes either of burning incenfe in other places, or of burning certain pieces of the fin-offering without the camp. *And the bullock for the fin-offering, and the goat for the fin-offering, whofe blood was brought in to make an atonement in the holy place, fhall one carry forth without the camp, and they fhall burn in the fire their fkins, and their flefh, and their dung*, Lev. xvi. 27. They fhall burn in the fire. What fire? The fire of the altar, no doubt; for it does not appear that common fire could be lawfully used in this solemn work, any more than it could be employed in burning incense. When the congregation saw one of the priests carrying fire of the altar in a censer without the camp, they would know that there was a sacrifice to consume with it; so when we hear of the great high Priest casting the fire of the altar into the earth, we may be sure he has a sacrifice to consume there, by this fire of divine judgments. He has persons to destroy, nations to afflict, churches to punish, and a sinful generation of his wrath in the earth, on whom he must take vengeance. Language similar to this is used by the prophet Isaiah, *The sword of the Lord is filled with blood, it is made fat with fatness, and with the blood of lambs and goats, with the fat of kidneys of rams; for the Lord has a sacrifice in Bozrah, and a great slaughter in the land of Idumea*, Isa. xxxiv. 6. Of the same import are the words uttered by the angel standing in the sun, relative to the last and most fearful execution of divine judgments on Christ's enemies, whereby he summons all the fowls that fly in the midst of heaven, saying to them, *Come and gather yourselves together unto the supper of the great God*, Rev. xix. 17. Since God has a sacrifice to consume on the earth, by the execution of his judgments on his enemies, the fire by which it is accomplished must be fire of the altar.

7th, These dispensations of God unto men are called by this name, because they are designed for the purification of the altar, and for the honour of those who are connected with it. Jehovah is nearly connected with the altar, it is before his throne, and he is worshipped there. For advancing his honour and glory, and for making men know that he is the Lord, are all his judgments executed on his enemies; and therefore they are the fire of the altar. Jesus Christ, the minister of the sanctuary and of the true tabernacle which the Lord pitched and not man, is also intimately connected with the altar. That his mediatorial glory may be advanced, his spiritual kingdom enlarged, and his gospel and cause vindicated, do these judgments come on men; on this account also are they fire of the altar. The servants of Christ belong to the altar, they minister daily there, and all their work as such is about this holy thing. For the vindication of the messages of grace which they have delivered, the calls to duty which they have given, and the threatnings which they have denounced, all in the name of the Lord and according to his word, ſhall days of calamity come on men; and therefore theſe viſitations are fire of the altar. The whole believing race are allied to the altar, for they have an altar at which they have no right to eat who ſerve the tabernacle. It is for the purpoſe of manifeſting the acceptableneſs to God of their profeſſion, teſtimony, holineſs, ſufferings and zeal that days of vengeance come on the wicked; and therefore theſe muſt be fire of the altar. For the purification of the altar alſo are judgments executed on thoſe who profane it. That the doctrines of the altar may be cleanſed from error, that the ordinances of the altar may be purified from human inventions, that the ſons of Levi may be refined as gold and ſilver to offer to the Lord an offering in righteouſneſs, that the worſhippers at the altar may be purged from their iniquity and be enabled to compaſs God's altar aright, and that every thing relating to the houſe of the God of heaven may be done according to his will, ſhall all theſe judgments found written in his word be executed in their ſeaſon; and ſurely all this glorious purification of the altar can only be effected by its own fire.

8th, Divine judgments are called fire of the altar to ſhew that God is well pleaſed with them, and that they tend to pacify him. When the fire of the antient altar conſumed the ſacrifices which were offered to God, he was pleaſed therewith, and it was a mean of reconciling him to the people. The judgments of God are called fire of the altar, becauſe they are pleaſing to him, and, after their execution, he is reconciled to the land. When divine judgments were executed on Achan and on all that he had, for his tranſgreſſion, on account of which the Lord was angry with all Iſrael, it is ſaid, *So the Lord turned from the fierceneſs of his anger*, Joſ. vii. 26. When the threatnings were fulfiled on Saul and his houſe, and on many of his adherants, it is declared, *After that the Lord was intreated for the land*, 2 Sam. xxi. 14. In the ſacred oracles, we have teſtimonies to this truth, of another nature than theſe; teſtimonies wherein the Lord repreſents the effect, which the execution of his judgments on his enemies, has upon himſelf. He declares that he is eaſed thereby. Iſa. i. 24. *Therefore ſaith the Lord, the Lord of hoſts, the mighty God of Iſrael; Ah, I will eaſe me of mine adversaries, and avenge me of mine enemies.* The Lord of hosts, the mighty God of Israel, speaking here after the manner of men, represents his enemies as a distressing burden to him, from which he eases himself, by taking vengeance on them. He also declares that he is comforted by the execution of his judgments on the workers of iniquity; *Thus shall mine anger be accomplished, and I will cause my fury to rest on them, and I will be comforted*, Ezek. v. 13. When the fire of the altar, in the judgments of his hand, breaks out, and destroys his implacable enemies, it is a comfort unto him; and therefore with these operations of his power, justice, holiness and truth, the eternal God is well pleased. Dispensations of this kind are also said to quiet his spirit; *Then cried he upon me, and spake unto me saying, Behold, these that go toward the north country, have quieted my spirit in the north country*, Zech. vi. 8. The execution of divine judgments, signified by the chariot of black horses going forth into the north country, as well as the bestowal of mercies, pointed out by the chariot of white horses that followed them, ver. 6. quiets the Lord's spirit, and brings glory to his name. Seeing these things are so, the judgments of God are with great propriety denominated fire of the altar.

9th, These operations of God on his enemies are represented by a censerful of fire taken from the altar, to shew that the wrath of God against sinners is only inflicted in part upon them in this world. When the ministers of the house burnt the sacrifices of the people without the camp with fire from the altar of burnt-offering, they did not carry away all the fire of the altar for this purpose, but only a small part of it. A censer full was only removed for this end, and a great quantity of fire remained burning continually on the altar. When Christ is represented as casting the fire of divine judgments on the earth, it is only a censer full of this fire of the altar which is taken for this design. The great mass of fire remains burning on the altar, which shall be cast upon them for their destruction and punishment, through the endless ages of eternity. As there was far more fire left at the altar than was removed in a censer, for burning sacrifices without the camp; so there is no proportion betwixt Christ's censerful of fire which he casts into the earth, in temporal judgments on men, and the infinite wrath of God which is reserved for the wicked in the place of misery. However awful the judgments of God may be, which the wicked suffer in this world, they are as nothing when compared with that unquenchable fire that they shall endure, in that place where the Lord's mercy is clean gone, where he has forgotten to be gracious, and where he will be favourable no more. Afflicting as temporal judgments may be to the children of men, and tedious as their sufferings are under their painful influence; yet the wrath of God that they shall endure hereafter shall be infinitely more distressing to them, and endless in its duration. In this world, it is only a censerful of fire of the altar that is scattered among them; but, in the world to come, they shall be laid on the altar, and the infinite mass of fire which burns continually there, shall eternally consume them, *for every one shall be salted with fire*, Mark ix. 49.

10th, Divine judgments are called the fire of the altar, because the wrath of God, which the wicked suffer both in this world and in the next, is the same in its nature with that which Christ endured and exhausted by his sufferings and death, in the room of his people. Jesus Christ not only stands at the altar of incense, *and makes intercession for the saints according to the will of God;* but he also stood at the altar of burnt-offering, *and gave himself for us an offering and sacrifice of a sweet smelling savour unto God.* As he fully executes his priestly office, in making intercession for us; so he completely fulfiled that office *when he appeared once in the end of the world, to put away sin by the sacrifice of himself.* His divine nature was the glorious altar, his human nature the sacrifice, and he, as God and man in one person, was the priest, who offered this sacrifice to God on this altar. When Jesus offered himself a sacrifice, the fire of divine wrath, which was due to the elect whom he represented on account of their sin, brake out upon him, and consumed his human nature in death. With respect to this infinite pouring out of divine wrath on him, we find him saying, *My heart is like wax, it is melted in the midst of my bowels*, Psal. xxii. 14. His human nature was melted and disolved in the pains of death, by the fire of divine wrath which he endured, for the salvation of his people. When he ministered at God's altar, as an atoning high priest, the fire of the altar took hold of him, and he, on account of the divine dignity of his person as the Son of God, intirely quenched this vindictive flame for all who believe in him to salvation. The judgments of God on men are called the fire of the altar, to shew that they endure the same wrath both here and hereafter, which Christ intirely finished in his sufferings and death, for the redemption of his people. And how can it be otherwise? As they reject the glorious and only Saviour, and exercise not a saving faith in his blood, their sin is not expiated, guilt remains on them, to the curse of the law they are liable, and they must suffer the vengeance of eternal fire, both in this world and in that which is to come. The fire of the altar must have a sacrifice; and as they reject the only propitiatory atonement, and are, by their daily rebellion against God, treasuring up wrath to themselves against the day of wrath, this fire will break out upon them and consume them. These divine judgments which the wicked suffer here, as well as their eternal punishment, are an execution of the same divine wrath on them, which Christ suffered for his people and for ever removed from them, when he was wounded for their transgressions, and bruised for their iniquities; and therefore it is called fire of the altar.

We now proceed to the

III. Head, which was to shew, what is imported in Christ's inflicting those judgments on the children of men; *He took the censer, he filled it with fire of the altar, and he cast it into the earth.*

1st, Christ's inflicting divine judgments on men imports, that all the agency which he employs about them, is in consequence of a delegated power over all things, which he has received from God the Father. He could have no official concern about the judgments of God, were it not given him by Jehovah. As he is the Son of God, and possessed of the divine nature and perfections, his necessary concern about all divine works toward the creatures, is the same with that of the Father, and the Holy Spirit. It is not of this, however, that the text speaks. Concerning that employment of the Lord Christ about these works of God, especially his works of judgment, which is peculiar unto him, does the text give us information. It is true, the Lord Jesus could have no ability for this official and peculiar work about either the judgments or the mercies of God, were he not possessed of that original and necessary concern about them, which belongs to him as a divine person. It is, therefore, of that work of Chrift about divine judgments which is peculiar to him, and which is official in its nature, that we are now fpeaking; and this he performs by virtue of a power over all perfons and things, which is given him of the Father. Ample and numerous are the teftimonies of the word of God, by which this truth is confirmed; a few of them only fhall be mentioned. In the vifion of Daniel this truth is clearly reprefented. *I faw in the night vifions, and behold one like the Son of man came with the clouds of heaven, and came to the antient of days, and they brought him near before him. And there was given him dominion, and glory, and a kingdom, that all people, nations, and languages fhould ferve him,* Dan. vii. 13, 14. Without particularly explaining thefe majeftic words, it may be obferved from them, that the Lord Jefus, *the one like the Son of man*, has received from Jehovah, *the antient of days*, *dominion*, power and authority, *and glory*, honour and renown, *and a kingdom*, fubjects to rule, *that all people, nations, and languages fhould ferve him*, that all mankind fhould be fubject to him, either in receiving the bleffings of falvation from him, or in having the fire of the altar fcattered among them by his hand. This power *is given him*, and it is given to him *who is like the Son of man*, to fhew that it is his official or mediatorial power, and not that divine power of which he is neceffarily poffeffed. On two very remarkable occafions, Chrift afferts this truth, in the hearing of his difciples. When the feventy returned with their joyful report, Jefus rejoiced in fpirit, and faid, *All things are delivered to me of my Father,* Luke x. 22. When he gave his fervants their commiffion, after his refurrection, he prefaces it with thefe words, *All power is given unto me in heaven and in earth,* Mat. xxviii. 18. Our mediator is the perfon to whom thefe things are delivered, and this power is given. Thefe things are delivered to him, and this power is given him, to fhew that it is an official or delegated power and charge that are here mentioned. The power that is given him is extenfive, it is all power in heaven and in earth; and the things which are delivered to him are univerfal, they are all things. The glorious perfon, who has delivered all things to him, and has given him all power, is his eternal Father. Twice does the Lord Chrift affert this truth in the fame difcourfe, *For the Father judgeth no man, but hath committed all judgment to the Son;* and again, *The Father hath given him authority to execute judgment also, because he is the Son of man*, John v. 22,—27. Jehovah the Father hath committed all judgment unto the Son, and hath given him, who is the Son of man, authority to execute judgment; by acquitting and blessing his people, and by condemning and punishing his enemies, both in this world, and in that which is to come. When our Redeemer addresses his holy and righteous Father, he uses the following words, *As thou hast given him*, thy Son, *power over all flesh, that he should give eternal life to as many as thou hast given him*, John xvii. 2. From these words it is evident, that our mediator has a gifted or delegated power over all flesh from the Father; that the principal end of his possessing and exercising this power over all flesh, in reference to the creatures, is that he may bestow the blessings of eternal life on the objects of the Father's love; and that, as his power extends over all flesh, he exercises it also in casting the fire of divine judgments into the earth, for the punishment of his implacable foes.

2d, Christ's casting the fire of the altar into the earth imports, that he inflicts judgments on men in the execution of his mediatorial office. He not only does so, by virtue of a power delegated to him of the Father; but he also accomplishes this work, in his mediatorial character. The inferior name, the angel, by which he is here called, clearly confirms this truth. As he is the Son of God he is never called by this name; but as he is our Mediator, God and man in one person, he is, in different parts of the divine word, represented in this manner. The casting fire of the altar into the earth, therefore, belongs unto the mediatorial work of Christ. The works which are ascribed unto Christ, in the two verses before the text, are purely mediatorial. It is only in his mediatorial character that he stands at the golden altar, like an officiating priest, has a golden censer, and receives much incense. It is as our Mediator only that he offers this incense with the prayers of all saints, on the golden altar, in his prevalent intercession for them before the throne. It is in his mediatorial character alone that the prayers of the saints, perfumed with his incense, can ascend with acceptance before God out of his hands. It is the same person, he is called by the same name, and is still employed about things which belong to the sanctuary, who is mentioned in the words of the text, and the angel took the cenſer, and filled it with fire of the altar, and caſt it into the earth; it muſt therefore be in his mediatorial character that he performs this ſtrange act.

3d, Chriſt's caſting the fire of the altar into the earth imports, that judgments are inflicted on men according to the purpoſe, and in obedience to the command of God. This work is performed by the Mediator according to the decree of God. The unalterable purpoſes of Jehovah are the rule, according to which he himſelf performs all things among the creatures. All his works, whether in creation, providence or grace, are an exact fulfillment of his decree; *For he worketh all things after the counſel of his own will*, Eph. i. 11. As the decree of God is a rule to himſelf, in all his diſpenſations toward the creatures; ſo this purpoſe is a rule to Chriſt, in all his mediatory adminiſtrations, both when he cauſes thoſe who love him to inherit ſubſtance, and when he throws the fire of divine anger upon his enemies. The purpoſe of God fixes the time, the objects, the inſtruments, the meaſures, and the duration of divine judgments in the earth; and from its appointments, in theſe and the like particulars, the Mediator, in his adminiſtrations, will never depart. As Mediator, he is perfectly acquainted with the divine decrees, and is a faithful ſervant to his Father, and, therefore, every part of that purpoſe muſt be exactly fulfilled by his operations. He hath ever been, and ever will be faithful as a Son over his own houſe, and faithful to him who appointed him to his mediatory office, deviations, therefore, from this ſupreme rule in his official work, are impoſſible.—As the decree of God is the rule of his mediatory adminiſtrations, ſo the command of God is the reaſon why he actually adminiſters, in the kingdoms of grace and providence. The words of Jeſus reſpecting his death and reſurrection apply to every part of his official work; *This commandment have I received of my Father*, John x. 18. When Chriſt takes the cenſer, fills it with fire of the altar, and caſts it into the earth, he may ſay, this commandment have I received of my Father. When Chriſt performs his official works in theſe particulars, he neither runs unſent, nor acts without proper powers; but he is clothed with a commiſſion, and is inveſted with authority from Jehovah for this purpoſe. Every operation of Chriſt, in bringing either mercies or judgments on men, is performed according to the purpose, and in obedience to the command of God.

4th, Christ's casting the fire of the altar into the earth imports, that it is done by the power or influence of God. The mediatorial administration of Jesus does not set aside the supreme working of the three one God. The Redeemer's giving eternal life to his people does not prevent the Father's gift of eternal life to them; *For the gift of God is eternal life through Jesus Christ our Lord.* Christ's judging the world, in his mediatorial character, does not contradict that truth, that God is the judge of all. The Mediator's inflicting divine judgments on the children of men, does not hinder the bringing these judgments on them to be supremely the work of God. There is no inconsistency betwixt the divine operations of the three one God, in governing all his creatures and all their actions, and the mediatorial administrations of Jesus Christ. These are connected together, and their consistency is asserted by Christ himself when he said, *My Father worketh hitherto, and I work*, John v. 17. It is impossible that Jehovah can surrender to any the supreme government of all things, either in the right or in the exercise of it; because it necessarily and essentially belongs to the divine nature. The mediatorial power and administrations of Jesus do not withdraw the supreme government of all things, either in the right or in the exercise of it, out of the hands of the three one God. His power as our Mediator, and his administrations in that character, both in grace and providence, are essentially different in their nature, from the power and operations of Jehovah, both among his saints and his other creatures. The latter is underived, the former is communicated; the one is essential, the other is official, this is supreme, that is subordinate. When Christ casts the fire of divine judgments into the earth, his Father worketh hitherto, or unto this end, and he also works. The power or influence of Jehovah, of which Christ as the Son of God is essentially possessed, is exercised in pouring divine judgments on men; while the Lord Christ, as our Mediator, has an official concern in casting them into the earth. Now, this work is accomplished by divine power, because the exercise of that power which is official, plainly supposes the exertion of that which is supreme; because he who is entrusted with mediatorial authority, as he is the Son of God, is poſſeſſed of this almighty power; and becauſe Jeſus in all his mediatorial adminiſtrations, reſpecting either his people or his enemies, is upheld and ſupported by the power of the three one God.

5th, The Mediator's caſting the fire of the altar into the earth imports, that the treaſures of wrath, as well as the treaſures of grace and ſalvation, are at his diſpoſal. As it hath pleaſed the Father that in him all fulneſs ſhould dwell, that out of his fulneſs his people might receive and grace for grace; ſo it hath pleaſed the Father alſo to commit all judgment unto him, that he might have authority to execute judgment alſo upon his enemies, becauſe he is the Son of man. He not only reigns over his church, by the ſceptre of his grace; but rules in the midſt of his enemies, and, with his iron rod, daſhes them in pieces like a potter's veſſel. He has not only a power to forgive ſins, and to exalt the law-condemned ſinner into a ſtate of juſtification before God; but he has alſo power over fire, and can cauſe it burn up his enemies. The fire of the altar is at his diſpoſal, and, therefore, he takes it into his cenſer and caſts it on the inhabitants of the earth. He is exalted as a prince and a ſaviour, not only to give repentance to Iſrael and the remiſſion of ſins; but alſo to avenge all the wrongs done by his incorrigible enemies to God, to himſelf, and to his church, by executing divine judgments upon them. That wrath by which God's enemies are deſtroyed, is not the wrath of him only that ſitteth on the throne; but it is alſo called the wrath of the Lamb. It is the wrath of the Lamb, becauſe they are the effects of the Mediator's diſpleaſure, as well as the effects of the anger of God, which are endured by thoſe who hate and oppoſe him. It is alſo the wrath of the Lamb, becauſe the wrath of God, in its terrible effects on his enemies, is inflicted on them by the agency of our Mediator, who is the Lamb in the midſt of the throne.

6th, The Mediator's caſting the fire of the altar into the earth imports, that every thing is done by Chriſt, which is neceſſary for the infliction of divine judgments on his enemies. Three actions are aſcribed to him in the text, relative to this work; and no more is neceſſary for its accompliſhment. He took the cenſer,—he filled it with fire of the altar,—and caſt it into the earth. There was no more needful to be done, by the prieſts under the former diſpenfation, to burn, without the camp, the bodies of thofe beafts, whofe blood was brought into the fanctuary by the high prieft for fin, than to take their cenfer, to fill it with fire from the altar, and to apply it to the combuftible materials, by which they were reduced to afhes. In like manner, Chrift has nothing more to do, for confuming the Lord's facrifice on the earth, or for deftroying thofe who have troden under foot the court without the temple and the holy city forty and two months, than to take the cenfer, to fill it with fire of the altar, and to caft it into the earth; and all thefe, the text affures us, the Lord Jefus does perform. It is an orderly, progreffive and complete fervice which is here reprefented. It is begun, he took the cenfer; it is continued, he filled it with fire of the altar; and it is finifhed, he caft it into the earth. This infpired reprefentation of the Mediator's work, which John faw in the vifions of God, being fo particular and full, plainly proves that every thing neceffary, for the execution of divine judgments on his enemies, fhall be performed by the Lord Chrift.

7th, Chrift's cafting the fire of the altar into the earth imports, that all the inftruments of the Lord's anger are under his command, and at his direction. When the Lord executes his judgments on his foes, he employs the agency of his creatures whether animate or inanimate. In his entrufting the Mediator with authority to execute judgment, he puts all thefe inferior agents under his power. Are the angels employed in this work? *Chrift is gone into heaven, and is on the right hand of God, angels, authorities, and powers being made fubject unto him,* 1 Pet. iii. 22. Is the agency of men employed by the Lord in deftroying his enemies? *The Father hath given him power over all flefh,* John xvii. 2. Is the inanimate creation fometimes employed by the Lord, in bringing to pafs his ftrange act of judgment? The winds and the fea obey our Redeemer, and *he hath put all things under his feet, and given him to be head over all things to the church,* Eph. i. 22. Whatever the creatures are whofe inftrumentality the Lord Jehovah is pleafed to employ, as inferior agents in his works of judgment, they are all *the armies which are in heaven*. And whom do they follow? At whofe direction do they move? They follow that glorious perfon who fat on the white horfe, who is called faithful and true, whofe eyes were as a flame of fire, on whofe head were many crowns, who had a name written that no man knew but he himſelf, who was clothed with a veſture dipt in blood, and whoſe name is called the word of God. This is a glorious deſcription of our Mediator, and it is immediately added, *And the armies which were in heaven followed him upon white horſes, clothed in fine linen, white and clean*, Rev. xix. 14. They follow him to receive their orders from him, and to act according to his will. They follow him to be uſed by him as he pleaſes, in bringing judgments on the children of men. That they follow him to a work of this kind, is evident from the remaining part of the chapter, and from the next verſe; *And out of his mouth goeth a ſharp ſword, that with it he ſhould ſmite the nations; and he ſhall rule them with a rod of iron; and he treadeth the wine preſs of the fierceneſs and wrath of Almighty God.*

8th, Chriſt's caſting the fire of the altar into the earth imports, that all the effects of divine judgments on the children of men are produced by his agency. As he caſts theſe burning coals from the altar into the earth, the effects they produce on men are cauſed by his mediatory adminiſtration. Since the bleſſings enjoyed by the church come to them through his work, as the interceeding high prieſt, ſtanding at the altar with the golden cenſer in his hand, and much incenſe to offer it with their prayers; the evils alſo which befal the children of men, ſuffering under the judgments of God, are brought on them by him who caſts the fire of the altar into the earth. The mercy and grace of God are the ſupreme foundation of the church's felicity, and his wrath and juſtice are the chief cauſe of the miſery of his enemies; but both are produced alſo by the miniſtration of the Lord Jeſus. He has an immediate, miniſterial and ſubordinate agency in the production of theſe things both to his friends and to his enemies; an agency to which he is honourably exalted becauſe he became the Son of man, and finiſhed in our nature the infinitely arduous work that was given him to do. Whatever, therefore, are the effects of divine judgments on the children of men, they are produced by the power and working of Jeſus. If they ſuffer by theſe judgments, in their perſons, in their wealth, in their honours, in their power, in their relations, or in their lives, all this accumulated woe is hurled on them, by his hand who caſts the fire of the altar into the earth. Are they overcome? It is the Lamb that overcomes them. Are they slain? It is with the ſword of him that ſat on the horſe. And are they troden in the wine preſs without the city? It is he who treadeth the wine preſs of the fierceneſs and wrath of Almighty God.

SERMON II.

Rev. viii. 5. *And the angel took the cenſer, and filled it with fire of the altar, and caſt it into the earth; and there were voices, and thunderings, and lightnings, and an earthquake.*

IN diſcourſing on the three foregoing heads, which have been already conſidered, it has been ſhewn in what reſpects the judgments of God are compared to fire, why they are called fire of the altar, and what is the import of Chriſt's inflicting divine judgments on his enemies. According to the method propoſed, we ſhall now proceed to the

IV. Head of the doctrine, which was to mention ſome of the effects of Chriſt's work, which are here repreſented by voices, thunderings, lightnings and an earthquake.

When the mediatorial angel caſts the fire of the altar into the earth, voices and thunderings ſhall be heard, lightnings ſhall be ſeen, and an earthquake ſhall be felt by the inhabitants of the world. When thoſe things happen together, they conſtitute a moſt dreadful tempeſt in the natural world. When the noiſe of loud ſounding winds and roaring thunders is heard, accompanied with frightful flaſhes of vivid lightning, which ſtrike the eye, and when theſe are attended with the ſhocks of a terrible earthquake, great terror ſeizes the minds of men, the earth ſeems to be convulſed, and much devaſtation is often brought upon the works thereof. By theſe outward tempeſts, which are brought on men by the hand of God, he has often executed his diſpleaſure upon his enemies; and Divine Providence may ſtill employ them to a conſiderable degree for pouring his vengeance on the wicked in the day of his recompences. In that part of the ſolemn tranſaction at Sinai, which was intended to repreſent the Lord's diſpleaſure at ſin, and his puniſhing ſinners, and to re-exhibit to that people the covenant of works, all theſe particulars are found; for the alarming voice of the trumpet and of thunders was heard, lightning and fire were ſeen, and the whole mount quaked greatly. When the kingdoms of this world ſhall become the kingdoms of our Lord and of his Chriſt, the temple of God ſhall be opened in heaven, and there ſhall be ſeen in his temple the ark of his teſtament, for the comfort and ſalvation of his people; but, at the ſame time it is declared, that there ſhall be, for the puniſhment of his enemies, lightnings, and voices, and thunders, and an earthquake, and great hail, Rev. xi. 19. When God's judgments ſhall be finiſhed on Turk and Antichriſt, with their ſupporters, we are told, *there were voices, and thunders, and lightnings; and there was a great earthquake, ſuch as was not ſince men were upon the earth, ſo mighty an earthquake and ſo great. And there fell upon men a great hail out of heaven, every ſtone about the weight of a talent*, Rev. xvi. 18, 21. Not in the words of our text only, but in other parts of Scripture alſo, the wrath of God, which is inflicted by his judgments on men, is ſet before us in theſe ſtriking repreſentations. From this it is evident, that the judgments of God on ſinners in various periods of time, though they may differ in their degree and duration, are yet the ſame in their cauſes, in their ſubſtance, and in the manner of their execution. The voices, thunders, lightnings, and the earthquake, mentioned in the text, are metaphors taken from theſe frightful occurrences in the world of nature, to repreſent the ſin-avenging judgments of the living God, and the awful diſpenſations of his Providence, by which the men of the world ſhall be diſtreſſed, and many of them deſtroyed. We ſhall now mention ſome of theſe divine judgments, which are repreſented by the voices, thunders, lightnings, and the earthquake, that are produced among men by Chriſt's caſting the fire of the altar into the earth.

1ſt, Theſe repreſent the judgment of diviſion. This is a ſore evil which is brought on men by the hand of God, and which often extends both to their religious and civil concerns. As it is a great mercy which the Lord has promiſed to his people, to give them one heart and one way; ſo it is a ſad ſtroke of his anger when he divides them in Jacob, and ſcatters them in Iſrael. How mournfully prevalent is the ſpirit of diviſion among the children of men, relative to religious things! Different voices are heard in the church of God. The watchmen do not ſee eye to eye in matters of religion, nor do they ſing together with the voice; but Ephraim is againſt Manaſſeh, and Manaſſeh is againſt Ephraim, and theſe together are againſt Judah. The Chriſtian people, inſtead of holding the unity of the Spirit in the bond of peace, are ſplit into parties, and altar is ſet up againſt altar in every corner of the land. Eccleſiaſtic teachers and rulers have been ſuffered, for a long time, to purſue meaſures, which have had a mournful tendency both to occaſion and confirm religious diviſion. We have divided away from the Lord, by turning from his truths and ordinances, and ſo have broken the ſtaff of beauty; he has therefore been provoked, as a puniſhment of our ſin, by ſending a ſpirit of diviſion amongſt us, to break the ſtaff of bands. The judgment of diviſion reſpecting our civil concerns is not leſs remarkable. To this token of the Lord's anger, nations are greatly ſubjected. Many are found, in the ſame country, rejoicing at events, which occaſion to others grief and mourning. Multitudes highly applaud ſome meaſures of public adminiſtration, which are reprobated by a numerous and reſpectable claſs of the ſame community. Almoſt every where, plans of government are purſued which occaſion the increaſe of political diviſion. The ſyſtems which are eſtabliſhed in nations, as they have many who are engaged in their ſupport, ſo there are others found who are endeavouring to pull them down. Theſe things are mournful evidences, that the Lord has brought the judgment of diviſion, in a remarkable way, upon the children of men: And a ſore judgment it is; for it prevents unity of affection, and of exertion for the public proſperity, both civil and religious; it makes every man, in ſome reſpects, his neighbour's enemy; and it gives us reaſon to fear, ſince we are thus divided, that we cannot ſtand.

2d, Theſe words contain the judgment of deſolating wars. The ſword of deſtructive war was often threatened by the Lord in the writings of the Old Teſtament, both againſt his own people, and the nations around them. By this judgment they were all often brought very low, and at laſt totally deſtroyed. It is in this calamity, that the fire of the altar, on many occaſions, conſumes the enemies of the Lord. Of this the inſtances, both in ſacred and profane hiſtory, are innumerable. A dreadful and deſtructive period of deſolating war is foretold, in the pouring out of the ſixth and ſeventh vials, by which the public enemies of Chriſt ſhall be overcome, and which is called the battle of Armageddon. All wars are in their nature a judgment of God on the children of men. Foreign wars, by which nation rises againſt nation, and kingdom againſt kingdom, are great calamities inflicted by the King of nations on the inhabitants of the world. Civil wars, or the inhabitants of the ſame kingdom riſing up againſt one another, and deſtroying each other's perſons and property, are alſo ſingular calamities from the hand of God. Long continued wars which are carried on by the obſtinacy and pride of both, or of one of the parties, to a diſtreſſing length, are great judgments on the inhabitants of the earth. Extenſive wars which are carried on by many nations at the ſame time, and in many places of the earth, are, in a ſpecial manner, divine puniſhments inflicted on ſinners. Wars which are proſecuted with uncommon bitterneſs and energy, producing frequent battles, great ſlaughter, and much local deſolation, are particularly the effects of the fire of the altar upon the earth. Wars attended with uncommon expence, whereby nations and their poſterity are ſubjected to great pecuniary burdens, are a ſore calamity from the righteous Judge. And above all, wars which have had for their effect the overturning the thrones of princes, and ſtill ſeem to have for their object further alterations of this kind, are peculiarly judgments from God, and ſhew that they are of the ſame nature with thoſe predicted in the ninth chapter of this book, which cauſed the world change its maſters, and brought dreadful diſtreſs on men. The wars by which the nations of the earth are at preſent ſuffering, have been, and ſtill are of the deſcription now mentioned, and therefore they muſt be the effects of the fire of the altar caſt into the earth.

3d, The words comprehend the judgment of famine This is another diſpenſation of God, by which he ofte inflicts his anger on the workers of iniquity. This w: one of the judgments with which God's antient people w: ſome times chaſtiſed, and it is one of the wrathful ſtrok which ſhall contribute to the deſtruction of antichri When the Lord, in his righteous providence withholds h bleſſing from the earth, prevents it from yielding its ſtreng to the ſinful generation upon it, and ſends unfriendly a barren ſeaſons, he is teſtifying his diſpleaſure in the plain manner, againſt the children of men. When the Lo prepares and employs the insects and reptiles of the earth; to devour a part of the fruits of the field, he is bringing this judgment on a land. This he did to his people of old, Joel 1, 3, 4. *Tell ye your children of it, and let them tell their children, and their children another generation. That which the palmer worm hath left, hath the locust eaten; and that which the locust hath left, hath the canker worm eaten; and that which the canker worm hath left, hath the caterpillar eaten.* When the Lord, by sending unnatural cold, excessive drought, or immoderate and unseasonable rain, refuses to bless the springing of the year, this calamity is brought on men. When the Lord makes the harvest an heap in the day of grief, and of desperate sorrow, by shaking winds, rotting rains, and destructive frost, he is visibly contending with the inhabitants of the earth. By these operations, he breaks the staff of bread, and sends amongst a people the evil arrows of famine, by which many come to be hardly bestead for those things which are needful to the body. The alarming scarcity and extravagant dearth of the necessary supports of human life are a great judgment from God; as thereby the outward situation of many is materially changed to the worse; the honest savings of better times are expended, hunger and nakedness are endured by many, and disease and death sometimes follow in the train. These isles of the sea to which we belong, are at present smitten with this sore judgment from the hand of God. He hath in the last season given us the blade and the ear, but he has withheld from us the full corn in the ear; whereby many have been reduced to great perplexity aud distress. Our iniquities have procured these things unto us. We have been unconcerned for the interests of his glory, and therefore has he brought this evil upon us, as he did upon his people of old; *Ye looked for much, and, lo, it came to little; and when ye brought it home, I did blow upon it; why? saith the Lord of Hosts, because of mine house that is waste, and ye run every man unto his own house*, Hag. 1, 9. The national support and countenance are bestowed upon many things in religion which are not the Lord's; and therefore he has laid this judgment upon us; for to us the words of the Prophet are applicable, *For she did not know that I gave her corn, and wine, and oil, and multiplied her silver and gold, which they prepared for*

Baal; therefore will I return and take away my corn in the time thereof, and my wine in the ſeaſon thereof, and will recover my wool and my flax given to cover her nakedneſs, Hoſ. xi. 8, 9. Our criminal abuſe of plenty which the Lord hath formerly given us, by luxurious eating, immoderate drinking, vain and expenſive clothing, and ſinful amuſements and diverſions, has alſo procured this evil unto us. Oh! that the children of men were religiouſly exerciſed under this ſore judgment, were not only crying what ſhall we eat? but alſo, what ſhall we do to be ſaved?

4th, Theſe words include alſo the judgment of the peſtilence, as another effect of the fire of the altar. With this judgment Iſrael was threatened; *And I will bring a ſword upon you, that ſhall avenge the quarrel of my covenant; and when ye are gathered together within your city, I will ſend the peſtilence among you: and ye ſhall be delivered into the hand of the enemy*, Lev. xxvi. 25. This judgment ſometimes accompanies war and famine, and at other times it comes by itſelf; but, in any of theſe ways, it is a moſt alarming diſpenſation of divine providence. By it many parts of the world, have been at different times dreadfully diſtreſſed. When the Lord ſends mortal and peſtilential diſeaſes among the children of men, it is a great evidence of his anger gone forth againſt them. By theſe many of them are cut off from the land of the living; and great terror and perplexity, inconvenience, and wordly loſs are endured by thoſe who eſcape. Of late years, different parts of the earth, and ſome of the armies of the nations have been, by the righteous hand of God, ſmitten with this ſore judgment, The nations have not been careful to counteract the diſeaſe of ſin, in its different appearances among them, whereby God is diſhonoured, and his law is broken; and therefore he may be provoked to ſuffer outward peſtilential diſeaſes to ſpread their contagious influence among men, till many of them are deſtroyed. When epidemical diſeaſes, occaſioning a ſlight and ſhort trouble, paſs through a land, they are warnings to the inhabitants thereof; becauſe he who has ſent them, can as eaſily ſend the peſtilence for our deſtruction. In the days of the Lord's vengeance upon men, when the fire of the altar ſhall be caſt into the earth, we are ſure that by this judgment, as well as by war and famine, many ſhall be deſtroyed. It is mentioned by the Lord Jesus, in the enumeration he gives of divine judgments, which shall come upon sinful nations in the times of the gospel; *And great earthquakes shall be in divers places, and famines, and pestilences,* Luke xxi, 11. Of the destruction of Antichrist it is said, *Therefore shall her plagues come in one day, death, and mourning, and famine,* Rev. xviii, 8. The noisome and destructive pestilence, is therefore one of the effects of the fire of the altar.

5th, National poverty and bankruptcy may be considered as another divine judgment on the children of men, which is included in these words. The public prosperity of nations is in itself a great blessing from the Lord; but when he dries up the sources of national wealth, and brings poverty and dependence upon men, the hand of the Lord, in his judgments, is against them. The former was promised to Israel, in their keeeping the commandments of the Lord; and the latter was threatened to them, in case of their departing from him. *The Lord shall open unto thee his good treasure, the heaven to give the rain unto thy land in his season, and to bless all the works of thine hand; and thou shalt lend unto many nations, and thou shalt not borrow,* Deut. xxviii, 12. In the 43d, and 44th verses of the same chapter, one of the judgments for their disobedience is expressed in the following words; *The stranger that is within thee, shall get up above thee very high; and thou shalt come down very low; he shall lend unto thee, and thou shalt not not lend unto him; he shall be the head, and thou shalt be the tail.* Whatever are the springs of a nation's wealth, the productions of the earth, the labour of their hands, or their extended commerce, the Lord can easily blast them, and overwhelm men with distress and perplexity. Antient Tyre, who was abundant in merchandize and in treasures, is a singular instance of the justice and power of God, in bringing upon nations, the most opulent and strong, great poverty and ruin. Both her prosperity and overthrow, are described by the Prophet Ezekiel, chap. xxvii. from which the following expressions are selected. *And thou wart replenished and made very glorious in the midst of the seas. Thy riches, and thy fairs, thy merchandize, thy mariners, and thy pilots, thy calkers, and the occupiers of thy merchandize, and all thy men of war that are in thee, and in all thy company, which is in the midst of thee, shall fall into the midst of the seas, in the day of thy ruin*, verses 25, 27. Our land has often suffered by the partial execution of this judgment. The stagnation of trade, as well as unfruitful seasons, occasioned by numerous bankruptcies, which circulate their hurtful influence through many orders of men, has sometimes brought us into great distress. When the fire of the altar shall consume Antichrist, this judgment also shall be found among her plagues. *And the merchants of the earth shall weep over her, for no man buyeth their merchandize any more*, Rev. xviii. 11.

6th, Popular commotions are a judgment from the Lord, which is pointed out in the words of the text. These are moral earthquakes, or violent shakings among rational creatures, and moral agents, which often prove a dreadful scourge to the children of men. When the Lord takes off the restraints of his providence from the minds of the multitude, and sets them loose against their superiors, or one another, it is a great judgment from God to the nation where it happens. These insurrections are lawless, ungovernable and violent; and the persons concerned in them are often carried to the greatest excesses. They greatly disturb the tranquillity of cities and of nations, and frequently occasion the destruction of much property, and the loss of many lives. In some parts of the world, these are more frequent and mischievous; and in others, they are both more seldom and moderate. Whatever may be the causes of these popular tumults, and however much sin may be committed in them; yet the holy and righteous God may order and overrule them, as a judgment of his hand, in punishing sinners for their iniquity. When the fire of the altar shall be thrown among men, there is reason to conclude, that by such dreadful moral earthquakes as these, he will arise and shake terribly the earth.

7th, The overturning the established systems of nations, is another effect of the fire of the altar, which is represented in these words. In the righteous judgment of God upon sinful nations, he sometimes overthrows both their civil and ecclesiastic establishments. These are spiritual and political earthquakes, which are brought on men, by the power and justice of God, as a punishment of their sin; and always occasion much distress to the inhabitants of the world. These alterations, relating as they do to the moſt important concerns of men, involve nations in ſore calamities; for they are accompliſhed by many voices, much thunderings, and frequent lightnings of the Lord's diſpleaſure. The kingdom of the ten tribes had this judgment executed on them, in their captivity by the King of Aſſyria. The kingdom of Judah ſuffered the ſame calamity in their captivity in Babylon. The kingdom of Babylon itſelf came under the ſame ſtroke, by the hand of the Medes and Perſians. It would be endleſs to enumerate the many inſtances of the execution of this judgment on the nations of the world. Almoſt every kingdom in the earth, at one time or another, has experienced earthquakes of this kind. Theſe have chiefly been brought on them, by means of the invaſion and conqueſt of a foreign power. In the new heavens and the new earth, for which believers do earneſtly look, and patiently wait, both civil and eccleſiaſtic tyranny ſhall be deſtroyed; and therefore ſpiritual and political earthquakes muſt happen in many lands, before the coming of that happy period. When the fire of the altar ſhall be ſent forth to deſtroy antichriſt finally, his ſpiritual ſyſtem ſhall periſh, and all that tyranny by which it has been upheld ſhall fade away. Theſe ſhall be the effects of the voices, thunders, lightnings, and earthquake under the ſeventh vial; for it is ſaid, *And the great city was divided into three parts, and the cities of the nations fell; and great Babylon came in remembrance before God, to give unto her the cup of the wine of the fierceneſs of his wrath*, Rev. xvi, 19.

8th, Natural earthquakes, ſtorms and tempeſts may belong unto the judgments of God, which are the effects of the fire of the altar. The Lord has often employed theſe, for viſiting on the children of men their aggravated iniquities. There have been dreadful deſtructions brought on ſinners, by theſe effects of Jehovah's power, and tokens of his wrath. The words may not only be underſtood in a figurative, but alſo in a literal ſenſe; and, in this view, they repreſent to us alſo the effects of the fire of the altar. By the natural winds, thunders, lightnings and earthquakes, the Lord has brought, and may yet bring judgments on men. With reſpect to the firſt of theſe, it is ſaid, *Thou didſt blow with thy wind, the ſea covered them; they ſunk as lead in the mighty waters*, Exod. xv 10. Relative to the second, we have the following declaration, *The adversaries of the Lord shall be broken in pieces; out of heaven shall he thunder upon them*, 1 Sam. i, 10. The operations of the third are stated in these words, *He shot out his lightnings and discomfited them*, Psalm xviii, 14. And with reference to the last we have the following account, *Yea, ye shall flee like as ye fled from before the earthquake, in the days of Uzziah king of Judah*, Zech. xix, 5. Tempestuous winds, destructive thunder and lightning, and the terrible earthquake are in the hand of God, and he can, by them as means, bring great desolations on the earth, and misery on the inhabitants thereof. By their operations, many have perished both by sea and land; and in days of fearful calamity on men for sin, there is reason to think, that they will again be the instruments of his wrath.

These are some of the judgments of God signified by the voices, thunderings, lightnings and earthquake, which are mentioned in the text, as the awful effects of Christ's taking the censer, filling it with fire of the altar, and casting it into the earth.

This subject shall now be concluded, by deducing some inferences from what has been said.

1st, From this subject we may see the awful nature of divine judgments. They are most solemn and tremenduous operations of Jehovah's holiness, power, and justice. A serious consideration of them, made the Psalmist say, *My flesh trembleth for fear of thee, and I am afraid of thy judgments*, Psalm cxix, 120. The greatness of God, who is the most high over all the earth, and with whom is terrible majesty, ought to impress our minds with the conviction of the dreadful nature of his judgments. The concern which the Lord Jesus, who is the lion of the tribe of Judah, has with their execution on men, may discover unto us their awful nature. The greatness of that guilt, which it is the design of these judgments to avenge on impenitent sinners, also discovers their terrible nature and effects. The representations of them in the text are calculated to affect our hearts with their awful nature. They are compared to fire, which is a most terrible, destructive and ragng element. They are the fire of the altar. When the fat and other parts of the sacrifices were burned upon the brazen altar, which stood in the court of the priests, at the door of the tabernacle of the congregation, it would ſend up a moſt vehement flame into the air, which the worſhippers, ſtanding in the court of the people, would ſee and conſider as an affecting emblem of that divine wrath, which they deſerved on account of their ſins. This is the metaphor, whereby the execution of divine judgments on men in this world is repreſented in the text; and certainly they muſt be very conſuming and deſtructive plagues. As they are compared to voices, lightnings, thunders, and an earthquake, which comprehend a moſt frightful ſtorm in the natural world, they muſt be very awful viſitations of Jehovah's arm and power on the children of men. Let none deſpiſe theſe doings of the Lord, either in the threatning or in their execution; but let all reverence God and fear his judgments.

2. This ſubject preſents to our view the evil nature of ſin. It is ſin that procures theſe judgments of God to the children of men. It kindles the ſire of the altar, cauſes Chriſt take the cenſer, fill it with this ſire, and caſt it into the earth; it muſt therefore be an evil and bitter thing to depart from the living God. The Lord is righteous and holy in all his words of threatning, and in all his works of judgment by which theſe are fulfilled; and ſeeing his temporal judgments on ſinners, and theſe which are eternal alſo, are cauſed by ſin, it muſt be a great evil. It is the procuring cauſe of the voices, lightnings, thunder, and the earthquake, by which the children of men are deſtroyed. Such is the nature of this evil, that God, to teſtify his abhorrence of it, hath laid the earth and all things therein under a curſe. For the ſame reaſon, the Lord, on ſpecial occaſions, ceaſes to exerciſe his patience with men, and brings on them the deſolating ſtrokes of his anger. In proportion as theſe judgments contain penal evil, ſo may we ſee the moral evil of ſin. The ſins of perſons, churches, and nations, are very heinous in their nature, various in their kinds, long continued in their duration, and exceedingly heightened by their aggravations; there is therefore no wonder that they bring down on their guilty heads, the awful judgments of God. O that we were made to ſee the evil of ſin, to hate it with perfect hatred, to mourn for it before the Lord, and to turn from it with all our hearts.

3. The glorious exaltation and work of our adored Me-

diator may be learned from what has been ſaid. He is now before the throne, and is ſtanding and miniſtering before the golden altar, which is in Jehovah's immediate and glorious preſence. Becauſe he humbled himſelf, and became obedient to death, even the death of the croſs, God the Father hath highly exalted him, and given him a name which is above every name. He hath given him authority to execute judgment alſo, becauſe he has, in our nature, finiſhed the work of redemption, in the purchaſe of it. As he miniſtered at the altar below, in the character of an atoning high prieſt, and hath then put away ſin by the ſacrifice of himſelf; ſo he is now ſet at the right hand of God, placed in the midſt of the throne, clothed with his royal robes, intruſted with all the treaſures of mercy and judgment, and employed in his mediatorial adminiſtrations. Theſe adminiſtrations are great and glorious, they comprehend his mediatorial work in his exalted ſtate, they are neceſſary to his Father's glory, his own honour, and his church's benefit, and they are proportioned to the honourable ſtation which he now occupies. In the holy place not made with hands, he adminiſters with reſpect to his people, by interceeding for them according to the will of God, by delivering them from all their miſeries, and by beſtowing upon them the bleſſings of eternal ſalvation. His adminiſtrations as our Mediator extend alſo to his irreconcilable enemies. With reſpect to them, he takes the cenſer, fills it with fire of the altar, and caſts it into the earth for their deſtruction. He threw the fire of the altar into the earth, an expreſſion which ſignifies that Jeſus performs this work with earneſt concern, with ſpecial care, with holy indignation, and with divine violence; with earneſt concern for the glory of God, and for bringing down the loftineſs of his enemies; with ſpecial care that no part of his wrath may fall upon his people, whom he keeps as the apple of his eye, but that it may alight upon, puniſh, and afflict the workers of iniquity; with holy indignation at the rebellion and wickedneſs of the children of men; and with divine violence that it may effectually conſume and deſtroy his irreclaimable foes. It is a great miſtake to confine Chriſt's miniſtrations to his redeemed church, and to exclude from his official rule his implacable enemies; for with reſpect to the latter, as well as the former, he has a glorious work to accompliſh. It is indeed an eternal truth, and full of consolation to the people of God, that Jehovah the Father has said unto Christ their Lord, *Sit thou on my right hand, until I make thine enemies thy footstool;* but he has also said to him, in the same affecting and solemn manner, *Rule thou in the midst of thine enemies*; and again, *Thou shalt break them with a rod of iron, thou shalt dash them in pieces like a potter's vessel.* Jesus is commissioned by the Father, both to give spiritual and eternal life to the objects of his everlasting love, and to execute judgment upon his enemies in this world, and even to turn the wicked into hell at last, with all the nations that forget God.

4. From this subject we may be informed, that the enemies of the Lord, and of his Christ, shall certainly be destroyed. The honour of the divine and mediatorial government requires it. In many of the prophecies and threatnings of God's word, this is plainly declared; and will he not do as he has said? *God is not a man that he should lie, neither the son of man that he should repent; hath he said, and shall he not do it? or hath he spoken, and shall he not make it good?* Numb. xxiii. 19. He hath not declared it in words only, but he hath assured us of it by most solemn and significant actions, which the servants of Christ have seen in the visions of God. Many of those are to be found in this book of the Revelations, and in other parts of scripture. The text contains three of them. John saw the mediatorial angel take the censer, fill it with fire of the altar, and cast it into the earth, which produced among men voices, lightnings, thunders, and an earthquake. Shall he not act those things in reality, which John saw him do in vision? To this the words of the prophet may be applied. *For the vision is yet for an appointed time, but at the end it shall speak, and not lie; though it tarry wait for it, because it will surely come, it will not tarry,* Hab. ii. 3. As the visionary representations of the work of Christ relative to his people, which are contained in the two verses preceding the text, shall be accomplished; so the significant actions, whereby his work respecting his enemies is exhibited in the text, shall be fulfilled in their season. Concerning the numerous and mighty hosts of foes with which his church is surrounded, and whereby his kingdom of grace is opposed among men, the Lord hath said, *To me be-*

F 2

longeth vengeance and recompence, their foot ſhall ſlide in due time; for the day of their calamity is at hand, and the things that ſhall come upon them make haſte, Deut. xxxii. 35. The belief of this truth ſhould be preſſed upon the minds of Chriſt's enemies, that they, forſeeing the evil, may hide themſelves, by abandoning their courſe of oppoſition to him, and by ſubmitting to the perſon, righteouſneſs, goſpel, and law of the Redeemer. The belief of this truth ſhould alſo be preſſed on the hearts of Chriſt's followers, to prevent them from ſinking into deſpondency, and giving way to unbelief and ſlaviſh fear during the period of the wicked's triumph; and to enable them to live in the exerciſe of an holy, joyful, and certain expectation of the accompliſhment of all the great and glorious things, which the Lord has promiſed to his church, both in this world and in that which is to come.

5. The great folly of the children of men, in oppoſing the intereſts of Chriſt in this world, is evident from what has been ſaid. Againſt whom are they acting? To whom are they making oppoſition? It is he who is God as well as man, who has all power in heaven and in earth, and who has the fiery judgments of God at his diſpoſal. Can they be ſafe in this courſe? Certainly not, for he muſt reign till his enemies are made his footſtool. He ſhall aſſuredly bring them low, by ſcattering theſe burning coals among them, and by caſting the fire of the altar into their boſom. To him the deſtruction of his enemies, even the moſt powerful and ſtubborn, is eaſy; for he has only to take the cenſer, fill it with fire of the altar, and caſt it into the earth, and inſtantly there ſhall be voices, lightnings, thunders, and an earthquake of perſonal or public judgments, by which they ſhall be overthrown. Their oppoſition to Chriſt contains the baſeſt ingratitude; for they are deſpiſing and rejecting him, who has come in the fleſh, and is now coming in the goſpel, not to condemn the world, but that the world through him might be ſaved. He is revealing to them ſtatutes by which they may live, and ſpeaking words by which they may be ſaved; and can they deſpiſe theſe ſtatutes of life, and reject this word of ſalvation, without being guilty of the greateſt folly and baſeſt ingratitude. In the words of Moſes they may be addreſſed, *Do ye thus requite the Lord, O fooliſh people and*

vain thing? Over them we may lament, in the words of that prophet, *O that they were wise, that they understood this, and that they would consider their latter end*, Deut. xxxii. 6, 29. This melancholy opposition to Christ, is managed by the children of men both in their personal and collective capacities. By the unbelief and enmity of their hearts, by their corrupt and erroneous sentiments, and by their immoral and ungodly lives they, as individuals, rage and imagine a vain thing against the Lord and his Christ. In their civil and ecclesiastical capacities, the children of men, by forsaking and opposing the concerns of the Mediator, and by practising and supporting these things which are contrary to his word, do set themselves and combine against the Lord and his anointed. All this will be found to be folly and presumptuous madness; for he that sitteth in the heavens will laugh, the Lord shall have them in derision; and the time shall come when he shall speak to them in his wrath, and shall vex them in his sore displeasure. How necessary and suitable then, to all ranks of men, must these exhortations be, and how worthy are they of their most hearty acceptation! *Be wise now therefore, O ye kings: and be ye instructed, ye judges of the earth. Serve the Lord with fear, and rejoice with trembling. Kiss the Son, lest he be angry, and ye perish from the way, when his wrath is kindled but a little: blessed are all they that put their trust in him*, Psal. ii. 10, 11, 12.

6. From this subject we may also see the safety of the people of God in a day of public calamity. When the fire of the altar is cast into the earth, not even the smallest sparks of it shall ever reach those who have fled for refuge, and laid hold on Christ by faith, as the hope set before them in the gospel. Their interest in Christ is the ground of their safety. By believing in him, they are for ever secured from the curse of the law, and the wrath of God; for they are brought within the bond of the covenant of grace, are clothed with the righteousness of Christ, are interested in the promises, and are entitled to the blessings which they contain. They are partakers of the infinite merit and satisfaction of Christ's obedience, sufferings, and death, whereby they are delivered from the guilt of sin, the condemning sentence of the law, and the stroke of divine justice. There is no fire at the altar for them; because their Surety has endured it on their account, and has removed it from them

entirely, and for ever. Christ will never cast the fire of the altar, the vindictive judgments of God, upon any for whose transgressions he was stricken. He will never cast any part of the fire of the altar into the earth, which he himself has endured, when he bare his people's sins in his own body on the tree. They are in him as their hiding place from the storm, and covert from the tempest, through which the wrath of God can never penetrate; they shall therefore enjoy perfect and eternal safety. An habitual improvement of Christ, by faith in his person, righteousness and grace, is necessary both unto our glorifying him, and unto our enjoying a comfortable sense of our safety in him. Our failing in this most important exercise, as it is greatly to the Redeemer's dishonour, so it will both deprive us of much spiritual comfort, and bring upon us days of darkness and sorrow. Those who live daily by faith on the Son of God, shall be enabled to sing, with holy joy and triumph, *God is our refuge and strength, a very present help in trouble. Therefore will we not fear, though the earth be removed, and though the mountains be carried into the midst of the sea, though the waters thereof roar, and be troubled, though the mountains shake with the swelling thereof.* They indeed may endure many trials, in a day when the Lord is shaking terribly the earth; but in these there is no part of the fire of the altar for them. The various tribulations which they may suffer shall, by the blessing of God, enlarge their spiritual exercise, promote their happiness and comfort, and prepare them for the inheritance of the saints in light. The consideration of the glorious person, to whom the execution of divine judgments is committed, and of their relation to him, may assure believers of perfect safety from the wrath of God, in the midst of public calamities. These are in the hands of the Lord Jesus Christ, who is their Redeemer and Saviour, their Head and Husband, their Shepherd and Physician, their Brother and Friend. Can it ever be supposed that he will suffer the dearly beloved of his soul to fall under the wrathful judgments of God? Shall ever any of those who stand in such blessed relations to him, fall under the effects of that wrath which he endured for their sake? How is it possible that the saints, whose prayers and other religious duties, are presented to God with acceptance by his mediatory intercession, can ever be smitten with any of these plagues which are prepared for his enemies, and of which he himſelf has the direction? When it ſhall hail, coming down on the foreſt, the city of the believing church of Chriſt ſhall aſſured be low in a low place.

7. The great cauſes of faſting before God, in which we are this day profeſſedly engaged, may be learned from what has been ſaid. Although the copy of the cauſes of our faſt, which was read to you at the beginning of the public work of this day, and the obſervations which were made thereon, may be ſufficient, in ſome degree, for laying theſe things before your view; yet it may be neceſſary alſo in a few words to ſtate ſome of thoſe grounds of humiliation, which are plainly ſuggeſted by the ſubject you have heard. When the fire of the altar is caſt into the earth, nations are guilty. This is mournfully the caſe in the times wherein we live. The nations of the earth, inſtead of ſerving and glorifying God in their national capacity, are oppoſing and diſhonouring him. The nations ſeek not the happineſs of one another, which is their duty to do; but by their conduct towards each other, in commerce, treaties and war, they diſcover diſpoſitions equally malignant with thoſe of individuals in private life. For thoſe things it becomes us this day to be afflicted, to mourn and to weep. When the fire of the altar is flaming among men, churches are corrupt. Our times are remarkable for producing this ſore evil. Were we to conſider carefully the ſtate of the nations, in their religious capacities, we will find ſuperſtition, idolatry and blaſphemy prevailing with many; ignorance, error, and infidelity raging in the earth; profanity, apoſtacy, and diviſion, increaſing among men; immorality and wickedneſs of every kind overſpreading the world; and the inſtitutions of God neglected and deſpiſed, while the inventions and laws of men are regarded, in matters which concern his ſpiritual kingdom. For theſe things we ſhould weep, our eye ſhould run down with water; becauſe the children of Sion are deſolate, and the enemy is prevailing. When the fire of the altar is poured on the earth, iniquity will be greatly abounding among men. This is another awful character of our times. How dreadful is the growth of all kinds of immorality in this generation. Their moral ſtate is clearly deſcribed in theſe affecting words of the Apoſtle: *This*

know also, that in the last days perilous times shall come; for men shall be lovers of their ownselves, covetous, boasters, proud, blasphemers, disobedient to parents, unthankful, unholy, without natural affection, truce breakers, false accusers, incontinent, despisers of those that are good, traitors, heady, high-minded, lovers of pleasures more than lovers of God, having a form of godliness, but denying the power thereof. On account of the prevalence of those evils let us afflict our souls before God. When the fire of the altar is cast into the earth, God is angry and displeased with the inhabitants thereof. Every divine judgment is an infallible sign that Jehovah's anger is gone forth against men. In these days there are many frowns of the Lord's countenance, and wrathful dispensations of his hand, so that he may run who reads his displeasure against the nations. The seven golden vials full of the wrath of God who liveth for ever and ever, are in these days pouring out on the nations, by which we may see his anger at the inhabitants of the world. On this account we should be religiously affected, and cordially occupied in fasting and prayer; saying, *Thou hast been displeased, O turn thyself to us again.* When the fire of the altar is falling on the earth, the Lord Christ is carrying on his wrathful mediatory administrations towards the nations. It is a clear evidence that Christ has taken the censer, has filled it with fire of the altar, and cast it into the earth, when the judgments of God are falling on men; for the one cannot be without the other. He whom the gospel reveals as the Lamb of God, who taketh away the sin of the world, is now manifested in his awful providences as the Lion of the tribe of Judah, who is marching through the world in indignation, and threshing his enemies in anger. As that season when Christ is executing his mediatory office, in the remarkable communications of his Spirit, grace, and salvation, to the souls of multitudes, is a time of much enlarged spiritual joy to the church; so the period of his executing that office, by taking vengeance on the nations for their iniquity, should be a time of much mourning and heaviness to the children of God. When the fire of the altar is burning in the earth, the nations are suffering by divine judgments. O how alarming are the judgments of God in our time, and how great are the sufferings of nations under the heavy stroke. Some have been suffering by the terrible pestilence, and their population has been diminiſhed greatly by untimely and ſudden death. Others are ſuffering by cruel war, either as being the place of its devaſtation and carnage, or as feeling the diſtreſſing effects thereof in many other reſpects. Some are ſuffering by the ſcarcity and dearth of the neceſſaries of life, which have brought upon multitudes the greateſt diſtreſs. And others are ſuffering by the ſtagnation of trade, whereby this ſea, or ſource of wealth and ſupport to many, is become like the blood of a dead man. In a word, all the judgments of God formerly mentioned, are in the earth, and ſhall we not afflict our ſouls for theſe calamities of men. When the fire of the altar is ſcorching the earth, the church is in a low condition, and the intereſts of religion are in a decaying ſtate. Were it otherwiſe, the Lord, by turning away his anger from us, would ſoon make the fire of the altar ceaſe to burn. Though the church is ſafe in a time of calamity, becauſe the Lord hath founded Sion, and on account of the preſence of her King in her; yet, in ſuch a time as this, ſhe is like a cottage in a vineyard, as a lodge in a garden of cucumbers, and as a beſieged city. Shall not this affect our hearts with godly ſorrow, and make us ſay, *If I forget thee, O Jeruſalem, let my right hand forget her cunning; if I do not remember thee, let my tongue cleave to the roof of my mouth; if I prefer not Jeruſalem above my chief joy. For the hurt of the daughter of my people am I hurt; I am black; aſtoniſhment hath taken hold on me.* When the fire of the altar is ſcattered among men, their ſouls are under the influence of many ſpiritual plagues. When the great majority of every claſs of men are under infatuation of judgment, blindneſs of mind, hardneſs of heart, vile affections, ſearedneſs of conſcience, carnality and ſenſuality of deſire, treacherouſneſs of memory, a reprobate ſenſe and the like, their ſpiritual condition is moſt forlorn and alarming. As thoſe ſpiritual judgments are very prevalent among men; ſo they operate both as provoking cauſes of the Lord's diſpleaſure, and as mighty hinderances to our improving religiouſly the tokens of his wrath. Since nations are guilty, churches are corrupt, and individuals are impure; ſince God is angry, and Chriſt is carrying on his awful adminiſtrations among men; ſince the nations are ſuffering by divine judgments, the church is in a low eſtate, and the ſouls of multitudes are infected with ſpiritual plagues, we certainly have the greatest reason to be in bitterness of spirit before the Lord.

8. It is of importance for us to consider from this subject, what should be our employment in a day of solemn fasting, when times are evil and perilous, both by sin and judgments. To lay this before your view, you may be referred to the accounts given of the exercises of the godly in the vision of Ezekiel, which was formerly mentioned. In Ezek. ix. 4. we are told that those who were marked for preservation, as the Lord's peculiar treasure, sighed and cried for all the abominations that were done in the midst of Jerusalem. Three parts of their exercise are here represented for our instruction. They were acquainted with these abominations, and they knew them in their contrariety to the nature and law of God. They were not inattentive to the abounding evils by which God's law was broken, and his displeasure incurred; but they saw and considered them with holy grief and indignation. They sighed for these abominations. They were troubled in spirit, they mourned and wept before the Lord, their souls were afflicted, their bowels were moved, and they were pained at their heart for the sins which prevailed in the land. They cried also on account of these. They cried before God by prayer and confession, and they cried before men by an holy life and a public testimony against these abominations. In the eighth verse of the same chapter, the prophet describes his own exercise on this awful occasion, when the coals of fire were scattered over the city; *I fell upon my face, and cried, and said, Ah, Lord God, wilt thou destroy all the residue of Israel, in the pouring out of thy fury upon Jerusalem.* For our imitation, the following exercises are contained in these words. Deep humility and great earnestness in his application to God; he fell on his face, and cried:—Earnest supplication to God for mercy to the church; and an holy expostulation and talking with God in prayer concerning his judgments. Let us study this day, in a dependence on the grace of Christ, to exercise ourselves in these particulars, that we may be found going forth by the footsteps of the flock.

If we consider the vision to which the text belongs, we will also find some peculiar parts of the exercise of the saints in an evil time, by which our duty is clearly exhibited. In Rev. vii. 3. the parties who are ſealed are called *the ſervants of our God.* We ſhould conſider it as our higheſt honour and principal concern to be the ſervants of God. By believing in Chriſt for ſalvation, enliſting ourſelves under his banner, devoting ourſelves to his ſervice, and walking in his ways, we ſhould ſay, *Oh, Lord, truly we are thy ſervants, we are thy ſervants, thou haſt looſed our bonds.* In verſe 9th, it is ſaid they were clothed with white robes, and had palms in their hands. Having renounced the filthy rags of their own righteouſneſs, they have ſubmitted unto, and put on the righteouſneſs of Chriſt; they have a pure heart by regenerating grace, the clean hands of a pure converſation, and are arrayed with an holy profeſſion of the goſpel and law of their Redeemer. In connection with theſe robes, they have palms, the ſigns of victory, in their hands. As perſons who have obtained many victories over their enemies, and who have victory ſecured to them in the promiſe of God, they bear in their hands the palm of joy and conqueſt, even before their triumph is complete. In the 10th verſe, they are employed in the duty of praiſe. They *cried with a loud voice, ſaying, Salvation unto our God, who ſitteth upon the throne, and to the Lamb.* Though they have great reaſon to mourn on account of ſin, yet they are not left without a ſong in the midſt of their ſorrow. A view of the righteouſneſs of divine judgments; of their end, which is to promote the divine glory, and of their tendency to overthrow the enemies of Chriſt, and to eſtabliſh his kingdom in the world, cauſes them to ſing, like the church of old, *Sion heard and was glad, and the daughters of Judah rejoiced becauſe of thy judgments, O Lord,* Pſalm xciv. 8. In the 14th verſe, it is ſaid, *they have waſhed their robes, and made them white in the blood of the Lamb.* Convinced of their guilt and impurity, and enlightened in the knowledge of Chriſt as their only Saviour, they, in the exerciſe of faith, receive from him the atonement, embrace him as the propitiation for their ſins, and come to the blood of ſprinkling. With theſe ſpiritual exerciſes the hearts of believers are familiariſed, and in them they have great delight. In the two verſes before the text, they are repreſented as a praying people. The Mediator could have no prayers of ſaints to preſent on the golden altar before the throne, if his people did not give themſelves to this important duty. It is therefore a very prominent part of their character, with an eye to the merit and interceſſion of Jeſus, to make mention of the Lord, not to keep ſilence, and to give him no reſt till he eſtabliſh, and till he make Jeruſalem a praiſe in midſt of the earth. Theſe are ſome of the duties in which we ſhould be employed on a day of public faſting, and at ſuch a time as this. If we, by the grace and Spirit of Chriſt, attain unto them in any ſuitable degree, we will have kept ſuch a faſt as the Lord hath choſen; but if our ſouls are ſtrangers to theſe exerciſes, we will have faſted unto ourſelves, and not unto him.

We ſhall now conclude with a few advices deduced from the ſubject, and anſwerable to the work of the day. Let it be your concern, O Chriſtians, to ſpend the whole of the day in the exerciſe of faſting before the Lord. The work of a day of humiliation muſt not be confined to the public ordinances, but muſt be carried on in the private and ſecret duties of your families and cloſets. Every exerciſe of public humiliation comprehends a family and perſonal faſt. It is impoſſible to be religiouſly exerciſed in public faſting, if we do not ſtudy humiliation before God, in our family and perſonal capacities. One great end of public ordinances this day, is to adminiſter direction and help to you in your private and ſecret duties. Pour ye out your hearts before God by prayer and confeſſion, accompanied with repentance toward God, and faith toward the Lord Jeſus Chriſt, in the duties of your family. Retire by yourſelves, and in the exerciſes of ſerious meditation, reading of the word, earneſt prayer, ſelf-examination, humble confeſſion, and dedication of yourſelves to God in Chriſt, faſt perſonally, maintain intercourſe with God, and pour ye out your hearts before him. Take a broad view of your ſins in their heinous nature, various kinds, and manifold aggravations. Study to affect your heart with real grief and ſorrow for your ſins, and be in bitterneſs for them, as one is for an only ſon and a firſt-born. Conſider how your ſins diſhonour God, pierce Chriſt, grieve the Spirit, and wound your immortal ſouls, and be filled with godly ſorrow, earneſt carefulneſs and vehement deſire to avoid all ſin, and holy indignation, zeal and revenge againſt it. Turn the eye of your faith to the mercy of God, and to the blood of Jeſus Chriſt his Son, which cleanſeth you from all ſin, that you may hear him ſaying to you, I have caused thine iniquity to pass from thee, and I will clothe thee with change of raiment. Pray for the Spirit of God, that under his influence you may have comfortable views of pardoning mercy, may attain to the renewed actings of faith on the death of Christ, may have sin subdued in you, and may be enabled in time coming to keep yourselves from all iniquity.

Be deeply affected with the sins of others, whereby God is so remarkably dishonoured, in the times in which you live. If you are properly afflicted for your own sins, you will also be concerned for the sins of others. Rivers of waters should run down your eyes, because they keep not God's law. If you expect to share of the privileges of the saints in a time of judgments, you must imitate them in their spiritual exercises. Both these are set before us in the words of Peter concerning Lot; *And delivered just Lot, vexed with the filthy conversation of the wicked; For this righteous man dwelling among them, in seeing and hearing, vexed his righteous soul from day to day, with their unlawful deeds.* His sorrow was great, for his spirit was vexed. He was active in promoting this frame of mind, for he vexed his own soul. It was his habitual exercise, for it was from day to day. The causes of his grief were the sins of others, the filthy conversation of the wicked, and their unlawful deeds. And the privilege of Lot is also mentioned, for the Lord delivered him from the destruction of the wicked. *For the Lord knoweth how to deliver the godly out of temptations,* to cause them escape wrathful calamities, *and to reserve the unjust unto the day of judgment,* the seasons of his wrath, *to be punished,* 2 Pet. ii. 7, 8, 9. Take a view of the sins of the lands of your nativity, and confess and mourn over them before the Lord. Direct your attention to the sins of the nations of the world, and lament that the King of nations is so much dishonoured among men; that you may be able to say with truth, *I beheld the transgressors, and was grieved; because they kept not thy word,* Psa. cxix. 158.

Let your hearts be also affected with the judgments of God which are in the earth. It is your indispensible duty to consider them most seriously, in their awful nature, in their present effects, and in their ultimate design. When the four first seals were opened by the Lord Christ, Rev. vi. 1, 3, 5, 7. the four living creatures, one after another, ſaid, *Come and ſee.* This repreſents the great duty of the miniſters of the goſpel, to invite the Chriſtian people to a ſolemn and ſerious conſideration of the judgments of God, both as they are revealed in the prophecy and threatning, and as they are fulfilled in the providence of God. Inattention to the judgments of God which are in the earth characteriſes thoſe, who are the guilty objects of theſe wrathful ſtrokes. *Lord, when thy hand is lifted up they will not ſee; but they ſhall ſee, and be aſhamed for their envy at the people, yea, the fire of thine enemies ſhall devour them,* Iſa. xxvi. 11. Perſons are further expoſed to the diſpleaſure of God by this ſinful neglect. *Becauſe they regard not the works of the Lord, nor the operations of his hand, he ſhall deſtroy them, and not build them up,* Pſal. xxviii. 5. By a careful performance of this neceſſary duty, the ſouls of Chriſtians obtain much ſpiritual good; *Whoſo is wiſe, and will obſerve theſe things, even they ſhall underſtand the loving kindneſs of the Lord,* Pſal. cvii. 43. Let it be your earneſt concern, therefore, O Chriſtians, rightly to improve the judgments of God, by conſidering them as holy operations of a God of wiſdom, mercy and power, who will direct them infallibly to their proper ends; for though the rings of the wheels of providence are high and dreadful, yet they are full of eyes round about them all.

Pray much for the Spirit of God to apply the goſpel to the ſouls of men, that individuals and nations may profit ſavingly by divine judgments. It is not by theſe fearful works, that the Lord accompliſhes any gracious deliverance for the children of men. If the judgments of God are not accompanied with the application of the goſpel, by the power of the divine Spirit, to the ſouls of men, theſe operations of Jehovah will do them no good. When Elijah heard a great and ſtrong wind, which rent the mountains, and brake in pieces the rocks, it is ſaid the Lord was not in the wind. When he felt a terrible earthquake, the Lord was not in the earthquake. And when he ſaw a devouring fire, the Lord was not in the fire. But when he heard a ſtill ſmall voice, the Lord was in it; for whenever he heard it, *he wrapped his face in his mantle, and ſtood in the entering in of the cave,* 1 Kings xix. 13. In like manner, when the voices, thunderings, lightnings and the earthquake of divine judgments prevail in the world,

God, in the gracious manifeſtation of himſelf to ſinners, is not in them. It is only by the ſtill ſmall voice of the everlaſting goſpel, accompanied with the power of the Spirit, that any gracious and ſaving bleſſings can be communicated, either to the ſouls of men, or to the nations of the world. Judgments may be the mean of humbling the pride of men, and of diſpoſing their hearts to give attention to the goſpel of divine grace; but further they cannot go. The other parts of the work the Lord performs by a very different inſtrument, even the goſpel of our ſalvation. Let us therefore cry unto him, that he may ſend the goſpel with divine power after his judgments, and may cauſe the chariot of white horſes to go forth after the chariot of black horſes, for the converſion and ſalvation of the nations.

Seek preparation for theſe trials, to which you may yet be expoſed, by the execution of divine judgments. Thoſe which we have already ſeen, and thoſe of which we have heard, may be only the beginning of ſorrows. We may be aſſured, that the pouring out of the ſeven vials of the wrath of God upon the earth, which is deſcribed in the xvi. chapter of this book, is begun, is going on at this time, and is not finiſhed. The evils which the nations are ſuffering, may be conſidered as a part of the accompliſhment of this viſion. As the work of judgment is not yet fulfilled, we may expect the calamities of men to become ſtill more extenſive and diſtreſſing. Whether the Lord will, without intermiſſion, carry on his ſtrange act, finiſh his work, and cut it ſhort in righteouſneſs, or give intervals of quietneſs to the nations betwixt the ſtorms of his anger, we cannot ſay; but certainly the word and providence of God concur in calling us to prepare to meet our God, as he is coming forth to execute judgments in the earth. By ſeeking an intereſt in the Lord as our God, and in Chriſt as our Saviour; by avoiding all diſcontentment with the holy providence of God; by being willing to ſuffer whatever he may bring upon us in the way of his judgments; by keeping the great and aſſured deſigns of God's judgments in view, which are his own glory, the honour of Chriſt, the overthrow of his enemies, and the ſalvation of his church; and by looking carefully into the word and providence of the Lord, let us endeavour to prepare to meet with our God, in whatever way he may come to us. O ye fearers of the Lord and ye lovers of Christ, come, then, enter into your chambers, shut your doors about you, and hide yourselves for a small moment till the indignation be overpast; for behold the Lord cometh out of his place to punish the inhabitants of the earth, for their iniquity, and the earth also shall disclose her blood, and shall no more cover her slain.

Study, O Christians, to grow in grace. Be diligent in your attendance on the ordinances of God. Forsake not the assembling of yourselves together, in any religious duty, but exhort one another, and so much the more, as you see days of fearful calamity approaching. Give yourselves unto prayer. Be concerned in this duty for the glory of God, for your own souls, for the ministers of the gospel, for the rising generation, for your Christian brethren, for your fellow-creatures, and for the interest of religion in the world. Keep yourselves from the evils that are abounding among men, and have no fellowship with the unfruitful works of darkness, but rather reprove them. Let the life which you live in the flesh, be by the faith of the Son of God, in a daily improvement of his person, offices, righteousness, fulness, covenant and promise; so shall you be enabled to see without dismay, the great Mediatorial Angel take the censer, fill it with fire of the altar, and cast it into the earth, though it should produce among men voices, thunderings, lightnings and an earthquake.

FINIS.

PRINTED BY FALCONER & WILLISON.

OBSERVATIONS

ON THE

PUBLIC COVENANTS,

BETWIXT

GOD AND THE CHURCH.

A DISCOURSE.

BY ARCHIBALD MASON,

MINISTER OF THE GOSPEL AT WISHAWTOWN.

From JEREMIAH xi. 10.

THE HOUSE OF ISRAEL, AND THE HOUSE OF JUDAH, HAVE BROKEN MY COVENANT, WHICH I MADE WITH THEIR FATHERS.

GLASGOW:

PRINTED BY E. MILLER.

1799.

OBSERVATIONS

ON THE

PUBLIC COVENANTS.

A DISCOURSE.

JEREMIAH xi. 10.

THE HOUSE OF ISRAEL, AND THE HOUSE OF JUDAH, HAVE BROKEN MY COVENANT, WHICH I MADE WITH THEIR FATHERS.

IN the days of Jeremiah's prophecy, the people of God had greatly corrupted their way, and expofed themfelves to fore judgments, which the Lord, during that period, actually brought upon them. His miniftry among them was defigned to convince them of their fin, to give them the knowledge of their duty, and to turn them from the evil of their ways unto the fervice of the Lord. Their acting in oppofition to the folemn obligations under which they were to be the Lord's people, and to ferve him, by the public national covenant which fubfifted betwixt God and them, was one of the principal ways in which they had contracted great guilt, carried on rebellion againft God, and incurred his difpleafure. The prophet, therefore, in the beginning of the chapter, receives a commiffion from the Lord, to fpeak to the men of Judah, and to the inhabitants of Jerufalem, concerning this covenant. His commiffion warrants him to make a declaration unto them concerning the origin of this covenant, which was the will and command of God;—the period at which Ifrael was firft brought under the obligation of this covenant, when the Lord delivered them out of the iron furnace of bondage in the land of Egypt;—the defign of this covenant as to them, their hearing the words of it, and giving obedience thereunto;—the mifery they would bring upon themselves by breaking this covenant, they should be exposed unto the curse of God;—and the happy effects of their religiously fulfilling their covenant obligations, they should be the Lord's people, he would be their God, and would perform the oath which he had sworn unto their fathers, in giving them the land of Canaan for an inheritance. When the prophet heard the author of this message represent it to his mind, he was constrained to express his hearty approbation of it; *Then answered I, and said, So be it, O Lord.*

In the 6th verse, the Lord renews his royal order unto the prophet, to proclaim in the cities of Judah, and in the streets of Jerusalem, all these words, and to say, Hear ye the words of this covenant, and do them. The 7th verse represents the condescending and importunate expostulation which the Lord, by the ministry of his servants, had employed with Israel, in their different generations, to excite them to keep, and to deter them from breaking their covenant obligations unto him. And the following verse exhibits to our view both their rebellious conduct, and their awful doom. The 9th and 10th verses contain that part of the prophet's message, which had a special respect to the men of that generation. A conspiracy is found among the men of Judah, and among the inhabitants of Jerusalem. A conspiracy, against the Lord and his anointed, against his authority and law, against the ordinances of his worship and the truths of his word, and against the purity, prosperity and interests of his church, was formed and acted upon by that people, upon whom the Lord had bestowed so many high and peculiar favours. The manner in which they executed the conspiracy against the Lord, is described in the verse which contains our text, in three awful charges which is brought against them. *They are turned back to the iniquity of their forefathers, which refused to hear my words; and they went after other gods to serve them; the house of Israel, andt he house of Judah, have broken my covenant, which I made with their fathers.* These may either be considered as three separate charges, which the Lord brings against his people; or the first and second may be viewed as evidences of the truth of the third. They have turned back to the iniquity of their forefathers, and gone after other gods, and in fo doing have broken my covenant. In this manner they had confpired againft the Lord, acted high treafon againft the God of Ifrael, and did what they could to dethrone him from his mercy feat. The laft of the particulars, which are contained in this verfe, being the fubject of our prefent exercife, to it we fhall now confine our attention. *The houfe of Ifrael, and the houfe of Judah, have broken my covenant which I made with their fathers.*

The fpeaker of thefe words is the Lord God of Ifrael. Although the prophet delivered them unto the people, he both fpake in the name of the Lord, and had his commiffion from him; and, therefore, he fays, verfe 9th, *The Lord faid unto me.*

The party addreffed by the Lord is the houfe of Ifrael and the houfe of Judah. The houfe of Ifrael has formerly broken my covenant which I made with their fathers. The kingdom of the ten tribes, who were now in a ftate of captivity, are moft frequently, in the writings of the prophets, called by this name, The houfe of Ifrael. If that part of the pofterity of Jacob is meant in thefe words, the Lord brings their breach of covenant into the view of the houfe of Judah, that they might take warning from the low ftate to which the ten tribes were now reduced, on account of this fin, by the hand of the king of Affyria. And the houfe of Judah; that part of God's antient people which continued fubject to the houfe of David, the tribes of Judah and Benjamin, who were yet fpared, notwithftanding of great provocations, to poffefs their poffeffions, in the land of promife. Or, by the houfe of Ifrael, and the houfe of Judah, we may underftand, the kingdom of Judah, with thofe of the ten tribes, who, on different occafions, had fled to the land of Judah, had taken up their refidence among them, and were incorporated with them; they and the houfe of Judah together have broken my covenant.

It is with refpect to God's covenant that the houfe of Ifrael, and the houfe of Judah, are here charged with fin. God's covenant in fcripture fometimes fignifies that everlafting covenant which he made with Chrift our mediator, from eternity, concerning the falvation of loft finners, which was to him a covenant of purchafe or redemption, but, as it is revealed and offered unto the children of men in the gospel, is to them a covenant altogether of rich, sovereign and free grace. But by God's covenant, in the writings of inspiration, we must, at other times, understand that covenant of duties which takes place betwixt God and the church, wherein they devote themselves to the Lord, and engage to serve him all the days of their life. It is in this sense that the Lord's covenant is to be understood in the words of the text.

The persons with whom the covenant was made are also mentioned; which I made with their fathers. The covenanting ancestors of the people of Israel are here meant. That generation with whom the Lord made this covenant at Horeb, and the other generations of Israel, in whose days the covenant was renewed, and who formally entered into the bond of it, may all be considered as their fathers, with whom the Lord had made this covenant.

The text likewise contains an account of the sin, with which the Lord charges the persons, to whom the prophet was sent; it is the breach of this covenant, they have broken my covenant. They have not kept my covenant; they have neither fulfilled their obligations, nor performed their vows unto me. They have broken my covenant, not by the omission of duties only, but by the commission of sin, and walking in those ways which they had solemnly sworn to avoid, and vowed to forsake.

Having thus endeavoured to explain the text, and taken some view of the verses of the chapter which precede it, we shall now enter upon a more particular consideration of the subject, by prosecuting the two following designs.

I. We shall attempt to illustrate a few general observations concerning the public covenants betwixt God and the church, chiefly taken from the text.

II. Some practical inferences shall afterwards be deduced from the subject.

I. An illustration of some general observations on the public covenants betwixt God and the church, chiefly taken from the text, is now to be attempted.

First, God and his church are the parties in these solemn covenants, and both of them perform their part, in their different capacities, for establishing them. This observation is evident from these words, which I have made with their fathers. The most high God, as a reconciled God in Christ, revealing himself as a God of mercy through the Redeemer, and as the glorious Lord, and King, and Governor of his people, is one party in these solemn covenants. The church or people of God, as a company of professed visible believers in the name of Jesus, subjecting themselves unto the authority, word, and ordinances of God in Christ, having hope of salvation thro' him, and conscientiously desiring and endeavouring to act for his glory, is the other party in these public federal transactions. In the establishing of these covenants both these parties are active, in their respective capacities. By looking into the scriptural account of those solemn deeds, both parts of this observation will be confirmed. The original transaction of this kind, which is largely recorded in the 19th chapter of Exodus, deserves first to be considered. In the third verse we are told, that Moses went up unto God, and the Lord called unto him out of the mountain, saying, *Thus shalt thou say to the house of Jacob, and tell the children of Israel.* From the five following verses, which you may read from your Bibles, it appears, that the Lord, having employed the ministery of Moses to Israel, on this occasion, through him proposes the covenant unto the church, states the terms of it, makes the promise thereof, and, by his authority, lays it upon them in all its duties and obligations. The church, on the other hand, are also active, on their part, by giving an explicit, solemn, and voluntary consent thereunto, entering into the covenant, taking the obligation upon themselves, and promising obedience. The same things are evident from that covenanting which took place in Israel, before the death of Joshua. It is represented, at large, in the last chapter of his book, particularly, from the 14th to the 28th verse. Joshua, acting at this time in the name of the Lord, exhorts the people to their duty, calls them to chuse whom they will serve, describes that God into whose service they were entered, and the nature of that obedience which he requires. The people, acting their part in the solemn business, engage themselves to this service, saying, *We will serve the Lord, the Lord our God will we serve, and him will we obey.* The consequence of which is declared, ver. 25. *So Joshua made a covenant with the people that day, and set them a statute and an ordinance in Shechem.* The instance we have of public covenanting, in the days of Asa, the fourth from David, which is mentioned in the 15th chapter of 2 Chron. confirms also the truth of this observation. The Lord begins the great work, by sending a prophet to the king and the people, upon their return from a most victorious conquest of the Ethiopians, who had come out against them, and he delivers to them, in the name of the Lord, a most affecting discourse, tending to encourage them in the work of reformation. The king immediately gathered all Judah and Benjamin, and the strangers with them out of Ephraim, and Manasseh, and out of Simeon. The people of the land, obedient to the call, assembled at Jerusalem, in the third month of the fifteenth year of the reign of Asa. The divine account of the people's conduct, at this time, is conveyed to us in the following words: *And they entered into a covenant to seek the Lord God of their fathers, with all their heart, and with all their soul. And they sware unto the Lord with a loud voice, and with shouting, and with trumpets, and with cornets. And all Judah rejoiced at the oath.* These instances are sufficient to prove, that the parties in public religious covenants are God and his church, and that each of them is active in their formation. All covenanting, in after-times, must be of the same general nature, a solemn transaction betwixt God and the church, wherein the parties are not concerned only, but also actively employed. By giving the church the revelation of his will respecting this duty in his holy word; by allowing them covenanting seasons, and calls from his word and providence to engage in that duty; by employing some to be active in leading the church in this solemn work; by stirring up the hearts of his people, at large, to vow and swear unto him; by carrying on the work among them in the course of his favourable providence; and by giving them infallible signs of his presence, acceptance, and blessing in this service,—does the God of the church perform his part in constituting these covenants? The people of God act their part in this great work, when they, being rightly informed about the nature of the duty, and convinced of the call which they have to perform it, do really vow and ſwear to the Lord to be his people, and to obey his voice; and in this manner join themſelves to the Lord in a perpetual covenant, that ſhall not be forgotten.

Secondly, The public covenants betwixt God and the church contain his gracious engaging himſelf to be their God, and to bleſs them; and their dutiful obliging themſelves to be his people, and to ſerve him. This is the nature of all religious covenants with God. If they are conſidered in any other light, they are miſunderſtood; and if they are held up to men in any other point of view, they are miſrepreſented. They come not at all in the room of the covenant of works, have no connection with it, or proper analogy unto it. They do not in any reſpect ſuperſede or corrupt the covenant of grace; but are built upon it, and tend to carry on its merciful deſigns among men. The covenant of grace is abſolutely neceſſary as the foundation upon which theſe covenants muſt reſt; and as the fountain from which they proceed. In order to an acceptable covenanting with God, either in a public or in a perſonal reſpect, faith in him as our God in Chriſt, is really eſſential. An individual Chriſtian in a perſonal, or a body of them in a public capacity, entering into a covenant with God, do it not with a view to obtain an intereſt in him as their God, to regain his favour, or acquire a title to his ſalvation; but, having received Chriſt by faith, and taken hold of the covenant of which he is the mediator for theſe purpoſes, they, in their covenanting with God, ſolemnly devote themſelves unto him, and vow or ſwear, in the ſtrength of his grace, to glorify and ſerve him with their bodies and ſpirits which are his. Were it not for the everlaſting covenant which God hath made with Chriſt for our ſalvation, the curſe of the law, and the wrath of God, which we have incurred by ſin, could not be removed from us; nor could we have acceſs in any reſpect into a ſtate of friendſhip or amicable intercourſe with him. While matters betwixt God and us remained in this ſituation, acceptable and profitable covenanting with him muſt be impoſſible. But the Lord Jeſus, having fulfilled the condition of the covenant of ſalvation, by his obedience, ſufferings and death, has both redeemed his people from the curſe of the law, and made peace betwixt God and them, by the blood of his croſs. When ſinners are enabled in the exercife of a true faith to believe in Chriſt, and to take hold of the covenant of grace for ſalvation, God actually becomes their God in Chriſt, and they are brought into the bleſſed relation of a reconciled people unto him. It is therefore in theſe relations, which God and his people bear unto one another, in Chriſt by the covenant of grace, that they act towards one another in theſe covenants, into the nature of which we are now enquiring. Our covenants with God, therefore, muſt reſt upon God's covenant of grace as their foundation, and be a mean of carrying on the bleſſed deſign of that covenant, betwixt God and his people, while they are in this world.

Chriſtians, in their covenanting with God, whether in a perſonal or public capacity, have various objects to diſclaim and abandon; a ſolemn renouncing of theſe muſt make a part of their covenanting exerciſe. In this work, Chriſtians have many objects which they are called to embrace and receive; a deliberate and cordial acceptance of them, pertains alſo to this ſolemn tranſaction. When the members of the church draw near unto God in this duty, they have many things to ſurrender unto him, their perſons, their time, their influence, their ſubſtance, their ſervice, &c. for this reaſon a dedication of ourſelves, all that we are, have, and can do, is included in our covenanting with God. As Chriſtians, in the performance of this ſervice, are to bind themſelves with a bond to be the Lord's people, and to ſerve him; their coming under ſolemn vows and engagements, to be for him and not for another, muſt be an eſſential branch of this important duty. Though there may be a difference betwixt the objects which a Chriſtian as an individual, and a body of them in their collective capacity are called, in their covenanting with God, to renounce, accept, and devote to the Lord, and alſo in the duties to the performance of which they do engage; yet the nature and tendency of theſe ſolemn tranſactions are, in both caſes, ſubſtantially the ſame.

The truth of this obſervation, and of what has now been ſaid for its illuſtration will appear from the repreſentations of this duty, with which we are favoured in the word of God. One of theſe is contained in Deut. xxvi. 17, 18, 19. *Thou haſt avouched the Lord this day to be thy God. and to walk in his ways, and to keep his ſtatutes, and his teſtimonies, and his judgments, and to hearken unto his voice. And the Lord hath avouched thee this day to be his peculiar people, as he hath promiſed thee, and that thou ſhouldeſt keep all his commandments. And to make thee high above all nations which he hath made, in praiſe, and in name, and in honour, and that thou mayſt be an holy people unto the Lord thy God as he hath ſpoken.* We ſaid, the public covenants which exiſt betwixt God and the church contain his gracious engagement to be their God and to bleſs them. Here we are told, that, in theſe covenants, the Lord avouches the church to be his people; which plainly imports his engagement to be their God, and that he will bleſs them, by making them high above all nations, who are not in covenant with God, in name, in praiſe, and in honour; which certainly ſignifies his engagement to bleſs them. We likewiſe ſaid, that, in theſe tranſactions, the church's obligations to be the Lord's people, and to ſerve him, is alſo comprehended. What elſe can be the meaning of theſe words, *Thou haſt avouched the Lord this day to be thy God*, &c. Thou haſt ſolemnly taken hold of the Lord to be thy God, profeſſed thy relation to him as his people, and engaged thine heart to ſerve him, by keeping his ſtatutes, judgments, and commandments. Another repreſentation of the nature of this duty, from which the truth of this obſervation may be confirmed, is found in 2 Chron. xv. 12, 15. *And they entered into a covenant to ſeek the Lord God of their fathers, with all their heart, and with all their ſoul.—And he was found of them, and the Lord gave them reſt round about.* Their covenanting exerciſe was a ſolemn engagement on their part, to ſeek and ſerve the Lord their God, who had been their fathers God; and, in this manner, to act as a people who belonged unto the Lord. Jehovah, on his part, was found of them, as the Lord God of their fathers, and the Lord their God, and conferred covenant bleſſings upon them; for he gave them reſt, peace and proſperity on every hand.

Thirdly, Public covenanting is a moral duty, incumbent upon the church in every age; during the new, as well as under the old dispensation of grace to the children of men. As this truth is greatly opposed in our day, we shall endeavour to confirm it; and which, we suppose, may be done, to the conviction of the unprejudized, by the following arguments.

1st, There is nothing in the nature of these covenants, which subsisted betwixt God and Israel, that renders them inapplicable unto the church in new testament times. If the things which are essential unto public covenanting were such, as rendered it peculiar to the former dispensation, and utterly unsuitable to the new testament state of the church, the morality of that duty in gospel days could not be maintained. But no such thing is found to be the case; on the contrary, every thing belonging unto the nature of that exercise, suits the condition of the church since the coming of Christ, as well as before that period. Was it the privilege of the antient church to have the Lord, by a public fœderal transaction, engaging himself to be their God, and to bless them? and does not the gospel church stand in need of the same distinguishing favour? Was it the exercise of the Israelites to engage themselves as in duty bound, to be the Lord's people, and to serve him? and is not this an employment perfectly suitable to the new testament church? There is nothing in the nature of the antient covenanting that was not purely moral, and consequently this exercise belongs to us as well as to them. Many of the ordinances of that dispensation, indeed, to the observation of which the church of old, in their covenanting, did bind themselves, are now abrogated; but there is a system of ordinances under the new dispensation, equally with them of divine authority, which we are commanded to keep as they have been delivered to us, to a due regard unto and improvement of which, we are to bind ourselves in our covenant transactions with God. The change which the Lord hath made in the outward ordinance of his worship, in his sovereign pleasure and according unto the state of the church under the different dispensations makes not the smallest alteration in the moral obligation, which his people, existing in these different periods, were under, both to observe the ordinances which were divinely authorized in their time, and, by covenanting with God, to promiſe and vow ſuch an obſervation of them as the Lord required. Since every thing eſſential to public covenanting, anſwers the ſtate of the church now, as well as before the times of the goſpel, it muſt be a duty incumbent upon the new teſtament church.

2*d* The morality of this duty in our times further appears from ſcripture precepts requiring it, which are of a ſtanding moral obligation upon the people of God in every age. The firſt precept in the moral law may juſtly be conſidered as a command unto men to avouch the Lord to be their God, and to devote themſelves unto his ſervice. Thou ſhalt have no other gods before me. Thou ſhalt have me to be thy God. Conſidering this precept in connection with the preface to the law, *I am the Lord thy God*, it certainly requires the exerciſe of our faith upon him as our God, an open profeſſion of our relation to him, our dedication of ourſelves unto him, and our ſpecial deſign of ſerving and glorifying him for ever. This precept, therefore, clearly comprehends all the parts of ſolemn covenanting with God; and this duty is one of the principal ways, whereby the church teſtifies that ſhe has the Lord to be her God.—Another precept of the divine word which has a reſpect to this duty is found, 2 Chron xxx. 8. *Yield yourſelves unto the Lord;* The ſame command is given to the church by an apoſtle, Rom. vi. 13. *Yield yourſelves unto God, as thoſe that are alive from the dead.* In the Chriſtian exerciſe of yielding themſelves unto the Lord, the renouncing of the other lords, which, beſide him, have had dominion over them; the embracing of him as their God; the dedication of themſelves to him; and their engaging themſelves to ſerve him, muſt be included. Since theſe particulars, which are the great ſubſtance of covenanting with God, are included in yielding ourſelves unto him, this precept muſt be a command warranting this neceſſary duty. As this precept is not given in the Old Teſtament only, but alſo required in the New, the duty of covenanting, which is contained in it, muſt be an exerciſe required of us as well as of believers under the former diſpenſation. The laſt precept I ſhall mention is the words of God by David, Pſalm lxxvi. 11. *Vow, and pay unto the Lord your God.* Two divine precepts are here given to the church; *Vow unto the Lord your God, and pay unto the Lord your God.* The former requires Chriſtians to come under ſolemn, voluntary obligations unto the Lord, by vowing and ſwearing unto him, or covenanting with him; and the latter enjoins that, as they have made their vows, they ſhould ſtudy to fulfil them every day. The precepts which have now been mentioned, as they plainly comprehend covenanting with God, ſo they are applicable to Chriſtians acting as a body, as well as in their individual capacity. By the precepts of the divine law then, we are required to exerciſe ourſelves in the duty of perſonal and public covenanting with God.

3*d*, The morality of this duty is alſo evident from ſcripture examples. If we are called to be followers of them, both in their perſonal and ſocial conduct, who through faith and patience inherit the promiſes; and if we find that the church of God, with his approbation, have been employed in this ſolemn duty; why ſhould we queſtion its being the way of the Lord? When God brought Iſrael out of Egypt, and carried them forward to mount Sinai, he brought them, in the moſt ſolemn manner, into a covenant relation with himſelf. In the days of Joſhuah, when the children of Iſrael were peaceably ſettled in the land of promiſe, this ſolemn covenant with God was publicly renewed, and the people again entered into the bond thereof. When Iſrael had made great defection from the law of the Lord, by falling into idolatry, and the other evils which uſually accompany it, they, in the days of Aſa, returned from their evil ways unto the ſervice of God, by entering into a ſolemn covenant with the Lord their God. In the days of Jehoiada the prieſt, when he had placed Joaſh upon the throne, and had put the king's mother to death for her murder, idolatry and uſurpation, the people of Judah, after a period of mournful apoſtacy from God, returned to him by public covenanting, of which we have the following account. *And Jehoiada made a covenant between the Lord, and the king and the people, that they ſhould be the Lord's people; between the king alſo and the people.* 2 Kings xi. 17. There is a twofold covenant here. A religious covenant, the design of which was that they should be the Lord's people, wherein the Lord was one party, and the king and the people the other. And a civil covenant between the king and the people, in which the parties, no doubt, engaged to perform their different duties to each other. The church of God were also employed in this solemn exercise in the days of Josiah. When the book of the law was found, and the message from Huldah received, this pious youth, having conveened at Jerusalem the whole inhabitants of the land, engaged in the great work of reforming his kingdom, abolishing idolatry, and setting up the worship of God; and all this he confirmed by entering into a covenant to walk after the Lord, and to keep his commandments, and his testimonies, and his statutes. When Judah returned from Babylon, and were again planted in their own land, they, under the conduct of Ezra the priest, and Nehemiah the tirshatha, did solemnly renew their covenant with God. Shall such glorious and profitable solemnities be the privilege of the church under the former dispensation; and shall nothing of the kind be permitted unto her, or found with her under the gospel? Having such illustrious examples before their eyes, shall any nation be accounted innocent, that has embraced the true religion, if they are found neglecting this solemn mean of glorifying God, and of promoting their own spiritual advantage? How unjust and impious must it be, to condemn the practice of our reforming ancestors, in joining themselves to the Lord in a solemn covenant, when their conduct is supported by such glorious precedents?

4th, Prophecies of the Old Testament respecting the gospel church, which foretel that public covenanting should be their exercise, prove the lawfulness of this duty in gospel times. Three of these shall only be mentioned. The first is found in the words of David, Psal. lxviii. 31. *Princes shall come out of Egypt, and Ethiopia shall stretch out her hands unto God.* The words are a prophecy concerning the conversion of the Gentiles, in the times of the gospel, to the knowledge of the Lord and of his Christ. Egypt and Ethiopia are mentioned to signify the Gentile nations at large. It is said, princes shall come out of Egypt, they ſhall forſake the idolatry of Egypt, and believe in Chriſt for ſalvation. Of Ethiopia it is ſaid, they ſhall ſtretch out their hand unto the Lord. This expreſſion denotes that the Gentile nations ſhould, in the days of the goſpel church, openly take upon themſelves the profeſſion of Chriſtianity, declare their ſubjection unto the law of the Redeemer, ſend up their ſupplications unto God in Chriſt, and vow and ſwear allegiance to the King of Zion.—Another prophecy which has a reſpect unto the days of the goſpel, and deſcribes the exerciſe of the new teſtament church, wherein public covenanting ſeems to be included, is recorded, Iſa. ii. 3. *And many people ſhall go and ſay, come ye, and let us go up to the mountain of the Lord, to the houſe of the God of Jacob, and he will teach us of his ways, and we will walk in his paths; for out of Zion ſhall go forth the law, and the word of the Lord from Jeruſalem.* The two preceding and the two following verſes belong to the ſame meſſage of grace, which was delivered by the prophet to the church, relating to goſpel times The mountain of the Lord's houſe, which ſignifies the new teſtament church, is to be eſtabliſhed by the power of God, in an elevated ſituation, exalted above her enemies, and all nations ſhall flow to it. The prophet here foretels that many nations, multitudes of perſons in the Gentile nations, and Gentile lands in their national capacity, ſhould go and ſay, Come ye, and let us go up to the mountain of the Lord, to the houſe of the God of Jacob; let us embrace the Lord, and take hold of the God of Jacob, by a public and ſolemn avouching him to be our God, and by a careful obſervation of the ordinances of his holy mountain. To this is added an account of the exerciſe of their faith on the divine promiſe, and their ſolemn reſolution, vow or covenant to ſerve him. *He will teach us of his ways, and we will walk in his paths.* The glorious foundation of all this religious exerciſe, among the Gentile churches, is alſo declared; *for out of Zion ſhall go forth the law, and the word of the Lord from Jeruſalem.* The goſpel of divine grace, as revealed in the word, as preached by the ſervants of Jeſus, and as ſavingly manifeſted by the Spirit, taking poſſeſſion of the ſouls of men, induces them as individuals to the exerciſe of perſonally devoting themſelves to the Lord; and, when this becomes general, cauſes them as a nation to engage in this ſolemn work. In Micah iv. chap. at the beginning, this viſion concerning the goſpel church is doubled, becauſe the thing is true; from which we may aſſuredly conclude, that a ſolemn public taking hold of God as their God, and the devoting themſelves to him to walk in his paths, which is the eſſence of public covenanting, is, and continues to be the duty of the church of God in every period of time.—Another prophecy to the ſame purpoſe, ſtill more explicit, you have in Iſa. xix. 18, 21. *In that day ſhall five cities in the land of Egypt ſpeak the language of Canaan, and ſwear to the Lord of hoſts.* The period when this ſhall be accompliſhed is here mentioned, in that day. The prophets frequently ſpeak of the goſpel times in this manner, and it muſt be conſidered as referring to that period. Five cities of the land of Egypt are the objects of this prophecy. Egypt is here mentioned to ſignify the Gentile world, a part is put for the whole, and one nation only is mentioned to ſignify the reſt of the Gentile nations. Five cities in the land of Egypt ſignify many cities in many lands. They ſhall ſpeak the language of Canaan. They ſhall become acquainted with divine revelation, know the glorious truths of the goſpel, and have the holy law made plain before them. By this work of grace the Lord ſhall turn to them a pure language. It is alſo declared, they ſhall ſwear to the Lord of hoſts. Upon no rational or religious grounds can it ever be denied, that theſe words are a clear prophecy, that public ſwearing to God, or covenanting with him, ſhould be the exerciſe of the church in new teſtament times. It is not a ſwearing by the Lord, but a ſwearing to him, of which the Spirit of prophecy here ſpeaks. In this religious oath, which the Gentile nations ſhould ſwear, the Lord is not merely the object appealed unto, as the witneſs and the avenger; but he is the object to whom the oath is made, and to whom it is to be fulfilled. Both theſe exerciſes which are mentioned here are explained in verſe 21. *And the Lord ſhall be known to Egypt, and the Egyptians ſhall know the Lord in that day — Yea, they ſhall vow a vow unto the Lord, and perform it.* The Egyptians ſpeaking the language of Canaan is the ſame with their knowing the Lord, and their ſwearing unto the Lord is of the ſame import with their vowing a vow unto him. The exerciſe of public vowing and ſwearing to the Lord continues to be a duty incumbent upon Chriſtians in new teſtament times, ſince the Spirit of God has expreſsly foretold, that, during this period, they ſhould be ſo employed.

5th, The relation which ſubſiſts betwixt God and the church ſeems to render her public covenanting with him a neceſſary duty. Although this relation is infinitely more glorious than any relation that takes place among men, yet ſuch is the goodneſs of God, that he condeſcends to repreſent it to us by theſe earthly relations; a few of which may be mentioned, and from each of them the morality and neceſſity of the church's covenanting with God may be demonſtrated. The relation betwixt a king and his ſubjects is a metaphor, which is uſed by the holy Spirit, to repreſent the relation betwixt God and the church. The language which the church holds concerning her God, when viewing him in his gracious relation unto her, is the following; *The Lord is my King of old, working ſalvation in the midſt of the earth; the holy One of Iſrael is our King; the Lord is our King, he will ſave us.* To the conſtituting of a moral relation betwixt an earthly king and his ſubjects, a public agreement, or ſolemn covenant is eſſential. When a perſon is advanced to this dignity and truſt over men, he not only receives the promiſe of ſubjection and obedience from the people, but he alſo gives them ſecurity by his ſolemn oath, to rule them according to the laws. This is the covenant which is neceſſary to eſtabliſh the relation betwixt a king and the people among whom he rules. In the ſame manner, there muſt be a public and ſolemn covenant betwixt the God of ſalvation, and his church; the former as her glorious King, and the latter as his willing and obedient ſubjects.—The relation between God and the church is alſo repreſented to us in ſcripture, by the relation betwixt huſband and wife. The Lord ſpeaks of himſelf as the church's huſband, and of the church as his ſpouſe, in many places of ſacred writing. *Thou ſhalt be called Hephzi-bah, and thy land Beulah, for the Lord delighteth in thee, and thy land ſhall be married; turn, O back-*

ſliding children, ſaith the Lord, for I am married unto you; for thy Maker is thine huſband; I will betroth thee unto me for ever. Betwixt the huſband and the wife there ſubſiſts a marriage covenant, by which the parties are ſolemnly engaged to one another, and have vowed and ſworn to fulfil mutually all conjugal and relative duties. Betwixt the Lord as the huſband of his people, and the church as his bleſſed ſpouſe, there muſt neceſſarily ſubſiſt a marriage covenant; and that not merely betwixt him and an individual believer, but betwixt him and the church as a collective body; for unto the latter, not indeed to the excluſion of the former, do the texts here quoted principally relate. To the relation betwixt a maſter and his ſervant, is the relation betwixt God and the church likewiſe compared. *A ſervant honoureth his maſter, if I be a Maſter, where is my fear, ſaith the Lord of hoſts.* This relation among men is conſtituted by a mutual covenant, either in the way of verbal agreement, or written and ſubſcribed indenture or articled contract; whereby the maſter engages to pay the ſtipulated reward, and the ſervant to perform the ſpecified work: the relation betwixt God and the church, being compared to this, muſt neceſſarily require, that, as he hath covenanted with them, for his glory and their ſalvation, in Chriſt to be their Maſter, they ſhould covenant with him, through the Redeemer, to be his ſervants for ever. I ſhall conclude this argument by obſerving, that the reaſoning here advanced is not founded upon a mere circumſtance in theſe earthly relations, to which the connection betwixt God and the church is compared. No doubt, there are ſome circumſtances in theſe relations, from which it would be very unſafe to reaſon, concerning the nature and tendency of the ſpiritual relation, of which they are metaphorical repreſentations. But our reaſoning here is taken from that which is eſſential unto theſe relations among men. We may therefore be certain, that, ſince the Spirit of God has compared the one to the other, there muſt be ſomething belonging to the ſpiritual relation, analagous to that which is eſſential to theſe relations among the creatures, by which it is repreſented to us; and this can be nothing elſe, at leaſt in its moſt formal and explicit ſhape, than a public and ſolemn covenant betwixt God and the church.

6th, The perpetual morality of the duty of public covenanting with God is evident, from the acknowledged morality of other duties, which are of the ſame ſpecific nature. It certainly will not be denied, that it is the duty of the church to form and expreſs holy reſolutions, relative unto their ſerving the Lord, and walking in his ways. Neither will it be refuſed, that the church is called to make and utter promiſes, in the ſtrength of grace, to cleave unto the Lord, and to walk in all the commandments and ordinances of the Lord. The morality of theſe religious reſolutions and promiſes is evident, from the ſcriptural account of the ſpiritual exerciſe of the church and people of God; becauſe their exerciſe, as recorded in the ſacred page, is full of ſuch reſolutions and promiſes, whereby they engage themſelves to be for the Lord, and not for another. Now, if it is the duty of the church to reſolve and promiſe, in the ſtrength of divine grace, to ſerve the Lord; where is the dictate of right reaſon, where is the precept in the book of God, that forbids them to make the things which they reſolve upon, or promiſe to perform, the matter of a vow or of an oath unto the moſt high God? If they may reſolve or promiſe to avoid, and endeavour to ſuppreſs any evil, or to perform and maintain any thing that is good; what can hinder them to vow, covenant, or ſwear to the Lord of hoſts, to do the ſame things? Theſe duties are the ſame in their general nature, only the latter partakes of a greater degree of ſolemnity. If it is lawful to do the one, it is impoſſible that it can be ſinful to do the other.

7th, The morality of public covenanting with God appears alſo, from theſe ordinances of divine appointment, and duties of his worſhip, which contain in them a ſolemn vow or oath unto the Lord. The ordination of the public office-bearers in the church of Chriſt, is an ordinance which contains a vow or oath unto the Lord. When the teaching and ruling elders of the church are ſet apart unto their ſacred office and work, they, in the preſence of the church and with their conſent, come under a ſolemn vow or oath unto the Lord, to perform the duties of that ſtation in which they are placed. If the ministers and elders of the church do vow and swear unto the Lord, why should it be thought improper and sinful for the church, in all her officers and members, to vow and swear unto the Lord to perform the duties, which, in their different stations, are incumbent on them? The ordinance of baptism also contains a vow or oath unto the Lord. What is it that the members of the church do, when they come unto this ordinance, with their children? Do they not profess to take the Lord, as he is reconciled in Christ, as their God, and the God of their seed; to act faith upon the blood and Spirit of Christ, presented to them in this ordinance, for justification and sanctification, both to themselves and their children; to devote themselves and their little ones unto the Lord, that they may be his; and to engage, by solemn promise, vow and oath unto the Lord, to perform all the duties incumbent upon them, particularly to train up their children in the nurture and admonition of the Lord? If an individual, in this ordinance, is permitted to do this, where is the evil of his doing the same things substantially, in company with the rest of his fellow Christians, by joining themselves solemnly unto the Lord, in a perpetual covenant that shall not be forgotten? If we take a view of the Lord's supper, it will appear, that a vow or oath unto the Most High is found in the Christian's exercise, while he is observing that most solemn ordinance. The name that was antiently imposed upon it, and that by which it is still commonly called, *a sacrament*, shews that this was the view which the Christians in the primitive times had, and which Christians still have of the nature of this institution. The word, from which this name sacrament is derived, signifies an oath, a covenant, or sacred obligation, under which persons bring themselves. It was used to signify the oath which the Roman soldiers sware, to be faithful to the rulers of the state, to their military leaders, and to interests of the Roman people. The nature of the ordinance itself, abstract from its ordinary name, shews us, that Christians therein embrace the Lord and his Christ as their God, and Saviour, and portion; and also come under solemn obligations to be the Lord's people. If this is the duty of Christians in this ordinance, by what law does it become sinful for them to do the same things, by binding their souls with a bond to be his people, in a public covenant with God?

8th, The morality of the duty of personal covenanting proves the morality of the church's covenanting with the Lord, in her collective capacity. Few will be disposed to deny, that personal covenanting with God is one of the sacred duties of religion, which Christians should perform, and in which they sometimes have much spiritual delight. Christians perform this sacred spiritual duty, when they, in the exercise of grace, solemnly renounce all false confidences for salvation, take hold of God's covenant, yield themselves to the Lord, and promise and vow, in his strength, to deny all ungodliness and worldly lusts, and to live soberly, righteously, and godly in the present world. The person who lives in the neglect of this duty, omits an exercise which is eminently calculated, and often signally blessed to promote the holiness and comfort of believers. If this is an employment which is competent to a believer in a solitary state, must it not be an exercise that is lawful for a company of them to perform in a social capacity? There are a variety of duties incumbent upon the church in her public state, which are, for the substance of them, the same with these exercises which belong unto an individual Christian. Public prayer, public fasting or mourning for sin, and public thanksgiving and praise unto God, correspond unto the exercises of secret prayer, personal fasting and thanksgiving. Since Christians, as individuals, are under a moral obligation to pray, confess or repent and mourn for sin, and praise the Lord for his goodness; we may conclude that they are morally bound to perform these duties in a public capacity. In like manner, since it is the duty of a believer by himself, to covenant with the Lord as his God in Christ; it must be the duty of a multitude of them to perform the same service, in a suitableness to their public character.

9th, The morality of this duty will further appear both from the absurdity and impiety of the contrary opinion, and the weakness of the reasons by which it is supported. Those who oppose that truth, for which we are now arguing, must hold it to be an immoral and unlawful thing, for a Chriſtian people to avouch the Lord to be their God, and to ſerve him; that they have no warrant in the word of God to reſolve, promiſe, vow or ſwear that they ſhall to the uttermoſt of their power maintain his goſpel, cleave unto his ordinances, obey his laws, ſupport the intereſts of his glory in the world, and oppoſe whatever is contrary thereunto; and that it is a criminal and unlawful thing for them to join themſelves unto the Lord in a perpetual covenant that ſhall not be forgotten. The mentioning of this ſentiment is ſurely ſufficient to expoſe it to the deteſtation of all ſpiritually illuminated and holy minds. As this opinion bears impiety and abſurdity in the very face of it, ſo the arguments by which its friends endeavour to ſupport it are fallacious and vain. One of them is this, That the public covenanting under the former diſpenſation was typical, and, when Chriſt the ſubſtance appeared, it fled away, with the reſt of the ſhadows of the ceremonial law. This is eaſily ſaid, but the proving of it has always been found to be impoſſible. Muſt the ſolemn exerciſe of the church of God, in taking him for their God in Chriſt, in devoting themſelves unto him, and in binding themſelves with a bond to ſerve and glorify him, be ranked among the carnal ordinances which were impoſed upon the church till the times of reformation, and make a part of that yoke which neither we nor our fathers were able to bear? The idea is utterly abſurd. It is eſſential unto all typical inſtitutions to have ſomething in the goſpel church with which it is connected as a ſhadow, and which it did prefigure. But what is this? where is its Antitype? There is nothing in the ſtate of the goſpel church, nothing among all her duties, or her privileges, with which you can aſſociate public covenanting under the old diſpenſation, but public covenanting under the new; and how abſurd it is, to make a moral duty under the law typical of the ſame moral duty under the goſpel, muſt be evident to all who know any thing about the truths of God. Beſides, it is eſſential unto every typical ordinance, to appear in the view of an intelligent Chriſtian, to be peculiarly ſuitable to the ſtate of the church before the coming of Chriſt, and to be utterly incompatible with her condition after the manifeſtation of God in the flesh. Now, what is there in the nature of the church's covenanting with God, that makes it peculiar to her state prior to Christ's incarnation, and inconsistent with her situation after it? Nothing at all; and therefore let the nature of this duty be what it will, typical it cannot be. Another of these arguments by which this opinion is attempted to be supported, is the following. Public covenanting in Israel was not a moral, but a positive institution, and was abolished at the death of Christ. What! shall the death of Christ abolish the great Christian duty of taking the Lord for our God, of giving ourselves unto him, and of solemnly resolving, vowing and swearing to wait upon the Lord, and keep his way? The death of Christ did indeed abolish the obligation of the Israelitish covenants with God, in so far as they bound that people to support and practise the legal ceremonies; but it did not abolish the obligation of their national oath to the most High, either to perform the duties of the moral law, which were included in it, or to receive and observe that system of more spiritual ordinances instituted by Christ, and which came in the room of the abrogated ceremonies. The death of Christ is the grand foundation of all the duties and privileges of his people. Shall it therefore abolish one of the most solemn duties, and one of the most important privileges of the church of the living God? The death of Christ is the meritorious cause of that new covenant relation that takes place betwixt God and his church, and of all its spiritual and eternal effects. Can it therefore abolish that solemn exercise of covenanting with God, by which the Lord avouches the church to be his people, whereby the church avouches the Lord to be their God, and wherein both parties recognize avow and act towards one another according to that relation? Certainly not. Far be it from us to harbour such a thought. To ascribe this to the death of Christ, is to blaspheme it, and to make it one of the ends thereof to abolish the law, with a witness.

In defence of this sentiment, it has also been urged, that public covenanting is not expressly enjoined upon Christians in the New Testament, and, therefore, it cannot be a moral duty in the days of the gospel. Were it not that this argument is ſtill ſinfully urged againſt the morality of public covenanting with God, under the New Teſtament, with a view to prejudiſe the inconſiderate againſt this ſolemn exercise, even by thoſe who cannot be ſuppoſed to be ignorant of the ſatisfactory anſwers which have been given to it, we would not have mentioned it at all. Public covenanting, as is very clear from the Old Teſtament, was once an ordinance of God, and the indiſpenſible duty of his church. It is, therefore, neceſſary for thoſe, who oppoſe its morality now, to prove in a clear manner, either from the nature of the thing itſelf, or from expreſs ſcripture declaration in the New Teſtament, that it is abrogated by the authority of God. Till this is done, which will never be accompliſhed, we are warranted to conſider it ſtill as an ordinance of God, and the duty of his church.—This argument takes it for granted, that all moral duties which are incumbent on the church, in goſpel times, are expreſsly enjoined in the New Teſtament; which is a groſs miſtake. There are other duties, beſides public covenanting, for which there are no expreſs precepts in the New Teſtament. The baptiſm of infants, ſecret prayer on the morning and evening of every day, family faſting, and family worſhip every morning and evening, are all mentioned in the Old Teſtament, but none of them are enjoined in the New. Now, if theſe duties, the obligation of which upon us cannot juſtly be denied, are not expreſsly required in the New Teſtament, how weak and inconcluſive muſt the argument againſt public covenanting be, which is derived from this ſource? If our obligation to perform the one is denied on this account; it will be impoſſible, for the ſame reaſon, to defend our obligation to practiſe the others. The real ſtate of the matter is this; the ſcriptures of the Old and New Teſtament, taken together, are a complete revelation of the will of God to the children of men, both with reſpect to truth and duty. Public covenanting, and the other duties formerly mentioned, are ſo clearly revealed in the Old Teſtament, that there is no neceſſity for their being expreſsly mentioned in the writings of the New. While there is nothing in the nature of the things themſelves inconſiſtent with the ſtate of the goſpel church, nor the ſmalleſt hint in the New Teſtament of their abrogation, we are to conſider the authority of God in the precepts of the Old Teſtament, which are illuſtrated and recommended to us by approved examples, as ſtill binding the church of Chriſt, in theſe laſt days, to perform the ſame ſolemn ſervices.

In ſupport of this opinion, it has likewiſe been ſaid, that the Lord Jeſus never performed the duty of public covenanting, and, therefore, this exerciſe cannot be a duty incumbent upon us. In anſwer to this it may be obſerved, that this argument plainly ſuppoſes that Chriſt examplified, in his own practice, all the moral duties which are incumbent on his people; which is not true. A variety of important moral duties, which belong unto Chriſtians, who ſtand in certain human relations to each other, were never performed by the Lord Chriſt; becauſe, it was not conſiſtent with his perſon, dignity, office and work, that he ſhould occupy any of theſe relations. The neceſſary duties of repentance for ſin, the mortification of it, and the exerciſes of the mind connected therewith, could not be examplified by him, becauſe he was holy, harmleſs, undefiled, and ſeparate from ſinners. Beſides, we find him refuſing to perform a moral duty, to which he was ſolicited, becauſe it belonged to the civil magiſtrate, which was a ſtation he did not fill. If Chriſt never performed the various duties now mentioned and alluded unto, and yet their morality remains unſhaken to the end; what argument can juſtly be drawn, from Chriſt's not having publicly covenanted in the days of his fleſh, againſt the morality of that duty? To this argument we further reply. Public covenanting with God is not a ſtated, but an occaſional moral duty, to be performed by the church, when the calls of divine providence point it out to them to be their preſent duty. As it is ſinful to neglect it, when the Lord by his providence is calling thereunto; ſo it is equally improper to engage in it, when the providence of God clearly manifeſts, that the performance of this ſervice would not anſwer the ends for which it is intended. This was exactly the caſe in the days of the Redeemer's incarnation, and, therefore, he could not poſſibly have any call to perform the duty of public covenanting with God. Among the many glorious ends of his coming into the world, this was one, to abolish in his death the ceremonial observances, and to set up a more excellent and spiritual system of gospel worship in its stead. If Christ and the church had entered into a public covenant with God, the ceremonial system behoved to have been recognized and sworn unto therein; as it was binding on the church till the death of Christ. To covenant with God for the support of a system which was just about to be destroyed, would have been to contradict the designs, appearances, and calls of his providence. If ever there was a time when public covenanting with God was unseasonable, it was when the fulness of the time was come, when God sent forth his Son made of a woman, made under the law, to redeem them that were under the law, that we might receive the adoption of sons. Let none say, this renders the obedience and example of Christ imperfect. By no means. The non-performance of occasional moral duties, when there is no call in providence thereunto, but rather providential obstructions in the way of their being done, can never be justly considered as a defect in the obedience or example either of Christ himself, or of his followers; but the performance of them, in these circumstances, would certainly be a blemish in both.

The last argument that shall be mentioned, in support of this opinion, is the following. The apostles and primitive Christians did not enter into public covenants with God, and, therefore, it cannot be a moral duty in New Testament times. Although it were granted, that the apostles and the primitive Christians did not publicly covenant with God, yet no argument can be drawn from this, that is of any weight, against the morality of that duty under the Christian dispensation. If they really did not covenant with God in a public manner, we may be certain that it was because they had not a call in providence to be employed in this duty. The situation and circumstances of the church may be such, as to render it inexpedient or unnecessary to carry forward the work of public covenanting. This is clear from the account we have of the performance of that duty in the times of the Old Testament. In the days of some of the most religious kings, and fome of the moft remarkable prophets of the Lord, it does not appear that the church performed this folemn duty. The reafon is plain, they had not thofe calls of providence, arifing from the peculiar ftate of the church, and from the particular difpenfations of God towards her, which are neceffary to make public covenanting the prefent duty of any people. Now, if the apoftles and primitive Chriftians did not perform this duty, we may certainly conclude that their circumftances, in the courfe of divine providence, rendered it either unneceffary or inexpedient for them to be fo employed. In a word, let the fituation and circumftances of the church in the wildernefs, before the death of Jofhua, in the time of Afa, in the days of Jehoiada, under the reign of Jofiah, and when the Jews returned from Babylon to their own land, be carefully confidered, and when the fituation and circumftances of the Chriftian church, at any time or in any place, clearly correfponds with either of thefe, public covenanting with God is their prefent duty; but when it is otherwife, this folemn exercife is not required at their hand. To this argument it may alfo be anfwered, that it does not appear to be true, that we have no example of public covenanting with God, in the days of the apoftles. There is certainly fomething recorded concerning one of the apoftolic churches, which fignifies their having publicly vowed unto, or covenanted with God. It is the conduct of the church of Macedonia, mentioned by Paul, 2 Cor. viii. 5. *And this they did, not as we hoped, but firft gave their ownfelves unto the Lord, and unto us by the will of God* The meaning of which muft be this, the Macedonian churches, having gathered their collection for the poor faints at Jerufalem, and having requefted us to take the charge of conveying it to them, before they actually put it into our hand, did firft of all, contrary indeed to our expectation, folemnly devote themfelves as a church unto the Lord, by a public vow unto, or covenant with him to be his people, and committed themfelves unto us, as the miniftering fervants of Jefus, in which exercifes they had a refpect unto, and complied with, the will of God. I defy any man to make common fenfe of the apoftle's words, if this is denied. It is unqueftionable, that this exercife of that church behoved to be done by them, in ſome public and ſolemn act of religious worſhip ; and it may eaſily be proved, that this act of worſhip could be no other than a public vow or oath unto the Lord, or covenant with him. This appears from the ſimilarity of the expreſſion here uſed unto the words of the Old Teſtament, by which Iſrael's covenanting with God is deſcribed. They are ſaid to *join themſelves to the Lord, in a perpetual covenant ;* Jer. l. 5 What elſe can the exerciſe of the Macedonian churches mean, when they gave their ownſelves to the Lord? Are not our joining ourſelves unto the Lord, and our giving our ownſelves to the Lord, expreſſions of the ſame import? If the former ſignifies our covenanting with God, the latter can mean nothing leſs. Iſrael's covenanting is alſo deſcribed in the following words; *And Jehoiada made a covenant between the Lord, and the king and the people, that they ſhould be the Lord's people ;* 2 Kings xi. 17. *And they entered into a covenant to ſeek the Lord God of their fathers, with all their heart, and with all their ſoul.* 2 Chron. xv. 12. The nature of the church's covenanting with God, was juſt a ſolemn engagement that they ſhould be the Lord's people, and that they would ſeek him with all their heart, and with all their ſoul. Is not all this comprehended in the exerciſe of the churches of Macedonia? It cannot be ſuppoſed that they could give their ownſelves to the Lord, without engaging to be the Lord's people, and to ſeek him with all their heart, and with all their ſoul. As this was the church's covenanting under the old diſpenſation, and as we have here the whole ſubſtance of it in the exerciſe of a church under the new; we therefore have a clear example of public covenanting under the goſpel ſtate of the church.—The truth of this will further appear, if we conſider that there is no other religious duty or exerciſe, by which the Macedonian believers could perform this work, as the apoſtle here repreſents it, but by a vow or covenant with God. The enemies of public covenanting have mentioned three ways, by which the Macedonians, on this occaſion, might have given themſelves to the Lord, without a religious vow or covenant. Let us now ſee how they will correſpond with the apoſtle's account of the matter. It has been ſaid, that the

Macedonians might give their ownselves to the Lord, by making *a public profession of Christianity*. We answer, they had made a public profession of Christianity before they had any thought of sending a supply to the poor saints at Jerusalem; they were daily making that profession, by abstaining from their former heathenish worship and religion, and cleaving to the truths and ordinances of Christ; this, therefore, could not be the exercise of that church of which the apostle here speaks. Besides, how could the apostle say, concerning this act of the Macedonians, that it was not as he hoped, if it contained nothing else than their professing Christianity? the apostle could never hope that they would not profess Christianity, when they had, on former occasions, solemnly taken this profession on themselves. In fine, where is the church's profession of Christianity ever represented, in the New Testament, by their giving their ownselves to the Lord? These things show the gross absurdity of this supposition. It has also been said, that they might give themselves to the Lord in the *ordinances* of baptism. To this we may answer, the members of these churches were certainly baptized before this time. The apostle is here speaking of a solemn act performed by the Macedonians, after they had gathered their collection for the church in Judea, and before they actually sent it away. Can it be supposed, that the believers in these churches had either referred their baptism for this juncture, or that they were all re-baptized on this occasion? could ever the apostle say that he did not hope that they would submit to the ordinance of baptism, if they were yet unbaptized? or where is the administration of baptism represented, in the word of God, by the exercise of a whole church giving their ownselves to the Lord? this supposition is equally absurd as the other. It has further been said, that the Macedonian churches might give their ownselves to the Lord, *by receiving the Lord's supper.* To this we reply, the apostle speaks of this act of the Macedonians as a thing that was singular, and contrary to his expectation If it was nothing more than their eating the Lord's supper, it could be no way singular; for this ordinance was common to all the churches of Christ. Nor could it be contrary to his expectation;

how could the apoſtle imagine that they would allow him to depart, with their collection to the Jewiſh believers, without diſpenſing to them the ordinance of the Lord's ſupper? beſides, the receiving of that ordinance is never repreſented, as is the caſe here, by different churches publicly giving their ownſelves unto the Lord, and committing themſelves to the care of the apoſtles, by the will of God. This deed of theſe churches, therefore, behoved to be ſome explicit, public, ſolemn, and religious act of worſhip, diſtinct from any of theſe which have been mentioned; and it is impoſſible to conceive of any other divine inſtitution, that can anſwer the apoſtle's deſcription, but a public religious vow, oath, or covenant with God.

Fourthly, The church's public covenants with God have an intrinſic and moral obligation to duty of themſelves, upon the conſciences of the covenanters, diſtinct from the obligation to the ſame duties, by the binding force of the moral law. As this truth is groſsly miſrepreſented by ſome, and flatly denied by others, it is neceſſary that ſomething ſhould be ſaid, both for explaining the nature of this obligation, and for proving its reality. The moral law is both the fountain, in ſome reſpects, from which the obligation of theſe covenants does proceed, and the rule of direction by which the church's covenanting exerciſes are to be regulated. The nature of the obligation of religious covenants with God may be underſtood, in ſome meaſure, if the following things are duly conſidered.

The great Jehovah poſſeſſes in himſelf, and exerciſes all that authority, by which the children of men are bound to obedience, and has given them his law as the regulating ſtandard of their actions; but, in order more effectually to promote the ends thereof among men, he has inſtituted in his word, vowing and ſwearing unto him, and covenanting with him, as his ordinances unto them, and has required in his law theſe exerciſes from them, as their indiſpenſible duty. He has given to Chriſtians a power over themſelves, or a right of ſelf-government, whereby they, in agreeableneſs to the preſcriptions of his law, diſpoſe of themſelves, and voluntarily engage themſelves unto his obedience. The church's covenanting with God, and vowing and swearing unto him, are the principal ways by which they exercise this right, and use this power which God has given them, by disposing of themselves as the law requires, in taking upon themselves the yoke of Christ which is easy, and his burden which is light. When Christians are convinced, by the light of God's word, that these exercises are their duty, and, in consequence thereof, do actually promise, vow and swear unto the Lord, or covenant with him, that they shall, in the strength of his grace, abstain from evil, and practise holiness; they are under obligation to obedience, by their own religious and voluntary promises, vows, oaths and covenants, as well as they are bound thereunto, by the infinite authority of God in his law.

It may tend to cast some light on this matter, to state a few of the differences betwixt the obligation to duty by the moral law, and that of the church's covenants. The obligation of the church's covenants is distinct from the obligation of the law. It s not independent of the law, nor separate from it; but the obligation of the one may be distinguished from that of the other. Christians are under an obligation to perform duties, by the authority of God in his law; and they are, at the same time, under an obligation to perform the same duties, by their own act, whereby they have bound themselves to practise them.—The obligation of the law is primary and supreme; that of the church's covenants is secondary and subordinate thereunto.—The obligation of vows and covenants, both as to the matter and manner thereof, may always be examined by the rule of the law; but that which we know to be the law of God is not, as to its rectitude and obligation, the subject of any such examination.—The obligation of the law is necessary unto the very being of the rational creature; that of our covenants is not so. It is impossible for them to exist, without being under the obligation of the divine law; but the greater part of them are not under the obligation of religious covenants.—An act of the creature is necessary to bring us under the obligation of vows and covenants; but no such act is requisite to subject us to the obligation of the moral law.—The obligation of our covenants with

God reaches to time only; but that of the law of God extends to eternity.—By the former, we bind ourſelves to ſincere, though but imperfect obedience, but by the latter, we are divinely bound to perfection.—In the law, God, who is its glorious author, binds us to obedience, by his own authority; but, by our promiſes, vows and covenants, we bind ourſelves to be the Lord's people, and to ſerve him.

The moral law is the directing ſtandard, by which theſe ſolemn tranſactions of the church are to be regulated. The regulations of the law, concerning theſe acts of the creatures, reſpect both the matter of them, and the manner of their performance. As the directions of the law reſpect the matter of our vows and covenants, they indiſpenſibly require, that the things we bind ourſelves to perform be agreeable to the law, and in nothing contrary to the precepts of the word. If they are otherwiſe, our vows and covenants are null and void in their obligation; and it is ſinful to fulfil them. Of this nature was that oath, which more than forty of the Jews had ſworn, that they would neither eat nor drink till they had killed Paul. The Chriſtian has no right or power to bind himſelf to do any thing, that is contrary to the infinite obligation under which he is laid, by the authority of God in his law. It is, therefore, neceſſary in order that our vows, oaths and covenants may have validity in them, and an obligation ariſing from them to bind our conſciences, that the matter of them be lawful, and agreeable to the commandments of God. The directions of the law extend alſo to the manner in which theſe ſolemn tranſactions are to be performed. The law of God requires that we vow or ſwear unto the Lord in truth, in righteouſneſs, and in judgment; by faith in him as our God in Chriſt; expecting acceptance with him in this, as in all other duties, through the Mediator; with holy fear and reverence of his majeſty and glory; in obedience to his holy law, which requires theſe duties of us; with a ſincere intention of fulfilling them, in the ſtrength of his grace; with a view to promote his glory; and with a deſign to advance the ſpiritual good of ourſelves and others. When the church of God, by uſing his ordinance, and performing their duty, do vow or swear unto the Lord, and enter into a covenant with him, which is, in the matter of it, agreeable to his law, and, in the manner of performing it, is such as he requires, these acts lay them under a real, formal and moral obligation to perform the duties to which they have engaged, and to eschew the evils from which they have bound themselves to abstain. The proof of this is now to be attempted, and its truth may be confirmed, by the following arguments.

1st, That there is an intrinsic obligation to duty in the church's vows, oaths or covenants, is evident from the words of the text, and other scriptures, wherein the children of men are charged with breaking or transgressing their covenant with God. *The house of Israel and the house of Judah have broken my covenant.* See also Jer. xxxiv. 18. Hosea vi. 7. In these scriptures, the church of God are said to break, and to transgress the covenant betwixt God and them. It is impossible that the covenant could be broken, or transgressed, if it did not lay an obligation to duty on the consciences of the covenanters. How could they break a bond, if it had no binding force upon them? or how could they transgress a covenant, if they were not obliged to duty, by that covenant? since the people of God are charged with breaking and transgressing their covenant, they must have been bound to the performance of duty by their covenant; and, if so, religious covenants must have an intrinsic and formal obligation to duty of themselves, by which covenanters are bound.

2*d*, The truth of this observation will also appear, if we consider, that the sin of the church of God, as it is a transgression of the divine law, and their sin, as it is a breach of their covenant with God, are distinguished from each other. Isaiah xxiv. 5. *The earth also is defiled under the inhabitants thereof; because they have transgressed the laws, changed the ordinance, broken the everlasting covenant.* The sin of Judah is here described, both as it is a transgression of the law, and as it is a breach of the everlasting covenant. This plainly imports, that they were under an obligation to duty by the authority of God in his law, and, therefore, their sin was a transgression of his laws; and that they were under another obligation to duty from their entering into covenant with God, and, on this account, their ſin is ſaid to be a breach of the everlaſting covenant. It is evident, that the divine law obliged them to obedience, and that they were under the obligation of it, when their ſin is declared to be a tranſgreſſion of that law; it is equally clear, that their covenant with God obliged them to obedience, and that they were under the obligation thereof, as their ſin is here ſtated to be a breach of that covenant. From this text of ſcripture, we have juſt as much evidence, for the obligation of religious covenants on the conſciences of men, as we have for that of the divine law upon them; for their ſin is not a tranſgreſſion of the law only, but alſo a breach of the covenant.

3*d*, The ſcriptural account of the nature of religious vows and oaths unto the Lord, fully confirms the truth of this obſervation. In the xxx. chap. of Numbers, this is repreſented in the cleareſt manner; we ſhall particularly attend to the 2d verſe. *If a man ſhall vow a vow unto the Lord, or ſwear an oath to bind his ſoul with a bond; he ſhall not break his word, he ſhall do according to all that proceedeth out of his mouth.* There are three things in this verſe. The exerciſes mentioned, vowing a vow, or ſwearing an oath unto the Lord.—The nature of the creatures vows and oaths unto the Lord, they are his binding his ſoul with a bond.—The duty of a perſon that has vowed or ſworn unto the Lord, he ſhall not break his word, he ſhall do according to all that proceedeth out of his mouth. It is the ſecond of theſe particulars which we have in view at this time, wherein the nature of vows and oaths unto the Lord is deſcribed; it is ſaid to be the perſon's binding his ſoul with a bond. This expreſſion is frequently uſed in the courſe of the chapter, as the deſcription, which the Spirit of God uniformly gives of the nature of thoſe religious exerciſes. If a perſon, by vowing and ſwearing unto the Lord, binds his ſoul with a bond, to do according to all that proceedeth out of his mouth, muſt there not be an obligation laid upon his conſcience to fulfil it, by his vow and oath? How is it poſſible that the ſoul can be bound with a bond by vowing and ſwearing to God, and yet there ſhall be no intrinſic obligation in his vow or oath? Words cannot be conceived more clearly and ſtrongly to expreſs the inviolable obligation of religious vows and oaths, than thoſe which are here uſed. By our religious vows, oaths and covenants with God, we bind ourſelves with a bond, we bring ourſelves under a moral obligation, diſtinct from that of the divine law, to do according to all that proceedeth out of our mouth. Let none ſay that theſe vows and oaths relate to matters of indifferency, to which the ſoul was not bound, by the divine law; for if our vows and oaths bind our ſouls with a bond, with reſpect to things of this nature, much more muſt they bind our ſouls with a bond, and lay obligation upon us, when they are interpoſed, as they ought to be, about matters of ſuperior moral importance.

4*th*, The intrinſic moral obligation of the church's vows and covenants with God is alſo evident, from the commands of the divine law, which require the children of men to fulfil them Some of the precepts of God's word, which require this duty, are the following: Deut. xxiii. 21. *When thou ſhalt vow a vow unto the Lord thy God, thou ſhalt not ſlack to pay it; for the Lord thy God will ſurely require it of thee, and it would be ſin in thee;* Pſal. lxxvi. 11. *Vow, and pay unto the Lord your God.* Eccl. v. 4. *When thou voweſt a vow unto God, defer not to pay it; for he hath no pleaſure in fools. pay that which thou haſt vowed.* Deut. xxix. 9. *Keep therefore the words of this covenant, and do them, that ye may proſper in all that ye do.* Jer. xi. 6. *Hear ye the words of this covenant, and do them.* In theſe portions of ſcripture, and in others of a ſimilar nature, the Lord requires the children of men to pay their vows, and to keep their covenant with him. This plainly imports, that our vows contain an obligation in them, whereby we are bound to pay them; and that by our entering into a covenant with God, we are bound to keep it. When the Lord commands us to obey his law, it ſhews us that the law obliges us to obedience; and when he requires us to fulfil our vows and covenants, it plainly diſcovers that they poſſeſs an intrinſic obligation which binds our conſciences. If the law laid no obligation upon us, God could not command us to obey it; and, if our vows and covenants did not bind us, the Lord could not enjoin us to fulfil them. It is not the command of God, requiring us to pay our vows and keep our covenants, that gives obligation unto them; this command only requires us to act according to that obligation, and warns us of the evil of violating it. The obligation arises intirely from the act of the creatures, using a divine ordinance, by vowing unto God, and covenanting with him, whereby they bind their souls with a bond to serve the Lord. The commands of God, relating to our vows and covenants, plainly suppose their intrinsic obligation upon us. In these divine precepts, the Lord clearly recognizes the moral obligation of these solemn deeds. Every one of these commands is a divine acknowledgment that our vows and covenants, which he requires us to fulfil, have an intrinsic obligation upon us. How could the Lord require his people to pay a vow, which did not at all oblige them to pay it? how could he command them to keep a covenant, which was void of all binding force upon them? The denial of the intrinsic obligation of our religious vows and covenants, renders the commands of God, wherein he requires us to pay the one and keep the other, absurd and senseless. It is as if the Lord should say unto his people; you have vowed a vow unto me, which indeed has no obligation in it, nevertheless you must pay it; you have entered into a covenant with me, which has no binding force upon you, yet you must keep it. Can the Lord interpose his authority in this manner? The supposition is blasphemous. The reverse is unquestionably the truth. These holy precepts of God's word are his declaration unto the children of men, to the following effect. You have vowed a vow unto me, and entered into a covenant with me, by which you have, according to my ordinance, bound your souls with a bond, which morally obliges you to fulfil it; see therefore that you keep your covenant and pay your vow, and beware of breaking your solemn engagements From these precepts of the Lord's word, it is evident that religious vows and covenants contain in them an intrinsic obligation to duty.

5th, This truth is also confirmed from the scriptural account of the views, which believers had of their religious oaths and vows unto God; a few of these shall be mentioned. Pſalm cxix. 106. *I have ſworn, and I will perform it, that I will keep thy righteous judgments.* This text contains the exerciſe, in which David had been employed, religious ſwearing unto the Lord; his reſolution reſpecting it, I will perform it; and what was the matter of his oath, not a matter of indifferency, to which he was not previouſly bound by God in his law, but a thing moral in its nature, that he would keep God's righteous judgments. David, having uſed the divine ordinance of ſwearing to the Lord of hoſts, reſolves to perform it, by keeping God's righteous judgments. His reſolving to perform his oath plainly ſhews, that he believed that he was bound by the oath he had ſworn, as well as by the divine law, to keep God's righteous judgments; and that his oath was a bond upon his ſoul, by which he had brought himſelf under a ſolemn and voluntary obligation to ſerve the Lord. Pſalm lvi. 12. *Thy vows are upon me, O God; I will render praiſes unto thee.* The former part of this verſe repreſents the ſituation of the holy man, he was under vows unto God; and the latter part of it expreſſes his fulfilling them, by praiſing and glorifying God. Thy vows are upon me; I have vowed unto the Lord, and the obligation of theſe vows conſtantly binds me. I am not under the obligation of thy law only, but the binding force of religious vows alſo, is upon my ſoul. Correſponding to this it is alſo ſaid, Pſalm lxvi. 13, 14. *I will pay thee my vows, which my lips have uttered, and my mouth hath ſpoken, when I was in trouble.* Theſe words contain the exerciſe of the holy man, he had vowed unto the Lord, his lips had uttered and his mouth had ſpoken them; the time when he had made his vows, it was a ſeaſon of trouble; and his reſolution concerning his vows, I will pay thee my vows. From this reſolution it is evident, that the holy man conſidered his vows as a debt-bond unto the Lord, which he was engaged to pay, and as containing an obligation to duty, which he was bound to fulfil. From theſe inſtances, and others which might be mentioned, and probably will be recollected, it appears that the ſaints of God conſidered their oaths and vows unto him, as containing an intrinſic obligation to duty; and certainly this is the view which the church ſhould entertain of them, till the end of the world.

6th, The obligation of our covenants with God is alſo evident, from the binding force of human contracts between man and man. It is a natural dictate of reaſon, which is confirmed by the word of God, that the promiſes, oaths and covenants of men with one another, oblige the parties to fulfil them; and that their failing therein, or acting contrary thereto, is a great evil. If our promiſes, oaths and covenants with our fellow creatures, bring us under a moral obligation, and bind us to fulfil them; muſt not our promiſes, oaths and covenants with the moſt high God, contain in them a moral obligation to perform duty to him? To allow the one and deny the other is certainly abſurd and impious. It is abſurd. Does not the divine law as expreſsly require us to fulfil our ſacred engagements to God, as it enjoins us to implement our common obligations to men? Does not the word of God promiſe rewards to them that keep their covenant with God, as well as to them who act according to their agreements with men? Does not the law of God threaten thoſe with judgments who break their covenant with him, as well as it denounces vengeance againſt thoſe who violate their engagements with their fellow creatures? How abſurd therefore muſt it be to allow an obligation in the one caſe, and deny it in the other. This opinion is alſo impious. It is to ſay, that the law of God guards the rights of men, more than the intereſts of its glorious author; that, if we open our mouth unto men we are bound, but though we open our mouth unto God, no obligation at all ariſes from it; and, that our fellow creatures have a claim upon us by our contracting with them, but the great God has no claim upon us by our covenanting with him. The groſs impiety of this muſt be evident to all.

7th, The obligation of religious oaths and covenants may be proved from the nature of our baptiſm, of the Lord's ſupper, and of a religious profeſſion. When we are baptized in the name of the Father, of the Son, and of the Holy Ghoſt, are we not brought under obligations to ſerve and glorify the three who bear record in heaven? When we ſit down at the table of the Lord, and ſhew forth his death till he come, do we not come under very particular engagements to be for the Lord, and not for another? When we take upon ourſelves a religious profeſſion, are we not bound to walk according to it? If theſe things are ſo, how much more muſt we be under an obligation to perform the duties of holineſs, by an explicit and formal vowing or ſwearing unto the Lord, and covenanting with him.

The lax and prevailing ſentiment by which this truth is oppoſed, is the following. Religious covenants are not formally, but only materially binding. They have no real obligation in themſelves, but we are bound to the duties therein, becauſe theſe duties are required in the moral law. This dangerous opinion appears to be imbibed by many profeſſed witneſſes for the covenanted reformation, by the influence of which, they ſeem to be precipitated into the gulf of public apoſtacy from theſe principles, which they formerly eſpouſed. It is impoſſible for a perſon to believe it, without entertaining a ſecret contempt of religious vows, oaths and covenants; and it is impoſſible for him to act upon it, without being involved in a practical oppoſition to them. Having already eſtabliſhed the contrary truth, it will not be neceſſary to ſay much for overthrowing this erroneous ſentiment. If this opinion were true, the houſe of Iſrael and the houſe of Judah could not be charged with breaking the covenant: they might be charged with breaking the Lord's law; but he could not have ſaid, they have broken my covenant. If Iſrael's covenant with God did not bind them, by an intrinſic obligation, their iniquity could not be a breach of the covenant, but only a tranſgreſſion of the law; nor could it be any way criminal from the relation it had to the covenant, but only from the reference it had to the law. We may eaſily know what to think of an opinion, which neceſſarily renders the charges the Lord brings againſt his backſliding people, abſurd and unjuſt.—Were this opinion true, there could be no ſuch thing among the children of men, as the ſins of perfidy, covenant-breaking or perjury. Though we may pledge our veracity, by religious promiſes and vows unto God, if there is no obligation in them, there can be no perfidy, or breach of faith in our diſregarding them. Though we may join ourſelves to the Lord in a ſolemn covenant, if that deed brings us under no obligation to fulfil it, the ſin of covenant-breaking can have no exiſtence. Though we ſhould enter into an oath to walk in the Lord's law, if this oath is not binding in itſelf, how can the ſin of perjury, or deſpiſing the oath of God, be charged upon us? We are certain that theſe ſins are mentioned in the word of God, and that they are committed by men; but this opinion deſtroys them for ever.—Were this ſentiment right, then all the ſolemn acts of believers as individuals, and of the church as a body, are rendered void and uſeleſs to all intents and purpoſes Of what uſe are promiſes, vows, oaths and covenants, if there is no obligation in them? If obligation to performance is refuſed to them, their very eſſence is deſtroyed. The mind cannot think on any of thoſe tranſactions without conſidering an obligation to do as we have ſaid, vowed or ſworn as eſſential to their being. Promiſes, without an obligation to fulfil them, vows, without an obligation to pay them, oaths, without an obligation to perform them, and covenants, without an obligation to keep them, are monſters both in divinity, and in morals, which are created by this more monſtrous opinion.—It is alſo the native import of this doctrine, that Chriſtians are under no other obligation to duty, after they have promiſed, vowed and ſworn unto the Lord, or covenanted with him, than they were before they engaged in theſe ſolemn and holy tranſactions. The man who can believe this, there is great reaſon to fear, is actuated by a deſire to break the bands of the Lord and his anointed, and to caſt away their cords from him. Theſe things both ſhew the groſs error of this ſentiment, and ſerve to confirm the truth of the contrary doctrine.

We ſhall conclude the illuſtration of this obſervation, by mentioning another opinion which has been urged, for overthrowing the obligation of the church's covenants with God. That the Chriſtian's vows and covenants have no obligation, except when they relate to things which are indifferent. When Chriſtians vow or covenant with God, either to abſtain from or perform any actions, to which they were not bound by the moral law, their covenants oblige them; but no obligation ariſes from them, when they contain articles that are moral in their nature, and to which they are previously bound by the divine law. I shall not take up time in shewing the wild absurdity of an opinion, which allows Christians a power to bind themselves to the performance of things which are indifferent, and denies them a right of coming under a voluntary obligation unto the Lord, relative to duties which are morally binding by his holy law. Upon this it is only necessary to observe, that in all the instances we have of covenanting in scripture, moral duties, to which the church was bound by the law of God, constituted the matter of their vow and oath unto him. In the covenanting that was carried on in the land of Judah, at different periods, the scriptural account of the matter of these transactions is contained in the following expressions. *And Jehoiada made a covenant between the Lord, and the king and the people, that they should be the Lord's people.* 2 Kings xi. 17. *And they entered into a covenant to seek the Lord God of their fathers, with all their heart, and with all their soul.* 2 Chron. xv. 12. *And the king stood by a pillar, and made a covenant before the Lord, to walk after the Lord, and to keep his commandments, and his testimonies, and his statutes, with all their heart, and all their soul, to perform the words of this covenant that are written in this book; and all the people stood to the covenant.* 2 Kings xxiii. 3. *They clave to their brethren, their nobles, and entered into a curse, and into an oath, to walk in God's law, which was given by Moses the servant of God, and to observe, and do all the commandments of the Lord our God, and his judgments, and his statutes.* Neh. x. 29. From these scriptures it is undeniable, that duties of a moral nature, such as the church was previously bound unto by the authority of God in his law, and these only, constituted the matter of their oaths unto God, and of their covenants with him. This opinion, therefore, plainly contradicting as it does the dictates of the Spirit of God, must be rejected with abhorence.

Fifthly, The church's covenants with God bind the consciences of their posterity.

This may be confirmed by the following arguments.

1st, The truth of this observation is evident from the words of the text; *the house of Israel and the house of Judah have broken my covenant, which I made with their fathers.* They are charged with breaking this covenant, and this covenant was made with their fathers. It is not ſaid that this covenant was made with themſelves perſonally, but with their fathers; and yet they are charged with breaking it. From this it is perfectly evident, that they were under the obligation of God's covenant, which was made with their fathers; that this covenant bound them to the performance of the duties which it contained; and that their ſins were as really a breach of this covenant, as the ſins of thoſe could have been, who had perſonally entered into it. What further proof can be required of the binding obligation of religious covenants upon the covenanters poſterity, for the matter is clear from the text. However, as the ſubject of this obſervation is of conſiderable importance, and is much controverted among Chriſtians, we ſhall endeavour to confirm it from ſome other arguments.

2*d*, The ſcriptural account of the covenant, which the Lord made with Iſrael at Horeb, confirms the truth of this doctrine. We find it in Deut. v. 2, 3. *The Lord our God made a covenant with us in Horeb. The Lord made not this covenant with our fathers, but with us, even with us, who are all of us here alive this day.* The covenant, of which Moſes is here ſpeaking, was made with the fathers of thoſe, to whom he was now addreſſing himſelf. The perſons with whom this covenant was made were all dead, or ſlain in the wilderneſs. This appears from Num. xxvi. 64. *But among theſe, there was not a man of them whom Moſes and Aaron the prieſt numbered, when they numbered the children of Iſrael in the wilderneſs of Sinai.* Moſes here declares, that the covenant was not made with their fathers, it was not made with them only, the obligation did not ly upon them alone; but it was made likewiſe with thoſe who were then before the Lord as their poſterity, and the obligation of it extended even unto them. The Lord entered into a covenant with Iſrael at Horeb, ſoon after he had brought them out of the land of Egypt, and Moſes, about forty years afterwards, when all who were above twenty years at the ſolemn tranſaction were dead and gone, informs the congregation of Iſrael, that this covenant was made with them, not with their fathers, but with them, even with them, who were alive at that day. From this ſcripture, the obligation of religious covenants upon poſterity is eſtabliſhed, beyond all poſſibility of reaſonable contradiction; and it is truly aſtoniſhing and mournful that any, who profeſs to believe divine revelation, ſhould deny it.

3*d*, We have ſtill further evidence concerning this important matter, from the account given us of that covenanting in Iſrael, which took place a little before the death of Moſes, the hiſtory of which is contained near the beginning of the xxix. chap. of Deuteronomy. We have a deſcription of the parties of which the aſſembly was compoſed, ver. 10, 11. *The captains of their tribes, their elders, and their officers, and all the men of Iſrael, their little ones, and their wives, the ſtranger in the camp, from the hewer of their wood, unto the drawer of their water.* Not one of the whole camp was abſent from the ſolemn convocation. We are informed alſo of the ſituation in which they ſtood, and the great end of their meeting, ver. 10, 12 *Ye ſtand this day all of you before the Lord your God, that thou ſhouldeſt enter into covenant with the Lord thy God, and into his oath, which the Lord thy God maketh with thee this day.* The deſign of this tranſaction is ſtated, ver. 13. *That he may eſtabliſh thee to day for a people unto himſelf, and that he may be unto thee a God.* The parties concerned in this tranſaction are deſcribed, ver. 14, 15. *Neither with you only do I make this covenant, and this oath; But with him that ſtandeth here with us this day before the Lord our God, and alſo with him that is not here with us this day.* Theſe two verſes divide all the parties who were connected with this covenant, and bound by its obligation into three claſſes; thoſe who were come to mature age, their children who were preſent, and their poſterity who were yet unborn. *Neither with you only do I make this covenant and this oath,* that is, it is not made only with you, who, by reaſon of age, are capable of entering, in your own perſons, into the covenant and oath of God; but with him that ſtandeth here before the Lord. Theſe are their little ones, who, though they were preſent, were, by reaſon of nonage, incapable of entering into the bond of God's covenant.—And alſo with him that is not with us this day; theſe ſignify their poſterity who were yet to be born. The two laſt claſſes, as well as the firſt, are here declared to be under the obligation of the covenant and oath of the Lord their God. From this it is evident, that the obligation of the church's covenants deſcend unto poſterity; as it is impoſſible to take any rational and conſiſtent view of this portion of ſcripture, without underſtanding it in this ſenſe.

4th, That the obligation of religious vows and oaths extends unto poſterity is evident alſo, from the names which the ſcriptures beſtow upon the church's covenants with God. They are called *an everlaſting covenant*, Iſa. xxiv. 5. and *a perpetual covenant*, Jer. l. 5. Theſe covenants are called an everlaſting covenant, and a perpetual covenant, becauſe their obligation is durable and permanent, and extends to future generations. If the obligation of theſe covenants periſhed at the deceaſe of actual covenanters, they would be temporary, fleeting and tranſient in their nature indeed, and could have no title to theſe honourable appellations beſtowed upon them by the Spirit of God.

5th, The obligation of public covenants with God may alſo be eſtabliſhed from the nature of the ordinance of baptiſm. In this ordinance, the members of the church do not come under obligations for themſelves only, but they bring their children alſo, under very ſolemn obligations, which partake of the nature of a covenant with God, or an oath unto him, and which they are bound to fulfil all the days of their life. Now, if an individual Chriſtian may, according to the ordinance and law of God, bring his children, acting as their deputed governor and repreſentative, under moral obligations to all duty, which ſhall bind them, in the baptiſmal covenant; may not a generation of Chriſtians, according to the divine ordinance and law, bring the following age, whoſe deputed governors and repreſentatives they are, under ſolemn bonds to be the Lord's people, by covenanting with God, which ſhall be obligatory upon them unto the performance of the duties contained therein? The whole of the riſing generation, belonging to the church, are actually brought under ſolemn obligations unto the Lord, by the deeds of their parents in the ordinance of baptiſm; and if they may do this in a ſolitary capacity, may not a company of them, in a ſocial ſtate, bring their poſterity under ſimilar bonds, in the ordinance of public covenanting? It is impoſſible to acknowledge the lawfulneſs of the one, without diſcerning, at the ſame time, the moral fitneſs and neceſſity of the other.

6th, The reaſonableneſs and propriety of the obligation of religious covenants deſcending to poſterity may be argued, from the power which belongs unto men to bind their children, in matters' that pertain to the preſent life. In very many inſtances, do the children of men bind their poſterity, both before and after they are born, by domeſtic contracts, ſocial engagements, and public treaties, which are obligatory upon them, either for a time, or during the whole of their lives. Shall theſe civil contracts, whereby they have bound their poſterity to their fellow creatures, have an obligation upon their ſeed; and ſhall their ſacred covenants, whereby they have brought them under obligations to the Lord their God, have no binding force upon the following generation? To ſuppoſe this, is certainly exceedingly unreaſonable. From the power that is beſtowed upon men to bring their poſterity under moral and lawful obligations, relative to their temporal concerns and intereſts, either by public or private contracts, the authority or warrant of Chriſtians, to bring their ſeed under engagements unto the Lord, by public covenanting with him is unqueſtionably evident. From the obligation of civil contracts upon poſterity, the binding force of religious covenants upon the following generation is equally clear. The truth is, the right of the children of men, in both caſes, is allowed and appointed in the law of God; and the precepts of that law, which require the parties concerned to fulfil their engagements, ſhew that both are obligatory.

It will be utterly vain for any to ſuggeſt, that this right of Chriſtians to bind their poſterity to duty, by public covenanting with God, and the obligation of theſe deeds upon the following race are an infringement upon the Chriſtian liberty of their ſeed, in matters of religion; becauſe no part of true Chriſtian liberty can be mentioned, which is, in the ſmalleſt degree, trenched upon thereby. This Chriſtian right, and the obligation under which poſterity is brought by their uſing it, do not deprive the following generation of their liberty to accompliſh a diligent ſearch, by every poſſible mean of information, to be fully ſatisfied in their own mind, as their fathers were, of the morality of the duty of public covenanting, of the call their anceſtors had to engage in it, of the binding obligation of the ſacred deed upon them, and of the agreeableneſs of the matter of their fathers oath or covenant unto the unerring ſtandard of God's law. It is not true Chriſtian liberty, but the dominion of ſin, by whatever name it may be called, which diſpoſes men to break looſe from thoſe ſacred moral obligations to duty which God has appointed in his word, and under which he, in the courſe of his favourable providence, has actually brought them.

It will be equally vain for any to object, that becauſe the deſcendents of covenanters did not conſent in their own perſons, unto theſe obligations, they cannot be binding on them; becauſe this principle would invalidate the lawful moral obligations binding poſterity in civil things, by the deeds of their fathers, which would turn the world into abſolute confuſion. It is not neceſſary unto the tranſmiſſion of the obligation of religious covenants unto poſterity, that every generation of Chriſtians ſhould be, in their own perſons, actual covenanters. We are ſure this was not the caſe with the ſeed of Iſrael, and yet their national covenant with God was binding upon them, in all their generations. The church may be very culpable in neglecting the duty of public covenanting, whereby they give a formal explicit conſent, in their own perſons, to theſe ſolemn obligations; or there may be ſeaſons paſſing over the church, in which they may not have a call to engage in this ſolemn ſervice; yet no neglect of this kind, whether ſinful or neceſſary, can hinder this obligation from deſcending to poſterity. Neither can the communication of this obligation to future generations be obſtructed, by the wickedneſs of a people, in withdrawing their neck from the yoke of God, in acting contrary to their ſolemn engagements, and in openly denying that this obligation is remaining on them. No doubt, all this was the caſe with ſome of the generations of the houſe of Iſrael and Judah, nevertheleſs they were under the obligation of the covenant which God had made with their fathers, and the obligation of it was even through them transmitted to their posterity.

Another prevailing opinion, that seems to be embraced by many, who wish to be considered as friends to public covenanting, is in direct opposition to what has been said; and which, if I understand it, I may express in the following words The obligation of public covenants with God upon posterity consists only in aggravating their sin, if they forsake these principles, for maintaining of which, their fathers showed so much zeal, as to enter into a covenant to preserve and defend them. It is easy to see, that this opinion intirely denies and destroys the proper obligation of a people's covenants with God, upon their posterity. The apostacy of a generation from the religious attainments, which have been reached in the days of their fathers, and which they have handed down unto them, will be a most aggravated evil, whether their fathers have covenanted with God or not. All covenants with God, and their obligation, are, by this opinion, rendered useless, as they respect the following age. It is not the design of the church's covenants with God to aggravate the sin of apostacy, either in the actual covenanters, or in their seed; but it is the design of these sacred transactions to render apostacy a sin, both in themselves and in their posterity, from the relation it has to their covenant engagements Apostacy from attainments in religion is a sin, by the law of God, since the following is one of its precepts; *Hold fast that which thou hast.* Apostacy is also a sin, by the church's covenant, seeing they have bound themselves thereby to cleave unto the Lord, and not to suffer themselves to be drawn away from the profession of his gospel, the obedience of his law, and the observation of all his ordinances. It ought to be bewailed bitterly, that men, from whom we had many reasons to expect better things, should employ themselves to devise and propagate vain schemes of doctrine, to loose themselves and the generation, from moral and sacred obligations, by which they are fast bound unto the service of God. In opposition, however, unto this erroneous and immoral opinion, we must assert, that the obligation of public covenants with

God, is ſubſtantially the ſame, as it now binds the conſciences of poſterity, and as it formerly bound the actual covenanters; and that as our fathers were bound by their deed of covenanting with God, ſo we their poſterity are equally bound by that deed, to the performance of covenant duties. This truth is clearly confirmed from theſe ſcriptures, which repreſent a generation of profeſſors, who have not perſonally covenanted with God, but whoſe fathers had done ſo, to be chargeable with the ſin of covenant-breaking This is done in the words of our text, and in other portions of ſacred writing. What more could be charged upon actual covenanters than this? If the charge, that is brought againſt non-covenanting poſterity, is the ſame with what the charge againſt covenanting anceſtors could really be, this will clearly demonſtrate that both theſe claſſes of men are equally under covenant obligations.—The truth of this aſſertion is alſo eſtabliſhed by theſe ſcriptures, which repreſent the puniſhment of the poſterity of covenanters for the ſin of covenant breaking. One of the principal evils, for which the kingdom of the ten tribes was carried into a diſmal captivity, by the king of Aſſyria, was, becauſe *they rejected his ſtatutes, and his covenant he had made with their fathers*, 2 Kings xvii. 15. The great cauſe why the kingdom of Judah was carried captive unto Babylon, their holy city burnt with fire, their temple deſtroyed, and their land made deſolate for ſeventy years, is repreſented in the following words of Jeremiah, chap. xxii. 8, 9. *Wherefore hath the Lord done thus unto this great city? And they ſhall anſwer, becauſe they have forſaken the covenant of the Lord their God, and worſhipped other gods, and ſerved them.* It is evident, that neither the generation of Iſraelites in the kingdom of the ten tribes, nor in the kingdom of Judah, upon whom theſe calamities came, were in their own perſons actual covenanters; yet the puniſhment of covenant breaking was inflicted upon them, in as remarkable a way, as it could have been brought upon thoſe who had actually covenanted with God. How can we account for this, without believing that they, as well as their covenanting forefathers, were under the ſame covenant obligation.—This truth, and the fallacy of that opinion by which it is oppoſed, will further appear, from the ſcriptural account of the connection which poſterity has with the covenants that are made with their fathers. The ſcripture repreſents this connection of non-covenanting poſterity with the covenants of their fathers, as we have already ſeen, that the Lord made this covenant with them, that is with poſterity, Deut. v. 2, 3. This is the very way, in which the connection of actual covenanters with the covenant, is repreſented in the text, and in other ſcriptures, that the Lord has made the covenant with them. Now, ſince the Spirit of God deſcribes that connection, which actual covenanters have with the covenant, and the connection which non-covenanting poſterity have with it, by the ſame words, it muſt undeniably prove that both the one and the other are equally under the obligation thereof. This being the caſe, there neceſſarily muſt be ſomething more, in the obligation of religious covenants upon poſterity, than this opinion, we are now oppoſing, will allow; and that can be nothing other than what we have aſſerted, that they are bound thereby, in a way, which is eſſentially the ſame, with the manner in which their covenanting fathers were thereby bound to the performance of covenant duties.

Sixthly, The church's public religious covenants with God may, and ought to be national. A people's covenanting with God may be ſaid to be national, in the three following reſpects. When the civil and eccleſiaſtic rulers or repreſentatives of a nation enter into a covenant with God; when the great body of the people enter themſelves into the bond of this covenant; and when an acknowledgement of the obligation thereof, with a reſolution to fulfil it, is made a fundamental law of the ſtate, ſo as no perſon, who is an enemy thereunto, ſhall be intruſted with the affairs of the nation in their hands, either of a ſpiritual or temporal nature. In theſe ſenſes, we affirm that the church's covenants with God may and ought to be national.

1*ſt*, The truth of this obſervation is evident both from the words of the text, and from the other inſpired accounts we have of Iſrael's covenanting with God. The houſe of Iſrael and the houſe of Judah, in their national capacity, are the party mentioned in the text, who was in covenant with God. The people without their rulers, the rulers without the people, or a part of the people without the concurrence of the reſt could not be called the houſe of Iſrael and the houſe of Judah. The bond of this covenant extended to the whole family of Iſrael and Judah, and therefore it reſpected them in their national ſtate. The more particular accounts which we have in the divine word, of the nature of the church's covenants with God, will further confirm this truth. It was Iſrael as a nation that ſtood before the Lord in Horeb, when he entered into covenant with them. Near forty years afterwards, and immediately before the death of Moſes, Iſrael again appeared before the Lord in their national capacity, and entered into a covenant with him. *In that ſolemn aſſembly, there were preſent the captains of their tribes, their elders, and their officers, with all the men of Iſrael, their little ones, their wives, and their ſtranger that was in their camp, from the hewer of their wood, unto the drawer of their water, who all entered into covenant with God, were thereby eſtabliſhed for a people unto him, and he engaged to be their God.* Deut. xxix. 10, 11, 12, 13 The covenanting that took place in the days of Joſhua, bears alſo clear marks of its being a national deed. The perſons concerned in it are mentioned in Joſhua xxiv. 1, 2. *And Joſhua gathered all the tribes of Iſrael to Shechem, and called for the elders of Iſrael, and for their heads, and for their judges, and for their officers, and they preſented themſelves before God. And Joſhua ſaid unto all the people, &c.* Here the people were not without their rulers, nor the rulers without the people; but the whole body of the nation entered into a covenant with the Lord, which is largely declared in the following part of the chapter. When their covenant was renewed in the days of Aſa, it was alſo a national tranſaction, as will be evident from the following account of it. *And Aſa gathered all Judah and Benjamin, and all the ſtrangers with them out of Ephraim and Manaſſeh, and out of Simeon.—And they gathered themſelves together at Jeruſalem.—And entered into a covenant to ſeek the Lord God of their fathers, with all their heart, and with all their ſoul.* 2 Chron. xv. 9, 10, 12. The ſame truth is clearly confirmed from the account of this ſolemn action in the days of Joſiah. The parties who covenanted with God on that occasion, are mentioned, 2 Chron. xxxiv. 29, 30. *Then the king sent, and gathered together all the elders of Judah and Jerusalem, and the king went up into the house of the Lord, and all the men of Judah, and the inhabitants of Jerusalem, and the priests, and the Levites, and all the people great and small, and he read in their ears all the words of the book of the covenant, that was found in the house of the Lord.* Upon the return of the captives from the land of Babylon, they again entered into a covenant with God, in their national capacity, as is evident from the x. chap. of Nehemiah.. In that chap. after expressing by name a considerable number of the priests, Levites, and heads of the people, it is added in the 28 & 29 verses; *And the rest of the people, the priests, the Levites, the porters, the singers, the Nethinims, and all they that had separated themselves from the people of the lands, unto the law of God, their wives, their sons, and their daughters, every one having knowledge, and having understanding; they clave unto their brethren, their nobles, and entered into a curse and into an oath, to walk in God's law.* These scriptures plainly prove that God's covenant with Israel was made with them, in their public national capacity. It was not made with one of the tribes, or with some individuals in all the tribes; but it was with the whole body of the people that this covenant was made, and to all of them its obligation extended. The covenanting, therefore, that is warranted, in the days of the gospel, to be carried on in Christian lands, may and ought to be transacted by them, in their public national character. It is not lawful for a few persons in a land only, when they come to be enlightened in the knowledge of the gospel, and have been determined to embrace it, to join themselves to the Lord in a perpetual covenant; but it is lawful for a people, in their national state, when they are brought to the knowledge or profession of the truth, to do the same thing. Since covenanting with God was a moral duty, incumbent upon his people, under the former dispensation, and was performed by them in their national character; it certainly must be the duty of the Christian church, when the Lord in his goodness brings her in any land unto a national form, to practise this moral duty in their public capacity.

2*d*, In order farther to confirm the truth of this observation, it ſhall be proved, that the ſcriptures repreſent the Gentile churches ſerving the Lord in their national capacity. Many ſcripture prophecies; which ſpeak of the Gentile church, plainly repreſent that they ſhall do ſervice to the Lord, and receive bleſſings from him in their national ſtate; from each of which the reaſonableneſs and neceſſity of national covenanting among them may be deduced. A few of theſe, out of many, ſhall be mentioned. Early did the Lord, by the ſpirit of prophecy, reveal this truth to the children of men; even as early as the days of Noah, by whom the following declaration was made, Gen. ix. 27 *God ſhall enlarge Japheth, and he ſhall dwell in the tents of Shem.* In what capacity did the ſeed of Abraham, who were the deſcendents of Shem, dwell in their tents, or enjoy religious and ſpiritual privileges from God? It certainly was in their national ſtate. When the poſterity of Japheth, by whoſe offspring the iſlands of the Gentiles were divided in their lands, did ſucceed to the privileges of Shem, and dwell in their tents, which began in the apoſtles preaching unto them; muſt not they alſo, in order to the full accompliſhment of this prophecy, enjoy privileges from God, and perform duties unto him in their national capacity? If the poſterity of Shem, when they dwelt in their own tents, had it as their peculiar honour to be, as a nation, in covenant with God; muſt it not be the diſtinguiſhing privilege of the offspring of Japheth, when they dwell in the tents of Shem, to enjoy the ſame bleſſedneſs?—This argument will be corroborated, by the words ſpoken by the Lord unto Abraham, Gen. xxii 18. *And in thy ſeed, ſhall all the nations of the earth be bleſſed* As theſe words ſecure the converſion of many in all nations to the faith of Chriſt, and their enjoying eternal ſalvation through him; ſo they alſo plainly foretel, that the goſpel ſhould become a national bleſſing unto them, and lay them under national obligations unto God in Chriſt.—Another of theſe prophecies is recorded, Pſal. xxii. 27. *All the ends of the world ſhall remember and turn unto the Lord; and all the kindreds of the nations ſhall worſhip before thee.* All the ends of the world, and all the kindreds of the nations certainly relate to people in their large public capacities; and their turning to the Lord, and their worshipping before him must signify, that public, solemn, and spiritual duties should be performed by them in that character.—That very important piece of prophetic information, which is contained in Isa. lii. 15. must not be omitted; *So shall he sprinkle many nations, the kings shall shut their mouths at him; for that which had not been told them shall they see, and that which they had not heard shall they consider.* After describing the humiliation and sufferings of Christ for the salvation of men, the prophet mentions the effect of these, in their application unto them by the hand of the Redeemer, so shall he sprinkle many nations. He shall reveal himself to many nations, bring them to the knowledge of his truth, the profession of his gospel, the obedience of his law, and subjection to his ordinances in their national capacity; as well as justify, sanctify and save multitudes of persons among them. The conduct of the civil rulers of these sprinkled nations is also declared, the kings shall shut their mouths at him. They shall no more oppose the propagation of the kingdom of Christ, no more thunder forth bloody edicts against his followers, nor persecute them on account of the profession of his truth; but should be silent before, and submit unto the Lord of the whole earth. The text also gives the best of all reasons for this change, which should be accomplished upon Gentile nations, and on their governors, *for that which had not been told them shall they see, &c.* Scriptural illumination in the knowledge of Christ, inducing them to a serious consideration, and to an affectionate embracing of him and his religion, shall effectually accomplish it. The Spirit of God assures us here, that Gentile nations, and their rulers shall be sprinkled by Christ, shall be enlightened in the knowledge of him, and shall submit unto him; and must not they, therefore, devote themselves unto and serve him in their national character.—The dictate of inspired prophecy which is recorded in Jer. iv. 2. may be also mentioned. *Thou shalt swear, the Lord liveth, in truth, in righteousness, and in judgment; and the nations shall bless themselves in him, and in him shall they glory.* In the beginning of this verse, the prophet describes the duty of Israel, Thou shalt swear, the Lord liveth, thou shalt ſwear unto the Lord, and in thy ſolemn oath unto him, ſhalt aſſert that he is the living God, that he is thy God, that he is the foundation of all thy hope, and is intitled unto thy obedience. The manner in which this religious oath unto the Lord ſhould be made, is here deſcribed; in truth, in righteouſneſs, and in judgment. The prophet proceeds to declare, in the end of the verſe, what ſhould happen among the Gentile nations; they ſhall bleſs themſelves in him, and in him ſhall they glory. The nations ſhall account it their higheſt privilege to know, ſerve and enjoy the living God, ſhall look unto him for the enjoyment of all bleſſedneſs, ſhall eſteem it their chiefeſt honour to be related and engaged unto him, and ſhall have it as their exerciſe to rejoice and triumph in him. The ſpiritual employment of Iſrael and of the Gentile nations which is here mentioned, though expreſſed in different words, is ſubſtantially the ſame; for when Iſrael ſware that the Lord liveth, they alſo bleſſed themſelves in him, and gloried in him; and when the Gentile nations do this, they muſt alſo be conſidered, as avouching the Lord to be the living God, and their God in Chriſt, by vowing and ſwearing unto him. Beſides, in the very ſame capacity in which Iſrael did ſwear the Lord liveth, the Gentile nations ſhall bleſs themſelves in the Lord, and glory in him, and this certainly was in their national ſtate; for, the party mentioned, in the beginning of the verſe, is called Iſrael in the context; and the party ſpoken of, in the end of the verſe, is called the nations; which ſignifies both their acting in their national character, and that many nations ſhould be thus employed.—The irrefragable confirmation of this truth, with which we are furniſhed, in the words that were ſpoken to Daniel, in the viſions of God wherewith he was privileged, muſt not be omitted; Dan. vii. 27. *And the kingdom, and the dominion, and the greatneſs of the kingdom under the whole heaven, ſhall be given to the people of the ſaints of the Moſt High, whoſe kingdom is an everlaſting kingdom, and all dominion ſhall ſerve and obey him.* The words now before us are a part of a moſt ſtupendous viſion, which Daniel ſaw, and wherein many of the moſt aſtoniſhing events of divine providence, yet to be accompliſhed, were clearly unfolded to his view. The deſign of this part of the viſion is to deſcribe the nature of that dominion, glory and kingdom, which were given unto the one like the Son of man, who came with the clouds of heaven to the Antient of days, in order that all people, nations, and languages ſhould ſerve him, which is clearly expreſſed in the 13 and 14 verſes of this chapter. The words of this verſe repreſent the exalted ſtate, to which the people of the ſaints of the Moſt High ſhould be advanced in this world, under Chriſt their redeeming Saviour, and ruling King The kingdom and the dominion ſhall be given unto them, which ſignify either the perfection of their power, or the different kinds of inſtituted authority, civil and eccleſiaſtic, which are the two anointed ones that ſtand by the Lord of the whole earth. The greatneſs of the kingdom imports the glory and proſperity to which civil and eccleſiaſtic authority ſhould be advanced in their hands. The extent of this is pointed out in the expreſſion, under the whole heaven; not confined unto one nation, as under the old diſpenſation, but ſpread over all the earth. This ſhall be given unto the people of the ſaints of the Moſt High, the profeſſors of his religion ſhall be exalted unto a national ſtate. They ſhall no more be in a low, oppreſſed and perſecuted ſtate, not being reckoned among the nations; but they ſhall take and poſſeſs the kingdom, and the nations ſhall be denominated from them. As this kingdom is extenſive, it ſhall alſo be permanent; for it ſhall be an everlaſting kingdom, continue to the end of the world, and remain in its perfect ſtate through eternity. It is added, and all dominions ſhall ſerve and obey him. All divinely inſtituted authority among men ſhall acknowledge Jeſus as their Lord, ſhall ſubmit themſelves to his goſpel, ſhall regulate their conduct by his law, ſhall promote the intereſts of his glory, and ſhall advance the proſperity of his church. The meaning of this prophecy is ſo clear, and the proof of the point in hand, which it contains, ſo concluſive, that nothing further need be ſaid for its illuſtration.—The prophetic declaration of Zechariah, chap. ii. 14. deſerves alſo our conſideration, *And many nations ſhall be joined unto the Lord in that day, and ſhall be my people.* The parties ſpoken of are many nations, the people who were ſitting in darkneſs, and in the region and ſhadow of death. The Gentile lands, in their national capacity, are the objects of this prophecy. What is ſaid of them? they ſhall be joined unto the Lord; they ſhall forſake the ſervice of idols, and the darkneſs of their heatheniſh ſtate; they ſhall believe in God through Chriſt, take upon them the profeſſion of his religion, and devote themſelves unto him in a ſolemn covenant. The expreſſion of the prophet ſeems to point at this public and ſolemn tranſaction; becauſe it is the ſame phraſe which is uſed by Jeremiah, when he is ſpeaking of this important duty; *Come, let us join ourſelves unto the Lord in a perpetual covenant, that ſhall not be forgotten.* The time when this ſhall be accompliſhed is alſo ſpecified, in that day. This is one of the expreſſions of the antient prophets, by which they uſually point at the times of the New Teſtament church; and we are ſure that this muſt be its meaning in this verſe, becauſe this prophecy is only fulfilled during that period. We are likewiſe informed of the bleſſed conſequence of their being joined unto the Lord, and they ſhall be my people. This privilege of the Gentile nations muſt be of the ſame nature with the bleſſedneſs of antient Iſrael, becauſe it is both expreſſed in the ſame words, they ſhall be my people, and founded upon the ſame ground, they ſhall be joined unto the Lord; and therefore it muſt ſignify, that theſe heathen lands ſhould become, in their national capacity, the Lord's profeſſing, privileged and covenant people.—The laſt prophetic declaration, that ſhall be mentioned, is recorded in Rev. xi. 15. *And the ſeventh angel ſounded, and there were great voices in heaven, ſaying, the kingdoms of this world are become the kingdoms of our Lord, and of his Chriſt, and he ſhall reign for ever and ever.* The part of the verſe alluded unto is that which records the precious truth, proclaimed by the great voices in heaven, the kingdoms of this world are become the kingdoms of our Lord, and of his Chriſt, and he ſhall reign for ever and ever. Theſe words deſcribe the ſituation of the nations of the earth, after the pouring out of the ſeven vials, mentioned chap. xvi. which immediately followed the ſounding of the ſeventh trumpet. The heathen, Mahometan, and antichriſtian nations, who were in many reſpects kingdoms of this world, corrupt, carnal and earthly, both in their constitutions and administrations, shall undergo, by the grace, Spirit, word, and providence of God, an holy and spiritual revolution, by which they should, as nations, become the kingdoms of the God of the church, and of his holy anointed One, devote themselves unto him, and submit themselves to his obedience, who should rule them by the sceptre of his grace while they live in this world, and dwell among them as their King in the heavenly glory to eternity. From these declarations of the Spirit of prophecy it is evident, beyond all contradiction, that the Gentile nations should submit unto and serve the Lord, and the blessed Redeemer in their national capacity; that their faith should be a national faith, their profession a national profession, their worship a national worship, their obedience a national obedience, and their covenanting a national covenanting.

3*d*, The truth of this observation will further appear, if we consider the nature of that service, which we are called to give unto God in Christ, in our different capacities, when we are enlightened in the knowledge of divine truth. When the grace of God comes into the heart of an individual, and instructs him in the knowledge of truth and duty, he is thereby bound, and will be chearfully determined to serve the Lord, in the performance of all the duties that are incumbent on him, in his personal capacity. When the members of a family are privileged with this illumination, it becomes their duty, and it will be their exercise to serve, to worship, and to promote the glory of God, in their domestic state. The inhabitants of a city, having heard the joyful sound, and embraced it, are thereby obliged to set up all the ordinances of Christ among them, and to serve and glorify God, in this more public capacity. If the light of the glorious gospel shall extend over all those who reside in a province, it is then their immediate and indispensible duty, in their more enlarged and public character, to submit to the faith, the ordinances and service of Christ. If the Sun of righteousness does arise and shine upon a whole nation, it surely becomes the duty of that people, in their national capacity, to make a public profession of the truth of God, to surrender themſelves unto him, and to obſerve all his laws. Chriſtianity is not framed for being the religion of an individual only, but it is calculated for ſocieties of men, whether great or ſmall. Such is the nature of ſome of its bleſſed inſtitutions, that perſons, acting in their perſonal capacity only, can have no acceſs unto or enjoyment of them at all. It is a religion that may be profeſſed by the children of men, whether they act in their perſonal, domeſtic, congregational, or national ſtate; and it lays obligations to moral duties upon them in all their different capacities. In all theſe capacities in which we are capable of acting, we are bound to perform all duties unto the Lord in that character. Covenanting has been already proved to be the duty of Chriſtians in New Teſtament times, therefore they are called to perform this ſolemn ſervice in their national capacity. In whatever character we have a relation unto or intereſt in God, we ought, in that capacity, to claim and improve this intereſt in him, and devote ourſelves to him as his people. When nations are enlightened with the goſpel, they come to have this intereſt in and relation unto God as a nation; their covenanting therefore, which is a claiming of this relation to him, and a devoting themſelves unto him, may and ought to be national.

Before this part of the ſubject is concluded, it may be neceſſary to take ſome notice of a very common and enſnaring objection, which has been urged againſt the truth for which we are now pleading. The nation of Iſrael was a theocracy, they were a people under the immediate and gracious government of God, and their covenant with him was their national oath of allegiance unto him; this is not the caſe with any Chriſtian nation in the world, and, therefore, all arguing for national covenanting among us, from its having been nationally performed among them, muſt be falſe and inconcluſive. This objection, whether it be valid or not, can militate only againſt the firſt argument, that has now been advanced for eſtabliſhing the truth of this obſervation, which was taken from the ſcriptural account of the antient covenanting, as being national, from which the duty of national covenanting under the New Teſtament was inferred; but it cannot at all affect what has been further ſaid in ſupport of this truth, which, if duly conſidered, might fully overthrow the objection. But let it be more particularly examined.

Our anſwer to the objection is this. When a nation is enlightened with the goſpel, comes to receive the truths of Chriſt, makes a profeſſion of his religion, and ſubmits to his ordinances and laws, it is as much a theocracy, a people under the immediate and gracious government of God, and are as much bound, by covenanting nationally with him, to ſwear an oath of national allegiance unto the Lord, as ever the houſe of Iſrael and the houſe of Judah were to perform this ſervice in the land of Canaan. Let us conſider all the ſuppoſible grounds of Iſrael's claim to a diſtinguiſhing theocracy, and we will find, that if they apply to them, they equally apply, in their ſubſtance, to Chriſtian nations. Suppoſe Iſrael was a theocracy becauſe they were all brought to the knowledge and profeſſion of the true religion in their national ſtate, and were all the deſcendents of one man whom the Lord, in a wonderful manner, called to the knowledge of himſelf. This, in its ſubſtance, is exactly the caſe with every Chriſtian nation. They alſo, in their national ſtate, are brought to the knowledge and profeſſion of the true religion. As to their not being the offspring of one man, who was called of God as was Abraham, this is a mere circumſtance in the caſe. Various are the ways which the Lord takes to bring nations to the knowledge and profeſſion of the truth; but, whether he cauſes the goſpel to make ſlow progreſs in a land till it, like the little leaven, ſhall leaven the whole lump, or makes a nation to be born at once, or even lays hold of one man till his poſterity becomes a nation, and ſets up his religion among them; yet, being brought to the knowledge of his religion as a nation, be it in what manner it will, they muſt equally be, in that capacity, under moral obligations unto the Lord.—It may alſo be ſaid, that Iſrael was a theocracy, becauſe they were a peculiar people, and no other nation knew the true God, and his truths and worſhip but themſelves. To this it may be anſwered, that their national duties and obligations unto God aroſe from their being nationally a church and people profeſſing the true religion, and not at all from its being peculiar unto them, or enjoyed by no other nation. Chriſtian nations are, therefore, under the very ſame obligations to ſerve the Lord, in their national character as Iſrael was, becauſe of their national privileges, which are the ſame in their nature and deſign with thoſe enjoyed by the antient church, and very far ſuperior unto them in their degree. Though many nations, in the days of the goſpel, are, at the ſame time, privileged, in their national character, with ſpecial bleſſings from the Lord; this cannot relieve them from the obligations they are reſpectively under to the Lord, nationally to profeſs his goſpel, nationally to obſerve his ordinances, and nationally to covenant with him. Each of theſe nations muſt be as much bound to the performance of national duties, from their enjoyment of national privileges, though theſe may be poſſeſſed by other nations, as they poſſibly could be, if no other nation were favoured with them but themſelves.—Were the Iſraelites a theocracy, becauſe God was the author of their peculiar laws, whereby their ſtate, in many particulars, was to be governed? Is not the word of God, which is now enjoyed by the church in its perfect ſtate, a light unto the feet, and a lamp unto the path of Chriſtian nations, both in the formation and execution of their laws? on account of which he may be called the Author of their laws, as well as he was the Author of the laws of Iſrael. The one is as much bound now, as the other formerly was, to regulate their civil and eccleſiaſtic adminiſtrations by the law, and by the teſtimony of God; and ſo far as it is otherwiſe, it evidences that there is no light in them. The ſubſtance of the matter, in both caſes is, in this particular alſo, exactly the ſame. —It may be alledged, that Iſrael was a theocracy, becauſe they held the poſſeſſion of the land of Canaan upon the condition of their obedience to the divine laws, and becauſe they were driven from the enjoyment of it for their rebellion. But was Iſrael the only nation that was, in the providence of God, exterminated from their land, on account of ſin? Were not all the ſurrounding nations viſited with the ſame judgment? Concerning this ſtrange work of God to Iſrael it cannot be ſaid, he hath not dealt ſo with any nation. Beſides, the word of

God, and the paſt diſpenſations of his providence plainly declare, that Chriſtian nations ſhall be viſited with the ſame judgments in their ſubſtance, which were inflicted upon Iſrael, if they, like them, fall into the ſins of apoſtacy from their religious attainments, of idolatry and error, of cruelty and oppreſſion, of infidelity and impiety, and of breaking the covenant which he had made with their fathers.

Some may ſay that Iſrael was a theocracy, becauſe the Meſſiah was to ſpring from them. To this it will be ſufficient to anſwer, that after the days of Jacob, this theocracy behoved to be confined to the tribe of Judah, for, at that period, the church was aſcertained that he was to ſpring from them; and after the days of David it ſhould have been reſtricted to his family, for then it was revealed to the church that Chriſt ſhould be of the ſeed of David according to the fleſh. If this, therefore, is the ground of their being a theocracy, the nation at large could have no connection with it at all, and it muſt have been very limited indeed.—But it may ſtill be affirmed that Iſrael was a theocracy, becauſe they were a typical people, many of their ordinances were of a typical and ceremonial nature, and were aboliſhed when Chriſt the ſubſtance appeared. It may be obſerved, that the ſyſtem of ordinances in the Chriſtian church is alſo for a ſeaſon, and ſhall be done away when the church is advanced to her heavenly and perfect ſtate. It was not becauſe they were a typical people, that they were under national obligations to the Lord; but becauſe they were brought to the knowledge and profeſſion of the true religion, in their national character. It was not becauſe many of their ordinances were ceremonial that they were nationally bound by the oath of God to obſerve them; but becauſe they were of divine appointment. Theſe duties, therefore, belong unto Chriſtian nations, as well as the Jewiſh ſtate; for the moral grounds of them are common to both. There was indeed, in the wiſdom and goodneſs of God, a change made in the ordinances, which were of divine authority, and ſuited to the nature of the two diſpenſations; but this did not make any change in the law, which formerly obliged the Jews, and now binds Chriſtians to hold faſt the traditions which have been delivered to them, to improve them for their own ſalvation, to tranſmit them to their poſterity, and to reſolve and promiſe, vow and ſwear unto the Lord, that they will endeavour to perform theſe neceſſary and important duties.—If any are diſpoſed to conſider the words of God unto Samuel. *They have rejected me, that I ſhould not reign over them.* 1 Sam. viii. 7. As a proof that Iſrael was a theocracy; it is only neceſſary to obſerve, that if this was the caſe, their theocracy behoved to end at the advancement of Saul to the throne of Iſrael; and, as there was national covenanting among them after, as well as before that period, it is hereby proved that this duty is not peculiar to a people, who are a privileged theocracy. From what has been ſaid it clearly appears, that this notion of the ſtate of Iſrael, from which men would conclude, that their national covenanting with God is not imitable by a people under the goſpel, who are nationally brought to the faith of Chriſt, is vain and fooliſh; and that it remains an eſtabliſhed truth, that covenanting, in Chriſtian lands, as well as among the Iſraelites of old, may and ought to be national.

Seventhly, The church's public covenants with God ſhould contain an engagement to perform all commanded duties. For the illuſtration of this obſervation, it is neceſſary to explain its meaning, to confirm the truth of it, and to overturn that ſentiment by which it is oppoſed.

When it is ſaid, that an engagement to perform all commanded duties, ſhould be contained in the church's public covenants with God, the meaning ſurely is very plain; but, leſt it ſhould be miſunderſtood, the following things are mentioned. By commanded duties we underſtand, thoſe things which are enjoined upon the children of men, by the authority of God in his law. If any actions cannot be traced up to the precepts of God's word, or to the approved examples recorded in the ſcripture, as their warrant, they are reprobate ſilver, and muſt not have a place in the church's bond to obedience; but whatever actions are agreeable to his law, theſe may and ought to have a place, either in general or in the detail, within the church's covenant engagements. The duties that are enjoined both in the firſt and second tables of the law, are equally admissible into a people's public vow unto the Lord. We are not warranted to engage, in our covenant with God, to perform the duties which we owe unto him only but we ought also to oblige ourselves, in these covenants, to the performance of these duties, which are incumbent upon us, both with respect to ourselves, and to our fellow creatures. Duties which are called civil, as well as those which have been denominated religious, must have a place in the church's oath of obedience to God. All these moral duties which belong unto men, in the different stations in which they are placed, whether as heads and members of the Christian family, as teachers and those who are taught in the Christian church, or as governors and those who are governed in the Christian state, ought to be comprehended in the church's public national covenant with God; and their covenant should contain their voluntary obligation to perform all commanded duties, both with reference to their civil and religious concerns.—The truth of this observation may be confirmed by the following arguments.

1st, Israel's covenant with God contained an engagement unto all commanded duties, and the obligation to duty, in all covenants with God among Christian nations, must be of the same extent. That Israel, in their covenanting with God, engaged themselves to all duties, will be evident from the scriptural account of these transactions, a few of which may be mentioned. In the first public action of this kind, which is recorded in the xix. chap. of Exodus, there are two things in the account of it, which confirm this truth; the words of the Lord by which he lays the covenant obligation upon Israel, and the words of the people whereby they took it upon themselves. The former is expressed in the 5. verse. *If ye will obey my voice indeed, and keep my covenant.* The voice of God contains all that the Lord spake to Israel for the regulation of their conduct, and includes the duties of the moral law which are recorded in the following chapter, with the great variety of precepts which are detailed at large in the three chapters that follow it, together with all that he had spoken, or might hereafter speak unto them for the same important purpose. The words of the people, whereby they come under the obligation, confirms the ſame thing; verſe 8. *And all the people anſwered together, and ſaid, all that the Lord hath ſpoken we will do.* It is evident that the voice of the Lord muſt comprehend all commanded duty, and the words of the people are of equal extent.—The inſpired record reſpecting the extent of the duties of the covenant, into which Iſrael entered in the days of Joſiah, contained, 2 Kings xxiii. 3. confirms the ſame truth. *And the king ſtood by a pillar, and made a covenant before the Lord, to walk after the Lord, and to keep his commandments, and his teſtimonies, and his ſtatutes, with all their heart, and all their ſoul, to perform the words of this covenant that were written in this book; and all the people ſtood to the covenant.* Iſrael's walking after the Lord, keeping his commandments, his teſtimonies, and his ſtatutes, and performing all the words of the covenant that were written in the law of Moſes, certainly ſhew that their covenant with God contained an obligation to perform all commanded duties both with reſpect to their civil and religious intereſts; with which the people practically complied, for it is added, that they ſtood to the covenant.—The account of the covenant tranſaction, in the days of Nehemiah, is of the ſame import. Neh. x. 29. *They entered into a curſe and into an oath, to walk in God's law which was given by Moſes the ſervant of God, and to obſerve and do all the commandments of the Lord their God, and his judgments, and his ſtatutes.* The law of God delivered to Iſrael by Moſes, all the commandments of the Lord their God, and his judgments, and his ſtatutes, comprehend all commanded duties both of a civil and religious nature, that were incumbent upon them in all the different ſtations and relations in which they ſtood, both with reference to God and one another. The obligation of public covenants with God, among Chriſtian nations, muſt alſo extend unto all commanded duties.

2*d*, The truth of this obſervation is alſo evident, from the extent of the obligation of the divine law upon the conſciences of men. By the authority of God in his law, men are bound to the performance of all duties, both civil and religious. There is not a ſingle duty incumbent upon men, or performed by them, in all the variety of stations which they can occupy, or circumstances in which they can possibly be placed, but it is comprehended and enjoined in the law of God. An impression of this truth upon the mind of the psalmist made him say, *Thy commandment is exceeding broad.* The original divine obligation to duty by the moral law being thus extensive, it is necessary that the church's voluntary obligation to perform duty in their covenant with God, should be of the same extent. All the duties which are comprehended in the law, may and ought to be contained in the church's public vow unto the Lord. It is utterly absurd to suppose, that God should require duties of the children of men, which they shall not be permitted to include in their resolution, promise, vow, or oath of obedience unto him. The law of God is not the rule by which the duties which the church obliges herself to perform, are to be tried as to their nature only, that they be agreeable to it; but it is likewise the standard by which these duties are to be measured as to their extent. In so far as our covenant obligations to God fail in this particular, they will be considered by him as defective. The voluntary and covenant obligations to duty, under which Christians bring themselves, must be equally extensive, as the original divine obligation is by the moral law. As every duty is contained in the one, so we should bind ourselves by the other, to all commanded duties.

3*d*, This observation may also be confirmed by viewing the extent of the obligation to duty, under which the Christian brings himself unto the Lord, when he personally covenants with him. When the Christian is employed in the spiritual exercise of covenanting with God in his personal capacity, by taking hold of God's covenant, yielding himself unto the Lord, and coming under a voluntary obligation to serve him, it will be found that this engagement of his extends to all the duties that are incumbent upon him. It will not be proper for him, neither will he, in a spiritual frame, be disposed unto it, to promise or vow the performance of religious duties only; but he will include, in his obligation to God, the observation of all those relative and civil duties, which are bound upon him by the divine law. He will be convinced in his mind, that both the divine glory and the profperity of his foul are concerned, in his fulfilling the one as well as the other; and therefore he will cheerfully come under an obligation, in the ftrength of divine grace, to perform them all. As the believer efteems all God's precepts concerning all things to be right, he will vow and fwear to have a refpect to all his commandments, faying, *I have fworn, and I will perform it, that I will keep thy righteous judgments.* Pfalm cxix. 106. If perfonal covenanting with God includes the believer's obligation to perform all commanded duties; muft not the church's public covenant with God be equally extenfive, in its obligation? If it is lawful and neceffary for the Chriftian, in his perfonal capacity, to bind himfelf to all duty; muft it not be equally lawful and neceffary for the church to comprehend duties of every clafs, in their public and folemn engagements to the Lord? fince it would be difhonouring to God, for the believer to come under a partial obligation to duty, it muft be ftill more provoking in the eyes of his holinefs, to fee his profeffing church partial in the law.

4th, The truth of this propofition may alfo be evident, if we confider the concern that the glory of God has in our performance of all commanded duties. No Chriftian will deny, that he is divinely bound to glorify God, with his body and fpirit which are his; and that whatfoever he does, to do all to the glory of God. The glorifying of God is the fupreme end which his moral creatures, and efpecially redeemed finners, fhould have in their view, in the performance of all commanded duties. It certainly muft be the great defign of the church, in her covenanting exercife, to bind herfelf to the obfervation of whatever fhall promote the divine glory. As it tends greatly to advance the glory of God, when a people regulate their civil concerns according to his law, as well as when their religious affairs are directed in agreeablenefs thereunto; it muft unavoidably follow, that, in their voluntary obligation to God, they fhould bind themfelves unto the duties of the former, as well as of the latter clafs. When the Lord has given a people, in his holy word, an infallible ftandard of moral actions, both of a civil and religious nature; muft it not be highly improper for them, when they covenant with him, to recognize the one, and pay no attention at all unto the other? The glory of God, in the extent in which it ſhould be promoted by a people, enjoying divine revelation, can never be duely advanced by them, while they act in this manner. The Lord was as really diſhonoured and diſpleaſed with the injuſtice, oppreſſion and murder which his antient people committed, in their civil capacity; as he was with their error, idolatry and profaneneſs, in their religious ſtate The former, as well as the latter, were charged upon them as a breach of his covenant; and on account of the one, as well as the other, he poured his judgments upon them. As the glory of God is greatly promoted among men, by a ſpiritually enlightened nation, when their civil affairs, as well as thoſe that are religious, are managed according to the divine law, and as he is greatly diſhonoured when it is otherwiſe; it muſt be indiſpenſibly incumbent upon them, when they enter into covenant with him, to bind themſelves to the duties which relate to their civil, as well as to their religious concerns.

5th, An argument, to confirm this truth, may be taken from the concern which the happineſs of the church has with the due performance of civil duties in the land. The proper regulation of civil affairs in a nation contributes greatly to the advantage of the church, and her members If the civi conſtitutions of nations are framed according to the word of God, and if their adminiſtrations are agreeable to this unerring ſtandard, the proſperity and happineſs of the church will thereby be greatly promoted. The ſtedfaſt adherence of a land to the rule of the word, in the ordering of their civil concerns, will greatly contribute to their obſervation of that rule, in their religious tranſactions. If a people make defection from the divine law, as a civil ſociety; it cannot be ſuppoſed, that they, as a church, will long walk according to the commandment. It certainly muſt be the duty of Chriſtians, in their covenanting with God, to engage themſelves to thoſe duties which are intimately connected with their own advantage. As the proper management of their civil matters is ſo eſſential to the proſperity of the church, it muſt be their duty, when they covenant with God, to engage themſelves unto the due performance of civil, as well as religious duties; and therefore the church's public covenants with God muſt contain an obligation to perform all commanded duties.

6th, The laſt argument that ſhall be mentioned, in proof of this point, may be taken from the different ſtations, in which thoſe perſons, whoſe duty it is to covenant with God, may, in his ſovereign providence, be placed In the honourable liſt of covenanters, the names of thoſe will be found, who exerciſe civil rule and authority over men; as well as the names of thoſe, who are public teachers of religion, and preachers of the goſpel of Chriſt. The perſons in whoſe hands the legiſlative and executive powers of a nation, relative to their civil affairs, are lodged; and the perſons who are paſtors, teachers, and rulers among them, as a Chriſtian church, will unite in the great and ſolemn work of public covenanting with God. The body of the people, who are bound together by ſo many relations civil and religious, and are obliged to the performance of ſo many duties to God and one another of various kinds, will alſo be found in the number of thoſe, who will join themſelves to the Lord in a perpetual covenant, that ſhall not be forgotten. It is eſſential to all covenanting with God, that the covenanters bind themſelves to proſecute the ends of their covenant, according to their different ſtations. It muſt therefore be neceſſary, that the duties relative to civil things make a part of our covenant-obligations. How is it poſſible that men in civil office can be covenanters, if the important duties of their honourable ſtation are excluded from the oath of God? If the civil rulers, ſupreme and ſubordinate, ought to unite with others in a covenant with God, the performance of the duties of their office muſt be included in the obligation of that covenant. What appearance can theſe dignified perſons make in a public vow unto the Lord, if no place is found, in the obligation thereof, for thoſe duties, which it is their principal employment to perform? The duties of civil rulers, as well as thoſe of the goſpel miniſter, being required in the divine law, being alſo for his glory and the advantage of men and Chriſtians, muſt be comprehended in a national vow unto and covenant with God.

Having endeavoured to confirm the truth contained in this obſervation, it is neceſſary now to ſhew the impropriety of that ſentiment by which it has been oppoſed, which is the following. "Religious and civil things "ſhould not be blended together in the oath of God, or "in a covenant with him; when this is done, the proper "diſtinction which ſhould be maintained between the "concerns of the kingdom of Chriſt, and the affairs of "the kingdoms of this world is deſtroyed; and hereby "theſe things are blended together in an abſurd man-"ner, between which there is a neceſſary and eternal "difference." Such is the language that is held, not by thoſe only who are the open and avowed enemies of public covenanting, but by thoſe alſo who pretend to be the moſt zealous friends of this ſolemn duty; on account of the latter, more than for the ſake of the former, it is neceſſary that ſomething be ſaid in defence of the oppoſite truth. The perſons, to whom we have now alluded, generally exert their ingenuity, to find out excuſes for our reformers, with a view to palliate the groſs blunders which they ſuppoſe them to have committed, in framing and entering into the national covenant of Scotland, and the ſolemn league of Scotland, England and Ireland; for in theſe public vows, no doubt, both the civil and religious intereſts and duties of the nations are contained. As we do not ſuppoſe that the conduct of our reformers ſtands in need of any excuſes, becauſe it was agreeable to the word of God, and the footſteps of the flock, we ſhall not take any notice of them; but proceed to examine this opinion, and in order to this, ſhall endeavour fairly to ſtate the queſtion.

With a view to clear the caſe, it is neceſſary to obſerve, that we are not ſpeaking of what is the duty, and ſhould be the exerciſe of a body of Chriſtians, in covenanting with God, who have been brought to the knowledge and profeſſion of Chriſtianity, in an unenlightened and unreformed land, where the great body of the people and their rulers have never nationally received, and ſubmitted unto the truth as it is in Jeſus. No doubt it is impoſſible for them, in theſe circumſtances, to carry on the duty of covenanting, in the manner in which it was done by our anceſtors, at the times of our reformation. Nor are we ſpeaking of the duty and work of a company of Chriſtians, about covenanting with God, who live in a land that was once nationally engaged to the Lord by covenant, but who are now completely apoſtatized from their covenanted attainments, and who are nationally diſregarding and acting contrary to their covenant obligations unto God. It is evident alſo that perſons, in this ſituation, cannot perform the work of covenanting, in the particular way in which it proſpered in the hands of our forefathers. But we are ſpeaking concerning the duty of the church of God, when ſhe is brought, in his merciful goodneſs to her, unto a national ſtate; when the great body of the people of all ranks, and their rulers are enlightened in the knowledge of the goſpel, and are become willing to take upon them the yoke of Chriſt. With reſpect to the duty of a people in this ſituation, notwithſtanding of all the clamour, either of profeſſed friends or open enemies of this ſolemn duty, it is believed and affirmed, that their covenanting with God ſhould include an obligation to perform all commanded duties, both with reſpect to their religious and civil concerns. Having thus ſtated the matter in diſpute, we ſhall now proceed to anſwer the objection, which may be done in the following particulars.

1ſt, If it is ſinful and abſurd to blend civil and religious concerns and duties together, in the church's covenant with God, how came it to paſs that theſe different things were mingled, by the direction and with the approbation of God, in Iſrael's covenanting with him? Certainly the Lord never commanded or approved of any thing that was ſinful, or even abſurd in the nature of it. No ſuppoſible difference betwixt the ſituation of the church under the former, and under the preſent diſpenſation, can ever make a thing that is ſinful and abſurd in its nature at preſent, to have been conſiſtent, beautiful and moral in the foregoing period. If they are now ſuch oppoſite and contrary things, that cannot lawfully be conjoined, in the church's oath of obedience unto God; it is impoſſible that they could ever be united, by divine authority, in a sacred vow unto him. This opinion casts a blasphemous reflection upon the wisdom and holiness of God, in his institutions and administrations with his antient people; and therefore ought to be rejected.

2*d*, If it is sinful and improper to blend together civil and sacred things in our covenant with God, whence is it that they are thus blended together in the moral law? If these are matters, betwixt which there is such an eternal difference, that they cannot stand together in a people's covenant obligation unto God; it is impossible to see how the Lord would have caused them to stand together in his holy revealed law, which is the rule of duty to the rational creature. What God has joined together in his law, no person or people are warranted to put asunder in this exercise of covenanting with him. Surely the example of God, in joining things together in the moral law, and in the precepts of his word, by which that law is explained, is a better directory to the Christian church, what things to unite with one another, in their bond of obligation to the Lord, than the vain imaginations of erring men.

3*d*, If it is absurd to blend civil and religious things in a people's covenant with God, whence is it that the members of the church are under an unavoidable necessity of blending them together in their Christian practice? Every day they live, the saints of God have an opportunity of performing duties, not only of a religious but also of a civil nature. The children of men are concerned necessarily with both tables of the law, in their conversation. They have civil rights, as well as religious privileges which they are daily enjoying, are bound to preserve the one as well the other, and have daily occasion to perform lawful moral actions, about the former as well as the latter. As these different duties are daily mingled in the obedience which they yield unto the divine law; will not this warrant them to comprehend them both in their covenant obligation unto God. Where is the absurdity of their being conjoined in our voluntary obligation to duty, when they are necessarily connected in our daily performance of it?

4*th*, A civil state, whose constitutions and administrations are regulated according to the word of God, is not that society, which the scripture calls a kingdom of this world; as is most improperly affirmed in the objection. The words of divine revelation where this name is used, have been considered already, and are found in Rev. xi. 15. *The kingdoms of this world are become the kingdoms of our Lord, and of his Christ.* This expression, the kingdoms of this world, does not refer to a nation, viewed merely as a civil society, managing their outward, political and civil affairs, but it describes a people who are carnal, earthly and corrupt in the constitution and management both of their civil and religious concerns. It must be in the former of these senses that it is used in the objection, as it is opposed to the kingdom of Christ, and as it is an objection against our solemn covenants; for it was the duties and concerns of the reformed civil state, that had a place therein. This however is not at all the meaning of the words, in this portion of scripture, which were uttered by the great voices in heaven. Let us try which of these senses of this scriptural name, is most agreeable to the meaning of the declaration with which it is connected. The civil and political societies of this world are become the kingdoms of our Lord, and of his Christ; or, the civil and political states of this world are converted into churches. Is not this to make the great voices in heaven speak absurdity and nonsense? How is it possible that nations, as they are civil bodies, can be transformed into ecclesiastic societies? But this, absurd and foolish as it is, must be the change predicted in these words, if the name, the kingdoms of this world, describe nations as they are political bodies. Let us now see how this name, in the sense in which we have viewed it, quadrates with the declaration of which it is a part. The nations of the world, which are carnal, earthly and corrupt both in their civil and religious capacities, are become the kingdoms of our Lord, and of his Christ. Is not this the very alteration which is here foretold, by the Spirit of prophecy? The great voices in heaven proclaim, that the time was fast approaching, when the antichristian, Mahometan, and heathen nations, that were kingdoms of this world, on account of their ignorance, error, superstition, idolatry, tyranny and immorality, should undergo such a change, by the light of the goſpel and the power of the Spirit, as would make them become the kingdoms of our Lord, and of his Chriſt. It is therefore moſt inconſiderate and improper, to reckon a civil ſtate, conſtituted and adminiſtering their affairs according to the ſcriptures, a kingdom of this world, the righteous management of whoſe outward and civil concerns, cannot make a part of that duty, to which a people, enlightened with the goſpel, ſhould bind themſelves in their covenanting with God.

5th, That civil and religious things are abſurdly blended together in the oath of God, conſtitutes the great charge contained in the objection, againſt this article of divine truth which it oppoſes. There is no doubt, civil and religious things may be ſinfully blended together, in different reſpects; but in none of theſe ways are they ſo blended, in our ſolemn national covenants. Civil and religious things are ſinfully and abſurdly blended together, when they are confounded with each other, and not duly diſtinguiſhed in their nature, objects and relative importance; when the place which belongs to the one is given to the other; when ſpiritual and religious ſervices are required from, or uſurped by civil rulers, and civil legiſlation or adminiſtrations are graſped by eccleſiaſtic perſons; when civil rulers become ſubject to churchmen, in things of a civil nature, as was the caſe in the dominion exerciſed by antichriſt over the kings of the earth; and when the teachers and rulers of the church are made the ſervants of temporal princes in religious matters, as is the caſe with all eraſtian ſtates, where the civil rulers exerciſe a ſupremacy over the church. Were civil and religious things blended together in any of theſe ways, by our forefathers, in their covenanting with God, there would be ſome ground for the objection; but when it is evident to all, that no ſuch thing is found in them, the objection muſt be utterly unreaſonable. Civil and religious things indeed ſtand together in theſe ſolemn tranſactions; but they are not, in any of theſe ways, blended with each other in them. Each of theſe claſſes of duties, in our public religious covenants, have their proper place aſſigned them, the neceſſary diſtinction between them is fully maintained, and the performance of them is aſcribed to the proper objects, without either the church-men's ſcandalous uſurpation of the prerogative and adminiſtrations of civil rulers, or the magiſtrate's eraſtian encroachment upon the duty and juriſdiction of the ſervants of Chriſt in his houſe. This being the caſe, it is impoſſible for any man to ſay with truth, that civil and religious things are ſinfully and abſurdly blended together, in the church's public covenants with God.

6th, With a ſhort repreſentation of the views of our reformers, by which their conduct, in framing and entering into our ſolemn covenants, ſeems to have been directed, which will appear to be reaſonable and ſcriptural, the anſwer to this objection may be concluded. In the firſt period of the reformation, when the national covenant was compiled, our anceſtors were emerging from popiſh darkneſs, idolatry and tyranny; and in the ſecond period, when the ſolemn league and covenant was ſworn, they were extricating themſelves from the errors, ſuperſtition and oppreſſion of prelacy; by both of which their political and eccleſiaſtic conſtitutions and adminiſtrations had been grievouſly corrupted. They were perſuaded, that purity, in their religious concerns as a church, could not be maintained for any time, if they did not acquire ſome ſuitable degree of conformity to the ſcriptural ſtandard, in their civil affairs as a nation. They were convinced, that a people, enjoying divine revelation, are bound by the authority of God, to eſtabliſh civil government among them, in the ſcriptural purity thereof; as well as to ſet up all the ordinances of the houſe of God in the church, according to his word. They were ſenſible, that both the magiſtracy in the ſtate, and the miniſtry in the church were ordinances of God, with the proper eſtabliſhment of which in the land, the ſcripture-law, the glory of God, and the good of men were eminently concerned; and that a people who profeſs to deſire and endeavour that the latter be enjoyed by them in purity, while they ſuffer the former to remain in a corrupt ſtate, act a part which is contrary both to ſcripture and reaſon. They were of opinion, that having attained this purity, it was their duty to preſerve it intire in their own day, and to uſe every ſcriptural mean to tranſmit the ſame unto the following generations; and that one of the principal means for these ends was, to enter into a solemn national vow unto the Lord, or covenant with him, attended with the instituted solemnity of an oath unto him, whereby they should bind themselves to perform all the duties of their different stations, that the nation might enjoy the benefit of the reformation purity both in church and state, and that all these attainments might be handed down to posterity. Influenced by views of this nature, our forefathers entered upon the great and necessary work of reforming both the civil throne, and the sanctuary of the Lord. They settled the church of God upon her true foundation, and fixed from his word her pure doctrine, worship, government and discipline. They established civil government among them in its purity, and specified the terms precisely upon which they conveyed, and their rulers received civil authority over them; and made provision, as far as it was in their power, that this constitution should produce corresponding administrations. Having accomplished this great work, they entered into a covenant with God, as a people that were reformed in their civil and religious capacities, both to carry into effect for their present good, and to preserve the fabric of reformation which they had been enabled to build; in which covenant the preservation of their civil and religious privileges, the promoting of their civil and religious interests, and the performance of all the duties belonging to their civil and religious concerns, are the objects to which they did solemnly engage themselves. What is there in all this that is contrary to scripture, or in opposition to reason? Is it not rather, in every part of it, perfectly proper, highly becoming, and absolutely necessary? Where would have been the propriety, of leaving out of their covenant-obligations unto God, the important duties of their civil concerns and administrations, of which the revealed law is the sacred rule, and to the performance of which they were solemnly bound by the authority of God in that law? How absurd would it have been, for them to have admitted the illustrious band of reformed Christian civil rulers into the oath of God, merely in the character of private Christians, without including in the national oath the important and necessary duties, with reference to the performance of which, it is their great employment to attend continually upon this very thing? Had the nation, in the days of our covenanting anceſtors, acted in this manner, would it not have been conſidered as a treating with national contempt the authority of God in his law, requiring them to expreſs due gratitude to him for their national civil privileges, and to bind themſelves to perform their various civil duties? Since the law of God requires the performance of civil duties, and the right management of civil adminiſtrations from men; and ſince the glory of God and the advantage of men are promoted by theſe, as well as by the right regulation and obſervation of thoſe which are of a more ſpiritual nature, our reformers muſt have done well, in ſo framing their public national covenants with God, as to include in their obligation, the performance of all commanded duties, both of a civil and of a religious nature.

Eightly, It is a precious privilege for a people to be in covenant with God. Who are the people that are mentioned in the text? They are the houſe of Iſrael and the houſe of Judah. The poſterity of Abraham, Iſaac and Jacob were highly privileged above all nations on the earth; but they were in covenant with God, and their covenant-relation unto him was the foundation of their enjoying ſuch diſtinguiſhing and peculiar privileges. Would we therefore ſhare of theſe bleſſings, we muſt alſo be in covenant with God. On this account, it muſt be a great privilege for a perſon or a people, to be in a covenant-relation unto the Lord their God.

The greatneſs of this privilege may be evident, from the words of God unto Moſes, when the Lord made the covenant with Iſrael at Horeb. Exod. xix. 4, 5, 6. *Ye have ſeen what I have done unto the Egyptians, and how I bare you on eagles wings, and brought you unto myſelf. Now therefore if ye will obey my voice indeed, and keep my covenant, then ye ſhall be a peculiar treaſure unto me above all people. And ye ſhall be unto me a kingdom of prieſts, and an holy nation.* When a people are brought into covenant with God, they are delivered from the dominion of error, idolatry, will-worſhip, and corruptions of various kinds; and are bleſſed with the knowledge of the truth refpecting the doctrine, worfhip, government and difcipline of the church of Chrift. This work the Lord performed for the lands of our nativity. He delivered them from popifh abominations, and from prelatic corruptions, and caufed the light of gofpel-truth to fhine on them; by which he delivered them from Egypt, bare them on eagle's wings, and brought them to himfelf. A people in covenant with God are a peculiar treafure unto him. He has a fpecial intereft in them, diftinct from that intereft which he has in other nations, and more excellent than it; for all the earth is his. A covenanted people become a kingdom of priefts, and an holy nation unto the Lord. Thefe names clearly import, that thofe who are in covenant with God are a people, who are freed from the corruptions which are in the world through luft, who are bleffed with eminent nearnefs unto the Lord, by whom he is peculiarly glorified, in whom he takes fpecial delight, and over whom he exercifes a particular care. In confirmation of all this, the words of the prophet Ifaiah may be mentioned; chap. lxii. 4. *Thou fhalt no more be termed forfaken; neither fhall thy land any more be termed defolate; but thou fhalt be called Hephzi-bah, and thy land, Beulah; for the Lord delighteth in thee, and thy land fhall be married.* A people who are not in covenant with God are forfaken and defolate. The fpiritual privileges, which are enjoyed by the church, are denied unto them; and the miferies, which pertain unto the nations which know not God, are found in their wretched lot. But the nation, that is in covenant with him, is the object of the Lord's delight, becaufe they are brought into a marriage-relation unto him, as their head and hufband. Let none object to what has been faid, becaufe it is taken from the words of the Lord, relative to his antient people. For, as there is nothing in the moral nature of the covenant-relation betwixt God and Ifrael, that is inconfiftent with, or unfuitable unto the condition of the church in New Teftament times; fo there is nothing belonging unto the temporal or fpiritual bleffings of the antient church, that may not be enjoyed by a covenanting people, under the gofpel-difpenfation. If thefe were the privileges of God's covenant people, under the darker adminiftration of grace to them; how much more ſhall they be enjoyed, by a people who have joined themſelves to the Lord in a perpetual covenant, under the clearer diſpenſation of goſpel-grace to the children of men? The only difference that can juſtly be made, relates unto the extent thereof. It was inconſiſtent with the former diſpenſation, to allow any nation but the ſeed of Iſrael to enjoy theſe bleſſings; but under the goſpel, the middle wall of partition having been taken down, there is nothing in the nature of things now to hinder any nation, nay, all nations from participating of this felicity.

The happineſs of a nation that is in covenant with God, and is acting agreeable to this relation, may be ſummed up in the following particulars.—They will have God in Chriſt to be their friend. In their covenanting with him, they have taken hold of him as their God, and have devoted themſelves unto the Lord to be his people. While they are enabled, by the grace that is in Chriſt Jeſus their Lord, to act like his covenant-people; *The Lord their God, who is mighty, will be in the midſt of them, he will ſave, he will rejoice over them with joy, he will reſt in his love, he will joy over them with ſinging.*—A people, in this ſituation, will have among them a great number of real, and very eminent ſaints. When the Lord carries on a glorious work of outward reformation, and covenanting in any land; he will, at the ſame time, accompliſh a work of ſaving grace in the hearts of multitudes, and cauſe the principles of grace advance to very high degrees in the ſouls of many. It certainly muſt be an extraordinary bleſſing unto any nation, when thoſe who are the pillars of a land, on whoſe account judgments are either averted or greatly ſhortened, who are the light of the world, and are the ſalt thereof who keep it from corruption, are found amongſt them in great abundance. If theſe are found in any land, it muſt be among a people who are in covenant with God; and if they are to be found at any time more than at another, it will be on ſolemn covenanting ſeaſons.—A people, that have publicly covenanted with God, will enjoy many precious and Chriſtian privileges from the Lord, among which the following may be mentioned. A church conſtituted among them according to the rule of the word; the preaching of the everlaſting goſpel, and the diſpenſation of the other ordinances of divine inſtitution, as means both for the converſion of ſinners, and for the edification of believers; the ſcriptural government of the church, and the proper ordering of her affairs, through the inſtrumentality of office-bearers, who are appointed by the Lord Chriſt; the faithful adminiſtration of the cenſures of the houſe of God, for the benefit of all concerned; kings who ſhall be nurſing fathers, and their queens who ſhall be nurſing mothers unto the church; and a multitude of benefits, ariſing from the holy example, religious advice, and effectual fervent prayers of the godly among them. Theſe are by no means ſmall privileges, they are bleſſings that are exceeding great.—Upon a nation in covenant with him, the Lord will beſtow many temporal benefits. When a nation's ways, in this reſpect, pleaſe the Lord, he cauſeth even their enemies to be at peace with them, and will remove war far from their borders. He will cauſe the earth to yield her increaſe unto them, and will lay no famine upon them. In all their concerns they ſhall have the bleſſing of God, and ſhall enjoy that proſperity in all things, that is for his glory and their real benefit. With reſpect to the bleſſedneſs of a people in this ſituation, we may ſay, *Happy art thou, O Iſrael; who is like unto thee, O people ſaved by the Lord, the ſhield of thy help, and who is the ſword of thy excellency?* A view of the privileges of a covenanted land, made David cry out, *Happy is that people whoſe God is the Lord.*

Ninthly, The Lord will ever remember and acknowledge the covenant, which exiſts betwixt him and his church. He ſtill kept in memory, and did recognize the covenant, which ſubſiſted betwixt him and his people Iſrael; and therefore he ſays concerning it, the houſe of Iſrael and the houſe of Judah have broken my covenant, which I made with their fathers. The words of the text diſcover the Lord's remembrance of the covenant, which he had made with Iſrael. Though they had forgotten this ſolemn and holy covenant, yet it was not forgotten of God. The text alſo imports that the Lord owned this covenant, and was ready at all times to acknowledge it. The Lord was not aſhamed of this covenant, nor was it ever the object of his diſapprobation.

Iſrael indeed acted as if they had been aſhamed of this covenant, and as if they had diſapproved of it; but the Lord, in the midſt of all that contempt with which his people treated their covenant with him, ſays of it, it is my covenant which I made with their fathers. The truth of this obſervation will be further evident, and its importance illuſtrated from the following conſiderations.

1ſt, The Lord remembered and did acknowledge his covenant with his people, by making honourable mention of it, in his addreſſes unto them. In the text and context the Lord ſpeaks to the ſeed of Iſrael concerning it, in the moſt reſpectful manner. This alſo the Lord did, by the miniſtry of all the prophets. Such is the repreſentations which the Lord gave his people of his covenant with them, on every occaſion, as will clearly prove his love and eſteem of it, and that he never would either forget or diſown it. Though the ſeaſon of the labours of extraordinary and inſpired men in the church of God, is come to an end; yet when the ordinary ambaſſadors of Chriſt, ſpeaking to his people in his name, and according to his word, declare the excellency, uſefulneſs, and obligation of theſe ſolemn deeds, the Lord is by their inſtrumentality, ſpeaking of the covenant, which exiſts betwixt him and his profeſſing people, with honour and reſpect.

2d, The Lord teſtifies his regard unto his people's covenant with him, by calling them to fulfil their obligations unto him. How often does the Lord, in his word and by the miniſtry of his ſervants, exhort a people, who have ſworn unto him, to keep his covenant, and perform their vows? In the 6th verſe preceding the text, the prophet receives a commiſſion from the Lord, to perform this work, in the moſt ſolemn manner. He was commanded to travel through all the cities of Judah, and every ſtreet of Jeruſalem, to publiſh Jehovah's royal proclamation to the inhabitants thereof, the great and important ſubſtance of which was, *Hear ye the words of this covenant, and do them.* The Lord, ſpeaking by David, calls his people not only to vow, but alſo to pay their vows unto the Lord their God. By the prophet Nahum, the Lord renews the call, in theſe very affecting words, *O Judah, perform thy vows.* If the Lord did not always remember, and acknowledge his covenant with his people, he would not, in fuch an earneft and frequent manner, put them in mind of their covenant-duties, and exhort them to the performance thereof.

3*d*, The Lord's remembrance and acknowledgement of his covenant with his people will alfo appear, from his encouraging them to keep his covenant, by promifing to blefs them in this courfe; and from his deterring them from breaking it, by theatening to punifh them for this fin. He does not only call them to fulfil their covenant by his authority, but allures and encourages them to this by his promife. The fum of his promifes to this effect, is contained in thefe remarkable words of Mofes, Exod. xix. 5 *Now therefore, if ye will obey my voice indeed, and keep my covenant, then ye fhall be a peculiar treafure unto me above all people; for all the earth is mine.* It is here promifed unto a people who are in covenant with God, that they fhall be the happy objects, in whom the Lord hath a peculiar intereft, in whom he taketh a peculiar delight, over whom he will exercife a peculiar care, upon whom he puts a peculiar value, and whom he confiders as making up his peculiar riches or inheritance. As the Lord teftifies his refpect unto his covenant, by giving his people abundant affurances of his favour and goodnefs, in fulfilling their obligations; fo the fame thing is difcovered by the revelation of the threatening againft covenant-breakers. The words of Jofhua to the tribes of Ifrael lay this matter before the children of men. When Ifrael's covenant with God was renewed, he faid unto the tribes affembled for this folemn exercife at Shechem, Jofh. xxiv. 20. *If ye forfake the Lord, and ferve ftrange gods, then he will turn and do you hurt, and confume you, after that he hath done you good.* Upon a people who break their covenant with God, the Lord here threatens to bring the evil of punifhment, which fhould wafte their comforts, render them miferable, and at laft confume them.

4*th*, He fhews his regard unto his covenant, by taking notice of the conduct of a people who have vowed unto him, that he may know whether they are fulfilling or breaking their folemn obligations. Did the Lord pay no regard to the behaviour of his church, by which his covenant is either kept or broken, it would manifest that the covenant itself was but little the object of his concern; but the reverse of this is the case. We find the church acknowledging this truth, Psal. xliv. 20, 21. *If we have forgotten the name of our God, or stretched out our hands to a strange god; shall not God search this out? for he knoweth the secrets of the heart.* Yes, his eyes are upon all the ways of his church, and he observes all their doings, not with respect to his law only; but with reference to their voluntary obligations also, that it may appear whether they are faithful or perfidious in his covenant.

5th, The Lord's bestowing upon a people, who keep his covenant, the blessings contained in the promise; and his inflicting upon them who break it, the misery found written in the threatening, prove his favourable regard unto these solemn transactions. When Israel walked in the ways of God, and kept his covenant, he was not to them a barren wilderness, or a land of drought; but freely and abundantly conferred upon them the rich blessings of his grace and mercy. Of this, the spiritual and temporal prosperity of the people of God, in the days of David, Solomon, Asa, Jehoshaphat, Hezekiah, and Josiah, are incontestible evidences. As he fulfilled his promise unto those who kept, he also executed his threatenings upon them who brake his covenant. All the calamities which were brought upon Israel, in their different generations, have this evil assigned as one of their procuring causes. Their different captivities out of their own land, which brought upon them accumulated disgrace and ruin, were occasioned by this sin. For the proof of this, it is necessary only to repeat the words of Moses, and of Jeremiah. Deut. xxix. 24, 25. *Even all nations shall say, Wherefore hath the Lord done this unto this land? what meaneth the heat of this great anger? Then men shall say, because they have forsaken the covenant of the Lord God of their fathers, which he made with them, when he brought them forth out of the land of Egypt.* Jer. xxii. 8, 9. *And many nations shall pass by this city, and they shall say every man to his neighbour, Wherefore hath the Lord done thus unto this great city? And they shall answer, because they have forsaken the covenant of the Lord their God, and have worshipped other gods, and served them.*

6th, The Lord's regard unto his covenant with the church, is also evident from the gracious issue which this relation to him shall take, by the exercise of his goodness, in recovering them from a state of apostacy and misery into which they had fallen. He will not finally cast off a covenanted people; but will remember mercy for them, deliver them from their low estate, and restore them to the enjoyment of his special goodness as their covenant God. Although a covenanted people may so far forget and disown their special relation unto God, as neither to be sensible of their voluntary obligation unto him, nor seek or expect covenant-blessings from him; yet the Lord will not in this manner, nor on that account, give up with his interest in, or relation unto them. What the Lord did for his people Israel, he will do, in his own time and way, for every Christian covenanted land; which is recorded, Lev. xxvi. 44, 45. *And yet for all that, when they be in the land of their enemies, I will not cast them away, neither will I abhor them, to destroy them utterly, and to break my covenant with them; for I am the Lord their God. But I will for their sakes remember the covenant of their ancestors, whom I brought forth out of the land of Egypt, in the sight of the heathen, that I might be their God; I am the Lord.* On all these accounts, it clearly appears, that the Lord neither forgets, nor disowns, but remembers and acknowledges, the covenant, which subsists betwixt him and his people.

Tenthly, It is an important duty, for a people to keep their covenant with God; and a very aggravated sin, to violate their sacred obligations unto him. Although the words of the text, and the nature of the things evince the truth of both parts of this observation; yet, that our minds may be the more affected therewith, a short scriptural illustration of each of them may be necessary. This shall be attempted in the following particulars.

1st, That it is the duty of a people, who are in covenant with God, to fulfil their obligations unto him, will be confirmed from the command of God which requires it. Were this not the case, the Lord would never interpose his authority concerning it, in such a positive manner as he does. Read his royal order relative to this matter, Deut. xxix. 9. *Keep therefore the words of this covenant, and do them;* and again Jer. xi. 6. *Hear ye the words of this covenant, and do them.* The ſovereign authority of the King eternal, immortal and inviſible, the only wiſe God binds the conſciences of the children of men, to the performance of their covenant-obligations; and, therefore, the duty muſt be of great importance.

2*d*, This truth will further appear, from the honourable way in which a people's conduct is mentioned in the Lord's word, who have endeavoured to fulfil their obligations unto him. Of the tribe of Levi, Moſes ſays, Deut. xxxiii. 9 *For they have obſerved thy word, and kept thy covenant.* Of the children of Judah, in the days of Aſa, it is ſaid, 2 Chron xv. 15. *And all Judah rejoiced at the oath, for they had ſworn with all their heart, and they ſought him with their whole deſire, and he was found of them; and the Lord gave them reſt on every ſide.* To the honour of the ſame people, in the days of Joſiah, the Spirit of God teſtifies, 2 Kings xxiii. 3. *And all the people ſtood to the covenant.* Since ſuch divine commendations are given to a people, for performing their covenant-engagements to the Lord, it muſt be a duty of great importance.

3*d*, The excellency of this duty may alſo be diſcerned, from the notice that is taken of it in the promiſe or prophecy of God's word. A very ſtriking inſtance of this is found, Iſa. xix. 21. *Yea, they ſhall vow a vow unto the Lord, and ſhall perform it.* Theſe words may be viewed both as prophecy and a promiſe of God to the church; and, in either of theſe conſiderations, the importance of this duty is abundantly evident. As the greatneſs and excellency of the duty of public covenanting clearly appears, from the Lord's having foretold that it ſhould obtain, in the days of the New Teſtament, among Gentile nations; ſo the vaſt importance of the duty of fulfilling our ſolemn obligations is evident, from its having been foretold by the Spirit, as it is in theſe words, that the goſpel-church ſhould perform their vows unto the Lord. Conſidering the words as a promiſe of God, the greatneſs of this duty will alſo be evident from them. Such is the excellency of this duty, that the God and Rock of our ſalvation has mercifully engaged himſelf, to communicate ſuch meaſures of grace unto the New Teſtament church, as will enable them, not only to vow a vow unto him, but alſo to perform it. The Lord having made the duty of fulfilling covenant-obligations unto him, the ſubject-matter of ſcripture-prophecy, and of a gracious promiſe, from this the importance of the exerciſe may be ſafely concluded.

4*th*, The excellency of this duty is alſo very great, becauſe the right performance of it is ground of comfort to the church, under adverſe diſpenſations of divine providence. When the church was ſorely tried with adverſity, the conſideration of this was one ſpring of her conſolation. This is expreſſed in Pſal. xliv. 17. *All this is come upon us; yet we have not forgotten thee, neither have we dealt falſely in thy covenant.* In the eight preceding verſes, the church repreſents the various troubles to which, at that time, ſhe was ſubjected; but it was matter of joy to her, that ſhe had been enabled, by the grace of God, to fulfil her covenant-obligations unto him. It was a comfortable reflection unto the church, that though the Lord had viſited her with great adverſity, yet ſhe had not dealt falſely in his covenant.

5*th*, The advantages ariſing from this duty diſcover its importance. Three of theſe ſhall be mentioned. Thoſe who fulfil their covenant-obligation unto God, he will advance unto the moſt diſtinguiſhed honour. Exod. xxx. 5. *If ye—keep my covenant—ye ſhall be a peculiar treaſure unto me.* What an inconceivable honour is it, for perſons to be a peculiar treaſure unto the ever bleſſed Jehovah, to be made up by him amongſt his precious jewels, and to compoſe a part of his portion, or the lot of his inheritance! Himſelf aſſures us that this ſhall be the bleſſedneſs of all who keep his covenant.—Thoſe who do ſo ſhall enjoy univerſal proſperity. Of this we are informed by the Lord's word, Deut. xxix. 9. *Keep therefore the words of this covenant, and do them, that ye may proſper in all that ye do.* Whatever they ſhould do, with reſpect to the concerns of this preſent life, they ſhall enjoy in it all neceſſary and profitable proſperity. And whatever they may perform, with relation to the intereſts of their ſouls, the Lord will make them to proſper therein, for his own glory, and for their ſpiritual and eternal good.—Chriſtians, who keep their covenant with the Lord, have reaſon to expect a bleſſing on their offſpring. This truth is declared unto us in the cxxxii. Pſ. ver. 12. *If thy children will keep my covenant, and my teſtimony that I ſhall teach them; their children alſo ſhall ſit upon thy throne for evermore.* A promiſe is here made unto the ſeed of David, which the Lord graciouſly confirms by his oath, that their children ſhould ſway the ſceptre of regal government over the kingdom of Iſrael, if they would conſcientiouſly fulfil their covenant-engagements unto him. This promiſe is not peculiar unto thoſe to whom it was primarily made; but belongs unto all, who, through the covenant of grace, have an intereſt in the ſure mercies of David. The ſame declaration of grace is renewed, Pſal. ciii. 17, 18. *His righteouſneſs is unto children's children, to ſuch as keep his covenant.* Would Chriſtians bequeath the bleſſing of the Lord, unto their dear and riſing poſterity, which certainly is their duty and will be their deſire, this is the way pointed out unto them, that in their own perſons, they be careful to keep the Lord's covenant.

As the duty of keeping covenant with God is highly important, ſo the ſin of violating ſacred obligations unto him is of great aggravation. The following ſcripture-quotations will abundantly confirm this truth.

From the 16th to the 40th verſe of the xxvi. chapter of Leviticus, we have a long liſt of awful and ſore judgments which the Lord threatens to bring upon his people Iſrael. The cauſe of all theſe is mentioned in the 15th verſe, which is their breaking his covenant. In the 25th verſe we have the following moſt pointed expreſſions; *And I will bring a ſword upon you, that ſhall avenge the quarrel of my covenant; and when ye are gathered together within your cities, I will ſend the peſtilence among you; and ye ſhall be delivered into the hand of your enemy.*—The greatneſs of this ſin is evident from the Lord's words unto Solomon, which are recorded, 1 Kings xi. 11. *Wherefore the Lord ſaid unto Solomon, foraſmuch as this is done of thee, and thou haſt not kept my covenant and my ſtatutes which I have commanded thee, I will ſurely rend the kingdom from thee, and will give it to thy ſervant.* The ſin of covenant-breaking was the cauſe of the Lord's dividing the choſen tribes into two nations; which was not only a puniſhment to the houſe of David, but a ſource of great affliction unto the whole people.—This mournful truth is also confirmed by the words of Hosea, chap. x. 4. *They have spoken words, swearing falsely in making a covenant; thus judgment springeth up as hemlock in the furrows of the field.* The sin here mentioned is covenant-breaking. They had indeed made a covenant, but they had broken it, and thereby they manifested that they had sworn falsely in making it. What were the effects of this? Judgments, in their number, like the luxuriant growth of hemlock; in their nature, noxious and destructive, like this poisonous herb, are the genuine fruits of this evil.—The manner in which the Lord speaks of this sin, as charged upon a people, discovers the peculiar criminality of it. In the lxxviii. Psalm 10th verse, the Lord charges the children of Ephraim with this sin in the following words; *They kept not the covenant of God, and refused to walk in his law* The whole congregation of Israel are, in the 37th verse, charged with the same evil, in a way that sufficiently expresses the greatness of this sin. *For their hearts were not right with him, neither were they stedfast in his covenant* From these words it is evident, that covenant-breaking is an obstinate refusing of God's law, and proceeds from an aversion of heart at him.—The Lord, by the prophet Hosea, chap. vi. 7. speaks of this evil in words still more remarkable. *But they like men have transgressed my covenant.* Or, as it is read by some, *But they like Adam have transgressed my covenant.* The heinous nature of this sin is manifest, from both these readings of the text. They who are my people, and by profession are an holy race, act like darkened, unrenewed and heathen men in transgressing my covenant. Or, according to the other reading of the words, The sin of my people, in transgressing my covenant, bears a great resemblance unto the first sin of Adam, whereby the covenant of works was broken, the favour and image of God were lost, and the whole human race brought and exposed unto temporal, spiritual and eternal misery —It may serve to illustrate the same truth to observe, that the sin of covenant-breaking is mentioned by the apostle, Rom. i. 31. and 2 Tim. iii. 3. amongst the most unnatural, abominable and scandalous offences. Thus it appears that keeping covenant with God is a moſt neceſſary and important duty, and that breaking our engagements to him poſſeſſes high degrees of criminality.

Having finiſhed the illuſtration of the doctrinal obſervations, it is neceſſary to add ſome practical improvement of the ſubject, which ſhall be done in the following inferences deduced from what has been ſaid.

1ſt, This ſubject informs us, that it is the duty of Chriſtians to bring themſelves under ſolemn and voluntary obligations unto the ſervice of the Lord their God. From the principles already laid down and proved, nothing can be a more plain or native inference than this. Beſides it appears to be a ſelf-evident propoſition. The reverſe of it cannot be viewed, without exciting abhorrence in all religious minds. That it is not the duty of Chriſtians to bring themſelves under ſolemn and voluntary obligations to ſerve their God, will never be believed by thoſe who have their ſenſes duly exerciſed to diſcern between good and evil. That comprehenſive duty which Chriſt requires of them, who have come to him, and have found reſt in him, *Take my yoke upon you.* Mat. xi. 29. plainly includes this important exerciſe. All thoſe who have come unto Chriſt for ſalvation, and have found reſt to their ſouls in him, will be conſtrained to take his yoke upon them which is eaſy and his burden which is light. This yoke of Chriſt is the yoke of obedience to his holy commandments, which is not grievous to thoſe who are renewed in the ſpirit of their minds. The taking Chriſt's yoke upon us comprehends, not only our external obedience to the law, but alſo thoſe exerciſes of the mind concerning that law, which muſt neceſſarily go before our fulfilling it. A ſpiritual knowledge, approbation and eſteem of the law; a clear diſcerning of its moral and perpetual obligation, by the authority of God, upon our conſciences; and an holy purpoſe of heart, and firm reſolution, in the ſtrength of Chriſt, both to keep ourſelves from the evils which the law forbids, and to practiſe the duties which it requires, are all neceſſary in order to our practical conformity unto it. All conſcientious and acceptable obedience to the law of God muſt follow theſe exerciſes of the mind, and cannot go before them, whereby the Chriſtian is brought to a moſt cordial reſolution, and a voluntary determination, to make the Lord's moſt holy precepts the rule of his converſation. Now, what is this Chriſtian reſolution or determination to obey the law, but the believer's bringing himſelf under a voluntary obligation, by his own act, to ſerve the Lord. This voluntary obligation is abſolutely neceſſary unto all acceptable obedience; it is the effect of the mind's perceiving the original obligation, under which the perſon is to obey the law, by the divine authority of the Lawgiver; it comes between the Chriſtian's diſcerning the original divine obligation, and his practical compliance therewith; itſelf is an act of obedience to the law; and it is greatly ſtrengthened, as it is daily renewed by the Chriſtian, through the courſe of his holy obedience. Whenever a perſon comes to be ſavingly enlightened in the knowledge of the law, and of its obligation upon him, he immediately reſolves upon obeying it. His obedience to the law commences with that act, whereby he reſolves that whatever others do, as for him he will ſerve the Lord. The Chriſtian cannot thus determine or reſolve without bringing himſelf under a voluntary obligation to obey. It is therefore evident, that both the diſcovery of the original divine obligation of the law, and the Chriſtian's willing engagement to fulfil it, are abſolutely neceſſary unto all acceptable obedience. If theſe may be formed in the mind, they may be expreſſed in words unto the Lord. Of this we have innumerable inſtances in the ſcriptures. If they may be expreſſed in words, they may be uttered in the form of a promiſe, vow, or oath unto the Lord. If theſe things may be done by an individual, they may be done by a company, conſiſting of few or many, even by a whole nation. It is, therefore, an important and neceſſary duty belonging to Chriſtians, either in their perſonal or collective capacities, to come under voluntary obligations unto the ſervice of the Lord.

2*d*, The evil of oppoſing the duty of public covenanting with God, is evident from this ſubject. Both the open enemies and the profeſſed friends of this divine ordinance have united their efforts, though not by mutual concert, to bring it into diſrepute, and to prejudize the generation againſt it. This oppoſition has been managed in various ways. By denying its morality in the times of the New Testament; by refusing its intrinsic obligation even upon the covenanters themselves; by rejecting the proper obligation thereof on posterity; by denying to the civil duties of a people a place in the oath of God; by maintaining that an acknowledgement of the perpetual obligation of our covenants should not be required as a term of communion, in a church which professes to stand on the footing of a testimony for the covenanted reformation; and by an unnecessary and frivolous objecting to some parts of the matter, and some circumstances in the form of these solemn deeds in the days of our fathers, in these ways this great and important duty has been chiefly opposed Many, who have been accustomed to speak of our solemn covenants with affection and respect, have their mouths now opened against them; and some from ignorance of their nature, and others from prejudices at them which they have contracted, cease not to pervert the right ways of God. This prevailing opposition to our solemn covenants is lamentable in the instruments by whom it is made, alarming as to the season in which it has appeared, and astonishing in the source from which it seems to have sprung.—It is truly lamentable if we consider the persons who have made it. This opposition to the public vows of the nation unto the Lord has been managed by men in sacred office, who professed to be witnesses for the covenanted reformation, and were solemnly bound, by their ordination-vows, to maintain it to the end; but are now appearing to act as if they were resolved to destroy, in this particular, whatever they or their fathers have built. When this religious party appeared at first, though they never gave a full testimony for the whole of the covenanted reformation, yet they were the means of reviving in the land the knowledge and remembrance of some of the parts thereof; but now, alas! it would appear, that they are likely to be the instruments of bringing that work of God for these isles of the sea, under contempt and reproach.—This opposition to our solemn covenants is alarming, if we consider the season in which it has appeared. It has been made at a time, when the Lord seems to be coming out of his place to punish the inhabitants of the earth for their iniquity, to be sending diſtreſs upon nations for their ſin, and to be bringing a ſword upon us to avenge the quarrel of his covenant. To behold, at ſuch a time as this, a new and formidable oppoſition made unto theſe public vows, which is rapidly ſpreading amongſt thouſands of the Chriſtian people, muſt be alarming to the ſerious mind. It will contribute to the filling up the cup of the nation's ſin, and to the haſtening forward of our affliction.—This new oppoſition to our public covenants is aſtoniſhing in the ſource from which it ſeems to have ſprung. Viſionary ſchemes of political reform, founded on deiſtical principles, and which have yielded ſuch melancholy fruits, have been, with reſpect to many, the parents by which it has been produced, nurſed and reared to maturity. The great evil of this oppoſition to our covenants conſiſts in its being a fighting againſt God, a contempt of his ordinance, an injury done unto his church, a ſtriking againſt pure and undefiled religion, and an endeavour to harden the generation in their ſin. Let all the friends of our ſolemn covenants, and of that reformation of which they were a conſpicuous part, ſay, with reſpect to all the oppoſers thereof, *O my ſoul, come not thou into their ſecret; into their aſſembly, mine honour, be not thou united.*

3*d*, This ſubject may remind us of the wonderful works which the Lord has wrought, for the land of our nativity. It was viſited in the early times of Chriſtianity, with the light of the everlaſting goſpel, which, in greater or leſſer brightneſs, was long continued in it. When the dark clouds of antichriſtian abomination covered the nations of the earth, the light of the goſpel remained in ſome remote parts of our land, during the moſt of that period. When the Lord was pleaſed to deliver ſome of the nations of the earth from the idolatry, blaſphemy, and cruelty of popery, at the ever memorable proteſtant reformation, the light of the goſpel returned to this land; and the Lord raiſed up many to appear for his work, to be active in promoting it, and bleſſed them with extraordinary ſucceſs. At this firſt period of reformation, notwithſtanding of much oppoſition, the church attained unto great purity in doctrine, worſhip, government and diſcipline, and entered into a ſolemn vow or oath unto God, called the national covenant of Scotland, wherein they renounced the abominations of popery, and engaged themselves to abide in the profession of the gospel and ordinances of Christ. When the land was again subjected to great corruptions and oppression, by the establishment of prelacy and arbitrary power, the Lord wrought a wonderful deliverance, and brought the nation to higher degrees of reformation. The work which had been begun in the former period was greatly perfected in this. More extensive and complete subordinate standards of doctrine, worship, government and discipline for the Christian church were compiled, in agreeableness to the word of God, and were solemnly adopted by civil and ecclesiastic authority. The church was established in great purity, and civil government was settled according to the light of the word of God, which shined brightly in the land. To confirm all these blessed attainments, and to render them permanent privileges to following generations, a solemn league and covenant with God was sworn, by all ranks of men in Scotland, England and Ireland, by which they bound themselves with a bond to be the Lord's people, to adhere unto the true religion, and to keep themselves from every thing that was contrary thereunto. Hereby our land became Hephzi-bah, and Beulah, a land married unto the Lord, and the object of his delight. By this solemn exercise, we, as a nation, did ask the way to Zion, with our faces thitherward, saying, *Come, let us join ourselves to the Lord in a perpetual covenant, that shall not be forgotten, either by ourselves, or our posterity.* To this day, the professors of religion are under the strongest obligations to bless the Lord, for the attainments of that period; for it is greatly owing to these as a mean, that any religious purity remains among us, in the midst of all our defections, at the present time.

4th, This subject represents to our view the state of the children of men in the land of our nativity, respecting the sacred obligation of public religious covenants with God; they are under that obligation. Our fathers have entered into a solemn covenant with the Lord, as their God in Christ, to be his people, and to walk in all his statutes, ordinances and laws. These covenants are consonant to the word of God, both in their matter and form. The public religious covenants of the church bind their poſterity. We therefore are, and our poſterity ſhall be bound by the ſacred obligation of theſe covenants, to proſecute the ends thereof in our ſtation, all the days of our life. Particularly, we are bound by the oath of God, to embrace and continue in the profeſſion, obedience and defence of the true preſbyterian reformed religion of Jeſus Chriſt, which is revealed in the ſcriptures of truth, and exhibited in the ſubordinate ſtandards of the church of Scotland, in the doctrine, worſhip, government and diſcipline thereof;—to endeavour to promote the knowledge, profeſſion and practice of this holy religion, in the covenanted lands of Britain and Ireland; —to abhor and deteſt, to reſiſt and extirpate all contrary religion and doctrine, errors and corruptions, as popery, prelacy, ſuperſtition, ſchiſm, profaneneſs, and whatſoever is contrary to ſound doctrine, and the power of godlineſs;—to maintain the juſt rights, privileges and honour of all perſons in lawful authority, whether civil or eccleſiaſtic in the ſtate or church;—to promote the happineſs, and to maintain the liberties and privileges, temporal and ſpiritual, of ourſelves and others, and to tranſmit the enjoyment thereof to poſterity;—to ſtudy the due performance of all the duties we owe to God and man, abſtaining from all ſin, and endeavouring real reformation;—to encourage the hearts, and ſtrengthen the hands of one another in the work of the Lord, and not to ſuffer ourſelves to be drawn away from it, or to become indifferent about it, but to continue ſtedfaſt therein unto the end;—and to have the glory of God before us as our ſupreme end, and the grace that is in Chriſt Jeſus as our ſtrength to enable us to perform our vows unto the Lord. Theſe are ſome of the duties contained in the national covenant of Scotland, and in the ſolemn league and covenant of the three kingdoms, to which we are bound, both by the authority of God in his law, and by our ſolemn covenants with him. Ignorance of the nature of theſe covenants, of their obligation upon us, or of the duties to which we are bound by them, cannot relieve our ſouls from their binding force. No enmity at theſe ſolemn deeds can deliver the conſciences of thoſe who hate them from their obligation.

No contempt and reproach, which we may pour upon our national vows, will avail to ſet looſe from the duties thereof, thoſe who have their mouths filled with hard ſpeeches againſt them. Neither can any practical contradiction of them, or apoſtacy from them ſet us free from their obligation. Ignorance or contempt of the moral law, enmity at it, and rebellion againſt it cannot reſcue the conſciences of rational creatures from the obligation, under which they are, to love and obey it; neither can theſe free covenanters or their poſterity from the obligation of religious covenants. A very conſiderable number of the inhabitants of theſe lands are under perſonal and ſolemn vows unto the Lord, from their partaking of the Lord's ſupper. A ſtill greater number of them are under obligations to duty, by taking upon themſelves ſome kind of religious profeſſion. Almoſt all of them are under covenant-obligations to the Lord, by their baptiſm. Theſe obligations are of the ſame nature, with thoſe of public covenants with God. The Lord, who fixes the bounds of our habitation, has brought us in to being in a land, which was ſolemnly devoted unto him, and he has cauſed us, in his merciful providence, to deſcend from thoſe who entered into a ſolemn covenant with him to be his people, and he is ſtill furniſhing us with the moſt ample means of information, relative to the ſolemn deeds of our fathers, and their obligation upon us; we therefore are certainly under the binding force of public covenants with God, and ought to make it our great concern to fulfil them all the days of our life. To the inhabitants of theſe lands, the words which Jeremiah proclaimed in the cities of Judah, and in the ſtreets of Jeruſalem, may with great propriety be addreſſed, *Hear ye the words of this covenant, and do them.*

5th, This ſubject leads us to conſider ſome of thoſe evils, by which we as a nation have broken the covenant, which the Lord hath made with our fathers. As the houſe of Iſrael and the houſe Judah had broken the covenant, which God had made with their fathers; ſo we, the inhabitants of theſe covenanted lands, have been guilty of the ſame tranſgreſſion. All the different ſteps of public apoſtacy from the reformation purity are, in their nature, mournful breaches of our covenants with God.

The nation began this melancholy course, by adopting, both by civil and ecclesiastic authority, the public resolutions, whereby the known enemies of the work of God were admitted into places of authority and confidence in the land, which has been continued to the present day. All the alterations which have been made, in the constitutions and administrations either of church or state, are breaches of our national vows. The civil magistrate's claiming and exercising, and the nation's giving to him, by public acts, a blasphemous headship over the church, and a supremacy over all persons, and in all causes, ecclesiastic as well as civil, in the realm, which took place soon after the restoration, constituted a most mournful breach of covenant; and, alas! from this erastian yoke, the church has never been fully delivered. In the cruel and bloody persecution of the saints and servants of God, for adhering to their covenant-obligations, and for testifying against the evils which prevailed in their day, the nation carried their breach of covenant to the highest degree. The nation's suffering a precious opportunity for returning to their covenanted establishments, which a merciful providence ordered at the revolution, to pass away, without their duly improving it; and their settling themselves upon a foundation, whereby the attainments of the second and purest period of the reformation were overlooked, were certainly both an abuse of the goodness of God, and a breach of our covenant with him. The re-establishment of prelacy in England and Ireland, and the toleration of it in Scotland must be viewed in the same light. The incorporating union of Scotland with England, on terms inconsistent with their former covenanted conjunction, and destructive of it, can be considered in no other view. The boundless and authoritative toleration of all sects and heresies in these lands, whereby the true religion is mournfully corrupted, and whereby the nation becomes a partaker with other men's sins, is also a mournful breach of our covenants with God. The restoration of the antichristian law of patronage, and the rigorous exercise of that law, whereby men are imposed, in the character of ministers of the gospel, upon professed Christian congregations, without their conſent, and in oppoſition to their warmeſt remonſtrances, is a moſt wanton and profane violation of the oath of God. The countenance which the nation has given to the blaſphemous religion of antichriſt, in tolerating it at home, and eſtabliſhing it abroad, is a moſt mournful and affecting breach of our public vows unto God. The fond attachment of the minds of many, to deiſtical or infidel forms of civil government, which have been eſtabliſhed in ſome parts of the world, amounts to the ſame thing. Our mournful church diviſions, which ſeem to be increaſing, are both awful tokens of the Lord's anger againſt us, and peculiar breaches of our covenant with him. The univerſal abounding in the land of groſs errors and immoralities, of ſuperſtition and idolatry, of infidelity and profanity, and of every thing that is contrary to truth and duty, may ſtrike our minds as viſible and practical breaches of our public covenants. Beſides, the want of theſe ſpiritual exerciſes of the heart, and of theſe holy endeavours in word and deed, which are neceſſary both to promote the intereſts of the true religion, and to fulfil our public vows, muſt be ranked amongſt our breaches of the oath and covenant of God. On account of theſe and the like things, for the inſtances of our covenant-breaking cannot be fully enumerated, the Lord may juſtly ſay of us, The inhabitants of Britain and Ireland have broken my covenant, which I made with their fathers.

6th, The ſituation of theſe lands, with reſpect to the diſpleaſure and the judgments of God, may be diſcerned from what has been ſaid; they are the objects of theſe. Since we as a nation muſt plead guilty to the charge, which is contained in the text; we are in danger of the execution of the threatening upon us, which is expreſſed in the verſe that follows it; *Behold, I will bring evil upon them which they ſhall not be able to eſcape, and though they ſhall cry unto me, I will not hearken unto them.* The evil, which is here threatened, is the evil of punishment, which he brings upon a covenant-breaking people for their ſin. It is brought upon them by the mighty hand of God, and they ſhall not be able, by all their policy and power, to turn it away. It ſhall be actually inflicted upon them, though they ſhould be conſtrained, in an unreasonable and improper manner, to cry to him for deliverance. These isles of the sea have long been under many divine judgments, both of a temporal and spiritual nature. There have been times in which the anger of the Lord has been more visibly manifested against us, but he has turned from the full execution of his judgments, and has given us space to repent, and to return unto him; but, alas! we have the more grievously departed from him. If we persist in our rebellion against him, the Lord will whet his glittering sword, his hand will take hold on judgments, he will render vengeance to his enemies, and will reward them that hate him. In the times which are now passing over us, the Lord seems to be performing, in a very remarkable manner, this strange work upon the nations. The awful declaration which is contained in Isa. xxxiv. 2, 3. appears to have been mournfully accomplished of late, and may still receive a more alarming fulfilment; *For the indignation of the Lord is upon all nations, and his fury upon all their armies, he hath utterly destroyed them, he hath delivered them to the slaughter; their slain also shall be cast out, and their stink shall come up out of their carcases, and the mountains shall be melted with their blood.* The reason of all these public calamities, which the Lord will bring upon men, is mentioned in the 8th verse. *For it is the day of the Lord's vengeance, and the year of recompences for the controversy of Sion.* In the righteous dispensations of divine providence, judgments of the most awful nature have been inflicted upon many lands, and there is reason to apprehend that these shall be followed with more universal devastation. The character of the times wherein we live, and of those which probably will follow them, is marked in the words of Christ, Luke xxi. 22. *For these be the days of vengeance, that all things which are written may be fulfilled.* When the judgments of God are thus abroad in the earth, it is our duty to be learning righteousness; for, on account of our manifold sins, it certainly is the divine call to us as a nation, *Therefore thus will I do unto thee, O Israel; and because I will do this unto thee, prepare to meet thy God, O Israel.*

7th, The prosperous and blessed state to which the church of Christ shall yet be exalted in this world, may be learned from what has been ſaid. We have ſeen that the religion of Jeſus ſhall be the religion of nations, that public covenanting ſhall prevail among them, and that the kingdoms of this world ſhall become the kingdoms of our Lord and of his Chriſt. This period of the church's proſperity is deſcribed at the beginning of the 20th chapter of the Revelation, and has been called the glory of the latter day. Many of the Old Teſtament prophecies, relating to the purity, extent and glory of the church, have never been fully accompliſhed; but we look for it in that happy period, which ſhall aſſuredly come in its ſeaſon. After the vials of the wrath of God, which contain the ſeven laſt plagues, ſhall be poured out upon their appointed objects, whereby the fall of antichriſt, of the falſe prophet, and of the cities of the nations ſhall be accompliſhed, ſatan ſhall be bound a thouſand years, and the church, during that time, ſhall have great proſperity. The bleſſed concerns of the church of God, whereby the divine glory, the Mediator's honour, the welfare of nations, and the ſalvation of immortal ſouls are ſecured, ſhall be eſtabliſhed among men, and ſpread through the earth; but the intereſts of the kingdom of ſatan ſhall live no more, till the thouſand years are fulfilled. Then ſhall the goſpel and its ordinances be enjoyed, by all nations, in purity and with power; and the deſpiſed ordinance of public covenanting ſhall prevail among them; *For they ſhall vow a vow unto the Lord, and perform it.* Though we may not live to ſee the introduction of this bleſſed ſtate of the church into the world, yet we may behold it in the promiſe by an aſſured faith, rejoice on the preſent appearances of its approach, and expect to hear of it, at its taking place, with heavenly delight, when our ſouls ſhall be mingled with the ſpirits of juſt men made perfect, before the throne of glory.

8*th*, This ſubject may inform us with reſpect to our duty, relative to the covenants, which the Lord hath made with our fathers. The text and doctrine plainly diſcover, that it is our duty to keep theſe covenants, and to perform the duties to which their obligation extends. —In order to this, the following exerciſes ſeem to be required of us.—It is our duty to obtain a proper knowledge of theſe ſolemn deeds. If we are ignorant of theſe, we muſt either be deſpiſers of them, or our attachment to them will not be judicious. In proportion as men are ignorant of the church's covenants with God, they are generally found treating them with contempt; and to them the words of Jude are applicable, ver. 10. *But theſe ſpeak evil of thoſe things which they know not.* Let Chriſtians, therefore, ſtore their minds with the ſcripture-doctrine, concerning the ordinance and duty of perſonal and public covenanting with God. Let them ſearch the ſcriptures, and receive from them that inſtruction with which they are furniſhed, by the precepts and promiſes of God, and by the example of the ſaints and of the church, relative to the nature, neceſſity, uſefulneſs and deſign of this important duty. It is alſo neceſſary, that we take the covenants of our anceſtors into our moſt ſerious conſideration. It is to be feared, that many who condemn them, and perhaps not a few who pretend to approve them, have never ſo much as read theſe covenants, with ſpiritual concern and attention. *My brethren, theſe things ought not ſo to be.* We can never have a proper knowledge of the ſolemn vows of the nation, unleſs we are informed as to both periods of the work of reformation, in their beginning and progreſs, in their nature and tendency, and in their parts and properties. In order unto this, a careful peruſal of the faithful hiſtories of theſe times, and a diligent ſtudy of the ſubordinate ſtandards which were then compiled, are abſolutely neceſſary. It is both ſurpriſing and mournful to ſee the negligence and indifferency of profeſſed Chriſtians, about theſe neceſſary duties; for if we are not ſtirred up to enquire into theſe things, our public covenants with God will never be underſtood by us.—It is alſo our duty to make ſure of our being perſonally in covenant with God. If we pretend to be friends to our public covenants, and profeſs ourſelves to be under their obligation; and are, at the ſame time, deſtitute of an intereſt in God, as our God in Chriſt, our public profeſſion, though never ſo right, will aggravate our condemnation at the laſt. Let us therefore be careful about the reality of our perſonal religion; for, if we want this, no profeſſion can compenſate the defect. In order unto our being perſonally in covenant with God, a knowledge and conviction of the miſery and guilt of our natural ſtate, by the covenant of works; of the way of our recovery thro' Jeſus Chriſt, by the covenant of grace; and a taking hold of him, and of that covenant of which he is the Mediator, in the exerciſe of a ſaving faith, are of abſolute and indiſpenſible neceſſity. O, then, let theſe things be our chief concern. Perſonal covenanting with God ſhould alſo be diligently ſtudied. It conſiſts in the Chriſtian's taking hold of God's covenant, as all his ſalvation and deſire, and in devoting himſelf unto the Lord, to ſerve and glorify him, in the ſtrength of his grace, all the days of his life. Theſe ſolemn tranſactions betwixt God and the ſoul tend greatly to promote the exerciſe of true religion in the heart, and contribute much to the Chriſtian's enjoying the comfort of it. It muſt be exceedingly abſurd, for perſons to profeſs a zeal for public covenants with God, who have never, in a religious and ſpiritual manner, entered into a perſonal covenant with him. Of all ſuch the Lord will ſay, *This people draweth nigh unto me with their mouth, and honoureth me with their lips; but their heart is far from me.* Let Chriſtians then be careful, while they manifeſt a becoming zeal for our public vows unto God, that they be perſonally intereſted in God, as their covenant-God in Chriſt.—It is likewiſe our duty to be ſenſible that the obligation of our public covenants is upon us, and that we act, in every reſpect, as perſons who are under ſuch ſolemn vows unto God. Since religious covenants are binding on poſterity, and ſince we, as the offſpring of a covenanted people, are under their obligation; it is of great importance to be duly convinced, by the word of God, that this is our ſituation. We ought not to receive this ſentiment, nor any other in religion, upon truſt; but ſhould imitate the example of the people of Berea, *Who ſearched the ſcriptures daily, whether theſe things were ſo.* Being convinced, on ſcriptural grounds, that the vows of God are upon us, it is our duty to walk according to theſe obligations. By avoiding every thing in our hearts and lives, which are a contradiction to the oath of God, and by carefully performing every duty which it binds us to obſerve, Chriſtians hear the words of God's covenant, and do them. Our covenant-obligations extend to the frame of our hearts, to our religious profeſſion, to our conduct with reſpect to that profeffion, to the fentiments we either adopt or reject, and to the whole of our moral deportment. Chriftians muft be careful, in all thefe particulars, to regulate themfelves according to their covenant-obligations. A mental or practical approbation of thofe things which our covenants with God oblige us to abhor and avoid, muft be a criminal breach of them; but a ftedfaft adherence to our covenanted principles, and a converfation confonant thereunto, muft be a fulfilling of them. In our abftaining from evil, and performing duties, with which our covenant-obligations have a concern, we ought to have a particular view to the fulfilling of thefe obligations. As we ought to make the law of God, in a fupreme refpect, the reafon as well as the rule of our obedience; fo fhould we, in a fubordinate fenfe, improve our covenants with God. The perfon who is inattentive to this, as he overlooks a fpecial inducement to duty, fo his obedience, on that account, muft be attended with a culpable defect.— It is alfo incumbent on us to mourn over the breaches of thefe covenants, whether they are of a perfonal, or of a public nature. In all the confeffions of fin and mourning for it, in which the faints have engaged, their own fins, as well the fins of others, were deeply impreffed on their minds. What perfon is innocent of the fin of covenant-breaking? Who can wipe his mouth and fay, that, in this particular, he has done no iniquity? Let individual perfons then mourn before the Lord, and confefs unto him their breaches of his covenant; and let them ftudy, in the ftrength of divine grace, to turn from their tranfgreffions. While Chriftians are thus exercifed about things that are perfonal, they are not to overlook the public evils, by which God's covenant is broken; but they muft imitate the example of thofe mourners in Sion, who fighed and cryed for all the abominations that were done in the land. Thefe courfes of apoftacy and fin, which have been long abounding, and are ftill increafing among us, fhould lead us to the exercife of the holy man who faid, *Rivers of waters run down mine eyes, becaufe they keep not thy law*, Pfal. cxix. 136. We cannot free ourfelves of the guilt of a covenant-breaking generation, we cannot approve ourfelves to God as zealous for holinefs, whereby he is glorified, or zealous againft fin, by which he is dif-honoured, unless the exercise of Lot is our study and attainment, of whom it is said, *For that righteous man dwelling among them, in seeing and hearing, vexed his righteous soul, from day to day, with their unlawful deeds*, 2 Pet. ii. 8. Let us go and do likewise.—It is also our duty to espouse and support a faithful testimony, against the covenant-breaking courses of the times, and in behalf of the covenanted attainments of our fathers. The necessity of this duty is evident, from the character which the Lord gives unto his people, Isa. xliii. 12. *Ye are my witnesses, saith the Lord, that I am God.* When he describes the character and work of his church, during the reign of antichrist, it is in the following words. *And I will give power unto my two witnesses, and they shall prophesy a thousand two hundred and threescore days, clothed in sackcloth*, Rev. xi. 3. In the same visions with which John was favoured, the martyrs of Jesus are said to be *slain for the word of God, and for the testimony which they held*, Rev. vi. 9. The word of God is one thing, and the church's testimony for the truths of that word is another thing; and it was for their attachment unto the word of God, and for the faithful witness which they bare unto the truths of it, that they were put to death by their cruel persecutors. The nature or extent of this testimony, which Christians are called to espouse and support, is fixed by the Lord's dispensations to the church, and is not left to the choice of the witness-bearers. The church's testimony must comprehend her public declaration both for the things of God, and against those things which are opposite thereunto. In the church's testimony for the things of God, his whole truths, and all her pure attainments must be witnessed unto, as objects which the church approve and maintain. If any of them are overlooked, her testimony for God must be partial indeed. In the church's testimony against courses of corruption and apostacy, all these must be expressed, or condemned and rejected by her; and, if any of them is passed over in silence, her testimony must be unfaithful. Though the testimony of the church may torment the men that dwell upon the earth, yet it is most friendly in its design, and beneficial in its tendency unto them. It has nothing less for its object than to promote the glory of God among them, to exhibit his truths unto them, to turn them from their sinful and ruinous courses, to bring them to the knowledge and service of God, and to promote their spiritual and eternal salvation. Let Christians, therefore, be careful religiously and cheerfully to espouse, and spiritually and practically to support a faithful testimony for the covenanted interests of religion, and against whatever is contrary thereunto.—It is certainly incumbent on Christians also, to be frequent and fervent in prayer to God, that he may, by his word and Spirit, by his grace and providence, raise his church from her low estate, and restore her to the enjoyment of her covenanted purity. He has promised to remember for a people, though sunk in degeneracy and wretchedness, the covenant of their ancestors, and to deliver them from this condition. On the footing of this promise, and others of a similar nature, let us plead with God to deliver the land from the guilt of covenant-breaking, and to restore us to our former purity and privileges. Let us set our face unto the Lord God, to seek blessings to the church, by prayer and supplications, with fasting, and sackcloth, and ashes. Let us cry unto him that the Spirit, as a convincing, quickening, enlightening and sanctifying Spirit, may be poured upon the inhabitants of these lands; that they may remember from whence they have fallen, and repent, and do their first works. With holy fervency of soul, and in the exercise of faith, let us say with the prophet. *O Lord, revive thy work in the midst of the years, in the midst of the years make known, in wrath remember mercy.* That so we may be brought into such a condition as a nation before God, as he may not have occasion to bring this charge against us. *The house of Israel and the house of Judah have broken my covenant, which I made with their fathers.*

THE END.

AN

INQUIRY

INTO

THE TIMES THAT SHALL BE FULFILLED

AT

Antichrist's Fall;

THE

CHURCH'S BLESSEDNESS IN HER MILLENNIAL REST;

The Signs that this Happy Season is at Hand;

THE PROPHETIC NUMBERS CONTAINED

IN

THE 1335 DAYS;

AND THE

Christian's Duty,

AT THIS

INTERESTING CRISIS:

IN

FIVE DISCOURSES,

BY

ARCHIBALD MASON,

Minister of the Gospel, Wishawtown.

GLASGOW:

Printed by Young, Gallie, & Company.

SOLD BY

M. OGLE; AND A. & J. M. DUNCAN, GLASGOW: OGLE, ALLARDICE & THOMSON; OLIPHANT WAUGH, & INNES; A. BLACK; D. BROWN; AND T. NELSON, EDINBURGH: G. CUTHBERTSON, PAISLEY: W. SCOTT, GREENOCK: J. MEUROS, KILMARNOCK; AND OGLES, DUNCAN, & COCHRAN, LONDON.

1818.

PREFACE.

DURING the last harvest, the Author, in ten Sermons, delivered to his Congregation the subject contained in the following pages. Corresponding to the general heads, it is now published in five Discourses. To give unity to the different branches, which were necessarily divided in the delivery, and to render the perusal more convenient, this arrangement has been adopted, without the least abridgement of what was spoken, or any material addition to it.

The Author was unexpectedly led to the consideration of this subject, by irresistible inducements, which, as they can be satisfactory to none but himself, he deems it improper to detail. A belief of the importance of the subject, a conviction of its suitableness to the times that are now passing over us, and the earnest desire of many who heard it, are the principal reasons for its publication. While he is sensible of the seasonableness of the subject, he is at the same time aware of the imperfection of the execution; on this account he solicits an indulgent perusal.

The inquiry into the times that will terminate, when systems of false religion shall be thrown down, exhibits the moral and penal evils from which mankind shall then be delivered.—The statement of some parts of the church's millennial blessedness unfolds the felicity to which, at that time, the nations shall be exalted.—By mentioning some of the signs of its approach, the saints' faith and hope may be encouraged, from those extraordinary appearances, in Divine providence.—The remarks on the numbers which are contained in the predictions, should induce believers to place their confidence on the more sure word of prophecy.—And the exhibition of the Christian's duty, to repent and believe the gospel, ought to animate us all to make due preparation for the coming of this day of the Lord. Christ's ministers are certainly warranted, in giving to subjects of this kind a place in their public ministrations; that they may promote the glory and interests of their Lord, and may prepare his people for all those dispensations, by which Divine predictions will be accomplished.

As this subject is equally adapted to Christians of every class, and contains many things about which their minds should now be employed, it is their duty to attend to it. Without neglecting at all the great concerns of personal religion, by working out their own salvation, with fear and trembling, for it is God who worketh in them both to will and to do of his good pleasure, Christians are called, both by God's word and providence, to meditate on those matters, to live in the expectation of the great things which God has promised to his church, to converse with one another concerning them, to pray earnestly for the COMING of their REDEEMER'S KINGDOM, to assist in keeping in operation the means that are employed for promoting it, and to observe attentively the doings of the Lord.

Though some, disregarding those things, may be disposed to say, "the days are prolonged, and every vision faileth;" it is his opinion, in concurrence with many others, that a solemn crisis is fast approaching, and that "the days are at hand, and the effect of every vision."

That those Discourses, by the Divine blessing, may be useful to the readers, for giving them some more "understanding of the times to know what Israel ought to do," is the earnest desire of their Author.

WISHAWTOWN,
16th March 1818.

CONTENTS.

DISCOURSE I.

DISCOURSE II.

DISCOURSE III.

DISCOURSE IV.

DISCOURSE V.

AN

INQUIRY

INTO

THE TIMES THAT SHALL BE FULFILLED AT ANTICHRIST'S FALL, AND AT THE CHURCH'S ENTRY INTO HER MILLENNIAL REST.

DISCOURSE I.

MARK i. 15.—*The time is fulfilled, and the kingdom of God is at hand: repent ye, and believe the gospel.*

IT seemed good to the Holy Ghost that some of Christ's discourses, and those also of his apostles, should be very summarily mentioned, in the holy Scriptures. The account of many of them does not contain a record of what was spoken, but a statement of the scope and substance of what they delivered to the church. When the day of Pentecost was fully come; when the apostles were filled with the Holy Ghost, and began to speak with other tongues, as the Spirit gave them utterance; when Peter had delivered, on that day, a most affecting discourse to the people; when his hearers were pricked in their hearts, and said, Men and Brethren, what shall we do; and when Peter had given them counsel suited to their present convictions, it is added, as an account of the sequel of his discourse, "And with many other words did he testify and exhort; saying, save yourselves from this untoward generation." When Paul re-visited the Macedonian churches, the account we have of his labours among them is stated in the following words.

"And when he had gone over those parts, and had given them much exhortation, he came into Greece." The same thing is done with respect to many of Christ's discourses. While some of them seem to be given at great length, as his sermon on the mount, and his addresses to his disciples immediately before his death; others of them are mentioned in a very general way. Of that discourse which he pronounced in the synagogue of Nazareth, after he had read from Isa. lxi. 1, 2, a remarkable prediction concerning himself, the following words contain all the account that is given of it; "He began to say to them, This day is this scripture fulfilled in your ears. And all bare him witness, and wondered at the gracious words which proceeded out of his mouth." Concerning that most seasonable and instructive address which he made to two of his disciples, on their way to Emmaus, this is all the scripture record; "Then he said unto them, O fools, and slow of heart to believe all that the Prophets have spoken! Ought not Christ to have suffered these things, and to enter into his glory? And beginning at Moses, and all the Prophets, he expounded unto them in all the scriptures, the things concerning himself." Of this the words of our text are a striking instance. Of the early part of Christ's public ministry, and in his first tour through the cities of Galilee, this is the very summary, yet most satisfactory, account of his labours; "Jesus came into Galilee preaching the gospel of the kingdom of God; and saying, The time is fulfilled, and the kingdom of God is at hand: repent ye, and believe the gospel." We ought to observe in all this, Divine wisdom and sovereignty. If all Christ's discourses and miracles, with those of his apostles after him, had been recorded at full length, the volume of inspiration would have been so large, that the world's inhabitants, for whose salvation it was revealed, could not have so readily searched it, so clearly understood it, so profitably improved it, nor so easily propagated it, both for the glory of its Divine Author, and for the good of themselves and others. The want of great prolixity in the sacred volume is no want of perfection; but must rather be considered as a special excellency of the Divine word. This may probably be the design of John's words with which his gospel history of Christ is concluded; "And there are also many other things which Jesus did, the which, if they should be written every one, I suppose that even the world itself could not contain the books that should be written." From the summary account which is given of some of those discourses, as well as from those that are recorded more in detail, the church may receive great instruction: so we should say concerning the information which is given in the one, and that which seems to be withheld in the other, "Even so, Father; for so it seemed good in thy sight."

In the text there are the following things to which your attention must be directed. The information which Christ gives to the people concerning the expiration of the season, which was then coming to an end; The time is fulfilled. The apostle Paul mentions this season, on two different occasions, in the words that follow: "But when the fulness of the time was come, God sent forth his son, made of a woman, made under the law;" and again, "That in the dispensation of the fulness of times, he might gather together in one all things in Christ, both which are in heaven, and on earth, even in him." This time as it is mentioned in the text, seems to have a respect to that season, as it should bring to an end that system which existed before it, and establish in its stead the gospel dispensation. In the former quotation from Paul, this time is considered as the season of those glorious transactions, in Christ's incarnation, obedience and death, by which the former system was set aside, and the meritorious foundation was laid for supporting the economy that should be introduced. The time mentioned, in the latter quotation from Paul, contemplates the same season in its effects. The new system having been introduced, and its sure foundation laid, the Lord should, from that very time, begin his glorious work of gathering together in one all things in Christ; a work which he shall carry on till the end of time, and perfect in glory for ever. As it is the view given of this time in Christ's words, with which I am now concerned, to it I shall confine myself. Jesus informs the people in his doctrine, that the time was fulfilled. The time which was appointed for the Mosiac dispensation, the time for confining the knowledge and worship of the true God to the seed of Jacob, the time of types and ceremonies in the church of God, the time of the universal reign and prevalence of ignorance, idolatry and wickedness among the Gentile nations, this time was now fulfilled. The time of the church's minority, when her members were children in bondage under the elements of the world, was now come to an end. The time that was to intervene betwixt the giving of the promises and predictions concerning the Messiah, and their accomplishment, in his appearance in our world, is now run out. The seventy weeks mentioned in Daniel are now nearly fulfilled. This is the information which Christ intimated to the people, when he declared to them, The time is fulfilled. Had Christ's hearers understood and believed this information, they would have recognized it as good tidings of great joy unto all people, and would have received the blessed announcement, as Simeon and Anna did, with rapturous delight and triumph.

In the text Christ gives his hearers further information; and the kingdom of God is at hand. He did not only assure them of the expiration of the foregoing season, and of the abolition of the ceremonial dispensation which belonged to it; but he unfolds to them the nature of the time which was now aproaching, and the happy state into which the church should be immediately introduced. "The kingdom of God is at hand." The gospel kingdom is now to be erected, the Son of God has now come out of Bethlehem Ephratah, and has begun his glorious work for the redemption of men. This work he will completely finish, go to the Father, commission his ambassadors, send his Spirit to the church, establish his kingdom of grace, purity and peace, gather multitudes into its fellowship, and preserve it in the world till the end of time. All this information to Israel is included in Christ's declaration; "and the kingdom of God is at hand." By this intimation, Christ assured the Jews, that the Lord was now about to fulfil that prediction, "And in the days of these kings shall the God of heaven set up a kingdom, which shall never be destroyed." This important information to Israel was the principal scope of John's message. "In those days came John the Baptist, preaching in the wilderness of Judea, and saying, Repent ye, for the kingdom of heaven is at hand." It was the great design of the early part of Christ's public ministry, which is evident from our text. It was the substance of the Apostles ministry, while their Master was on earth; for from him they received this command, "And as ye go, preach, saying, The kingdom of heaven is at hand." Of the ministry of the seventy whom Jesus also sent out, this was likewise the chief end; for their commission is expressed in those words, "And say unto them, The kingdom of God is come nigh unto you." The design of all those intimations which were made to the Jews, by those different persons, at different times, was to bring them to be properly affected with those great and astonishing alterations, which God was about to introduce.

The text represents also the duty to which the professors of religion were called, at that important season; repent ye, and believe the gospel. Be ye exercised in a suitableness to the great change that is to be accomplished. Prepare yourselves for the coming of this kingdom. Be ye ready to welcome, with all your heart, the glorious deliverance. Repent ye. Humble yourselves on account of your sin, confess to the Lord your transgressions, and look to his mercy for the pardon of your iniquity. Believe the gospel.

Give credit to the truths that are now revealed to you, concerning the coming of the Just One, and that kingdom that he will set up. Embrace the new revelation that is to be made, and submit to the new dispensation which is to be established. By the exercise of faith and repentance, be ye prepared for those great and astonishing operations which God will accomplish before your eyes.

These are the things to which the text did primarily refer. I mean however to apply it to the things that are coming to pass in our own day; to the coming of the kingdom of God in the glory of her millennial state, and the following considerations will warrant us, in that application.

Many portions of the old Testament, which predict the church's deliverance and prosperity, and which express the duty of her members concerning them, apply primarily to the Jews' return from Babylon, find their accomplishment, in a higher sense, at the erection of the christian dispensation, shall be fulfilled also when the church shall enter on her latter day glory, and will be completely perfected in heaven. Our text may also be applied in the same way. There are three periods of the church to which the text, in all its parts, may be applied; the erection of the gospel dispensation, the introduction of the millennium, and the season immediately preceding the consummation of all things. Since the ancient Prophets declared to the people the approach of the church's deliverance from Babylon, and called them to those duties which were suited to that time; since Christ and his Apostles announced to the Jews the coming of the kingdom of God in her gospel form, and enjoined on them duties answerable to their state; since it will be the duty and the employment of Christ's servants who shall exist in the church, near the end of the world, to apply those very words to the circumstances in which they shall be placed, saying to the people, All time is now to be fulfilled, and the kingdom of glory will soon be manifested, repent ye and believe the gospel, that ye may be prepared for judgment and eternity;

it certainly must be the duty of gospel ministers, living near the church's deliverance, and her latter day glory, to carry this message to mankind, by an application of the text to their present situation, The time is fulfilled, and the kingdom of God is at hand: repent ye, and believe the gospel.

The meaning of scripture is one; but, as no prophecy of the scripture is of any private interpretation, it is no breach of that unity to apply them to situations and circumstances which correspond exactly with the church's condition, for which they were primarily intended. The denial of this would deprive the saints and the church of God of much of that direction and comfort which the scriptures are calculated to give, and which they receive from them. Though there will be no change of dispensation at the latter day glory, as there was at Christ's appearance in our world; yet there shall be such a glorious alteration in the church's condition, as will warrant the application of the text, to the things which will come to pass in those days. Some scriptures which refer to the church in one state of things, may, by fair analogy and unforced accommodation, be applied, with equal propriety, to the church's condition which is of the same description. At the coming of Christ, a long and dreary time was fulfilled, the kingdom of God did come, and men were called to prepare for that joyful event by repentance, and faith in the gospel; so at the church's entry into her millennial rest, a most dreadful period of darkness shall come to an end, the kingdom of God will gloriously appear, and the members of the church must study preparation for the solemn season, by the exercise of repentance toward God, and faith toward our Lord Jesus Christ. From these considerations we are authorized to apply Christ's words in the text, to the present circumstances and expectations of the church. If it was the work of John, of Jesus, of the twelve, and of the seventy, at the death of the legal dispensation and at the birth of the gospel economy, to proclaim to men, the time is fulfilled, and the kingdom of God is at hand, repent ye and believe the gospel; it must also be the duty of gospel ministers, when the decease of Antichrist and the revival of the church are approaching, to sound an alarm on God's holy mountain, by applying these very words to the glorious events.

In the text, according to this application of it, there is information concerning the ending of that time which God has fixed, and which prophecy has revealed to us. "The time is fulfilled." The time that must run out before the church can be delivered from her enemies, and advanced to her state of peace and purity. The time that must come to an end before that dreadful and systematic corruption of christianity, which has been set on foot and maintained by the antichristian church, shall be put down. The time during which the Gentiles shall possess the court that is without the temple, and tread under foot the holy city. This time shall then be fulfilled.

We have information also concerning the deliverance of the true church, which is the object of all this opposition, and which is depressed during its continuance; "the kingdom of God is at hand." The time of the church's universal extent, glory, purity and peace is fast approaching. The time when the predictions and promises, which relate to the church's happy condition in this world, shall be accomplished, is drawing near. The season of the Lord's answering the prayers of his saints, who have incessantly cried at his throne of grace, "Thy kingdom come," is at hand.

The duty of christians, who are living in the near prospect of this deliverance, is also contained in the text; repent ye, and believe the gospel. Be ye diligently exercised in the duties of religion, and prepare to meet thy God, O Israel.

In discoursing on this subject, it is proposed,

I. To mention some of those times that shall be fulfilled at Antichrist's fall, and at the church's entering on her millennial rest.

II. To describe the happy condition of the church during the thousand years of her glory and purity.

III. To mention some of those signs which indicate this blessed condition of the church to be at hand.

IV. To make some remarks on the prophetic numbers of Daniel and John, which are contained in the one thousand three hundred and five and thirty days, mentioned at the end of Daniel's prophecy.

V. To speak of the Christian's duty at this important crisis, Repent ye, and believe the gospel.

I. I am now to mention some of those times that shall be fulfilled at Antichrist's fall, and at the church's entering into her millennial rest. This time, considered as a period of duration, is one; but, viewed in its characters, may be many. By mentioning some of its most prominent features, I am now to describe it.

1. The time for exercising secular tyranny over the nations shall then be fulfilled. Scripture predictions warrant us to believe, that the general complexion of civil government, till the time of the church's deliverance shall arive, will be tyrannical. "Daniel's explanation of Nebuchadnezzar's vision of the great image, chap. ii. 36; his own vision of the four Beasts, chap. vii. 2; and John's visions in his revelation, clearly indicate this state of things. The vision of the King and that of the Prophet relate to the same time, and to the same objects, and comprehend a period of nearly 2500 years, from the days of Nebuchadnezzar when the visions were seen, to the downfal of the Roman Beast, both secular and ecclesiastic. The golden head of the image was the Babylonian Monarchy, which was then in existence; the silver breast and arms, the empire of the Medes and Persians; the brazen belly and thighs, the kingdom of the Greeks; and the iron legs, and the feet and toes of iron and clay, the empire of the Romans. The stone which was cut out without hands, and smote the image on its feet, that

part of it which represented the Roman empire in its decline, and then became a great mountain, which filled the whole earth, symbolized the kingdom of Christ. In Daniel's vision, he saw the same objects represented by other symbols. The golden head is, in this vision, represented by a lion with eagle's wings; the silver breast and arms, by a bear, with three ribs in the mouth of it; the belly and thighs of brass, by a leopard having on the back of it four wings of a fowl; and the legs and feet and toes are symbolized by an extraordinary beast, which was dreadful and terrible, and strong exceedingly, having great iron teeth, devouring and breaking in pieces, and stamping the residue with the feet of it. This beast was different from all those who were before it, as it appeared at first in the form of a republic, having ten horns, answering to the ten toes which were upon the image, in the king's vision. These frighful representations exhibit their arbitrary and tyrannical government over their own subjects, and their unjust cruelty to one another. Every one of them destroyed the empire of the one that existed before him, till all was swallowed up by the devouring beast of Rome. Before John saw his visions, three of those beasts had perished from the earth, and the fourth, or Roman beast, was at the height of its power, and therefore, his predictions were entirely confined to it. Of this beast we have an account, Rev. xiii. 1—8. John saw it rise out of the sea, having seven heads and ten horns, and upon his horns ten crowns, and upon its heads the name of blasphemy. It was like a leopard, its feet like those of a bear, and its mouth like that of a lion. It made war on the saints, and overcame them; and power was given to it over all kindreds and tongues and nations. In John's revelations, we find a description also of his ten horns. "And the ten horns which thou sawest are ten kings, which have no kingdom as yet; but receive power as kings one hour with the beast. These have one mind, and shall give their power and strength to the beast. These shall make war with the

Lamb." Rev. xvii. 12—14. These ten horns are identified with the Roman beast, and their government is arbitrary and tyrannical like his own. All these predictions inform the church of God, that during this long period, the men who shall have in their hands the government of the nations, shall, in their administrations, resemble the lion, the bear, the leopard, and a great monstrous beast, having seven heads, and ten crowned horns. The history of mankind represents a full accomplishment of these predictions. It clearly proves that the prophetic picture has not been overcharged, and that every feature in it has been completely fulfilled. Although the violence of the storm may be somewhat broken, as the beast is now in its old age; yet the same spirit continues to actuate it, and as far as its power will permit, the same courses are pursued. The rulers of the earth in general, disregarding the rights, liberties, property, and lives of their subjects, and seeking their own aggrandizement, and the establishment of their own dynasties, pursue such measures of rule, by oppression, persecution and war, as render their administration, a source of calamity to men. Were we to take a view of some of the collateral visions in those books, as that of the ram and the he-goat, Dan. viii. the devastations by Alexander's successors, Dan. xi. or the ravages of the Saracens and Turks, Rev. ix. it would farther demonstrate that this long and dreary season, from the beginning to the end of it, has been, and will continue to be, a time of injustice, cruelty, tyranny and blood. But shall this sword devour forever? No; the time of its slaughter shall be fulfilled. As the predictions concerning the existence and prevalence of those beasts upon the earth have been exactly accomplished; so the prophecies concerning their destruction shall be fulfilled in their season. The time will come when the stone "which was cut out without hands, shall smite the image upon his feet of iron and clay, and break them to pieces; when the iron, the clay, the brass, the silver, and the gold shall be broken in pieces together, and become as the chaff of the summer threshing floor, and the wind shall carry them away, that no place shall be found for them; and when the stone that smote the image shall become a great mountain, and shall fill the whole earth." The time will come, "when he that leadeth into captivity, shall go into captivity, and when he that killeth with the sword, shall be killed with the sword." Then the time of secular tyranny over the nations shall be fulfilled.

2. The time of Antichrist's reign in the earth, and his power over the church of God shall then be fulfilled. The existence and dominion of this enemy are foretold by the prophet Daniel, and by the apostles Paul and John. "I considered the horns," says Daniel, chap. vii. 8, 21, 25, "and, behold, there came up among them another little horn, before whom there were three of the first horns plucked up by the roots, and, behold, in this horn were eyes like the eyes of a man, and a mouth speaking great things." "I beheld, and the same horn made war with the saints, and prevailed against them. And he shall speak great words against the Most High, and shall wear out the saints of the Most High, and think to change times and laws; and they shall be given into his hand, until a time, and times, and the dividing of time." "Let no man deceive you by any means," says Paul, 2 Thes. ii. 3, 4. "for that day shall not come, except there come a falling away first, and that man of sin be revealed, the son of perdition; who opposeth and exalteth himself above all that is called god, or that is worshipped; so that he, as God, sitteth in the temple of God, shewing himself that he is God." Two of John's visions of this ecclesiastic beast of Rome must also be mentioned. He saw it rise, chap. xiii. 11. "And I beheld another beast coming up out of the earth; and he had two horns like a lamb, and he spake as a dragon. And he exerciseth all the power of the first beast before him, and causeth the earth, and them that dwell therein, to worship the first beast, whose deadly wound was healed." At the

beginning of the seventeenth chapter, another vision of the same object is recorded. "So he carried me away in the spirit into the wilderness, and I saw a woman sit on a scarlet-coloured beast, full of names of blasphemy, having seven heads and ten horns. And the woman was arrayed in purple and scarlet colour, and decked with gold and precious stones and pearls, having a golden cup in her hand full of abominations, and filthiness of her fornications. And upon her forehead was a name written, Mystery, Babylon the great, the mother of harlots and abominations of the earth. And I saw the woman drunken with the blood of the saints, and with the blood of the martyrs of Jesus; and when I saw her I wondered with great admiration." These are some of the predictions concerning the rise, character, and conduct of the ecclesiastic beast of Rome. The history of the Romish church, and of the Popes who have been at the head of it, clearly shews, that, black and frightful as the representations are, they have not been exaggerated. It is not necessary that every feature in this prophetic drawing, should be found in this beast at his childhood, nor that they should all prominently appear in him in his old age; sufficient certainly it must be, if they are all applicable to him, in the course of his life and actings. His rising up among the ten kingdoms into which the Roman empire was divided, his pretending to be Christ's vicegerent, and the sovereign head of the church on earth, his claim to infallibility in his doctrines and decisions, and his usurping and exercising a power to depose and set up kings, and to dispose of crowns and kingdoms, fulfil many of the things that are contained in these predictions. His hatred of the true church of Christ, the thundering anathemas and violent edicts which he has denounced against her, the cruel persecutions which he has carried on against her members, the dreadful massacres of them which he has contrived and executed, and the bloody wars, which have been undertaken and conducted among the nations, on his account, or at his instigation, verify the application to him of other parts of those prophecies. The worldly wisdom which has been exercised in forming the antichristian system, the profound policy and dissimulation with which its affairs have been conducted, the support which it has received from the kings of the earth, and the wealth it has gathered from its subjects in every land, prove the same thing. The blasphemous names which he has taken to himself and bestowed on others, the abominable idolatry which he has introduced and established, the gross errors which he has contrived and propagated, the hateful immoralities which he has practised, countenanced, indulged, and pretended to pardon, demonstrate, that, as face answers to face in a glass, so do these inspired predictions delineate the abominations of popery. But the time of his existence and power shall be fulfilled. Those Prophets whom the Lord employed to foretell his rise and reign, predict also his fall and ruin. Concerning the little horn, these are Daniel's words, chap. vii. 26. " But the judgment shall sit and they shall take away his dominion, to consume and destroy it unto the end." The words of Paul are equally expressive, 2 Thes. ii. 8, "And then shall that wicked be revealed, whom the Lord shall consume with the spirit of his mouth, and shall destroy with the brightness of his coming." In many parts of his visions, John saw the fall of this system presented to him; one of them only shall be mentioned. "And a mighty Angel took up a stone like a great milstone, and cast it into the sea, saying: Thus with violence shall that great city Babylon be thrown down, and shall be found no more at all." Such shall be the end of that lamb-horned, but dragon-mouthed beast, which has successfully propagated error, idolatry, immorality, and persecution on the earth.

3. The time of the church's low condition shall then be fulfilled. If the wicked walk on every side when the vilest of men are exalted; it is not to be supposed that Christ's church, at such a time as this can enjoy prosperity and peace.

While both the secular and ecclesiastic beasts exist, practise, and prosper, the interests of true religion must be low, and the outward condition of its professors must be afflicted. Accordingly, Scripture predictions represent the followers of the Lamb, at this season, to be "troubled on every side, yet not distressed; perplexed, but not in despair; persecuted, but not forsaken; cast down, but not destroyed." In these predictions the church is represented by the symbol of a woman, who, having been lately delivered of a man-child, and now is persecuted by the dragon, flies into the wilderness, with two wings of a great eagle. There she is nourished by her Lord, for a time, and times, and half a time; and is preserved in safety from the face of the serpent. She is also symbolized by two witnesses, prophesying a thousand two hundred and threescore days, clothed in sackcloth, wearing the black garb of mourners, and the coarse raiment of poverty. She is exhibited as under the power of the little horn, which prevailed against her. She is exposed, through this long season, to the wrath and cruelty of the secular and ecclesiastic beasts, which have all along endeavoured, according to their ability and opportunities, to cut her off from the earth. "And the dragon was wroth with the woman, and went to make war with the remnant of her seed, which keep the commandments of God, and have the testimony of Jesus Christ." The history of the Christian church, under this period, verifies sufficiently those predictions, which foretell her state. During this time, the number of her members has been small, their outward situation, by the oppression and persecution of the enemy, has been uncomfortable, and her testimony, for the glory of her Lord, has been disregarded and opposed. But out of this trying condition, they shall be delivered. "And the kingdom," says Daniel, after he had spoken of the judgment that shall sit upon the horn, chap. vii. 27. "And the kingdom, and dominion, and the greatness of the kingdom under the whole heaven, shall be given to the people of the saints of the most High, whose kingdom is an everlasting kingdom, and all dominion shall serve and obey him." When she shall be delivered from the power of the little horn, when she shall emerge from the wilderness, finish her witnessing prophecy, and put off her sackcloth, she shall hear that call; " And a voice came out of the throne, saying, Praise our God, all ye his servants, and ye that fear him, both small and great." This call she will instantly obey; for John immediately " heard as it were the voice of a great multitude, and as the voice of many waters, and as the voice of mighty thunderings, saying, Alleluia, for the Lord God omnipotent reigneth. Let us be glad and rejoice, and give honour to him for the marriage of the Lamb is come, and his wife hath made herself ready," Rev. xix. 6, 7, 8. At that joyful season, the days of the church's mourning shall be ended.

4. The time of Satan's deceiving the nations shall then be fulfilled. The Scriptures assure us, " that this enemy walketh about as a roaring lion seeking whom he may devour." Having accomplished the fall of man, by seducing our first parents, ever since that mournful event, he has reigned over the far greater part of the human family. On this account he is designated " the god of this world, the prince of the power of the air, the spirit that now worketh in the children of disobedience." As he assaults individuals with temptations, that he may direct their personal conduct, and lead them to sin; so he deceives them as societies and nations, by influencing their public deliberations, that he may regulate their important measures. With great success did he deceive the Gentile nations, when he tempted them to erect and submit to tyrannical governments, and gross idolatry which have so long prevailed among them. With equal success did he deceive those nominal christians, who were the principal instruments, in his hand, of forming the Christian religion after the model of the pagan mythology. When this transformation had far advanced, he next

deceived the nations, by the revelation of the man of sin, "whose coming was after the working of Satan, with all power, and signs, and lying wonders; and with all deceivableness of unrighteousness, in them that perish." After the creation of this kingdom of darkness, he continued to deceive the nations, by causing their rulers to give their power to the beast, and their subjects to wonder after him, to countenance his idolatries, to practise his immoralities, to believe his false doctrines, and to submit to his antichristian power. He is still deceiving the nations, by making them cleave to superstition, error, and various kinds of iniquities which abound among them. The last deception which he shall practice on the nations, prior to the church's deliverance, will be when that prediction shall be accomplished; "And I saw three unclean spirits like frogs come out of the mouth of the dragon, and out of the mouth of the beast, and out of the mouth of the false prophet: For they are the spirits of devils working miracles, which go forth unto the kings of the earth, and of the whole world, to gather them to the battle of that great day of God Almighty," Rev. xvi. 13, 14. The issue of that battle is declared, chap. xix. 20. "And the beast was taken, and with him the false prophet that wrought miracles before him:—These both were cast alive into a lake of fire burning with brimstone." This time shall be fulfilled, when the church shall enter into her millennial rest; according to that vision at the beginning of chap. xx. "And I saw an Angel come down from heaven, having the key of the bottomless pit, and a great chain in his hand. And he laid hold on the dragon, that old serpent, which is the Devil, and Satan, and bound him a thousand years." An attempt to renew his work, at the expiration of the millennium, will end in his entire and everlasting ruin. "And the devil that deceived them was cast into the lake of fire and brimstone, where the beast and the false prophet are, and shall be tormented day and night for ever and ever," ver. 10.

5. The time of the Jews' dispersion among the nations, and of their enmity at Christianity shall then be fulfilled. When the Jewish nation, had crucified the Lord of glory; when they had rejected his gospel, the preaching of which began at Jerusalem; when they had persecuted his apostles and followers; and when they had, in all these things, done despite unto the Spirit of grace; then was that prediction accomplished on them, "My God will cast them away, because they did not hearken to him; and they shall be wanderers among the nations," Hos. ix. 17. At the destruction of Jerusalem, by the Roman army, their final and complete dispersion was accomplished. Then were they entirely driven from their own land, scattered through the earth, and placed in such a situation as rendered it impossible for them to observe their Father's religion, to which they still professed to adhere. Then our Savour's predictions were literally fulfilled on them; "And they shall fall by the edge of the sword, and be led away captive into all nations; and Jerusalem shall be trodden down of the Gentiles, until the times of the Gentiles be fulfilled," Luke xxi. 24. Continuing in their dispersion in all quarters of the globe to this day, they are still attached to the typical and abrogated system of Moses, ignorant of their Messiah, to whom all their prophets did witness, and enemies to his religion which brings glory to God in the highest, peace to the earth, and good will to men. Being without Christ, in their present state of unbelief, they are also aliens from the commonwealth of Israel, and strangers from the covenants of promise, having no hope, and without God in the world. But shall the seed of Jacob abide still in unbelief, and remain as a people, in this low and disorganised state for ever? The inspired predictions assure us of their recovery. After Hosea had feelingly predicted their dispersion, "The children of Israel shall abide many days without a King, and without a Prince, and without a sacrifice, and without an image, and without an ephod, and without ter-

aphim:" He triumphantly adds; "Afterward shall the children of Israel return, and seek the Lord their God, and David their King, and shall fear the Lord and his goodness in the latter days," chap. iii. 4, 5. As the Jews have never obtained any deliverance, that can be considered to be a fulfilment of this prediction; as it is Jesus Christ, who is David's son and Lord, both his root and offspring, whom they shall seek; as it is to take place after a long and mournful state of deprivation of privileges, of freedom from gross idolatry, and of suffering many privations; and as the period of its accomplishment is the latter days, we may be assured that this blessed deliverance of Israel is yet to come. Daniel also predicts this important deliverance, and gives a character of the time at which it shall be effected; "And at that time shall Michael stand up, the great prince that standeth for the children of thy people, and there shall be a time of trouble, such as never was since there was a nation even to that same time; and at that time thy people shall be delivered, every one that shall be found written in the book." "And I heard the man clothed in linen, who was upon the waters of the river, when he held up his right hand and his left hand unto heaven, and sware by him that liveth for and ever, that it shall be for a time, and times, and an half; and when he shall have accomplished to scatter the power of the holy people, all these things shall be fulfilled," chap. xii. 1, 7. The time of unexampled trouble, ver. 1. signifies the judgments at the last scene of the vials of wrath; and the Lord's accomplishing to scatter the power of the holy people, ver. 7. signifies his bringing his judgments on the Jews, both in their dispersion and unbelief, to a final termination. The complete effusion of the vials, and the restoration of Israel are so connected, that in verse 1st, the former is mentioned as a description of the time when the latter shall take place, and, in verse 7th, the latter is stated as a mark of the season, when all these things, belonging to the last plagues, shall be fulfilled. Paul likewise predicts the restoration of the Jews, and states the means by which it shall be brought about; "Even so have these also now not believed, that through your mercy they also may obtain mercy," Rom. xi. 3. The New Testament Scriptures, and the preaching of the gospel, which belong to the mercy of the Gentiles, shall then be made effectual, by the power of the Holy Spirit, for recovering the posterity of Jacob.

6. The time of executing God's judgments on his incorrigible enemies, shall then be fulfilled. Although those calamities are foretold by Daniel, in the triumph of the stone in Nebuchadnezzar's vision, in the judgment that shall sit on the fourth beast and the little horn, in Daniel's own vision, and in his words which are quoted above; yet they are more particularly represented in the visions of John. In them we have more general, and more particular, accounts of those judgments—At the sounding of the seventh trumpet, or the coming of the third and last wo, it is said. "And the nations were angry, and thy wrath is come. And there were lightnings, and voices, and thundering, and an earthquake, and great hail," chap. xi. 18, 19. A most affecting description is given of the same objects, at the opening of the sixth seal, chap. vi. The same awful scene is exhibited to our view, in the vision of the vintage, at the end of chap. xiv. These fearful calamities, are also disclosed in the proclamation of the angel, and in the lamentations of those who beheld them, chap. xviii. These fearful plagues are further represented by the dreadful battle, an account of which is given in the eleven verses, with which the xix chapter is concluded. But the most complete and systematic exhibition of them is found in John's vision of the seven angels, who had the seven last plagues in which was filled up the wrath of God. He saw them, in chap. xv. prepared for their work, coming out of the temple in glorious attire, and receiving seven golden vials full of the wrath of God, who liveth for ever and ever. In chap. xvi. he heard them receive their commission to "go and pour out the vials of the wrath of God upon the earth;"

and he saw them execute their office, in pouring, by an orderly succession, these vials of wrath on the objects, which were destined to receive their contents. Now, all those sad calamities shall be wholly overpast, when the church shall be introduced into her prosperous state. No dregs of the vials of wrath shall remain to be poured out, no voices or thunders shall be heard, no lightnings shall be seen, no concussions of the earthquake shall be felt, no drops of the wine of the fierceness of his wrath shall be tasted, and no part of the shower of the terrible hail shall fall, when the church has entered into her millennial rest. Immediately before this happy time, the operations of the wine press shall be finished, the battle will be fought, and the cries of lamentation and sorrow shall be heard no more; for, at Antichrist's fall, the season of judgments shall be ended.

7. The time of heathenish idolatry, and mahometan delusions shall then be fulfilled. Many parts of the earth are still subjected to the darkness of paganism; and many portions of the globe are deluded by the absurdities of Mahomet. The pagan idolatry and many of its rites, are so irrational and cruel, and the dogmas, and pretended revelations of the Prophet of the East, are so gross and ridiculous, that the subjection of any part of mankind to those systems, furnishes a mournful proof of the darkness and corruption of human nature. But this time also shall come to an end. The universal conversion of the nations to Chrstianity, which the predictions warrant us to expect, assures us that heathenish and mahometan lands shall be enlightened. The voices in heaven proclaimed, "The kingdoms of this world are become the kingdoms of our Lord and of his Christ" Rev. xi. 15. Of the song of Moses and the Lamb, this is a part; "For all nations shall come and worship before thee; for thy judgments are made manifest." Rev. xv. 4. The objects mentioned, are the kingdoms of this world, and all nations. Of them it is said, they shall become the kingdoms of the Lord and his Christ, and shall come and worship before him. The

time at which this great change shall be produced on the nations is also revealed in the prophecy. At the end of the third wo, and when God's judgments are made manifest, by the execution of them. This exactly agrees with the time of Antichrist's fall, and the commencement of the churches prosperity. The manifestation of God's judgments in their execution does not only characterize the time of their change, but states also a special mean by which it shall be effected. The complete execution of those judgments will roll stumbling blocks out of the way of their turning to the Lord, and will so enlighten their minds and impress their hearts, as to dispose them to embrace that religion, of the truth of which, these plagues are a clear confirmation. Pagans and Mahometans constitute the greater part of the world's population, and occupy the larger portion of its surface. It is impossible, therefore, that those predictions can be accomplished, if pagans and mahometans continue in their ignorance and unbelief. The Old Testament contains predictions equally clear, concerning the extent of the kingdom of grace, in the latter days. "Arise, O God, judge the earth; for thou shalt inherit all nations," Psal. lxxxii. 8. To inherit all nations as their Creator, Preserver, and moral Governor, is the necessary and essential prerogative of God; it, therefore, cannot be the matter of a prophecy. But to inherit all nations as the God of salvation, he being their God, and they becoming his people through the Mediator, must be the thing intended. Isaiah, when speaking of the mountain of the Lord's house being established in the top of the mountains, and exalted above the hills, in the last days, adds, "And all nations shall flow unto it," Isa. ii. 2. Since there are predictions in both the Old and the New Testaments, which foretell the conversion of all nations to the true religion; we may be assured that the time is coming, when heathen and mahometan nations shall turn to the Lord, and when the idolatry of the one, and the delusions of the other shall perish from the earth. Besides, the Old Testament mentions places, whose inhabitants shall turn to the Lord; places which necessarily direct our minds to Pagans and Mahometans. Assyria, Ethiopia and Egypt, are the nations to which I allude. Of two of them it is said, " Whom the Lord of hosts shall bless, saying, Blessed be Egypt my people, and Assyria the work of my hands, and Israel mine inheritance," Isa. xix. 25. Of the other it is foretold, " And Ethiopia shall stretch out her hands unto God." Psa. lxviii. 31. Since those nations whose conversion is here predicted, are inhabited at present by Pagans and Mahometans, have we not abundant warrant to believe, that, at the latter day, the idolatry of the one, and the delusions of the other shall come to an end.

8. The time of the mixture of Antichristian corruptions with the constitutions and administrations of Protestant churches shall then be fulfilled. In the prophecies of Jeremiah, concerning ancient Babylon, which was a type of popery, called Babylon the great, we have the following prediction, which applies to the latter, as well as to the former; " Behold I am against thee, O destroying mountain, saith the Lord, which destroyest all the earth; and I will stretch out my hand upon thee, and roll thee down from the rocks, and will make thee a burnt mountain. And they shall not take a stone of thee for a corner, nor a stone for foundations, but thou shalt be desolate for ever, saith the Lord." chap. li. 25, 26. After the destroying mountain of Babylon the great, has begun to shake and totter, and after the fire of Divine judgments has begun to consume its foundations, which commenced at the protestant reformation, stones have been taken from her both for corners and foundations, in other ecclesiastical buildings. But after the Lord has completely rolled down this mountain from the rocks, and, by the fire of his judgments, at the time of the end, has reduced it to a burnt mountain, none shall ever after, take from it a stone for a corner, or a stone for foundations. The former of these, is the present situation of protestant established

churches. They have broken off from Babylon the great, but as she is not yet rolled down from the rocks, and made a burnt mountain in her final destruction, they have taken from her stones for corners and foundations. At the reformation the protestant churches retained, both in their constitutions and administrations, many corruptions which had their origin in popery. Instead of improving by time, experience, and the increase of light, they have in some things, rather deteriorated. The popish corruptions which have been admitted into the constitutions of these churches, the popish errors which are found in the doctrine of many of their members, the superstitious rites and ceremonies which belong to their modes of worship, the antichristian laws which regulate their government, and the popish usages which are practised in their exercising the censures of God's house, are dishonouring to Christ, hurtful to the church, and grieving to serious Christians, both within and without their communion. These corruptions will continue, there is too much reason to fear, till Antichrist's fall; but when that system shall be rolled down from the rocks, and be made a burnt mountain, and when the church's millennial glory shall commence, every one of them, with the system which gave them existence, shall pass away for ever.

9. The time of mournful divisions among the professors of true Christianity shall then be fulfilled. The popish corruptions, which are retained in the churches of the reformation, have been the cause of those divisions, which have subsisted between them and the different bodies of dissenters. Conscientious scruples about approving and practising those corruptions, on the one side; and a refusing to let them go, or a rigorous enforcement of them on the other, have caused the greater number of those separations from the churches that are established by law. As these corruptions have been the cause of divisions between dissenters and the churches on the establishment; so they have also been the mean of producing that disunion which subsists

among the dissenting bodies themselves. The different views which have been entertained of the corruptions of popish origin, by the bodies of dissenters, have divided the dissenting churches from one another. The contention between dissenting bodies has sometimes been so sharp, and the alienation of affection from one another so great, that they appear to have had more aversion at the cause of one another, than at the corruptions of that church, from which they have separated, on nearly the same grounds. In popish corruptions, by which the truths, institutions, and laws, of Christ, are opposed, it is very easy to find the mournful cause of all those divisions which exist among the professors of true Christianity. By those contentions and separations, the reformed churches at the presentt ime, are like God's ancient people. "When Manasseh was against Ephraim, and Ephraim against Manasseh, and they together were against Judah." But this mournful time shall also be fulfilled. The causes of division shall be removed at Antichrist's fall, and the divisions themselves shall cease. When the church shall enter into her millennial state, she shall enjoy that precious and most desirable blessing, which is contained in that promise; "The envy also of Ephraim shall depart, and the adversaries of Judah shall be cut off, Ephraim shall not envy Judah, and Judah shall not vex Ephraim." Isa. xi. 13.

10. The time of unprovoked and offensive war, with all its ruinous effects, shall then be fulfilled. The whole time of Antichrist's reign, especially the season of pouring out the vials, has been, and will continue to be, a time either of actual war, or of the nations' groaning under its dismal consequences. Wars which have been undertaken and prosecuted, as they generally are, to gratify the resentment, to humour the pride, to increase the power, the territories, and the wealth of the rulers of the earth; to support false religion, to prevent the progress of reformation, and to fasten the yoke of oppression more firmly on the necks of

the human race, bring great guilt upon a nation, and expose its population, of whatever degree, to the Almighty's wrath. In the formation of armies, great injustice is done to the young and the simple, by depriving them of their liberty, tearing them from their relations, and inuring them to habits of irreligion and profligacy. In the march of armies, injustice is often done to the persons and property of the peaceable inhabitants, and destruction marks their path. In the operations of armies, in battles, or in besieging fortified towns, what desolations are brought on the dwellings of men, what sufferings are endured by those who survive and pine away in their wounds, what blood is shed, how many lives are taken away, and what a multitude of immortal souls is dispatched in a moment to God's tribunal! By the reduction of armies, which have been collected for the purposes of war, it often happens that those who have, by a military life, contracted habits of wickedness, spread among those, in whose neighbourhood they take up their residence, the poisonous infection of the most degrading and destructive immoralities. These wars have a mournful tendency to increase national antipathies, to augment national debt and public burdens, and to give to the dispositions and character of men a ferocious quality. Besides all this, how dreadful is that responsibility to the God of the whole earth, which those who contrive and determine, and those who voluntarily conduct such shocking scenes, bring upon themselves! But this dark and dismal time of war, of blood and slaughter among the nations, shall be fulfilled, when the kingdom of God shall come. At that happy time, that prediction shall be accomplished; "And he shall judge among the nations, and shall rebuke many people," by pouring on them the vials of his wrath, "and they shall beat their swords into plough-shares, and their spears into pruning-hooks; and nation shall not lift up sword against nation, neither shall they learn war any more." Isai. ii. 4.

11. The time of Antichrist's wickedness, and of God's long-

suffering patience with those transgressors, shall then be fulfilled. As the judgments of the vials are the punishment of sin, the time of their effusion, as well as the times going before, will be a season of abounding iniquity. When the Lord brought on the inhabitants of the earth, the waters of the flood; "all flesh had corrupted his way upon the earth." When Judah was carried into captivity in Babylon, "the chief of the priests and the people, had transgressed very much, after the abominations of the heathen, and had polluted the house of the Lord, which he had hallowed at Jerusalem. They had mocked God's messengers, and despised his words, and misused his prophets, until the wrath of the Lord arose against his people, till there was no remedy." When the Lord brought on Jerusalem a sore and enduring destruction, "the Jews had killed the Lord Jesus and their own prophets, and had persecuted the apostles, they pleased not God, and were contrary to all men; forbidding them to speak to the Gentiles that they might be saved, and, having thus filled up their sin, Divine wrath came upon them to the uttermost." As it was in the days of Noah, of Zedekiah, and of the Jews; so shall it be with Antichrist, at the effusion of the vials. The angel of the waters said, when the third vial was poured out, "Thou art righteous, O Lord, which art, and wast, and shalt be, because thou hast judged thus. For they have shed the blood of saints and prophets, and thou hast given them blood to drink; for they are worthy." At the effusion of the fourth vial, it is said, "And men blasphemed God, who hath power over these plagues; and repented not, to give him glory." A similar account of them is given, when the fifth vial is poured out. "And they blasphemed the God of heaven, because of their pains and their sores, and repented not of their deeds." When the vials are finished, the same account is given. "And men blasphemed God because of the plague of the hail; for the plague thereof was exceeding great." While the vials are in progress they continue to blaspheme, and when the last, and most destructive judgment is inflicted, they, like some hardened criminals among men, shall die and go into perdition, in the very act of blaspheming the God of heaven. Long has Divine patience and forbearance been exercised with that woman, whose name is, Mystery, Babylon the great, the mother of harlots, and abominations of the earth; but the time of her wickedness, and of his long-suffering with her shall then come to an end. The Angel who came out from the altar, and had power over fire, shall then utter a loud cry to him who had the sharp sickle, saying, "Thrust in thy sharp sickle, and gather the clusters of the vine of the earth; for her grapes are fully ripe. And the Angel thrust in his sickle into the earth, and gathered the vine of the earth, and cast it into the great wine-press of the wrath of God. And the wine-press was trodden without the city, and blood came out of the wine-press even unto the horse-bridles, by the space of a thousand and six hundred furlongs.

12. The time of the Lord's trying the faith and the patience of his saints shall then be fulfilled. After John had seen the vision of the beast that rose up out of the sea, after he had foretold his persecution of the saints, and had predicted his destruction, he adds, "Here is the patience and faith of the saints," Rev. xiii. 10. Here is the object which shall exercise the saints' patience in sufferings, and their faith in the threatening of his ruin, and in the promise of their deliverance from his power. During the time of Antichrist's reign, their patience and faith shall be tried; but, when he shall fall, that season of trial shall come to an end. The nature of the Antichristian system, the violence with which it has been maintained and propagated, the sufferings of the church under its power, its long continuance, the threatenings concerning its destruction, the promises of the church's deliverance, and the deferring of this hope, furnish abundant opportunities for the trial and exercise of the patience and faith of the saints. The system of popery

being of such a nature, as to corrupt and oppose every thing in true Christianity, its precious doctrines, its simple and spiritual worship, its Divinely instituted government, and its pure and purifying censures, the existence of it in the world must be a great trial to the saints' faith and patience. The introduction, the support, and the propagation of it, having been carried on with such a high hand, and with such extraordinary success, must also have been, and still continues to be, a distressing trial to their faith and patience. The church's sufferings in various ways, under its power and cruelty, have so severely tried their patience, that nothing but a strong faith in God through Christ by the promise, could have prevented the saints from fainting, in this day of adversity. The long continuance of this system adds to the church's trials. It is not like the twenty years of the Ark's partial concealment in Kirjath-jearim, which all the house of Israel accounted long, and lamented after the Lord; nor is it like the captivity of Judah for seventy years in Babylon; but it must continue, from its beginning to its ending, for the long period of one thousand, two hundred, and sixty years. The threatenings of its destruction, and the promises of the church's deliverance and prosperity furnish ample scope for exercising the faith of the saints. In the fulfilment of those predictions there may be such seeming delays, as will induce them to cry, in the language of the souls under the altar; "How long, O Lord, holy and true, dost thou not judge and avenge our blood, on them that dwell on the earth." The Lord assures his people of deliverance, he intimates to them the manner of its approach, he unfolds their duty, and he declares their happiness and danger in those words; "Behold, I come as a thief. Blessed is he that watcheth," in the exercise of faith and patience, "and keepeth his garments, lest he walk naked, and they see his shame." When Antichrist shall fall, and when the church shall come out of her wilderness, and shall enter into her pleasant land; then shall all those trials of her faith and patience come to an end; and she shall say, Thou hast tried me, and hast brought me forth as gold.

I shall now conclude this discourse, by mentioning some reflections, from this part of the subject.

1. From it we may be convinced of the Divine authority of the Holy Scriptures, and the truth of the Christian religion. I have had occasion to mention several prophecies, which are contained both in the Old and New Testaments, and men have both seen and felt their accomplishment. The book that contains them must have been written, therefore, by the inspiration of God. While the Lord claims it as his peculiar prerogative, "to declare the end from the beginning, and from ancient times the things that are not yet done;" He challenges all pretenders to deity, to "shew the things that are to come hereafter, that we may see that ye are gods." Has Jesus plainly foretold the dreadful slaughter of the Jews, their complete dispersion among all nations, and the occupation of their city and land by a different people; has the Lord, by the component parts of a human body, represented to Nebuchadnezzar in a dream, the four secular monarchies, which should successively rule and oppress the earth, for more than two thousand years, and enabled Daniel to recover and explain the vision; did he double and diversify the vision, in another vision, concerning the same objects, to Daniel himself; did Paul foretell the rise, the character, and the conduct of the man of sin, the son of perdition; did John predict the rise, continuance, and actings of both the secular and the ecclesiastic beasts of Rome; have all these predictions been circumstantially fulfilled, in the providence of God; and has nothing that has the smallest resemblance to these prophecies, ever appeared among men, since the world began, and, on account of all this, are not we abundantly warranted, to believe, to embrace, and to improve the Bible, as an infallible

revelation of the will of God to men for their everlasting salvation? To these prophetic witnesses to the truth of divine revelation, it were easy to bring forward many more, especially those which relate to the Redeemer himself, and to his gospel kingdom; but those which have fallen in our way, when prosecuting this part of the subject, may certainly be sufficient. O, how irrational and inveterate must that enmity at the Scriptures be, which compels men to wrestle through those obstacles that are mercifully placed to obstruct their entry and progress on the rugged and destructive paths of infidelity! What abundant reason have those who believe the Scripture, to rejoice in the word of God; and to say every time they peruse it, Speak Lord, for thy servant heareth!

2. This subject informs us, that it is vain to expect either temporal or spiritual prosperity among the nations, till the word of God, and the gospel of our salvation, shall, by the power of the Spirit, subdue the earth. Till the weapons of our warfare, which are not carnal, but mighty through God, pull down the strong holds, cast down imaginations, and every high thing that exalteth itself against the knowledge of God, and bring into captivity every thought to the obedience of Christ, the hurt of the Redeemer's church will not be recovered. All these times, that have been mentioned, are fulfilled only at Antichrist's fall; it must, therefore, be evident, that while he exists, they will be continued. Evil and perilous times shall be the lot of the church and of the world, while the popish system remains on the earth. Till the dawning of the millennial day of light and purity, times of a quality opposite to those cannot be introduced. The defiling nature of popish errors, idolatry, and immoralities renders this impossible. The execution of judgments on men will be continued, while that system exists; and, therefore, permanent prosperity and peace, either in our temporal or spiritual concerns, are not to be expected. One scene of judgments shall come to

an end, only to make way for the entrance of another equally distressing; the truth of which is now verified in our sorrowful experience. Let us beware then of seeking or promising to ourselves great things; for the Lord will yet bring evil upon all flesh.

3. The absolute need which the nations have of civil, as well as ecclesiastic reformation, is evident from this subject. In the xiii. chap. of the Revelation, we have an account, first of the secular, and afterwards of the ecclesiastic beast. They both united in blaspheming God, in corrupting religion, in persecuting the church, and in enslaving men. Popish abominations could neither have prevailed nor continued, without the support of the secular beast; nor could he have maintained his tyranny over the nations, without the aid of the ecclesiastic monster. They have gone hand in hand, they have co-operated cordially in the execution of their unrighteous designs, and have, by the unity of their operation, succeeded in their gigantic enterprises. The corruption, therefore, exists both in the civil and ecclesiastic departments. At the fall of Antichrist, civil and ecclesiastic rulers shall cordially unite, in promoting the good of nations, and the prosperity of the church. When the Jews returned from Babylon, there were, at one time, Joshua the high priest, and Zerubbabel the governor of Judah; and, at another time, Ezra the priest, and Nehemiah the Tirshatha, who co-operated cordially in the work of the Lord. It shall be so, when the church is delivered from Babylon the great. At that blessed day, ministerial "Angels shall fly in the midst of heaven, having the everlasting gospel to preach, to the men that dwell on the earth;" and the ten horns which John saw upon the Beast, "these shall hate the whore, and shall make her desolate, and naked, and shall eat her flesh, and burn her with fire."

4. From this subject we may clearly see the nature of the times in which we live. Antichrist still exists, many of

the Kings of the earth are yet giving their power to him, and every part of his system is in full operation All the times which shall be fulfilled, and come to an end at his downfal, must, therefore, be still in existence. We live in times of secular tyranny, and ecclesiastic domination; when the church is low, when Satan is deceiving the nations, and when the Jews are yet scattered and in unbelief; while God's judgments are falling upon men, and heathenish idolatry and mahometan delusions are prevailing in the world; when the reformed churches are defiled with popish corruptions,* and when divisions prevail among the lovers of the Lord; when the nations are still learning war, when God's patience is still exercised to his Antichristian enemies, and the church's fiery trial is continued. Both as to sin and danger, our times, therefore, must be evil and perilous. Christians have great reason to adopt the exercise of David, "Yea, in the shadow of thy wings will I make my refuge, until these calamities be overpast," Psal. lvii. 1. and to say with Paul, "I go bound in the Spirit unto Jerusalem, not knowing the things that shall befall me there; save that the Holy Ghost witnesseth in every city, saying, That bonds and afflictions abide me." Let us all endeavour to add with him; "But none of these things move me, neither count I my life dear to

* The civil Magistrate's supremacy over the church, the consubstantiation of the Lutherans, the antiscriptural episcopacy of some of them, the civil power of the Lords spiritual, their formal liturgies, their kneeling at the Lord's supper, their using the cross in baptism, the antichristian law of patronage, their substituting pecuniary fines instead of public censure, their deposing from the ministry some of Christ's faithful servants, and their acquital or slightly censuring those who have taught the most pernicious errors, are some of the popish corruptions with which Protestant churches are contaminated. These are the evils which assimilate our churches to the popish system, and not the personal imperfections of some weak and uninformed protestants; imperfections which have been of late most injudiciously contrasted with the constitutional abominations of the church of Rome.

myself, so that I may finish my course with joy," Acts xx. 22, 23, 24.

5. That popery is ruinous to mankind, and will prove the destruction of those civil dynasties which support it, must be very evident from this part of our subject. It is ruinous to the temporal, but especially to the spiritual concerns of men. It detains them under slavery, and spiritual bondage. It keeps them in ignorance, it involves them in idolatry, it encourages them in sin, and it exposes them to Divine wrath. The threatening which is denounced against its incorrigible votaries is dreadful. "And the third angel followed them, saying with a loud voice, If any man worship the beast and his image, and receive his mark in his forehead, or in his right hand; The same shall drink of the wine of the wrath of God, which is poured out without mixture into the cup of his indignation; and he shall be tormented with fire and brimstone in the presence of the holy angels, and in the presence of the Lamb," Rev. xiv. 9, 10. It will be the ruin also of the kings of the earth. "And I beheld then," says Daniel, "because of the voice of the great words which the horn spake; I beheld even till the beast was slain, and his body destroyed, and given to the burning flame." It is not said, because of the voice of the great words which the horn spake, it was broken and destroyed; but because of its words the beast himself out of which it grew, the Roman secular tyranny by which it was supported, was slain, and his body, with this horn in its head, and all the other horns among which it sprung up, was destroyed, and given to the burning flame. The blasphemy, idolatry, and wickedness of popery shall be the cause of ruin to the kings on the Roman earth. With this prediction, several parts of John's visions do perfectly agree. The capture and destruction of the beast and the false prophet, or Antichrist who was signified by the little horn, are not the only effects of the great battle between Christ and Antichrist; but we are assured, that, as the

consequence of it, "All the fowls that fly in the midst of heaven shall eat the flesh of kings, and the flesh of captains, and the flesh of mighty men, and the flesh of horses and of them that sit on them, and the flesh of all men, both free and bond, both small and great," Rev. xix. 18. All this misery shall overtake them because they have been partakers of her sin, and shall, therefore, receive of her plagues, Rev. xviii. 4. Their great sin against God, and the principal cause of his judgment on them, are found in their giving their power to the beast, by making the existence and profession of his religion, essential to their civil constitutions, and its support and prosperity a chief object of their administrations. By the one, they devote their power to Antichrist; by the other, they exercise it for him. Oh, that the kings and judges of the earth knew their sin and danger, in giving any countenance or support to this mystery of inquity; and that they would "Kiss the Son, lest he be angry and they perish from the way, when his wrath is kindled but a little; Blessed are all they that put their trust in him."

6. The happiness of the church in her millennial state, is evident also from what has been said. Since all these times shall then be fulfilled, the church will be prosperous and joyful. Those things which shall be removed at that time being the very bane of all civil and religious society; the church must be blessed, when they shall depart from the earth. None of those evils shall then remain; for Antichrist having fallen, their time shall be fulfilled. The happiness of the church, on the removal of those evils, must be very great. There shall be nothing to hurt nor to destroy in all God's holy mountain. Though this is only the negative part of her prosperous state, yet it is both necessary and very considerable. The spiritual salvation of believers comprehends a deliverance from those evils to which they were exposed, as well as the enjoyment of those blessings to which they are advanced; so shall it be with the church at that happy

time. She shall be delivered from those evils under which she has long groaned, and shall be advanced to the enjoyment of those blessed privileges which are provided for her. The part of the subject which has been discussed, unfolds the former; and that part of it on which we are next to enter, may give us some view of the latter. In the mean time, let us seriously consider the church's distress and danger while those evils are continued, and her happiness and safety when the time of their existence shall be fulfilled; tnat by searching the Scriptures, meditation, prayer and religious c nference, we may be prepared both for suffering according to the Divine will, and for rejoicing at the prospect of those glorious things which are spoken concerning the city of God.

AN

INQUIRY

INTO

THE CHURCH'S HAPPY CONDITION DURING THE THOUSAND YEARS OF HER GLORY AND PURITY.

DISCOURSE II.

MARK i. 15.—*The time is fulfilled. and the kingdom of God is at hand: repent ye, and believe the gospel.*

WHEN men are agreed about the reality and general nature of any object, and are not of the same mind as to some material circumstances and qualities which belong to it; their descriptions of it may be very different, and even contradictory. The one class will be disposed to give such an account of it, as does not sufficiently embrace and exhibit its excellencies; and the other may carry their description of it above its real properties. The low representation of the former, may excite the other to exaggerate its glory; and the lofty account of the latter, may influence those of a different opinion, to underrate its value and importance. It has happened thus with the church's blessed condition, which the Scriptures warrant us to expect, at the latter day. While some writers have given a description which is too grand, by ascribing to it things which the Scriptures do not reveal; the representations of some others have certainly been too general, and have fallen short of its great and peculiar splendour. In conducting an inquiry into this subject, it were desirable, could it be attained, to avoid extremes, either on the one side, or on the other.

Having endeavoured to mention, in the foregoing discourse, some of those times which shall be fulfilled at Antichrist's fall, and at the church's entry into her millennial rest. I am now,

II. To describe the church's happy condition, during the thousand years of her glory and purity.

1. The holy Scriptures and the preaching of the gospel, accompanied with Divine influence, shall then be enjoyed by all nations. These are blessings which are absolutely necessary, and infinitely precious. To what other cause than the enjoyment of them, can we ascribe the religious, moral, ecclesiastic and political improvement of the nations who are previleged with their light? Whence is it, that most absurd and abominable systems of religion, gross and abounding immoralities, and civil and ecclesiastic tyranny prevail in popish, pagan and mahometan nations, where those blessings are not enjoyed? Scripture prophecy fortells the spread of spiritual light among all nations, by bestowing on them the Divine word and a preached gospel. This was intimated to Abraham and frequently renewed, "In thee, and in thy seed shall all the nations of the earth be blessed." Isaiah and Micah predict, that "in the last days, all nations shall flow into the mountain of the Lord's house." Isaiah and Habakkuk say, "That the knowledge of the Lord, and the knowledge of the glory of the Lord, shall fill the earth, as the waters cover the sea." Our Saviour declares, "And this gospel of the kingdom shall be preached in all the world, for a witness unto all nations, and then shall the end come." Matth. xxiv. 14. In John's visions, it is dedeclared that "The kingdoms of this world shall become the kingdoms of our Lord and of his Christ;" that "All nations shall come and worship before the Lord;" and that at the beginning of the church's prosperity, the saints who shall

praise the Lord for that deliverance, shall be, "of all nations, and kindred, and people, and tongues." What less than these enjoyments, can be imported, in that prophetic description of this happy time, by the symbols of Satan's binding, the saints' sitting on thrones, reigning with Christ, and the wicked not living, all for the long period of a thousand years. When the word of God, and the preaching of the gospel were put in operation, after Christ's ascension, they were the mean of enlightening many in every land to which they were sent, in the knowledge of the only way of salvation, through our Lord Jesus Christ. When the gospel had thus begun to illuminate mankind, nothing did prevent it from enlightening the whole world, but that dreadful corruption of Christianity, which ended in the establishment of the Antichristian apostacy, which has prevailed so universally, and has continued so long. The change produced on the nations by the labours of the apostles, and of those who succeeded them, cannot be considered as a full accomplishment of those predictions. It was but a part of the nations that was then enlightened, it was only a small number of their population that submitted to Christ's sceptre, the church was still exposed to persecution, the time of its continuance was of short duration, and it took place before the existence of the grand apostacy; all which is inconsistent with a full accomplishment of those predictions. We are, therefore, warranted to expect this complete fulfilment, at the time of the destruction of that wicked one, whose rise and reign prevented gospel light from spreading, and filled the world with darkness. The change which the nations shall undergo, according to those predictions, is of such a nature, that nothing but the Divine word, and the preaching of the gospel, with the Holy Ghost sent down from heaven, can accomplish it. What else can be the mean of causing them to be blessed in Christ, the seed of Abraham; to be filled with the knowledge of the glory of the Lord, to flow into the mountain of the Lord's house; to become the kingdom of the Lord and of his Christ; to come and worship before the Lord; to celebrate his praise, in a triumphant song, for his marvellous works in their deliverance; and to sit on thrones, and reign with Christ, a thousand years. We may, therefore, most confidently expect, that after the fall of Antichrist, all nations shall be enlightened with the word of God, and the preaching of the gospel; "when the light of the moon shall be as the light of the sun, and the light of the sun shall be seven fold, as the light of seven days."

2. The kingdom of Christ shall then be erected, and the pure worship of God shall be celebrated, in all nations Of their enjoyment of the Divine word, and a preached gospel, these shall be the happy effects. The kingdom of Christ shall be established in the nations; for, at that time, they shall become the kingdoms of our Lord, and of his Christ. This honour and blessedness of the nations are imported in those parts of the church's song; "Thou hast taken to thee thy great power, and hast reigned—Now is come salvation and strength, and the kingdom of our God, and the power of his Christ, for the accuser of our brethren is cast down."—"The marriage of the Lamb is come, and his wife hath made herself ready" By the grand solemnities of a coronation, and by those of a royal marriage, is represented to us, the erection of the gospel kingdom among the nations. The instituted worship of God in Christ shall then be celebrated in all the earth. All nations, says the blessed company standing on the sea of glass, with the harps of God in their hands, "All nations shall come and worship before thee." With a view to this happy season, Malachi, the last of the prophets, utters, in the name of the Lord, this delightful prediction: "For from the rising of the sun even unto the going down of the same, my name shall be great among the Gentiles; and in every place incense shall be offered unto my name, and a pure offering; for my name shall be great among the heathen, saith the Lord of hosts." The parties who are concerned in this prediction are the Gentiles and the heathen,

nations who had not been called by his name. The employment in which they should engage is stated; offering incense to the Lord's name, and a pure offering. The spiritual worship of the gospel church is signified by the incense and the pure offering, words taken from the services of the old dispensation, under which the prediction was given. The extent of these religious services among the nations is also affirmed. From the rising of the sun even to the going down of the same, and in every place. On all the nations that are enlightened with the light of the natural sun, on them shall the Sun of Righteousness arise, with healing in his wings. The reason of this glorious change in the condition and religious employment of the nations is also contained in the prediction. For my name shall be great, by the revelation of the word, and the preaching of the gospel, accompanied with the Spirit's influence, For my name shall be great among the heathen, saith the Lord of hosts. The nature of that worship which all nations shall then give to the Lord may be distinctly learned from this prophecy. As the burning of sweet incense before the Lord, and the bringing offerings unto him, were of Divine institution under the law; so the acts of religious worship, which shall then prevail in all the earth, shall not be those which originate in human device, but shall be such as are instituted in the word of God. The kingdom of Christ is erected, and Divine worship is celebrated in a land, when its inhabitants cordially receive and publicly profess the faith of Jesus; when they acknowledge themselves to be taught by him as their infallible Prophet, to be redeemed by him as their great high Priest, and to be governed by him as their mediatorial King; when they set up among them the instituted administrators of Divine ordinances, pastors and teachers, helps and governments; and when they carefully observe all the ordinances of Divine worship, and submit to all the administrations of his spiritual kingdom which he has established among them. This shall be the blessedness of all lands, when the kingdom of God shall come.

3. God's ancient people, the Jews, shall then flourish in the midst of the earth, as an holy and prosperous Christian church. The apostle Paul assures us, in the 11th chapter of his epistle to the Romans, that though they have been diminished, yet they shall in due time enjoy a fulness; though they have been cast away, there will also be a receiving of them, which shall be to themselves and others as life from the dead; though they were broken off, they shall again be grafted into their own olive; though God has shut them up in unbelief, he will yet have mercy upon them; though blindness in part has happened unto them, yet all Israel shall be saved, and there shall come out of Sion the Deliverer, and shall turn away ungodliness from Jacob; and though the Gentiles have obtained mercy through their unbelief, yet the time shall come, when, through the mercy of the Gentiles, they also shall obtain mercy. It is quite natural to suppose, that, when the darkness and misery of their rejection shall be finished, and when the happy time of their spiritual illumination in the knowledge of Christ shall come, their faith in his gospel which they have rejected, their love to his person whom they have blasphemed, their obedience to his law which they have transgressed, their zeal for his glory which they have profaned, their admiration of his grace which they have despised, and their attachment to his religion which they have opposed, will be altogether singular and extraordinary. At that time they shall obtain a complete deliverance from all the misery which is contained in the threatening, that, for so long a period, has been executed on them. Their unbelief and dispersion, with the evils which proceed from both, comprehend it all. They shall be delivered from their unbelief, when Christ shall come by his word and ordinances, applied to them by the Holy Ghost, giving them a sight of their guilt and danger, manifesting himself savingly to them, implanting faith in

their hearts, enabling them to believe in him, taking away all their sins, and giving them an interest in the blessing of Abraham, in the sure mercies of David. This work, the glorious Deliverer will carry on among them, till the body of that people shall repent and believe the gospel, and till it grow up to a national salvation. They shall also be restored to their own land, and continue as a blessing to the rest of the nations, in the midst of the earth, till the end of the world. Our Saviour's prediction, concerning the Jews, contains two proofs of their return to their own land. "They shall be led away captive into all nations." The dispersion of the Jews is, therefore, a part of their punishment. - When the Deliverer rescues them from their misery, he must turn back their captivity like streams in the south, otherwise the seed of Israel, after they are turned to the Lord, must still exist under a very conspicuous part of their calamity. Our Saviour adds, "And Jerusalem shall be trodden down of the Gentiles, until the times of the Gentiles shall be fulfilled." The times of the Gentiles are fulfilled at Antichrist's fall, at the conversion of the Jews, and at the church's entry into her state of glory and purity. This prediction, therefore, assures us that from the destruction of Jerusalem, in the first century of Christianity, to the fall of Antichrist in the nineteenth, Jerusalem and the holy land shall be possessed by a people, very different from the seed of Abraham; and we have seen the exact fulfilment of the awful threatening. But this prediction further assures us, that when the times of the Gentiles shall be fulfilled, none of them shall any more tread down Jerusalem; but they shall surrender it to its former possessors. If the Jews do not return to their own land at the latter day, then the Gentiles must continue to tread it down, or occupy it, after their times are fulfilled, which is contrary to our Saviour's prediction. The words of Daniel prove the same thing; "And when he shall have accomplished to scatter the power of the holy people, all these things shall be fulfilled." God's scattering the power of the holy people signifies the period of their dispersion, when they continued without a king, without a prince, without a sacrifice, and without an ephod. His accomplishing to scatter their power must therefore mean, their being gathered to their own land, and existing in it as an independent power, both in their civil and ecclesiastic capacities. Without this, the scattering of their power cannot be accomplished, or brought to an end. Many Old Testament prophecies fortell such a return of Israel to their own land, as would never be followed with a general dispersion, for a partial captivity. "Thou shall no more be termed forsaken, neither shall thy land any more be termed desolate." Isai. lxii. 4. "Then shall Jerusalem be holy, and there shall no strangers pass through her any more. Judah shall dwell for ever, and Jerusalem from generation to generation." 17, 20. "And I will plant them upon their land, and they shall no more be pulled up out of their land which I have given them, saith the Lord thy God." Amos. ix. 15. "And men shall dwell in it, and there shall be no more utter destruction; but Jerusalem shall be safely inhabited." Zech. xiv. 11. These predictions assure us that the Jews shall enjoy a glorious return to their own land, after which they shall never be forsaken, nor their land become desolate, after which no strangers shall pass through them any more; after which they shall never be pulled up out of their land; and after which there shall be no more utter destruction, but Jerusalem shall be safely inhabited. As the Jews, in their present state, are deprived of all the privileges which those predictions promise them; there must be another restoration to their own land contemplated in those prophecies; a restoration, after which they shall possess it till the end of time. We are, therefore, authorized to believe, that when the Lord shall set up an ensign for the nations, on the gospel millennial day, "He shall assemble the outcasts of Israel, and gather together the dispersed of Judah from the four corners of the earth." Isai. xi. 12.

4. Great purity shall be obtained both in the civil and ecclesiastic constitutions and administrations which shall then exist in the world. In that happy time, Christ's church, both Jew and Gentile, " shall suck the breasts of kings, and they shall be their nursing fathers, and their queens their nursing mothers;" and " the kings of the earth shall then hate the whore;" they will therefore discountenance false religion, and encourage and support that which is of God. The restraints which shall be laid on Satan, the overthrow of popery, the spread and knowledge of the holy Scriptures, and the great increase of true religion and morality will all contribute to accelerate and confirm civil and ecclesiastic reformation. An important change shall then take place in the constitutions and administrations of civil governors. Their constitutions shall no more be popish, prelatic, or erastian. The conditions on which they shall receive their power, will not oblige them to maintain, and to be members of popish and superstitious churches. An antichristian supremacy over the church shall no longer be given to them, or exercised by them as an inherent or constitutional right of their crowns. The exercise of their power in their administrations shall be of such a kind, that the ravenous beasts of the desert, or the horns of a monstrous animal shall not, in any sense, be the appropriate symbols of their government. In the dispositions and conduct of the kings of the earth, at that glorious season, the words of David shall, in a high degree, be verified;—He that ruleth over men must be just, ruling in the fear of the Lord. And he shall be as the light of the morning when the sun riseth, even a morning without clouds; as the tender grass springing out of the earth, by clear shining after rain." 2 Sam. xxiii. 3, 4. As the millennial nations shall become " an habitation of justice," so the Christian churches, at that time, shall be " a mountain of holiness." The church's doctrine shall then be evangelical and sound, her worship pure and spiritual, her government shall be regulated by the word of God, and her censures shall be

administered according to the Divine rule, for the glory of God, the good of the offender, and the edification of all. Every thing in the house of the God of heaven shall then be conducted according to his law. Popery, error, superstition, persecution, infringing on the rights of the christian people, divisions, and abounding immoralities, shall be, to the milennial churches, former things, that have passed away. At that time the Redeemer's kingdom shall look forth as the morning, fair as the moon, clear as the sun, and terrible as an army with banners. The saints shall have in their hands all civil and ecclesiastic rule. After the judgment shall sit on the beast and the little horn, "the kingdom and dominion, and the greatness of the kingdom under the whole heavens," all kinds of authority through the whole earth, shall be given to the people of the saints of the Most High." In John's vision of the same object, he saw them on thrones, living and reigning with Christ a thousand years. Filled with the knowledge of God and love to his glory, conscious of their obligations to act according to the law and the testimony, and studious of the welfare of men, and the good of the church, such rulers, though they had the opportunity, could not have the inclination to pervert the government, either in church or state.

5. Universal and permanent peace, both among the nations of the earth, and the churches of the living God shall then be maintained. It is mentioned as the effect of all nations flowing into the mountain of the Lord's house, when it shall be established on the top of the mountains, and exalted above the hills, that "they shall beat their swords into plowshares, and their spears into pruning hooks; nation shall not lift up sword against nation, neither shall they learn war any more." This vision is doubled, in the prophecy of Micah, because the thing is true, and shall be fulfilled in its season. This prophecy cannot be accomplished while there exists on the earth any of the four secular monarchies, which were represented in Nebuchadnezzar's vision of the great

image, and in Daniel's vision of the four beasts; the time of its accomplishment, therefore, is yet to come. The distinguishing mark of the season of its fulfilment is stated by Isaiah and Micah in the following words; "And many nations shall go and say, come ye, and let us go up to the mountain of the Lord, to the house of the God of Jacob; and he will teach us of his ways, and we will walk in his paths; for out of Zion shall go forth the law, and the word of the Lord from Jerusalem." These words, which can only receive their accomplishment when the scriptures and the preaching of the gospel shall enter all nations, as they characterize the time, so they state the grand instrumental cause of this universal tranquillity. The purifying and peaceful influence of the gospel, on the rulers and inhabitants of the earth, shall be so powerful, as will dispose them to live peaceably with one another, to love us brethren, and to seek the universal happiness of mankind. When the nations are enjoying comfortable peace, the churches of Christ will not be distracted with religious discord. Ecclesiastic peace as well as national tranquillity is predicted for that happy time. "The wolf also shall dwell with the lamb, and the leopard shall lie down with the kid, and the calf, and the young lion, and the fatling, together; and a little child shall lead them; and the cow and the bear shall feed; their young ones shall lie down together; and the lion shall eat straw like the ox; And the sucking child shall play on the hole of the asp, and the weaned child shall put his hand on the cockatrice den;" To show that those astonishing symbols of harmony and peace, relate to ecclesiastic concord, it is added; "They shall not hurt nor destroy in all my holy mountain." To shew likewise that the instrumental cause of ecclesiastic peace is the very same with that which produces national tranquillity, it is also said, "For the earth shall be full of the knowledge of the Lord, as the waters cover the sea." Isa. xi. 6, 7, 8, 9. We are not to imagine that those prophetic symbols are hyperbolical exaggerations; for there shall be many instances of persons of different situations, principles and dispositions, joyfully harmonizing at the church's deliverance, which will be as great a mystery in grace, as the things mentioned in the prophecy, were they to happen, would be a wonder in nature.

6. The number of the world's inhabitants, and of God's saints shall then be exceeding great. The inhabitants of the earth shall then be greatly increased. This is evident both from scripture and reason. It is confirmed by the word of God. The scriptures assure us, that when a people are the objects of Divine favour, and when they endeavour to walk in his way, that a great increase of their number is a blessing, which he will bestow on them. After the rebels were destroyed in the wilderness, their posterity, to whom the promise of enjoying Canaan was accomplished, obtained this blessing; for to them Moses said in the plains of Moab, "The Lord your God hath multiplied you, and, behold, ye are this day as the stars of heaven for multitude." Deut. i. 10. God's promise to his people is, "I will multiply them, and they shall not be few," Jer. xxx. 19. To Israel does Ezekiel say, chap. xxxvi. 38. "As the holy flock, as the flock of Jerusalem in her solemn feasts; so shall the waste cities be filled with flocks of men; and they shall know that I am the Lord." The ordinary inhabitants of the waste cities should resemble, in their number, those who were in Jerusalem, when the greater part of Israel's male population repaired to it, at their solemn feasts. If the Lord acted in this manner to Israel, when they enjoyed his favour and walked in his fear; we have abundant reason to conclude, that the nations of the earth, when they shall be converted to Christianity, and shall live according to the doctrines and precepts of the true religion, will then enjoy an extraordinary increase of inhabitants. The principles of reason, as well as the promises of God, support this conclusion. If secular misrule, ecclesiastic oppression, cruel wars, famines, pestilences, destructive immoralities, and such other things that

waste a nation's population, shall then be banished from the earth; it must follow as a necessary consequence, that mankind will rapidly increase, and that their number will become exceedingly great on the face of the earth. But the number of the saints also will be greatly increased. The visions that John had of the millennial church, and which he records at the middle of the seventh chapter, and at the beginning of chap. ninteenth, clearly shew that the saints, in those days of blessedness and rest, shall be very many. In the former of those representations, his words are the following; ver. 9. "After this," the vision of the sealed company, "After this I beheld, and, lo, a great multitude, which no man could number, of all nations, and kindreds, and people, and tongues, stood before the throne, and before the Lamb, clothed with white robes, and palms in their hands." While the saints who were sealed, are represented by an hundred forty and four thousand, those who shall rise up in the church at the beginning of the millenium, are said to be a great multitude, which no man can number, out of all the nations of the earth. As far as an hundred and forty and four thousand are exceeded by a number that baffles all human calculations; so far shall the number of the saints, at that time, exceed the number of them, who have lived in the age before it. In the other vision, their number is mentioned in the first and sixth verses. "And after these things," the lamentations of the kings and merchants of the earth, and the captains and sailors on the sea, over Babylon's fall. "After these things, I heard a great voice of much people in heaven, saying, Alleluia; And I heard as it were the voice of a great multitude, and as the voice of mighty waters, and as the voice of mighty thunderings, saying, Alleluia; for the Lord God omnipotent reigneth." How loud, how solemn and majestic is the voice, of this much people, of this great multitude, who shall then worship and praise the Omnipotent God! The number of the singers may be understood from the loudness, the solemnity, and the majesty of the song. As all nations shall know and profess the true religion, there is reason to conclude that a great part of their inhabitants shall be true believers, and the saints of the most High God. Since all nations shall be enlightened with the word, and the preaching of the gospel; and since every land shall possess a greater number of real christians, than ever existed in any land, of equal population, since the world began; the number of the saints, at that time must be altogether inconceivable. Such, however, is the idea of their number, which the scriptures warrant us to entertain. How glorious and frequent must conversion then be! The apostolic success will then be revived, continued, and exceeded. As it is difficult, in the present state of the world and the church, to be a christian in reality; so it will be difficult, in the condition to which the church and the world shall then be advanced, for any person to be an hypocrite, or a nominal professor.

7. The holiness, the religious exercises and blessedness of the saints shall then be of the most exalted order. As their number shall be exceeding great, their spiritual attainment shall be very high. John's two visions of the millennial church referred to already, for an account of their number, must be considered again, that from them we may learn the nature of their exercises and attainments. As they warrant us to conclude that their number will be immense; so they prove that their religious enjoyments will be extraordinary. In those visions, their dignity, their position, their attire, their employment, their associates, and their entertainment, are disclosed to our view. When the glorified church was after this revealed to John, her dignity was marked by her relation to her Lord, "Come hither, and I will shew thee the Bride, the Lamb's Wife;" so when the millennial church is set before him, her dignity is asserted in the same manner, "The marriage of the Lamb is come, and his Wife hath made herself ready." Though true believers, and the church of God have, in

every age, enjoyed this blessed relation to their spiritual Husband; yet there shall be such peculiar solemnities attending the celebration of the nuptials betwixt Christ and his millennial church, as will reflect on him the highest glory, and confer on her the greatest dignity.—They shall also have an honourable position. John saw them "standing before the throne, and before the Lamb." Having been brought to the throne of grace, they stand before him who sits on it, and before him who is in the midst of it, they approach to God through the blood of the Lamb, they devote themselves to God and the Lamb, and depend, for all Divine influence, on "the seven Spirits who are before his throne." John saw them also "in heaven." Delivered from the earth, and belonging to the spiritual heavens, they shall enjoy that state of the church, which bears the nearest resemblance to the heavenly glory, that can be attained in this world.—When presented to John in vision, "they were clothed with white robes, and had palms in their hands. And to her it was granted that she should be arrayed in fine linen, clean and white; for the fine linen is the righteousness of saints." Delivered from the defilements of the foregoing season, they now appear in a holy and purified state. Clothed with Christ's righteousness, adorned with regenerating grace, and beautified with the sanctification of the Spirit, they are justified in their state, faithful in their profession, and holy in their conversation. They also had palms in their hands, as the symbols of victory over Satan, Antichrist, and all other enemies, as the tokens of triumph before God and the Lamb, and as the ensigns of peace and rest in their blessed condition. —They are also described from their employment: They are not engaged in fasting, mourning and girding with sackcloth, for the Bridegroom is with them, and the days of their mourning are ended. They "cried with a loud voice, saying, Salvation to our God, and unto the Lamb." The great voice of much people said, "Alleluia, Salvation, and glory, and honour, and power, unto the Lord our God. And again they said, Alleluia." "And the four and twenty Elders, and the four beasts, fell down and worshipped God that sat on the throne, saying, Amen, Alleluia." The voice of the gréat multitude cried, "Alleluia, for the Lord God Omnipotent reigneth; Let us be glad and rejoice, and give honour to him, for the marriage of the Lamb is come." In these words, there are four periods of singing. The first, when the judgments of God against his enemies shall assume a decisive aspect; the second, when they shall be terminated in the destruction of Antichrist; the third, when the millennial church shall visibly appear; and the fourth, when she shall obtain consistence and stability. The reasons assigned for these different songs demonstrate the truth of this statement. The first is sung for the Lord's judging the great whore; at the second, her smoke rose up for ever and ever; the third is connected with a call to the servants of the Lord, and to those who fear his name, to engage in the work of praise; and the fourth song is sung on account of the reign of the Lord God Omnipotent, and the coming of the marriage of the Lamb. These exercises of religion are of the highest kind, thankfulness, praise, adoration, extolling and magnifying God. These characterize their spiritual frame from which they proceed, their holy thoughts of which they are the expression, and their heavenly deportment to which they have a powerful tendency to excite them. These exercises of praise demonstrate their bright views of the Divine glory, their deep impressions of his omnipotent power, their high sense of his mercy and faithfulness, and their vehement desire to shew forth the praises of him, who, both in their conversion, and in the church's deliverance, has called them out of darkness into his marvellous light.—They will have active associates in this delighful work. They will not sing alone. "And all the Angels stood round about the throne, and about the Elders and the four Beasts, and fell before the throne on their faces, and worshipped God; saying, Amen, Blessing, and glory, and wisdom, and thanksgiving, and honour, and power, and might, be unto our God for ever and ever, Amen." If the holy Angels participate in the joy of the rising millennial church, the spirits of just men made perfect will neither be ignorant nor silent; on this solemn occasion.—Their entertainment is also mentioned; for they shall be "called to the marriage supper of the Lamb." The spiritual provision, on which the saints have all along been fed, shall be administered to them in a plentiful manner. On Christ the bread of life, on the fulness of the blessing of salvation shall they delightfully feed. With the marrow, and fatness, and goodness of God's house they shall be satisfied abundantly. For the exercise of grace in their hearts, for the performance of religious duties, for the habitual nature of their spiritual frames and enjoyments, for the holiness of their conversations, for their love and usefulness to one another, and for the extent of their knowledge, the strength of their faith, the fervour of their love, the warmth of their zeal, and their comfortable death, the millennial saints will be peculiarly eminent.

8. The goodness of God to the world's inhabitants, in the provision he will make for their bodily wants, shall then be great and astonishing. Among the many judgments which the Lord has threatened to inflict on nations for their iniquities, famine is frequently mentioned; and among the calamities which guilty nations have suffered on account of their transgressions, it has often been one of the most distressing. In the holy scripture, and in the common history of mankind, we have abundant information, that famine has often been God's rod, and the punishment of his rebellious creatures. Many of the sins of men, which provoke the Lord to anger against them, consist in their abuse of his outward goodness; it must, therefore, be a righteous dispensation of providence, to deprive men, in a greater or lesser degree, of that Divine bounty which they use to his dishonour. Besides, for the sin of despising the bread of life, God's

taking away from us the bread that perisheth, is a most appropriate correction. But when that happy time shall come, in which the greater part of men shall be holy, those promises shall be accomplished; "I will also save you from all your uncleannesses; and I will call for the corn, and will increase it, and lay no famine upon you. And I will multiply the fruit of the tree, and the increase of the field, and ye shall receive no more reproach of famine among the heathen." Ezek. xxxvi. 29, 30. One of Sion's songs, in which the inspired writer contemplates the latter day glory, contains the following words; "O, let the nations be glad, and sing for joy. Let the people praise thee, O God; let all the people praise thee. Then shall the earth yield her increase, and God, even our own God, will bless us. God shall bless us; and all the ends of the earth shall fear him." Psalm lxvii. If the Lord caused the land of Canaan, small as it was, to yield abundant sustenance for the many thousands of Israel, when their ways pleased him; shall he not make the earth bring forth and bud, and yield fruits of increase for the comfortable support of its inhabitants, when it shall be filled with the knowledge of his glory, as the waters cover the sea. Of the millennial church it shall be said, "Blessed of the Lord shall be their land, for the precious things of heaven, for the dew, and for the deep that coucheth beneath, And for the precious fruits brought forth by the sun, and for the precious things put forth by the moon, and for the precious things of the ancient mountains, and for the precious things of the lasting hills; And for the precious things of the earth, and the fulness thereof; and for the good will of Him that dwelt in the bush;"—all those blessings shall come upon the head of those generations of the righteous, and on the top of the head of those whose lot shall fall in that day, when the kingdoms of this world shall become the kingdoms of our Lord and of his Christ. God's goodness to them in temporal things will bear some proportion to his peculiar kindness to them in spiritual things.

Living under the influence of the gospel, walking in the fear of the Lord, and enjoying the comforts of the Holy Ghost; "they shall eat in plenty, and be satisfied, and praise the name of the Lord their God, who hath dealt wonderously with them; and they shall never be ashamed."

9. The glory of God shall then be illustriously manifested to the children of men. When the wilderness and the solitary place shall be glad for them; when the desert shall rejoice and blossom as the rose; when it shall blossom abundantly, and rejoice even with joy and singing; and when the glory of Lebanon shall be given unto it, and the excellency of Carmel and Sharon, which shall be the spiritual condition of all the nations at the latter day, then they shall see the glory of the Lord, and the excellency of their God. Jehovah's glory and excellency the saints shall see, by contemplating both his works of judgment against his enemies, and his works of mercy in behalf of his church. Of the church's singing, Alleluia, and ascribing to him salvation, and glory, and honour, and power, this is the cause; "For he hath judged the great whore, which did corrupt the earth with her fornication, and hath avenged the blood of his servants at her hand." In these strange acts the saints shall understand, admire, and praise the Lord for the displays of the glory of his wisdom, sovereignty, justice, power, holiness, and faithfulness. In the wonderful deliverance he will work for his church, in her vast extent, her high elevation, the number of her members, the glory of her privileges, and the fulness of blessings which shall be enjoyed by believers, the saints shall see the glory of all those attributes, in connexion with the brightest display of his goodness, mercy, love, and grace, to his own people in Christ Jesus. Of this glory of the great God, in those wonderful events which the church shall behold, the minute accomplishment of his own predictions, and the exact fulfilment of his promises and threatenings, will be a most delightful display, and a special object of their contemplation.

In those glorious works, they shall see his word realised, and will clearly discern the time, the manner, and circumstances, of accomplishing those important predictions, concerning which we dare not now positively determine, and can only see as through a glass darkly. In the view of his admiring saints, O what glory will then surround him, as the God of providence, as the king of nations, as the God, the Father, and the Portion of his church! To them will that call be peculiarly applicable, and the reason assigned for it, completely verified; "Arise, shine, for thy light is come, and the glory of the Lord is risen upon thee." At this happy time, as well as at the important season to which our text did primarily apply, that promise shall be eminently fulfilled; "And the glory of the Lord shall be revealed, and all flesh shall see it together; for the mouth of the Lord hath spoken it." Isai. xl. 5. At this time the Lord, in a most singular manner, will build up Sion; and when he does so, "he shall appear in his glory." As the manifestation of his glory is one of the greatest blessings which God bestows on men; so a spiritual sight and impression of that glory is one of the highest attainments, to which the church, or the children of God can reach. Since, therefore, the displays of the Divine glory, at the millennial day, shall be peculiarly eminent, the spiritual felicity of believers at that time must be inconceivably great.

That the displays of the Divine glory, at this time, will be altogether extraordinary, is evident from Daniel's vision of it, chap. vii. 9, 10. "I beheld till the thrones were cast down, and the Ancient of days did sit, whose garment was white as snow, and the hair of his head like the pure wool; his throne was like the fiery flame, and his wheels as burning fire. A fiery flame issued and came forth from before him; thousand thousands ministered unto him, and ten thousand times ten thousand stood before him; the judgment was set, and the books were opened." In these verses, the represenations of the Divine glory at the fall of Antichrist and the revival of his church, are set before us in such a manner, as bears a strong resemblance to the appearance of his glory, at the final judgment of the last day. John's vision which corresponds with this, is found Rev. xi. 14—19. At the time of this judgment, the Son of Man shall ask, and the Father shall give him the heathen for his inheritance, and the uttermost ends of the earth for his possession. "And there was given him dominion, and glory, and a kingdom," ver. 14. At the time of this judgment, the Great God shall punish his antichristian enemies. "But the judgment shall sit, and they shall take away his dominion, to consume and to destroy it unto the end," ver. 26. And at the time of this judgment he shall give reward to his servants; "And the kingdom, and dominion, and the greatness of the kingdom under the whole heaven, shall be given to the people of the saints of the Most High," ver. 27. In all these solemn transactions, at Antichrist's fall, the Lord's glory shall eminently appear to his millennial church.

10. The glory of Christ, the Mediator, shall then appear in a very bright and wonderful manner, to the children of men. He who is represented, in the visions of Daniel, as the Son of Man, coming in the clouds of heaven, to the Ancient of days, and receiving from him dominion, and glory, and a kingdom, that all nations and languages should serve him, whose dominion is an everlasting dominion that shall not pass away, and his kingdom that which shall not be destroyed," shall then appear in his glory unto men, as the prophet, priest, and king of his church. This prediction, concerning the peculiar aggrandizement of our Mediator, relates to the period of time which we are now contemplating; because this season of his glorious manifestation to men will come at the fall of Antichrist, and at the church's enlargement in her millennial state. The former of these is evident from verse eleventh, in Dan. vii. where the vision is recorded: "I beheld then, because of the voice of the great words which the horn spake; I beheld even till the beast

was slain, and his body was destroyed, and given to the burning flame." The latter description of this time is also clear from verse eighteenth. "But the saints of the Most High shall take the kingdom, and possess the kingdom for ever, even for ever and ever." At the time when judgment shall be executed for pulling down civil and ecclesiastical corruption and tyranny, and at the time when the church shall receive deliverance, enlargement, and prosperity, at that very time the glory of the Lord Jesus shall be brightly displayed among men. This blessed day will not be the commencement of his reign, nor the beginning of the display of his mediatorial glory to his people; but it will be the season of a more remarkable exercise of his power, and of a more illustrious display of his glory. Having overcome all his antichristian enemies, having bound the Dragon who is called the Devil and Satan, having sent his word and gospel to the uttermost ends of the earth, having received the subjection of all nations to the sceptre of his grace and rule, and having begun to execute his offices in the establishment and prosperity of his church in all nations, and in the spiritual salvation of believers of every kindred, tongue, and people, he will then make such manifestations of his glory, and of the glory of God in him, as will fill the earth with the knowledge of it, as the waters cover the sea. In the number of places where it shall be displayed, in the multitude of persons to whom it shall be manifested, and in the bright discoveries that shall be made of it to every believer, Christ's glory will then be peculiarly illustrious. The Lord Jesus will then, by his word and Spirit, manifest himself in such a manner, and will, through the medium of the word and ordinances, be discerned by his people with such bright illumination, in the glory of his person as God manifested in the flesh, in the glory of his offices, general or particular, in the glory of his righteousness for the justification of believers, in the glory of his fulness for supplying his church and his children's wants, in the glory of his salvation which contains the blessings of eternal life, and in the glory of his administrations to his church both on earth and in heaven, as will constrain them to cry out, " And we beheld his glory, the glory as of the only begotten of the Father, full of grace and truth." He will be glorified in the overthrow of his enemies; for they shall fall by " the wrath of the Lamb." He will have honour in his church's song; for they will say, " Salvation to our God that sitteth on the throne, and to the Lamb." At that time also he shall perform a glorious work for his people's comfort and salvation, " For the Lamb, who is in the midst of the throne, shall feed them, and shall lead them unto living fountains of waters; and God shall wipe away all tears from their eyes."

11. The glory of the holy Spirit shall then be most illustriously displayed in the church. This Divine person is called the seven spirits, which are before his throne, from whom, as well as from him who is, and was, and is to come, and from Jesus Christ, grace and peace come to the saints. In his enlightening, purifying, and warming influences, he is represented by that most significant emblem of " seven lamps of fire burning before the throne." The seven eyes of the Lamb in the midst of the throne, " are the seven spirits of God sent forth into all the earth." At that blessed season, the Spirit of God shall be sent forth, in a peculiar manner, into all the earth. The sphere of his special operations shall then comprehend the whole world. The subjects of his gracious influence shall then be in all the earth. The effects of his glorious power, in the conversion, sanctification, comfort, and establishment of sinners in the ways of God, shall then be conspicuous in all nations. Those words of God shall have, at that time, a more extensive accomplishment, than ever they had in the days of the apostles. " And it shall come to pass afterward, that I will pour out my Spirit upon all flesh." The influence of the holy Spirit was exerted, and his glory was displayed in reviving the church, after she returned from her captivity in Babylon. Zechariah was

commissioned to say, "This is the word of the Lord to Zerubbabel, saying, Not by might, nor by power, but by my Spirit, saith the Lord of Hosts." Haggai, who prophesied at the same time, was sent to declare to Zerubbabel, to Josuah the high Priest, and to all the people of the land, to strengthen and encourage them in the Lord's work; "According to the word that I covenanted with you when ye came out of Egypt, my Spirit remaineth among you; fear ye not." If the holy Spirit was glorified by his operations among the captives, when they returned from Babylon; how much more gloriously will he manifest himself, when the Christian churches shall be delivered from Babylon the great, and when all nations, through his influence, shall bow to the Redeemer's sceptre? At the erection of the gospel dispensation, he also performed glorious administrations. At the day of Pentecost, there appeared unto the apostles cloven tongues, like as "of fire, and it sat upon each of them; And they were all filled with the Holy Ghost, and began to speak with other tongues, as the Spirit gave them utterance." When the apostles afterwards were enduring much persecution, and were assembled for solemn prayer, it is said; "And when they had prayed, the place was shaken where they were assembled together; and they were all filled with the Holy Ghost, and they spake the word of God with boldness." Acts iv. 31. When the apostles preached the gospel through the world, it often happened, that the Holy Ghost fell on all them who heard the word, communicating to many saving grace, and to some extraordinary gifts. If the holy Spirit performed such glorious operations, and exerted such Divine influence, for overcoming Jewish prejudices, for removing heathenish darkness, and for establishing the Christian religion; we may certainly conclude that he will perform similar operations, and will exert the same influence, when "All the ends of the earth shall remember and turn unto the Lord, and all the kindreds of the nations shall worship before him." To this truth, an holy apostle gives a direct testimony. "And then shall that wicked be revealed, whom the Lord shall consume by the Spirit of his mouth, and shall destroy with the brightness of his coming." 2 Thess. ii. 8. The holy Spirit, accompanying the word with Divine power, exhibiting to men the glory of Christ as a Saviour, and displaying to them the glory of God in him, shall be the Great Efficient cause of destroying the abominations of Popery, and of establishing the Redeemer's kingdom in all the earth. Then shall the Spirit of the Lord appear in the glory of his distinct personality, of the divinity of his character, and of his special work in the scheme of redemption. Then shall all nations be baptized in the name of the Father, and of the Son, and of the Holy Ghost; And then the grace of our Lord Jesus Christ, and the love of God, and the communion of the Holy Ghost shall be with them all, Amen.

12. All this blessedness, which has been mentioned, shall be the church's enjoyment, not-for a short space, but for a very long time. When we are assured that the time, which is fixed for our enjoyment of any good, is very short, it will diminish both its value, and our pleasure in the possession of it. But when we know that the time of our enjoyment of it is long, it augments its worth in our estimation, and enlarges our satisfaction in the fruition of it. The saints' happiness, at this blessed time, will be increased, by the consideration of the long continuance of their prosperity and peace. The number by which this season is marked in the visions of John is one thousand years. Whether this number signifies exactly so many years, or a long time, cannot be positively ascertained; but, from either of these views of it, we may be assured that the church's glory and purity will be continued for a very long time. That opinion, however, which considers each day in the thousand years, to signify a year, by which the duration of the millennium is extended to three hundred and sixty thousand years, being out of all proprotion to other prophetic num-

bers, and to them all put together, has not, so far as I know, been adopted by many.* This number of one thousand years is mentioned six times in as many verses, at the beginning of Rev. xx. It is mentioned in ver 2d, to fix the time during which Satan shall be bound; it is mentioned again in ver 3d, to state the time in which he shall be restrained from deceiving the nations. The same number is repeated in ver. 4th, to mark the duration of the church's living and reigning with Christ. It is still mentioned in ver. 5, as stating the time in which the rest of the dead, or the wicked, lived not. It is contained in ver. 6th, to describe the time during which, those who have part in the first resurrection, shall be priests of God and of Christ, and shall reign with him. It is brought before us, for the last time, in the 7th verse, to shew that when it shall expire, Satan shall be loosed out of his person, for a little season. As no other prophetic number is ever used in Scripture, to represent the church's blessedness in the latter day, as it is always employed without any alteration in its form, and since it is so clearly and frequently applied to the different things that are connected with that happy season, there seems to be some reason to conclude, though it must not be asserted positively, that the church's state of happiness and prosperity will continue exactly one thousand years, and may perhaps constitute the last day in the week of time, and the millennial sabbath, which the Lord our God hath blessed and sanctified for himself.

With some inferences, this part of the subject may be concluded.

1. Christ's kingdom, in this world, shall be victorious over all her enemies. By the light of Divine predictions and promises, we have seen some of the great things which are prepared for her; she shall, therefore, be victorious. The church may be low, but deliverance and enlargement are secured to her. Since Christ, her glorious Head, has spoiled

principalities and powers, and has triumphed over them; since every believer in him shall be made more than a conqueror through Christ Jesus; the church as a body shall also obtain the dominion. The purpose and promise of her God, the purchase and power of her Saviour, and the quickening Spirit who dwells in her, secure to the church victory and triumph over her enemies. Indeed, the enemy may say, "I will pursue, I will overtake, I will divide the spoil: my lust shall be satisfied upon them, I will draw my sword, my hand shall destroy them." But in the appointed time, "He will blow with his wind, the sea shall cover them, and they shall sink as lead in the mighty waters." Embrace the promise by faith, live in the hope of its accomplishment, and beware of doubting the church's deliverance and prosperity; for of old time, He has declared, with great solemnity, "As truly as I live, all the earth shall be filled with the glory of the Lord." Num. xiv. 21.

2. The change that will take place among men, at the coming of the kingdom of God, shall be exceeding great. As the alteration of the circumstances of Israel, from what they were in Egypt, or in the wilderness, was very great, after they were possessed of the land of promise; as the change in their situation from their being captives in Babylon, to their dwelling safely in Jerusalem, in the cities of Judah, and in the country which flowed with milk and honey, was very great; so the change in the church's condition, when she is delivered from spiritual Egypt, and from Babylon the great, and brought into her millennial rest, shall be incomparably great and glorious. The change on the Jews shall be extraordinary, when they shall emerge from their unbelief and dispersion, return to the Lord, and take possession of Canaan. To the protestant churches the change shall be remarkable also, when they shall receive that deliverance, which shall be like life from the dead. By the removal of popish darkness, idolatry, and wickedness, and by their obtaining the word, the gospel, the worship, and the salvation

of God, the change on the Antichristian nations will be most conspicuous and beneficial. What an alteration shall be produced on the mahometan world, when the mussulmans shall be delivered from the absurd doctrines, the irrational precepts and carnal promises of their Impostor; and shall enjoy the light of the glorious gospel of the grace of God! How great will be the transformation that shall be made on pagan nations, when they shall be turned from their gross ignorance of God, their irrational and cruel idolatry, and their abominable wickedness, to the knowledge and worship of the living God. All nations shall then be changed both in their ecclesiastic and civil interests, and placed under the reign of religion and righteousness. By the grace and power of God, the righteousness and intercession of Jesus, the Divine operations of the Holy Ghost, and by the word, the ordinances, and providences of the Most High, shall these changes be produced among men. How important, how advantageous, and how desirable must those changes be! How earnestly should we pray without ceasing, "that his way may be known upon the earth, and his saving health among all nations!"

3. The privileges and enjoyments of the church in the latter day, shall differ from those of the church in the foregoing ages, not in kind, but in degree. Whatever the church shall then profess, we really enjoy the same, as it were, in miniature. Every gospel privilege and christian enjoyment which belong to us, shall be inherited by them, in its highest perfection. No new dispensation of Divine grace to men, shall then be introduced; but that dispensation shall be perfected, both in its extent, and in its efficacy. No further or additional revelation of the Divine will shall then be enjoyed, nor is it necessary; but that revelation will be better understood. No other doctrines of salvation shall then be preached; but their beauty shall be more clearly seen, and their influence more sensibly felt. No other ordinances of Divine worship shall then be administered; but they will

be more purely dispensed, and more remarkably blessed for the conversion and edification of men. No other form of church government shall then be used, than that which now exists according to the Divine institution; but the administration of it shall be more conscientious and spiritual. No other ordinances of censure different from those already revealed and practised; but they shall seldom be needed, and when they are employed, the offenders will be truly penitent, and the spectators will fear. There shall be no other administrators of gospel ordinances, than the present Christian ministry, whose office is appointed in the Divine word; but, in knowledge, holiness and fervour, they will far excel those who now labour in word and doctrine. There shall not be any other office-bearers in the church, than those helps and governments which God hath already set in her; but their ability and faithfulness for the important work will then be greatly increased. To the Christian church, in all the periods of her existence, there is one body, and one spirit, and one hope of the Christian's calling. One Lord, one faith, one baptism. One God and father of all, who is above all, and through all, and in you all. Though there are diversities of gifts, it is the same Spirit, differences of administrations, it is the same Lord; and diversities of operations, it is the same God who worketh all in all.

4. Though the spiritual exercises and enjoyments of believers in the millennial church shall be very high, they will still be imperfect saints and militant Christians. The believer's perfection, both in blessedness and service, is reserved for that time, when Christ shall come, and receive them to himself, that where he is, there they may be also. Every believer while in this world, even in the most prosperous state of the church, will find it necessary to adopt Paul's words, "Not as though I had already attained, either were already perfect, but I follow after, if that I may apprehend, that for which also, I am apprehended of Christ Jesus," Phil. iii. 12. They will even then be exercised in the spiritual

warfare, finding a law in their members warring against the law of their mind. They will still find imperfection attending them, in all their religious duties, and in all their spiritual enjoyments; because though their attainments shall be high, there are still greater things laid up for them in heaven. They will be exercised in the life of faith on the Son of God, and in the study of that holiness without which no man shall see the Lord. To all the ordinary trials of human life, and to the common difficulties of the Christian's religious duty and exercise they will be exposed; though, on account of their high degrees of holiness and comfort, they will be less burdensome to them, than they are to us. They will still feel mortality working in their bodily frame, and will in the end put off their tabernacle, as the Lord Jesus has appointed unto them.

5. Christians should endeavour to employ themselves in those religious duties which are suited to their present situation. In the day of prosperity they ought to be joyful, and in the day of adversity they should consider. The millennial saints will be placed in the most comfortable circumstances, having the wonderful works of God before their eyes, and enjoying abundantly the blessings of his favour; the spiritual employment which is ascribed to them, therefore, consists in praise, thanksgiving, adoration, wonder and delight. The wisdom that cometh from above is profitable to direct Christians in the knowledge of their situation, and of those duties which that situation requires. The Divine injunction, which ought to guide our way in this important concern, is expressed in the following words; "Is any among you afflicted? let him pray. Is any merry? let him sing psalms," Jam. v. 13. The millennial church will be directed, wisely to observe this infallible rule. It is an effect of that spiritual madness, which is naturally in the hearts of all men, to be ignorant of our condition, and to neglect those duties which are suited to it. Of this the following account of the ancient church is a melancholy illustration. "And

in that day did the Lord God of hosts call to weeping and to mourning, and to baldness, and to girding with sackcloth. And, behold, joy and gladness, slaying oxen and killing sheep, eating flesh and drinking wine." Isa. xxii. 12, 13. O let us study to avoid this sore evil, and to endeavour to be employed before the Lord, according as the state of the church, the situation of our relatives, and our own personal condition do demand.

6. The church enjoys the greatest purity and happiness, when she is favoured with the brighest displays of the Divine glory. The church of the latter day will behold the Divine glory, by his works of judgment, and of mercy, in an extraordinary manner. The manifestations of that glory, and their spiritual discernment of it, will be principal causes, both of their holiness and comfort. They will have an experimental enjoyment of that apostolic privilege; "But we all with open face, beholding, as in a glass, the glory of the Lord, are changed into the same image, from glory to glory, even as by the Spirit of the Lord." The appearance of God's glory, is the greatest good that can exist among his creatures, and their perception of it is their highest privilege. In those days, therefore, when God gives to the church bright discoveries of his glory, by his Spirit, his word, and his works among them, the assembly of his saints will be highly privileged with consolation in the Lord, and with conformity to him. As it is with the church as a body, so will it be with individual believers. When he who commanded the light to shine out of darkness, shines into their heart, by the Spirit's application of the word to their souls, to give them the light of the knowledge of his glory, in the face of Jesus Christ, they act faith in him for their salvation, they see the beauty of the Lord, they love him with all their heart, and they have a blessed enlargement in holiness and comfort. All this glory is seen in the person, and through the mediation of Christ, discerned by the Christian's knowledge, applied by the Christian's faith, and inwardly felt by

the Christian's spiritual experience. Let us, therefore, improve the Divine word, the ordinances of Divine grace, and the duties of religion, that by them, as means prepared by himself, we may behold the glory of the Lord, and the excellency of our God.

7. Christians have need to be prepared for the coming of those glorious days. The first vision that John had of the millennial church, chap. vii. 9, was introduced by a vision which he had of another company, consisting of 144,000, who were sealed with the seal of the living God. This privilege consists in the powerful operations of the Spirit by the word, conveying to believers sanctifying, comforting, and establishing grace. By this privilege they are enabled to continue in the exercise of faith and the practice of holiness; to adhere to his truths, and to wait for his coming; to suffer for his name's sake, and to reverence his judgment; to rejoice in hope of the coming of his kingdom, and to observe the signs of its approach. As those who have the mark of the beast in their right hand, or on their fore-head, belong to him and are devoted to wrath and destruction; so those who are sealed by the angel ascending from the east, belong to God, and are marked out for preservation and safety, whether in a time of calamity, or in the season of prosperity and rest. "The sun shall not smite them by day, nor the moon by night." If we are among the company of true believers, we belong to the 144,000 who are sealed for the season of judgments, in the effusion of the vials; and are also prepared for the coming of the church's glory and purity. If the vision that John had, at the beginning of that chapter, of four angels holding the winds, that they should not blow on the earth, nor on the sea, nor on any tree, be now fulfilled, in that providential dispensation, by which the four great powers in Europe, by their military occupation of France, are preserving national tranquillity; If this application of the providence to the prediction, which has lately been made by one of the most able writers on Prophecy in

modern times, be correct, and indeed on the side of it there is high probability, what reason have we, at this time, to be seeking the application of the seal of the living God to our souls, that if we live to see the end of those wonders, we may joyfully mingle among the innumerable company, and join them in their triumphant song; and, if this is denied to us, we may anticipate the song, by praising God for the revelation of the predictions, and promises concerning those glorious days, in the faith and desire that he will accomplish his own word, " The Lord will hasten it in his time."

AN

INQUIRY

INTO

THE SIGNS WHICH INDICATE THE CHURCH'S HAPPY CONDITION TO BE AT HAND.

DISCOURSE III.

Mark i. 15.—*The time is fulfilled, and the kingdom of God is at hand: repent ye, and believe the gospel.*

When the Lord is about to accomplish any extraordinary dispensation among men, he often gives them those providential warnings which indicate its approach. By Christians, who have the direction of his word, those intimations of his sovereign designs ought to be carefully considered, and clearly understood. It is recorded to the honour of the men of Issachar, that they, on a very trying occasion, "had understanding of the times to know what Israel ought to do," 1 Chron. xii. 32. When the Redeemer dwelt among men, it is stated to the disgrace of the Jews, that though they could discern the face of the sky, they were not able to discern the signs of the times. A proper attention to those signs, therefore, is an important duty, and a just view of them is a great spiritual attainment. As God has appointed many natural signs, as premonitions of the approach of occurrences in nature; so he has established moral signs which no less clearly indicate to us, that some great spiritual change is at hand. When God exercises his condescension, by favouring us with those signs of his coming, it is most criminal to neglect or despise them, and most reasonable to observe and to receive instruction from them. It becomes us therefore, with deep humility, to investigate those Divine operations, and to cry to him, by fervent prayer, that he may enlighten our minds in the knowledge of his ways. When Christ informed his disciples of the destruction of the temple and city of Jerusalem, they said to him, "What shall be the sign when all these things shall be fulfilled." To their inquiry Jesus made a particular reply; and, as he often does to his people, above what they can ask or think, he added a variety of important directions how they were to act, at that interesting crisis. From those things it is evident, that the members of the church are abundantly warranted to observe the events that are coming to pass in their day, that they may so understand and apply those signs, either of mercy or of judgment, as will enable them to know if their Lord is delaying his coming for their deliverance, or is on his way to bestow the kingdom on his chosen people.

Some of those times which shall be fulfilled at Antichrist's fall, and some of the parts of the church's blessedness in her millennial state having been mentioned, that which was proposed next for consideration is,

III. To mention some of those signs which indicate this blessed condition of the church to be at hand.

1. The exertions that are made to translate the holy Scriptures into all languages, to print and to publish them throughout the world, are a sign that this kingdom of God is at hand. To the saints who have lived in the foregoing ages, and in the early part of this generation, it has often been a matter of wonder, what method Divine providence would employ, for sending his word to the darkened nations of the earth. Sensible of the indispensible necessity of their enjoying the Scriptures, in order to their spiritual illumination, and to their turning to God; and convinced of the difficulty of their obtaining the

sacred oracles, they have often been disposed to say, How can this be accomplished? By bringing into operation the Bible Societies which have been established, both at home and abroad, God, in his over-ruling providence, has answered this perplexing question, and has overcome those seemingly insurmountable difficulties. If we consider the object, the exertions, the extent, the success, and the co-operation of Bible Societies, we will see in them a sign that the kingdom of God is at hand.—The object of those societies is to furnish Christians and Jews, Mahometans and Pagans, with the holy Scriptures in their own language, without note or comment. May we not stand still and wonder at this object! Can any object be conceived that has a tendency more directly to promote the glory of God, and the spiritual and eternal salvation of his rational creatures? To send to spiritually dead sinners the word of life, to give to the darkened nations that which God has revealed for a lamp to the feet, and a light to the path of mankind, for guiding them infallibly to the knowledge, the service, and the enjoyment of God, must be an object of the highest importance. We may wonder also at the magnitude of this object. To furnish all nations with this precious word is a work which is not more remarkable for its utility, than it is for its grandeur.—The exertions that are made for effecting this object make a part of this sign. How many are now actively employed in translating the Scriptures, in printing them, and dispersing the sacred volume among the nations? We have every reason to believe that their number is great, that their diligence is unwearied, that their faithfulness is conscientious, and their labour is unremitting. The assiduous study, the fatiguing travail, and the daily labour of many persons, are employed to accomplish this object.—The extent of those exertions is truly astonishing.—In Europe, Asia, Africa, and America, these societies have greatly increased, and are still increasing. They have been erected in all parts of the earth, excepting those which are so remote that they have not yet heard of them, or so ignorant as not to understand their object, or so interested in keeping men in ignorance, idolatry and error, and in a state of corporeal and mental slavery to the power of men, as to give to this grand object, the illumination of mankind, a most malignant opposition. The success of those societies is also most encouraging. How many thousands, and tens of thousands of copies of God's word, either in whole or in part, have been distributed among the nations! Into a very great number of languages, and dialects of the same language, the holy Scriptures have been translated, printed and published in the earth, since the erection of the radical Bible Society at London, in 1804.—The co-operation of those societies is also worthy of our notice. Though they are established in parts of the earth which are very distant from one another, and among people of very different dispositions, yet there is such an unity of object among them all, such friendly communications maintained among them, and such mutual assistance given to one another, as to cause their exertions to bear as directly on the same grand design, as if all their operations were guided by the wisdom and energy of one mind. Now, since it is the word of God that must enlighten men in the knowledge of the way of salvation, since it is the mean by which the systems of darkness shall be removed from the earth, since it is the instrument of erecting Christ's kingdom in the world, and since God, in his wise and powerful providence, has begun and so far carried on this blessed scheme, have we not reason to conclude that the kingdom of God, which this word is appointed to promote, is at hand? Can we suppose that the Lord will withhold his blessing from those means which are so eminently calculated to promote his glory, and the salvation of men? We may, therefore, believe, that as the morning dawn indicates the approach of the ruler of the day; so the spreading of the Divine word among the nations is the harbinger of the rise of the Sun of Righteousness on them, with healing in his wings, and that the kingdom of God is at hand.

2. The extraordinary endeavours that are now made to publish the glad tidings of salvation to the nations, by preaching the gospel to them, are also a sign that the millennial state of the church is at hand. It is long since Christians in different nations attempted to spread the knowledge of the gospel among some of the heathens; but the endeavours that have been made for this purpose, during the last twenty years, are truly extraordinary. A great number of powerful societies have been established in these lands, and in other nations, which have it as their object to send forth evangelical missions to the most distant parts of the earth, that they may preach the gospel to the benighted inhabitants. These societies occupy different fields, and some of them send their labourers to different parts of the earth. Societies have also been formed, and have been for some time in active operation, for sending persons, duly qualified, to preach the gospel, to the darkened parts of the nations to which we belong. Many men who appear to be actuated by a concern for the glory of God, the honour of Christ, the propagation of the gospel, and the salvation of immortal souls, are now actively employed in almost every nation of the earth, in preaching the gospel to the heathen world. The word of God is not only given to the nations, but persons are sent to preach its doctrines, to explain and to apply that word to the consciences of men. As Jesus, at one time, sent forth the twelve Apostles, and, at another time, sent forth seventy disciples to preach in Judea, the doctrines of the kingdom of God; as the church of Jerusalem sent Barnabas to visit the Gentiles who had received the word of God; and as the church at Antioch, by the command of the Spirit, sent forth Paul and Barnabas to go to the Gentiles, who had not yet heard of Christ's name; so the duty of sending forth persons who are properly qualified, to preach the Gospel to the heathen, must be of indispensible obligation on Christians. Those men who from a conscientious regard to the glory of God, and the good of immortal souls, forsake

their relations, endure privations, encounter difficulties and danger, and suffer fatigue and trouble, that they may publish the doctrines of salvation to a perishing world, ought to be esteemed among the most useful servants of Jesus Christ. As great success attended the first publication of the gospel to the nations; so we are encouraged to hope, that if these endeavours are conscientiously made and continued, that the same success shall attend them, till, by the blessing of the Spirit, the knowledge of the glory of the Lord shall fill the earth, as the waters cover the sea. Since God in his holy providence has excited Christians to form societies for this important purpose, since so many who appear, in some good degree, to be qualified for this work, have devoted themselves to it, and have voluntarily engaged in it, and since some comfortable effects have been produced in many parts of the earth, we may consider this as a sign that the kingdom of God is at hand. Can we suppose that God's own ordinance, for the conversion of the heathen, will be put in operation among them, and that he will refuse to work with it, and with them who dispense it? May we not rather conclude that, in his own time, as well as by his own power, he will make it effectual for completely evangelizing the darkened parts of the earth. As this is one of the means of accomplishing this change, and as it is now applied in a far more remarkable manner, than at any former period, we may contemplate it as one of the signs that the kingdom of God is approaching.

3. The efforts that are now made to promote the rapid and universal education of mankind, and to circulate among them evangelic catechisms and tracts, are a sign that the kingdom of God is at hand. The education of men is an object of the highest importance. Those nations, whose population are blessed with education, excel other nations, in knowledge, in religion, in morality, in wealth, in liberty, and in the useful arts, to an inconceivable degree. Those nations, therefore, who make the most extensive and wise

provision for the education of their population, do best promote the honour of God, the happiness of posterity, and their own good. Those parents, and guardians of youth who neglect the education of the children, who are under their care, manifest little concern either for their temporal or spiritual welfare. Those who have obtained a common education, such as is given in our parochial schools, have it in their power, by a right improvement of that blessing, to acquire such treasures of knowledge in every thing that is truly valuable, as almost places them on a level with those who have enjoyed a liberal education. By an ability merely to read the scriptures, persons are enabled to promote both their own spiritual good, and the conversion and salvation of others. As the blessing of education is very great, it is no wonder to see religious and philanthropic men engaged in devising and executing schemes for effecting it. Since the prevalence among men of ignorance and brutality is favourable to the kingdom of Satan and of darkness; the advancement of knowledge and information in the world must be advantageous to the kingdom of Christ and of light. Extraordinary efforts, therefore, to spread education among men, must be a sign that the kingdom of God is at hand. In our times, these efforts are strenuously made. On the evening of the Lord's day, schools, which, in some circumstances of places and of persons, and when properly conducted, are both lawful and expedient, have been erected and carried on in many parts, greatly to the advantage of those who have attended them. Most useful and efficient societies have been formed, and are in active operation, whose object it is gratuitously to educate the young and the old, in the highlands of Scotland, in the kingdom of Ireland, in the principality of Wales, and in other places. By the invention and improvement of new methods of teaching, the instruction of youth has been facilitated greatly, and one person is enabled, in the same time, to instruct a much greater number. By the exertions of the British and Foreign

School Society, in patronizing this method of teaching at home, and promoting it in other nations, it is likely to be the mean of bestowing the blessing of education more expeditiously, upon uninstructed places of the earth. Besides all this, the evangelical missions to the heathen, having catechists and teachers attached to them, set up schools among them, for the instruction of the young and the old, and those who preach the gospel, either superintend those schools, or labour in them as teachers; so that many are instructed, wherever those missions are established. With those laudable endeavours, the exertions of the Tract Societies are closely connected. To print in different languages, catechisms and tracts, which exhibit a summary view of gospel doctrines and christian duties, or illustrate and apply important parts of revealed truth; and to circulate them at home and in foreign nations gratis, or at a very low price, are the principal objects of those Societies. By these means, the reading of vain and immoral ballads and tracts is counteracted; the minds of youth, and of others, are directed to the things which belong to their everlasting peace; a mean is used to convince the erroneous and immoral of the sin and danger of their principles and conduct; an opportunity is furnished to those who have acquired the habit of reading, to exercise it for the instruction of themselves and others; and to those who have obtained the holy scriptures, an help is administered to understand their contents. By all those different and extended exertions, we may hope that many have been plucked as brands out of the burning, have been delivered from ignorance, profanity, idleness, and immorality, and have been brought to the knowledge both of the gospel as the object of their faith, and of the law as the rule of their obedience. Since God has put it into the hearts of men to exert themselves, in this extraordinary way, to promote the education, the religious and moral instruction of men, far and near, we must conclude that, by those means, he will work among the nations that change, which will prepare them for the glory of the latter day.

4. The establishment of Christian societies, for the instruction and conversion of the Jews, is a sign that the kingdom of God, in its millennial state, is at hand. The deliverance of God's ancient people from their infidelity, their embracing Christianity, and their restoration to their own land, will be a very distinguished part of that Divine operation, by which God will introduce and establish the reign of righteousness in the earth. The illumination of the nations will be accomplished, when the Lord shall bind up the breach of his people, and heal the stroke of their wound. On this account, the existence and operation of those societies, for convincing and converting the Jews, is also a sign that the millennial day is drawing near. The object of those societies is to use every eligible mean in their power to convince the Jews, that the Messiah is come, that it is vain for them to look for another, and that Jesus of Nazereth is the very Christ. By giving Christian instruction to as many of themselves, and their children as will receive it; by endeavouring to present before them the arguments which prove that the Messiah is come, and that all the predictions of the Old Testament are fulfilled in Jesus, the Christian Saviour; by furnishing them with the New Testament in the Hebrew language; and by endeavouring to induce them carefully to peruse those sacred oracles, Christians are now applying their mercy to the Jews, that they also may obtain mercy. This is the ordinance of God for the Jew's conversion; and this, Christians are warranted and encouraged to use, for that end. When the Jews shall obtain mercy, it shall be accomplished by the instrumentality of the mercy, which is now enjoyed by the Gentiles. The word and Spirit of God are the great substance of the Gentiles' mercy. The former is in the church's hands, and the latter is the gift of God. Let the church, therefore, use the instrument which God has given her, and cry to him for the Holy Spirit to accompany the means with power, for turning the seed of Abraham to the knowledge

of the truth; and then, though the success at the beginning of their endeavours may be small, their latter end shall greatly increase.

5. The attention which seems to be given to the word of God, and to public religious instruction, by Pagans, Mahometans and Jews, is a sign that the kingdom of God is at hand. For information on these matters we are indebted to the reports of those societies which are employed on those objects, and to the accounts which they receive from those whom they have sent to execute their work. In them are found encouraging accounts of that attention which is given to the Scriptures, and to the gospel, when it is preached among them. An extraordinary desire after the Divine word has been manifested, wherever it has been distributed; and a diligent improvement has been made of it, by those who have received it. They do not reject it, they are not indifferent unto it; but they shew an earnest concern to obtain it. They crowd around the persons who are employed to distribute the Scriptures, they express much joy when they receive the Bible, and discover much grief when their applications cannot be answered; so that the only distress of those who distribute the Scriptures has often been the fewness of the copies which they had to give away. The use they make of the Bible when they have obtained it, is also sufficiently attested. They read it both for their own benefit, and for the instruction of others. They read it at home, they read it in public, by which one copy becomes a common good, and a mean of instruction to many. They converse about its sacred contents among themselves, and, in many instances, apply for explanation to those from whom they have received it. They are also very attentive to the preaching of the gospel. The accounts which have been received of their concern to hear the word in many places, and of the effects which have been produced on their minds and their conduct in life, are highly encouraging. Many of them also shew a concern to obtain educa-

tion, by attending the schools that have been erected among them, for bestowing on them this inestimable blessing. There is reason to believe, that the success is fully proportioned to the means which are employed; and that, if the latter were increased, the former would be much more abundant. Some Mahometans and Jews are also shewing a concern for the word of God. The Scriptures in the Turkish language is beginning to enter among the former; and the New Testament in Hebrew is beginning to attract the attention of the latter. To bring those things to any desirable perfection, must be a work of time; but when the ordinary means are used, and some good effects produced on a few, we may hope that the Lord, when his time is come, will pour out his Spirit on all flesh, so that the earth shall be made to bring forth in one day, and nations shall be born at once. A religious observation of those Divine providences, and a trust in the promise and power of God, will constrain us to consider such extensive operations, with their effects, as a token that all the ends of the world shall soon remember and turn to the Lord, and all the kindreds of the nations shall worship before him.

6. The prevalence of public opinion in favours of true rational Christian liberty, and in opposition to every species of thraldom, is a sign that the kingdom of God is at hand. When the dark system of popery prevailed universally in Europe, and when the court of Rome, consisting of the Pope and his Cardinals, exerted its power over men, the human mind was subdued under a most degrading and unnatural bondage, in matters of religion, and of politics, and even of philosophy. No liberty was given to discuss articles of faith, or modes of worship, in opposition to their blasphemous doctrines, their unscriptural decrees, their unholy traditions or their abominable idolatry. No permission was granted to animadvert on the science of government, or to canvass the measures of the political administrations. No allowance was made for the improvement of the philosophy

of those ages. The human understanding and will were completely kept in bondage, to the dominion of civil and ecclesiastic despotism. The Roman Antichrist, aware that the word of God was directly against his system, took it entirely from the people, removed the key of knowledge, and left his votaries to wander in gross spiritual darkness. Fearful also of the exercise of human reason, this spiritual Despot made war with it, and forbade its exertions on all subjects that were any way connected with the religion or government of the nations. The Christian world was in this dismal condition, when God, in his holy providence, employed those men, who were the instruments in his hand to introduce that happy reformation, which commenced three hundred years ago. Then men found themselves at liberty to think, to speak, and to write, on all those important subjects which promote the glory of God, and the good of men. Then the human mind, liberated from its prison, began to exercise itself on matters of religion, politics, and philosophy, and filled the nations with light. The holy Scriptures were again put into the hands of the christian people, who, from wandering in ignorance, were now conducted into the paths of faith and holiness. Since those days, great alterations have taken place in the sentiments of men, both with respect to religion and civil liberty. There have been particular times, in which the human mind has been greatly enlarged in the knowledge of the one, or the other, or of both. The second religious reformation in Britain, the memorable Revolution, the first American war, and the revolution in France have been the chief of those periods. To produce this beneficial change on the sentiments of men, in favours of religion, of true liberty, and human rights, and in opposition to tyranny and slavery, each of these important events has greatly contributed. For discovering to men the difference between true liberty, civil and religious, on the one hand; and licentiousness, impiety, and profligacy on the other, the last of those events has been also eminently useful. This alteration in the opinions of men is a great blessing to the nations. They are objects of vast importance about which the change of opinion is made. The prevalency of them among mankind is necessary to raise them from that state of degradation in which they have existed, during the reign of the Roman beast, and his little horn. The providential prevalence among men of right sentiments on these things is also a sign that the kingdom of God is at hand. However inimical the exercise of human reason may be to the Popish system, which is full of absurdity; it never can be detrimental to the kingdom of Christ. The age of true reason will be the age of pure religion; and the prosperity of religion will raise human reason to its most exalted exercise.

7. The measures which the court of Rome, and its clergy have adopted, with a view to counteract that system of means, which the God of the whole earth is employing, for the illumination of mankind, are a sign that the kingdom of God is at hand. Their opposition is principally directed against Bible societies, and the schools for the education of youth. To some of their dignified clergy, who have countenanced Bible Societies, and encouraged the circulation of the Scriptures among their people; the head of that council has sent bulls, prohibiting them from assisting those Societies, and from giving the Scriptures to the people; branding the publication of the word of God, by those Societies, with the most odious names; commanding them to condemn what they have done; endeavouring to flatter and cajole them into obedience; and intimating, not obscurely, what punishment he is able to inflict on them, if they continue in those practices. Their clergy have prohibited the people from receiving the Scriptures, which some Societies, from pity to their perishing souls, have gratuitously offered to them. They would not even allow their people to receive the Scriptures, printed according to their own approved

translation, which was generously offered to them gratis, if the clergy would suffer it to be done. They have forbidden their people to send their children to those schools, which were opened in the places of their residence for the free education of youth. Some of those who continued to send their children to the schools, contrary to their command, they have excommunicated, in the most frightful forms. To what extent this opposition may be carried, and what effects it may produce, time only can declare; but in it we may see a sign that the kingdom of God is at hand. It is such a sign, as it discovers the Popish church to be a kingdom of darkness, supported by ignorance; a kingdom of impiety, being enemies to the holy Scriptures; a kingdom of cruelty, managed with tyranny; and a miserable kingdom, which is supported by the sufferings of men. It is also such a sign, because it proves, that bestowing education on men, and placing in their hands the word of God, are the means which are well calculated to destroy that perversion of Christianity, which is the essence of their religion. A conviction of this must have induced them to venture upon such a public, unreasonable, and shameful opposition to an object, which must recommend itself to the approbation of every other rational creature. This opposition is a sign of the coming of Christ's kingdom, because it demonstrates the suitableness and efficacy of those means for introducing the reign of light, of truth, and of righteousness, on the earth. We are, therefore, encouraged to hope, that God will over-rule this opposition, and use it as a mean for giving such discoveries to the nations of the evil of that idolatrous system, as will, in due time, constrain the people to forsake it, and induce their Rulers to make it desolate and naked, to eat its flesh, and to burn it with fire.

8. The judgments, which God has executed, and is still executing, on the nations, are a sign that the kingdom of God is at hand. Divine predictions assure us, that the nations

must suffer the effects of the Lord's anger, on account of their sin, before they can enjoy that peaceful and prosperous state, which is contained in the promise. Before the conversion of the Jews, "there must be a time of trouble, such as never was since there was a nation, even to that same time." Dan. xii. 1. It is Jehovah's determination, to gather the nations, that he may assemble the kingdoms, to pour upon them his indignation, even all his fierce anger, and all the earth must be devoured with the fire of his jealousy; before he will turn to the people a pure language, that they may all call upon the name of the Lord, to serve him with one consent. Zeph. iii. 8, 9. The judgments that are contained in the third wo must be executed on men, before the kingdom of this world shall become the kingdom of our Lord, and of his Christ, Rev. xi. 14, 15. The seven vials of Divine wrath must be poured out upon the earth, before the church shall be delivered completely, from her wilderness condition, or bring to an end her sackcloth prophecy, Rev. xvi. The terrible war, which is signified by the slaughter of Armageddon, must be accomplished among men, before the church can sing on the lovely heights of her millennial Sion These judgments are necessary for vindicating God's government, for fulfilling his holy word, for destroying his implacable enemies, and for trying and purifying his church. A time of judgments has often been, by the Divine blessing, a season of good to mankind. As a time of private correction, from the Divine hand, is frequently to believers, a season of great spiritual good; so is it with the children of men, in a day of public calamity. "When thy judgments are in the earth, the inhabitants of the world will learn righteousness," Isa. xxvi. 9. Since the Divine judgments must be poured out, before the kingdom of God shall come; we may conclude, that the execution of them will be a sign of its approach. All the nations, that are principally concerned in the vials of wrath, have suffered, in the most extraordinary manner, by the judgment of war, and its various attendants, for more than twenty years. If we review in our minds, the way in which this war commenced, the objects for which it was undertaken, the incessant and violent nature of the struggle, its wide spreading circuit from nation to nation, the length of time in which it continued, the desolations it brought on the earth, the character of the nations and persons who were the greatest sufferers, the dreadful destruction of human lives which it accomplished, the uncommon waste of national wealth which it occasioned, the manner in which it has terminated, and the effects it has produced on the nations that were involved in it, we will clearly see, that this season of war has been a time of recompences for the controversy of Sion. As the church is not yet delivered, as the Jews are not yet brought in, and as the Antichristian church, and her secular supporters are not yet removed, we may be certain that the storm of judgments has not passed away. The greater and more dreadful part of the scene, remains yet to be acted. Since the Lord prefaces the account of the seventh vial with those remarkable words. "Behold I come as a thief," there is reason to apprehend that it will approach suddenly, and when men are secure. This season of judgments that has passed over us is another sign that the millennial kingdom is near.

9. The tottering state of the throne of Antichrist, and of the thrones of some of the Antichristian princes, is a sign that the kingdom of God is at hand. The Pope of Rome was lately dethroned, and was obliged to live as a wandering man, in solitude and degradation. The greater part of the kings, who ruled in the Roman earth, were also driven from their thrones, and forced to seek shelter and protection in foreign lands. In these dispensations of providence, He, by whom kings reign, and princes decree justice, has given his church an earnest, an emblem, and a presage of what he will finally accomplish on them, when the kingdom of God shall come. The Pope has now been restored to his civil power, to his ecclesiastic authority, and to his seat at Rome. For their exertions in order to his restoration and establishment, Pro-

testant princes must give an account to Him who hath said, "Be ye not partakers of her sins, that ye receive not of her plagues." The less efficient exertions of Catholic princes, for accomplishing this end, will no doubt procure their ruin, when they shall fall with him. The restored dynasties, civil and ecclesiastic, do not appear to have much stability; and this we are bound to consider as a sign, that the kingdom of God is at hand. With respect to the Pope, his power is weakened, his revenues are impaired, his authority is despised, his exertions are feeble, his spiritual kingdom is divided, and there is no very great security for his retaining his seat, or the exercise of his power. On him these words must soon have their accomplishment; "Whom God shall consume with the spirit of his mouth, and shall destroy with the brightness of his coming." With violence shall he be thrown down, and shall be cast alive into destruction. With reference to the restored civil dynasties, as little stability seems to belong to them. Two of them, for the security of their thrones, seem to depend on the troops of foreign nations which occupy their territory. A third appears to be in danger of a revolt among his subjects at home, and is overwhelmed with a rebellion in a distant part of his dominions. A fourth is still in a distant part of his states, to which he was obliged to go for safety. There is as much difference between the present power of the Pope and of those popish princes, and the power which they formerly were able to exert; as there is between the vigour of a person in the prime of his life, and that of a man, to whom, by age and debility the grasshopper is a burden. In all those dispensations of providence, by which God has weakened the power of his church's enemies, we may see a sign that her deliverance and prosperity are drawing near.

10. The uncommon exertions which have lately been made to turn the attention of men to the scripture predictions which relate to the church's deliverance, and to the fall of Antichrist; and to those Divine providences, which seem

to be a fulfilment of those predictions, are a sign that the kingdom of God is at hand. This is mentioned as a sign of the time, when all those things shall be fulfilled. "Many shall run to and fro, and knowledge shall be increased," Dan. xii. 4. It is a certain mark of the time of their end, when many persons are excited, in the providence of God, to employ their time and abilities in the investigation of Divine predictions, in the observation of Divine providences, and in the application of the one to the other, that they may know, and declare to the church, how far inspired prophecy is accomplished, by the things that have come to pass in our days. During the last twenty-five years, many books of this description have been published, and several of them have been republished, with corrections and additions. Many of them have been very generally read, their contents have been carefully considered, and, by their means, a great degree of knowledge, on those important matters, has been extensively diffused. Though these publications do not possess equal merit, yet few or none of them have altogether failed, in contributing something to our stock of knowledge, on those interesting subjects.—Some of them indeed have been excellent, and have, in a very high degree, attracted the public attention. The differences of opinion, on some important articles, which have been entertained by the Authors, and the calm and manly discussions which those differences have occasioned, operated as a mean, to render our knowledge, on those points, more certain and correct. The progress of Divine providence has contributed greatly to explain the predictions, and has enabled those Authors to discern and to correct some mistakes, and to add some new and important discoveries. We are bound to consider those things as a sign that this happy season will soon arrive. Since God in his providence has employed so many, and has enabled some of them so well to accomplish the difficult work of explaining the predictions of his holy word; he is favouring Christians with suitable means to excite them to a proper concern for the coming of his kingdom, to give them an understanding of the nature and fulfilment of prophecy, to animate them to those duties which this state of things requires, and to stir them up to preparation and watchfulness, that those days of trial and deliverance may not come upon them unawares. As nothing similar to this, of the same extent, in the same variety, and with the same perspicuity of application to the operations of Divine providence, has ever happened in the Christian church; we will not be attentive to the Lord's tokens that he is setting in the midst of us, if we refuse to consider these occurrences as a sign of the coming of his kingdom.

11. The very general expectation which has been entertained, by christian professors, of the speedy coming of Christ's kingdom, in its millennial glory, is also a sign that it is at hand. When any signal mercy is bestowed on the church, an expectation of it is often produced in the hearts of those, who fear and serve the Lord. This is demonstrated by the exercise of the saints, both at the coming of Christ into the world, and at the deliverance of the Jews from their captivity in Babylon. When Christ was, for the first time, brought into the temple, it is said of Simeon, "That the same man was just and devout, waiting for the consolation of Israel, and the Holy Ghost was upon him." Of Anna the prophetess, on the same occasion, it is said, that "she spake of Christ to all them that looked for redemption in Jerusalem." Besides these two eminent persons, there were others who expected Messiah's appearance at that time, and who looked for the Redeemer's coming, Luke ii. 25, 38. Concerning Joseph of Arimathea, that honourable Counsellor, it is recorded, that "he waited for the kingdom of God." Mark xv. 44. He had an expectation raised in his soul, that Christ's kingdom, in its New-testament form, should be immediately set up. When the seventy years of the Jews' bondage were coming to an end, an expectation of deliverance, at that time, was entertained in the minds of the religious captives. As this is attested of Daniel, we may con-

clude that it was the hope of many others; as we must not suppose that he would keep to himself the discovery he had made, or conceal from his brethren the hope he had founded on it. "In the first year of his reign, I Daniel understood by books the number of the years, whereof the word of the Lord came to Jeremiah the prophet, that he would accomplish seventy years in the desolations of Jerusalem. And I set my face unto the Lord God, to seek by prayer and supplications, with fasting, and with sackcloth and ashes." Dan. ix. 2, 3. As there was an expectation of deliverance from their captivity excited in some of the Jewish captives, which hope was a sign that their liberation was drawing near; and as there were many pious Jews, at the day of Christ's incarnation, and in the time of his public ministry, who looked for redemption in Israel, and waited for the kingdom of God, as a sign that the Redeemer was come to accomplish the work of our redemption, and to establish the gospel kingdom in the earth; so when there is a very general expectation existing in the minds of those who fear God, that Christ's kingdom, in her millennial glory, is soon to be established in the earth, we may consider it as a sign that this blessed deliverance is at hand. If the nature of this expectation, its extent among Christians, and the ground on which they rest their hope, are duly considered, it will appear to be an unquestionable sign, that the desired object is near.—It is not a mere speculative opinion, or a bare conjecture; but it is a religious hope founded on the Divine promises, creating in them an earnest desire that God, for the glory of his name, and in mercy to immortal souls, would speedily send his gospel to the uttermost ends of the earth.—This hope is also become very general among Christians, and multitudes of them are now looking for redemption to the church, and waiting for the kingdom of God.—The ground of their hope is the same with that of Daniel. Like that holy Prophet, they understand by the books of inspired prophecy, that the number of the years which God would accomplish in the desolations of his church is now coming to an end. The existence, therefore, of such an expectation in those who are truly religious and well informed, is a sign that the millennial day is at hand.

12. The prayers and thanksgivings that are offered to God, for success to the means of accomplishing this great work, and the very liberal contributions which have been made for supporting them, by Christians of every denomination, and of every land, are a sign that this kingdom of God is at hand. As it is the duty, we ought to believe it has been the exercise of Christians, to offer to God fervent prayers for the progress of this great work, in time to come; and to give him thanks for the success of it, in time that is past. Something of great importance has already been done. An opening has been made into the kingdom of darkness. Light has begun to shine among men. Great exertions have been made, and much success has attended them. For these, let us bring our sacrifices of praise into the house of the Lord. There is reason to hope, that Christians are not negligent in this important duty. Every degree of success that has attended the endeavours, which have been employed to circulate the Scriptures, to preach the gospel, or to promote education among men, is entirely of God; for it is He alone who gives the increase. But as this great work is only at its beginning, there is much need also for prayer. When the Lord intends to bestow a blessing on the church, he usually pours out his Spirit on her members, constraining them to cry mightily at the throne of grace for that blessing. Respecting this important concern, such, we hope, is the dispensation of God to his people, and such is their exercise before him. Prayers in secret, in private, and in public; prayer, by concert, and without it; prayers stated and occasional, we have reason to believe, are offered to God by Christians every where, and of every profession, for the advancement of his kingdom in the world. This may be considered as a sign that the day of the Redeemer's triumph is

near. Oh, that Christians would abound more and more in these duties.—The extraordinary contributions which have been made for supporting this wonderful work are a sign of the same thing. On no former occasion, was there ever so much of the property of man devoted to purposes of this kind, than there has been, during the last twenty years. Multitudes of persons of both sexes, persons in every station, persons of every age, persons of every religious profession, and persons in almost every nation have contributed of their substance for those purposes, and have consecrated part of their gain to the God of the whole earth. Contemplating the various plans which have been adopted for the religious instruction of men, considering the labours that have been undergone in executing them, and calculating the vast sums which the liberality of Christians has provided for supporting them, we may say, with wonder and praise, it is the Lord's doing, and it is marvellous in our eyes. However numerous and grand their objects have been, and however expensive, they have still been supported by those free contributions; and, it is hoped, they will continue to receive efficient support, till, through their instrumentality, the world shall be enlightened, and the millennial day shall dawn.

Some reflections from what has been said, on this part of the subject, must be subjoined.

1. The wants of the unenlightened nations are many and great. They want the word of God, the preaching of the Gospel, and the other ordinances of Divine grace. They want the knowledge of the God of salvation, of Christ who is the purchaser, and of the Spirit who is the applier of that salvation. They want the knowledge of the covenant of works, by the breach of which the human family have been brought into a state of sin and misery, and the covenant of grace, of which Jesus is the Mediator and Surety, and which is all the salvation and desire of them who believe. They want regenerating and converting grace, justification into

the favour, adoption into the family, and sanctification into the moral image of God. Without these, their condition must be deplorable, their lives immoral, and their end, misery for ever. They want faith in Jesus Christ, and repentance of sin unto spiritual and eternal life. These blessings, according to the ordinary and appointed dispensation of Divine grace, are bestowed upon men, only by means of the word and ordinances. As their wants are many, so they are exceeding great. What human wants are to be compared with those which are spiritual and eternal? "For what is a man profited, if he shall gain the whole world, and lose his own soul? or, what shall a man give in exchange for his soul?" To those who are Christans indeed, but not to those who are such only in profession, will the wants of the darkened nations appear, in all their magnitude and variety. Though the unconverted persons, among the enlightened nations, labour under numerous and important wants, yet enjoying the revelation of grace, the offers of Christ, the promise of the Spirit, and the command to believe, they are not without hope in the world; but the heathen are destitute of these. Let their situation impress our minds, and fill our souls with pity.

2. The means that are now used for supplying the wants of the darkened nations, possess a suitableness, and a fulness, for answering that end. The word of God, the preaching of the gospel, the schools for education, the circulation of evangelic catechisms and tracts, and the various opportunities for their improvement, which necessarily accompany their enjoyment of them, constitute that system of means which is now employed, for accomplishing this great end. The human mind cannot conceive any means that are better adapted to their religious improvement. How suited are they to enlighten their minds, to renew their hearts, to rectify their conduct, and to train up the youth in the ways of the Lord! There is also a fulness, or perfection in those means. If this system is considered, it will not be easy to

conceive of any thing that can render it more complete. Reading and hearing the word, meditation, conversation and prayer, are connected with their enjoying the Scriptures, and evangelic catechisms, and religious tracts. Public preaching and hearing the gospel, prayer, praise, and other ordinances of worship, accompany their enjoyment of the Christian ministry. Reading, hearing, catechising, occasional explanations, exhortation and prayer, belong to the exercises in the schools. Besides, the private intercourse that must subsist, between the preachers and their people, the teachers and their scholars, and the people who are privileged with those means, among themselves, and with others, must be of vast advantage to their religious and moral improvement. All these things taken together form a most complete system of means, for supplying the wants of the darkened parts of the earth. Who would not desire, that since it is so perfect in its nature, it were more perfect in its extent? These constitute the grand engine which God hath instituted, and which Christians are now employing, for the illumination of the benighted world.

3. The success that has attended the application of those means, is sufficient to encourage Christians to persevere in the use of them. Their attempts have not been fruitless, the means have not been blasted, nor has their labour been in vain. They have been instrumental already of much good. They have had great success both in providing, and in applying the means. They have had this success, in the publication of the Scriptures, in the evangelic missions, in the circulation of tracts, and in the schools. In those operations, this success has attended them both at home, and in foreign nations. What a multitude of Bibles, in many languages, have now been printed and circulated in the world! They have the prospect, as certain as human contrivance and exertion can make it, of publishing a much greater quantity, in the space of a few years. The evangelic missions are prospering, their number is increasing; and their

success is great in the Lord. The schools are also prospering exceedingly, and they will soon be brought into operation in places where they have not formerly existed, and where their salutary effects have never been enjoyed. These are promising appearances, (the particular facts I cannot here detail,) and they should stimulate Christians to the most vigorous exertions, that all the ends of the earth, may see the salvation of their God.

4. The object that Christians are endeavouring to accomplish among the nations, by their extraordinary and united exertions, is great and glorious. The excellency of an object adds dignity to the means, and spreads a lustre over the exertions that are made, by the use of the means for accomplishing it. To no other object can this truth more truly apply, than to that which is now before us. To deliver mankind from their present state of darkness, idolatry, alienation from God, gross immorality, and, at last, from everlasting misery; and to bring them to the knowledge of the only true God, and Jesus Christ, whom he hath sent. May I not express it in the Redeemer's own words to Paul? "To open their eyes, to turn them from darkness to light, and from the power of Satan unto God, that they may receive the forgiveness of sins, and inheritance among them which are sanctified by faith that is in me," Acts xxvi. 18. Their object contains something which is still higher than this. The object in view is to promote the glory of the God of salvation in the earth; to exalt the Saviour's honour among men; to be instrumental in accomplishing God's gracious purposes, and in fulfilling the predictions of his word; and to give occasion to the holy angels to raise the celestial song, and an opportunity to contemplate those objects among men, which they desire, with holy delight, to look into. The object to be attained by those means is the demolition of the kingdom of Satan in the world; and the erection and establishment of Christ's kingdom on its ruin; that God may be glorified, and that sinners may be saved in the Lord, with

an everlasting salvation. Such is the object that Christians have in view, and such shall be the effects of its accomplishment. It is, therefore, great and glorious. Who would not desire to have some concern in effecting it?

5. When the Lord is working, in his providence, for the illumination of the Gentiles, he is not unmindful of his ancient and peculiar people, the Jews. He is also making provision for them. Among their dry bones are begun a noice and shaking, which will terminate in their spiritual resurrection. Some of them are active members in some Bible Societies. Some of them are searching the New Testament in their original language, so far as it has advanced. Not a few of them have turned to Christianity in other nations, and hopes are entertained of many more. The present exertions of Christians in printing the Scriptures have excited in some of them the hope of their Messiah's speedy appearance. In this hope they will not be disappointed; though he may come in a way that they do not expect. In all these things, it is evident, that God is remembering them in their low estate, for his mercy endureth for ever; and that he will deliver them from the hand of their enemies, for his mercy endureth for ever.

6. The Divine government is truly wonderful, and his agency is brightly displayed, in those new and strange operations. "All things are of God," not in creation only, but also in providence and grace. This agency of God, the prophet describes, Hag. i. 14. "And the Lord stirred up the spirit of Zerubbabel the son of Shealtiel governor of Judah, and the spirit of Josuah the son of Josedech the high priest, and the spirit of all the remnant of the people, and they came, and did work in the house of the Lord of hosts their God." In the existence, operations and success of the Bible Societies, the evangelic missions, the school societies, the tract societies, and the attempts to awaken the Jews, He has exerted the same supernatural influence on the spirits of men. By turning the attention of men, to those great objects, enab-

ling them to devise schemes for accomplishing them, putting it into the hearts of multitudes to contribute of their substance for their support, disposing the minds of many to engage in laborious services for bringing those plans into operation, encouraging and assisting them in their arduous work, and by giving to those schemes extraordinary increase, he has stirred up the spirits of men to come, and to work in the house of the Lord of hosts their God. Some have thought it wonderful that these schemes have not been devised, and those attempts made at a more early period; and viewing them in one light, it may be true; but, considering them as the fruit of Divine agency, and as the ordering of Divine wisdom, we may be assured, that they have been brought into existence at the most seasonable, because at the appointed time. They are all the execution of his decree, the fulfilment of his word, and the effects of his special providence concerning the Redeemer's church. Let us ascribe to the Lord the glory of their being, activity and success; and trust in him for their continuance and prosperity, till all nations shall submit to the sceptre of Christ.

7. There is a duty incumbent on Christians with respect to those endeavours that are now made, to enlighten and convert to true Christianity the nations of the earth. As this is a work for the accomplishment of which the Lord must make bare his arm, or exert his power; prayer to him for this blessing, must be our indispensible duty. The first three petitions in our Lord's prayer, all bear upon this most important object. " Hallowed be thy name,—Thy kingdom come,—Thy will be done on earth, as it is in heaven." O, therefore, let us cry to the Lord, in every prayer of ours, that he would enlighten the world, erect his kingdom on the earth, and bless the means that are, or may be employed, to promote those ends. As great labour must be performed in carrying on this work, much expense must be incurred; it is, therefore, the duty of Christians to contribute cheerfully for defraying it. Our lot is fallen in a time, when Christians

are called, according to their religious attainments and worldly substance, to contribute, by fervent prayers and liberal donations, for promoting this great work of God. Some persons may incline to support one, some another, some more than one, and some even all of those societies. Of his duty in this matter, let every Christian be fully persuaded in his own mind, and perform it faithfully, as in the sight of God. On a particular occasion, Jesus sat over against the treasury, and beheld how the people cast in money into it, and many who were rich cast in much. He beheld a certain poor widow deposit her two mites in the Lord's treasury, and gave her a peculiar commendation. The omniscient Jesus still sits over against the treasury, to observe, who contribute, and if their contributions, for the relief of the poor, and for the promotion of his kingdom in the world, are proportioned to his providential bounty to them, and are made from proper motives. Since God has assured us his kingdom shall come, since he is giving us signs that it is at hand, since so many means are applied in our day to promote its increase and establishment among men, and since we have calls and opportunities to glorify God with our substance, "let all that be round about him, bring presents to him that ought to be feared."

8. Time, sufferings and the increase of knowledge in the world, have not produced any favourable alteration in the system of Popery, or in the principles and conduct of its supporters. When God gives men space to repent, and they do not turn from their evil ways, but still persist in their iniquity; their sin is greatly aggravated, and their condemnation will be more awful. When he corrects men for their iniquity, and they still continue in their rebellion; peculiar criminality attaches to their disobedience. When men enjoy the means of improvement, and harden themselves in their opposition to God; they render their sin exceeding sinful, and expose themselves to the righteous judgments of God. All these things may be applied to

Antichrist and his votaries. They have enjoyed much time to consider their ways, they have been sorely chastised, and means of information have been administered to them abundantly; "but they repented not of the works of their hands, that they should not worship devils, and idols of gold, and silver, and brass, and stone, and of wood, which neither can see, nor hear, nor walk. Neither repented they of their murders, nor of their sorceries, nor of their fornications, nor of their thefts." They are still mad upon their idol worship, and adhere to all their antichristian errors. Cruelty, tyranny, and persecution, still characterise their administrations. The most wicked decrees of their former councils are still the rule of their government, and their abominable traditions, equally with the Scriptures, if not above them, are the rule of their faith. That most cruel and wicked court, the Inquisition, is again in full operation, in many popish countries. That most destructive order of their clergy, the Jesuites, have been again restored to existence in that church. Their enmity at the holy Scriptures is still manifested clearly. The bulls of the Pope, against Bible Societies are a proof of this. Besides that Popish power which is the image of the Roman Empire, has prohibited the entrance and sale of Bibles from foreign Societies, in some parts of his dominions. In these ways they are increasing their guilt, and hastening their terrible fall.

9. For accomplishing his merciful and righteous purposes, the great God performs very different works among men, at the same time. Of this, the providences of God to the nations, during the last twenty-five years, are a satisfactory demonstration. Those years have been a season of Divine judgments unto men. The cup of God's anger has gone round among the nations, and has produced such effects, as should cause our souls remember the wormwood and the gall of those calamities, and be humbled in us. But in those very years, that glorious and Divine work, of which we have been speaking, has had its origin, and a part

of its progress. When the councils of the nations were deliberating about war, and conquest; many bodies of Christians were consulting about the means of sending the word of God, and the gospel of Christ through the world. When the armies of the nations were attacking one another, and the confused noise of the warrior was heard, and garments rolled in blood were seen; the Societies of Christians were "wrestling against principalities, against powers, "against the rulers of the darkness of this world, against "spiritual wickedness in high places." When the Lord was threshing the nations in his anger, He was at the same time, giving birth and energy to a complete work, by which, spiritual darkness shall be dispelled, and the whole earth shall be lightened with his glory. These two dispensations of God shall contribute, in different ways, to accomplish the same end. This simultaneous movement of Divine providence stamps both dispensations with peculiar grandeur and significancy. It hath pleased him, at the very time when he poured the vials of his wrath upon the earth, to send forth his word and gospel, the rod of the Redeemer's strength, into all the earth, that his people may be made willing, in the day of his power. Since God has put the means for enlightening the world into activity, at that time, when he seems to be pouring out on the nations the vials of wrath; it encourages our hope, that these means shall introduce the glory of the latter day. Since he has brought those sad calamities on the earth, at the very time when he stirred up the minds of Christians to exert themselves, in an extraordinary way, for the conversion of the world; it strengthens our belief that those judgments are destined for the destruction of Antichrist. As there was a long preparation for the rise of Popery, in the church's gradual defection from the truth and purity of Christianity; so there shall be a long preparation for the millennial day, in the continued use of the means which are now in operation. As the church still grew worse and worse till the man of sin was placed in his seat; so those means shall become more and more efficient, and our signs shall brighten, till the millennial day shall break upon the world. Let Christians then work, and wait, and pray, and hope; let them cast out their anchors, and wish for the day; for God's combined operations of mercy and judgment may assure them, that his kingdom, in her millennial glory, is at hand.

AN

INQUIRY

INTO

THE PROPHETIC NUMBERS WHICH ARE CONTAINED IN THE THOUSAND THREE HUNDRED AND FIVE AND THIRTY DAYS, MENTIONED AT THE END OF DANIEL'S PROPHECY.

DISCOURSE IV.

MARK i. 15.—*The time is fulfilled, and the kingdom of God is at hand: repent ye, and believe the gospel.*

IN some Scripture predictions, God has condescended to reveal both the events that shall come to pass, and the time at which they shall be accomplished. This he has done with respect to the wandering and suffering condition of Abraham and his posterity, from the time of the Patriarch's departure from Haran, till the time of Israel's deliverance from Egypt, Gen. xv. 13, Exod. xii. 40, 41. This method is taken, with respect to the Jews captivity in Babylon, Jer. xxv. 11, 12. It pleased the Lord, concerning that most important of all events, the death of Christ, to do the same thing. "And after three-score and two weeks shall Messiah be cut off, but not for himself," Dan. ix. 26. In those predictions which relate to the rise and fall of Antichrist, and to the church's sufferings under that power, and to her deliverance from it, the character and conduct of the former, and the condition and actings of the latter are described, and the duration of both the one and the other is also distinctly marked. If we had a certain knowledge of the time, at which these events began, it would be very easy to fix the season at which they shall terminate. But, in the dispensations of his wise and holy providence, God, whose way is in the sea, and his path in the mighty waters, and his footsteps are not known, has so ordered events, at the beginning of that time, as casts a veil of darkness over it; in consequence of which considerable uncertainty about it rests on the minds of men, and different opinions have been held by those who have investigated it. Since the prophetic numbers are revealed, and the principal occurrences are on record, it is the church's duty to search after the knowledge of the time, when her greatest earthly enemy shall fall, and when she shall enjoy her promised felicity. With the deepest humility, with the most profound reverence, and with the strongest dependence on Divine direction, should imperfect and erring man engage in searching into the mysteries of the word and providence of the Most High God. Desiring these dispositions, though not possessing them in any high degree, let us now proceed to consider the

IV. Branch of this subject.—To make some remarks concerning Daniel and John's prophetic numbers, which are contained in the thousand three hundred and five and thirty days, mentioned at the end of Daniel's prophecy.

1. The 1335 days are Daniel's gross number, which has a respect to the church's low condition, and to the reign and tyranny of the Antichristian horn. It is mentioned Dan. xii. 12, "Blessed is he that waiteth and cometh to the thousand three hundred and five and thirty days." In this number there are three other numbers included, and they are brought before us in this chapter. The first of them is mentioned in verse 7; "That it shall be for a time, times, and an half." This number, as will afterwards be proved, contains three years and half a year, or 1260 days. The second of these numbers is stated in verse 11. "There shall

be a thousand two hundred and ninety days." In this number there is an addition of 30 days made to 1260 days. Those 30 days constitute Daniel's second number. The third number is discovered by what is said in the 12 verse. "Blessed is he that waiteth and cometh to the thousand three hundred and five and thirty days. From this it is evident, that 45 days are added to the 1290 days which raise that number to 1335 days. The period of 45 days forms Daniel's third number. This is Daniel's statement of the times which represent Antichrist's rise and ruin, and the church's sufferings and deliverance. First 1260 days, then 30 days, and afterwards 45 days, making in all 1335 days. This gross, or general number contains the period, which Daniel's predictions contemplate, and they will not be completely fulfilled till the 1335 days expire. Daniel's three particular numbers, being the component parts of his gross number, are entirely successive, and each of them shall begin at the day when the number before it did end. The only number mentioned by John, in the book of his Revelations, relating to the continuance of Antichrist's power, and to the sufferings of the church is the 1260 days, which corresponds exactly, in duration with Daniel's first number. These are the numbers which we are now to consider.

2. The 1260 days are twice mentioned by Daniel, and he states this number in the same form of words. In chap. vii. 25, it is, "A time, and times, and the dividing of time." In chap. xii. 7, it is, "A time, times, and an half." This number is once mentioned by John, in the same way, In Rev. xii. 14, it is, "A time, and times, and half a time." John also states this number in two other forms, and twice in each of them. We have the following account of it, Rev. xi. 2, "And the holy city shall they tread under foot forty and two months." And again, chap. xiii. 5, "And power was given to him to continue forty and two months." The third form in which John represents this number, is found, chap. xi. 3. "And they shall prophesy a thousand two

hundred and three-score days, clothed in sackcloth." He also represents in the same way, chap. xii. 6. "That they should feed her there, a thousand two hundred and three-score days." Those different representations describe a number of the same duration. The time, and times and an half, signify one year, two years, and half a year; or three years and a half. This number contains exactly forty and two months; and, allowing thirty days to each month, according to the Jewish manner of calculating time, both the three years and an half, and the forty two months contain exactly one thousand two hundred and sixty days. The beautiful harmony of those descriptions of this number establishes the truth of this explanation of them, and shows that they describe a period of the same duration. This will also appear from the events which are predicted to happen under all those descriptions of this time. That the time, and times, and half a time, of John, are the same with his one thousand two hundred and three-score days, is confirmed by Rev. xii. 6. 14. In verse 6, it is said, "And the woman fled into the wilderness, where she hath a place prepared of God, that they should feed her there, a thousand two hundred and three-score days." In verse 14, it is said, "And to the woman were given the wings of a great eagle, that she might fly into the wilderness, into her place, where she is nourished for a time, and times, and half a time, from the face of the serpent." Since the church's low condition, in her wilderness state, and God's care of her there, are represented both by the 1260 days, and the time, and times, and half a time; we must therefore conclude that those two representations must describe the same portion of time. The time, and times, and an half, mentioned by Daniel, signify in general, the same time that is mentioned by John's forty and two months; because, the former describes the season in which the church is given up to the little horn of the Roman beast, and the latter signifies the period during which the Gentiles shall tread under foot the holy city, and when the beast, which is the head of those Gentiles, shall have power to continue in his blasphemy, persecution and war. As the sufferings of the church under the little horn, are the same with the witnesses prophesying in sackcloth, and the woman's remaining in the wilderness, both of which is for 1260 days, this period must in general coincide with Daniel's three years, and a half. From this agreement in their signification, the similarity of the meaning of these representations of this number is satisfactorily demonstrated.

3. Each of the days, which is contained in the number of 1260, and in the additional numbers of 30 and 45, is the prophetic symbol for one year. According to this view of the first number the time of the beast's war with the church, and of her depressed state must continue for the long season of 1260 years. Besides, there are two other numbers, which must be added to Daniel's 1260 years, one of 30, and another of 45 days, which must expire before the church's happy condition will begin. The 30 days must also signify 30 years, and the 45 days must represent 45 years; and these, being added together, form Daniel's gross number, of one thousand three hundred and five and thirty years. From the nature of the predicted events, this method of reckoning the prophetic numbers, is necessary. Since the predictions will not apply to the providences, unless this method is observed; it plainly proves, that this was the design of the Spirit of prophecy, in making those revelations to men.—Besides, this application of a day for a year, is of Divine institution. To the Prophet Ezekiel the Lord said, "I have appointed thee, each day for a year," Chap. iv. 6. The same thing is intimated by the Lord's word to Israel, Num. xiv. 34. "After the number of the days in which ye searched the land, even forty days, each day for a year, shall ye bear your iniquities, and ye shall know my breach of promise." As the writers on prophecy, are agreed in this view of the numbers, and as Christians, who exercise themselves on

those subjects, are understood to be of the same opinion, further discussion on it is unnecessary.

4. Distinct and important events, which will be most conspicuous accomplishments of Scripture predictions, will commence at the expiration of each of Daniel's three numbers, which are contained in his 1335 years. The sitting of the judgment will begin at the expiration of his time, and times, and half a time, or his 1260 years. In Dan. vii. 25 we are assured, that, "the saints shall be given into the hand of the Antichristian horn, until a time, and times, and the dividing of time." Again, in ver. 21, 22, it is said, "I beheld, and the same horn made war with the saints, and prevailed against them; Until the Ancient of days came, and judgment was given to the saints of the Most High." From these texts, it is ascertained, beyond the possibility of a doubt, that Antichrist's domineering power over the church will continue till the end of Daniel's 1260 years; and that his war with the saints, and his prevalence over them are terminated, at the coming of the Ancient of days, and when the judgment shall begin to sit. These two events must happen together, at the end of Daniel's time, and times, and the dividing of time. His successful war with the church must cease, and the judgment to take away his dominion, to consume and destroy it to the end, must begin, when Daniel's 1260 days, or years, expire. The prophetic symbol by which the Prophet is directed to represent Antichrist's destruction, is that of a judge sitting on the judicial trial of a great state criminal. As among men, a capital criminal is rendered incapable of re-acting his crime, is suffered to live, and is permitted to defend himself, while the judgment is sitting on him; so the Antichristian beast while the judgment sits on him, shall be restrained, shall be permitted to exist, and shall be allowed to act in his own defence, till the judgment is finished, and the sentence is executed on him. The sounding of the seventh trumpet, and the coming of the third wo, in John's predictions, are the same with the sitting of the judgment, in those of Daniel.

These are mentioned, Rev. xi. 14, 15, "The second wo is past, and behold the third wo cometh quickly. And the seventh angel sounded." The seventh trumpet introduces the seven vials, and the third wo comprehends all the seven last plagues which are contained in the seven golden vials, full of the wrath of God. It follows then that the sitting of judgment, to destroy the dominion of Antichrist, will commence; and the effusion of the seven vials on the Roman earth will begin, at the expiration of Daniel's 1260 years. The effects produced by the sitting of the judgment, in Daniel's prophecy, are the destruction of the Roman beast, and his little horn; and the saints possessing the kingdom. The effects produced by the effusion of the vials are the division of the Antichristian city into three parts; the fall of the cities of the nations, and great Babylon's drinking the cup of the wine of the fierceness of the wrath of God; and the introduction and establishment on the earth of the millennial song, the marriage of the Lamb, and his marriage supper. From this it appears, that the sitting of the judgment in Daniel's prophecy, and the effusion of the vials in the visions of John, relate to the same transactions, shall be fulfilled at the same time, and will produce the same glorious results.

That public and solemn transaction which will commence at the expiration of the 30 years, or, counting from the beginning of the time, as Daniel does, the 1290 years, must now be considered. It is the opinion of some writers on prophecy, that those 30 years are the time in which the vials of Divine wrath shall be poured on the earth. As those years belong to the season when the judgment shall sit, they must be a part of that time, which is appointed for the effusion of the vials; but that those judgments of God on his enemies shall terminate, when these years expire, is more than we are warranted to assert. Let us attend to the Prophet's words, in which this number is mentioned. "And from the time that the daily sacrifice shall be taken away, and the abomination that maketh desolate set up, there shall be a thousand two hundred and ninety days;" these words very plainly describe what shall be done, at the commencement of the 1290 years, and characterise the time, from which they are to be dated. When the Christian religion, in the purity of its doctrine, worship, and administrations, shall be suspended; and when the Antichristian abomination, which spreads dessolation over the church, shall be established; at that fatal time these 1290 years begin. In the text, however, nothing is said concerning the event which shall happen at their termination. As nothing is said of this number in any other part of Scripture, we must either remain ignorant of the event which will be brought to pass at its conclusion, or fix it by mere conjecture, or endeavour to come at the knowledge of it from the preceding context. While we, in considering prophecy, should avoid all conjectures, and be willing to remain ignorant, when God is pleased to withhold information; yet we are warranted to employ the light, which the prophecy in general spreads around us, for explaining any of its parts. If we look into the foregoing part of this chapter, Daniel xii. we will find that the deliverance of the Jews is mentioned once and again, as a special object, concerning which Daniel received information. We may, on that account, consider it as the event which will commence, at the expiration of the 1290 years In this view of the matter, the eleventh verse may be supplied from the first and seventh verses, in the following way. And from the time that the daily sacrifice shall be taken away, and the abomination that maketh desolate set up, till the time that thy people shall be delivered, every one that shall be found written in the book, and the time when he shall have accomplished to scatter the power of the holy people, there shall be a thousand two hundred and ninety days, or years. We cannot conclude on this with absolute certainty, but from this connexion of things, we have some reason to hope, that at the expiration of Daniel's 1290 years, 30 years after the judgment begins to sit, and the vials begin to be poured out, the conversion, and the restoration of the Jews to their own land, will have a conspicuous commencement.

We have no reason to doubt of that glorious transaction, which shall be accomplished among men, at the expiration of Daniel's number of 45 years, or counting from the beginning of this time, his 1335 years. The words of Daniel, where this number is mentioned, sufficiently explain it. "Blessed is he that waiteth, and cometh to the thousand three hundred and five and thirty days," or years, ver. 12. The period of great blessedness shall then be introduced. It is not the blessedness of believers in general, which Daniel records in this verse. All those who wait in faith, though they should not come to the 1335 years, are blessed; yea, and they shall be blessed. But it is the peculiar blessedness of those who wait and come to the 1335 days, that Daniel's vision describes. The blessedness of the millennial season, the glory of the millennial church, and the felicity of the millennial saints are here declared. By this part of the vision, Daniel's question, what shall be the end of these things? is fully answered. This is the same with that which is mentioned in Rev. xix. 9. "And he saith unto me, Write, Blessed are they which are called unto the marriage supper of the Lamb: And he saith unto me, These are the true sayings of God." Then shall the church completely emerge from the wilderness, put off her sackcloth, and finish her witnessing prophecy. Then shall she celebrate her millennial song, partake of the marriage supper, and begin her reign with Christ a thousand years. Then shall the church be entirely delivered from the great words, the war, and the dominion of the Roman beast, and his little horn. "And then shall the kingdom and dominion, and the greatness of the kingdom under the whole heaven be given to the people of the saints of the Most High."

5. From this view of Daniel's numbers, and the transactions that will begin at the expiration of each of them, we may be positively assured, that the judgment will begin to sit, or in the Prophet's words, the judgment shall be set, and the books opened, at the expiration of his first number, 1260 years. This shall also be the time when that great voice shall be uttered from heaven; "saying to the seven angels, Go your ways, and pour out the vials of the wrath of God upon the earth." That at the expiration of his second number of 30 years, which being added to 1260, makes up his 1290 years, we have some reason to hope, that Israel's deliverance will begin. And at the expiration of his third number, of 45 years, which, being added to the other numbers, makes 1335 years, we are assured the glorious season of the church's purity and rest, shall take its auspicious commencement. The Prophet's words warrant us to believe, that the last year of the 45 years, or, which is the same, the last year of the 1335 years, will be the first year of the blessed millennium. It cannot begin sooner; for the church is not blessed till she wait and come to that year: It cannot be delayed till a following year; for when that year shall arrive, her blessedness shall begin. If we add Daniel's two last numbers together, 30 and 45, we will have 75 years. As the last of those years belongs to the millennium it must be taken from that number which will leave the number of 74 years. This is the time during which the judgment shall sit on the little horn, and the vials shall be poured out on the Roman earth. These, we are certain, will commence, when Daniel's 1260 years shall expire, on the first year of the thirty years, or which is the same thing, on the first year of the 74 years. As there is no interval between the complete destruction of the little horn with the Roman beast, and the saints possessing the kingdom; as there is no interval between the final ruin of Antichrist with the lamentations of the kings, of the mer-

chants, and the sailors over it, and the church's millennial song, but the latter is represented, both by Daniel and John, as immediately succeeding the former; the final sitting of the judgment, the last drop of the vials, the decisive stroke. of the armageddon war, or the consummating effect of all the three, shall take place in the 74th year, or, calculating from the beginning of the times, which is the very same thing, in the 1334th year. This work of judgment being finished, the glorious millennium shall begin in the 75th year, or in the 1335th year, according to the infallible declaration of the Spirit of prophecy, speaking in Daniel, "Blessed is he that waiteth, and cometh to the thousand three hundred and five and thirty days." These conclusions are deduced with confidence, and reasonable contradiction seems to be impossible.

6. Different dates have been assigned for the commencement, and the termination of the 1260 years. On this important matter, writers on prophecy have not agreed. There were different times of the Jews captivity to Babylon, and as many corresponding periods of their return. As Babylon was a type of Antichrist, and the sufferings of the Jews in Chaldea, prefigured the church's low state under popery; it is not unreasonable to suppose, that something of the same kind may be found in the church's liberation from Babylon the great. As there was one principal captivity to Babylon, and one most general and public return, in which Jeremiah's predictions were visibly fulfilled; so there must be one period for Antichrist's rise, and a corresponding one for his fall, at the former of which the church is brought into bondage, and at the latter she obtains deliverance, in which the predictions of Daniel and John shall have their principal and most conspicuous accomplishment. There was about the space of 1260 years, between the time of Constantine, who, by his extravagant favours bestowed on the Christian clergy, early in the fourth century, laid the foundation for antichristian domination, and the establish-

ment of the Protestant reformation, a little after the middle of the sixteenth century. Though there is no reason to consider the former of those events as the rise, or the latter as the fall of Antichrist; yet the one was such a preparation for his coming, and the other such a presage of his destruction, as render both those occurrences in Divine providence worthy of our serious consideration. Some valuable writers have fixed the date of Antichrist's rise at the middle of the eight century, when Pepin, King of France, in the year 756, raised him to the dignity of a temporal prince. This period will carry us forward, for the ending of the 1260 years, to the twenty-first century, and it would terminate in the year 2016. As the Pope's possession of civil power is not essential to his Scriptural characters, as the Man of Sin, the Antichrist, and the false Prophet, and as the grant of Pepin rather raised him to his height, than gave him birth, there does not seem to be any valid reason for considering that period to be the rise of the Papacy. Something, however, may take place in the millennial church, at the time which corresponds with this period of the Pope's aggrandisement, near the beginning of the twenty-first century, which may be very remarkable. About that time, perhaps, the unexplored parts of the earth, where the foot of civilized man has never trodden, may submit to the sceptre of Jesus; such as the interior of Africa, of the American Continents, of New Holland, and some parts of Assia, or the undiscovered islands of the sea. There are other two dates of the rise of popery, and, of course, also of its fall, about which modern writers on prophecy are divided in opinion. One of these dates is in the year 533, when the Emperor Justinian constituted the Bishop of Rome, the Head over all the churches. The other date is in the year 606, when the Emperor Phocas declared the Bishop of Rome to be the Head of the church. Of the decree of Phocas, it is affirmed, there is no record; it is only mentioned in history. Of the decree of Justinian there is a solemn record, and all the accompanying documents are yet extant. It has also been said, that the decree of Phocas was only a ratification of Justinian's decree, and rather confirmed to the Bishop of Rome the supremacy over the church, than conferred on him that Antichristian dignity. According to this view of Antichrist's rise in 533, Daniel's 1260 years have expired, the seventh trumpet has sounded, the third wo has come, the vials have begun to be poured out, and the judgment began to sit in the year 1792, when that most uncommon, general, destructive, and judgment-like war, that Europe ever saw, had its dismal commencement. From 533 till 1792 inclusive of these years, we have Daniel's number of 1260 years. The 30 additional years, and the number of 1290 years, will terminate in 1822, when the public conversion and restoration of Israel will probably begin. The second additional number of 75 years, and the gross number of 1335 will come to their end in 1867, exactly 50 years from the present time; when Satan's kingdom, in its heathenish, mahometan, and popish forms, shall have fallen as lightning from heaven; when the conversion of Jacob's seed, and their return to their own land will be perfected; when the protestant churches will be revived and purified; when the pagan, mahometan and antichristian nations will be enlightened and turned to the Lord; and when the church, in her millennial glory, purity and rest, will be established on the earth.

7. It is humbly submitted, if the two dates last mentioned, about which modern writers differ, may not be perfectly reconciled, by the following view of the predictions of Daniel and John. Let us suppose, that the 1260 years, mentioned by Daniel, began at 533, the first of those dates; and that John's 1260 years commenced at 606, the second date. In this scheme John's number will end in 1866, and Daniel's three numbers, reserving the last year in them for the first of the Millennium, will end in the very same year, in 1866. This singular coincidence in the dates, and their answering

so exactly to the numbers of the Prophet, and to the number of the Apostle, so as to cause both of them terminate in the same year, certainly deserves our attention. The reasons for suggesting this idea of the times are the following:

The additional numbers of 30 and 45 are necessary, in the prophecies of Daniel, to express the time that must elapse, from the rise of Antichrist till the beginning of the millennium. No notice is taken of those numbers—no reference is made to them in the visions of John. From this we conclude, that these additional numbers are not to be employed in explaining John's number. Since John does not mention Daniel's gross number of 1335, nor his additional numbers of 30 and 45; they were not contemplated by him, as belonging to his scheme, nor must they be introduced by us, in order to explain it. John's prophecies, being the last, are the most full and particular; they illuminate the predictions of Daniel. They are, however, two different schemes of prophecy, in which, though they most harmoniously agree, different numbers and symbols are employed. John mentions his number five several times, and in three different forms, and mentions no other number; the symbolical representation of his scheme of prophecy is larger and more systematic than that of Daniel; and by detached visions different parts of his scheme are sometimes exhibited in miniature, and are sometimes amplified; can we therefore suppose, if the superadded numbers of the Prophet had been necessary to explain the predictions of the Apostle, that they would not be mentioned in his visions?

There is a necessity that John's number of 1260, and Daniel's number of 1335 should terminate at the same time; but there does not appear to be the same necessity for their commencing together. They must terminate at the same time, because John's 1260 years must continue till the beginning of the millennium, as he does not mention any other number which intervenes betwixt the end of the former, and the commencement of the latter. In John's 1260 years, the time of the vials, or the season of judgment, must be included, because his prophecy mentions no other number of years, in which these transactions are to be accomplished. Daniel's number of 1335 years exceeds John's 1260 years, by 75 years. As the last of those years belongs to the millennial period, it must be separated from the number, and we have 74 years. Since the only wise God, as the Author of prophecy, has given us two schemes of time, the one of which exceeds the other by 74 years; and since He, as the God of providence, has given us two conspicuous dates, whose claim to be the rise of Antichrist is so nearly equal, and whose distance from one another, inclusive of the first year, is exactly 74 years, there appears to be good reason, from this remarkable coincidence of time, to adopt this method of reconciling them.

Besides, if Daniel's numbers do not begin at 533, that most conspicuous and best attested date of Antichrist's rise is altogether overlooked in prophecy; which is a conclusion that those who have a due regard to Him, who is the giver of prophecy, and the God of providence, will not be easily persuaded to believe. If it is maintained that Daniel's 1260 years do not commence till 606, the judgment will not sit, the Ancient of days will not come, the seventh angel will not sound his trumpet, and none of the vials included in the third wo will be poured out till 1866; for Daniel undoubtedly fixes the sitting of the judgment, at the expiration of his time, and times, and the dividing of time, or at the end of the 1260 years, as they are mentioned by him. This is a conclusion entirely at variance with the opinion of those, who plead for Antichrist's rise in 606. If there is not a scheme of prophecy which contemplates the rise of Antichrist at 606, then that providential dispensation, which took place in that year, is also disregarded in Divine predictions, which reflects no honour on Him whose works are the fulfilment of his word. Since God, in his holy providence, has furnished us with two conspicuous dates, for the entering of the man of sin into the Lord's temple; and since he, in his holy word, has revealed a double scheme of numbers relating to the rise and fall of Antichrist, and to the subjugation and emancipation of his church, one of which dates exactly agrees to the numbers of Daniel, and the other to the number of John, and both harmoniously terminate in the same year, it must be exceedingly probable, if not absolutely certain, that it was God's design to mark out to the church that most important era, by this twofold account of it.

No valid objection can be made against the accuracy of those calculations, arising from our beginning Daniel's numbers with the 533d year of the Christian era, and not at the termination of that year; or from our beginning John's number, at the end of 606, and not with that year. The former was the eastern mode of calculating time, when Daniel's predictions were delivered, and when the seat of empire was established in the east. The usage of the time, and place of Daniel's visions must necessarily be employed, in explaining his prophetic numbers. The latter was the western mode of computing time, when John saw his visions, and when the seat of empire was transferred to the western part of the earth. The custom of that time and place must also be observed, in explaining the commencement and termination of John's number.

Since this method of explaining and reconciling those numbers, so far as I know, has not been formerly used; since it may have a tendency to unite the opinions of authors, on this interesting enquiry, concerning the beginning and the ending of those numbers; since it seems to lay a solid foundation for our hope, concerning the time when all those things shall be fulfilled; and since it appears to display the wisdom and harmony of the word and works of God, it is most respectfully submitted to the consideration of Christian professors.

With a few reflections which the foregoing remarks seem to suggest, this disourse shall be concluded.

1. We must carefully distinguish between a Divine prediction and an human explanation of it; betwixt scriptural numbers mentioned in prophecy, and men's calculations concerning their beginning and ending The one is perfect and certain, the other may be very imperfect and false. Though human interpretations of prophecy should prove fallacious, the error attaches, not to the prediction, but to the explanation of it; not to the Author of prophecy, but to the fallible interpreter. Though human calculations should prove erroneous, the prophetic numbers themselves are without error. Our disappointment, by a false explanation of a prediction, ought not to engender in our minds any prejudice or objection at the prophecy itself Very unreasonable it will be to undervalue the prediction, because of the error of its explanation; and to charge God foolishly, on account of the mistakes of men. Though Divine providence should sweep away, to their very foundations, the explanations and calculations of men; the Divine prediction will still stand sure like an immovable rock, and will be accomplished in its season, and in all its parts. Divine predictions and human explanations must be distinguished also as to our esteem of them. All our esteem of that which is human, should centre on that which is divine. Any regard we may have for the labours of men, on those subjects, should increase our love and admiration of the Author of prophecy, who only could reveal it, and who alone can make it come to pass. There is also a difference between these two objects, in the manner in which we should examine them. In our examination of scripture prophecy, reverence for the glorious Author of it, a certain belief of its truth, and an humble desire to know the mind of God, by the light of his own Spirit, should fill our hearts. In coming to an examination of an explanation of prophecy, the Christian's mind, not being freed from the fear of error in the object of his

consideration, ought to exercise guarded suspicion, and ought rather to delay, than rashly to form his opinion.

2. In scripture prophecy, there will be found such a mystery, majesty, and beauty, as should raise our admiration of its Author, and attract our attention to itself. Of all Divine predictions, this is the infallible description; "For the prophecy came not in old time by the will of man; but holy men of God spake as they were moved by the Holy Ghost." Holy persons who were sanctified of God, uninfluenced by their own will, and guided and taught by the Divine Spirit, delivered those messages of God to men, messages which are full of mystery, majesty, and beauty. Of all scripture predictions, there are none which possess those qualities more eminently than the prophecies of Daniel and John, respecting the grand Antichrist, and the church of the living God. The symbols that are used to represent those very different objects, are most appropriate and significant. Their diversity in the two schemes hurts not their unity, darkens not their meaning, but rather illustrates and confirms their application to the objects which they represent. The different numbers that are mentioned cordially harmonise, and tend to confirm our minds in the truth of their application. Systematic forms of representing a long series of events, by a long war, and the solemn session of a court of judgment, by the opening of seven seals, the sounding of seven trumpets, and the pouring out of seven vials; and by collateral visions, some of which give a more summary, and others a more detailed description of the same things, plainly mark the whole structure of the predictions, to be the offspring of Divine wisdom, and the fulfilment of it, to be the effect of Divine power. As the millennial church shall praise him for its accomplishment; let us thank him for its revelation, and wait its issue.

3. Divine predictions shall be assuredly fulfilled. The giver of prophecy is the God of providence. He does what he will in the army of heaven, and among the inhabitants of

the earth. Prophecy contains promises and threatenings; promises when it respects the church, and threatenings when his enemies are the objects of it. His faithfulness and power are engaged to fulfil his promises to his people; prophecy, so far as it contains a revelation of good things to the church, shall, therefore, be fulfilled. The Divine veracity and power are also interested in executing the threatenings against his enemies; prophecy, therefore, in so far as it exhibits them, shall assuredly come to pass. " To me belongeth vengeance and recompence; their foot shall slide in due time, for the day of their calamity is at hand, and the things that shall come upon them make haste. For the Lord shall judge his people, and repent himself concerning his servants, when he seeth that their power is gone, and there is none shut up or left." Very considerable parts of those predictions have been already accomplished, and shall we suspect the fulfilment of the rest? The most dismal parts of them, concerning the rise and reign of the enemy, have come to pass; we should not, therefore, hesitate about the accomplishment of those parts of the prediction, which are more glorious and joyful. As the time of Antichrist's elevation has come, so the season of his destruction shall arrive. Since the predictions concerning the church's sufferings have been fulfilled, those which relate to her blessedness and glory shall likewise be accomplished. " God is not a man, that he should lie; neither the son of man, that he should repent: hath he said, and shall he not do it? or hath he spoken, and shall he not make it good?" Num. xxiii. 19.

4. The present appearances in the religious world encourage the hope, that some great and happy change among men is fast approaching. The extraordinary endeavours that are now made, to send the word and gospel of Christ into all the earth, seem to be the harbinger of this change, and the means by which it will be effected. These endeavours are of such a nature, of such variety, of such extent, and have produced already such wonderful effects, as render

it very probable that the grand millennial season may arrive at the time, to which our view of the prophetic numbers has conducted us. The Bible Societies, for instance, have existed only thirteen years. There are precisely four times that number of years from the present time till the year 1867. If those Societies have accomplished such great things in these thirteen years, in part of which period the scheme has been in its infancy; what may we suppose it will accomplish, if it is continued, with the Divine blessing, for fifty years longer? It is not at all unreasonable to suppose, that by the time that the Sixty-second annual Report of the British and Foreign Bible Society shall be published, all the parts of the earth will have been, for a considerable time, in possession of the holy Scriptures. If they shall be in possession of the Divine word, may we not hope, that they shall also be turned from dumb idols, to the service of the living God, through our Lord Jesus Christ. Respecting the evangelic missions, the schools, the circulation of religious tracts, and the endeavours to graft Israel into their own olive-tree, the same method of reasoning might be adopted. If these different attempts to set up the Redeemer's kingdom among men, have, in the short time that is past, done great and wonderful things; may we not confidently expect, if their labours are continued half a century longer, the blessing of God, and the working of the Spirit accompanying them, that all the ends of the earth may then see the salvation of our God. From these things it appears, even by the light of human probability, that we have reason to expect, that the great and glorious day of the Lord may come at the time that was mentioned. If the view that we have taken of the prophetic numbers be correct, as we hope it is, then it may be said; "We have also a more sure word of prophecy; whereunto ye do well that ye take heed, as unto a light that shineth in a dark place, until the day dawn and the day star arise in your hearts."

5. The knowledge of the particular stage, in the church's journey, at which she has now arrived, and in which she is now moving forward to the promised land of her millennial rest, is a very desirable, and important attainment. Though it would be most unbecoming, to speak with presumptuous confidence, or in the language of absolute certainty, concerning the precise time; yet a fair application of the predicted events, and the prophetic numbers, to the past and present operations of providence, and to the seasons in which the Lord has brought them to pass, will enable us, with strong probability, to answer those weighty interrogations, " Watchman, what of the night?" How long shall it be to the end of these wonders? Our opinion is this—That Daniel's 1260 years, began with the 533d year of the Christian era, and ended at 1792; that his additional number of 30 years, which makes his first number 1290, beginning where the former ended, will expire in 1822; and his third number of 45 years, which completes his gross number of 1335 years, will end in 1867, the last year of which will be the first of the blessed millennium. With this calculation, John's number perfectly agrees, when dated from 606, the second date of the rise of popery; because from 606 to 1866 there are 1260 years. The judgment against the little horn, and for the church's deliverance and exaltation, has been sitting, and the vials have been pouring out since 1792.—These will be continued till 1866, and will be completely finished on that year. The blessed state of the church will commence in 1867, the year, to which those who wait and come are blessed. This happy period of the church shall be continued 1000 years, or, for a long time. After which the millennial day will have a short evening, called " a little season", which will be followed by the general judgment. These are the conclusions to which we are led, by this investigation of the prophetic numbers. That they are perfectly correct and infallibly true, we dare not assert; but that they are probable, and worthy of our

consideration, there is some reason to believe. According to this view, we have now passed through one third part of the time of the sitting of the judgment, and the effusion of the vials; and two thirds of that time, or 49 years, from the expiration of this year, 1817, remain yet to be fulfilled. The 25 years of this season, which have now passed over us, have been most eventful, both for the Divine judgments which have been on the earth, and for the means that have been employed for illuminating and converting the nations to the faith of Jesus. The 49 years of this season that are yet to come, will also be full of most important events. During that time, the Lord will, on the one hand, perform the remaining part of his strange work of judgments, of one kind or another, on his Antichristian enemies, till they are removed from the earth; and, on the other hand, he will give increasing activity and success to the means of grace that are and shall be used, for filling the earth with the knowledge of the glory of the Lord, till all nations are prepared for entering into the millennial glory, when "there shall be one fold and one shepherd, one Lord and his name one."

6. An humble examination of the predictions of God's word, and a religious observation of the dispensations of his providence, constitute a necessary part of that duty which is incumbent on Christians especially at such a time as this. The command to search the Scriptures comprehends the former, and the injunction to regard the operations of his hands includes the latter. The neglect of either of them must be a great evil. Let us, therefore, turn our attention frequently to the word and to the works of God. To his word which foretells the events of those times, and to his works which fulfil his word. Indifference and inattention to those things are sinful and profane. The want of zeal for the Divine glory, and a concern for the kingdom of Christ and the salvation of men, are the causes of this criminal negligence. Religious exercise about the words of his

mouth, and the doings of his hand, even though we may be disappointed in some of our expectations, is unspeakably better than a careless neutrality in the cause of God and religion. The difficulties which attend this investigation, should not deter us from essaying it. In your meditation on those things, cry to the Lord, by prayer, for his counsel and direction. Take the help of your Christian brethren's knowledge and experience in those matters, by familiar conversation about them with one another. Compare different parts of Scripture together, and separate dispensations of providence with each other; that the light you obtain from all, may help you to understand that which seems most difficult and dark. Be not discouraged by the want of success in any one attempt; but renew your endeavours, in the hope of succeeding better, through grace, on another occasion. Let not your searchings into God's words and works, lead you to vain speculation; but make such an use of them as will influence your inward exercise, and direct your outward conduct. Happy will you be, if those endeavours you exert in searching his word, and in observing his operations, impress more deeply on your souls, those words of Jesus; "The time is fulfilled, and the kingdom of God is at hand; repent ye, and believe the gospel."

AN

INQUIRY

INTO

THE CHRISTIAN'S DUTY AT THIS INTERESTING CRISIS.

DISCOURSE V.

MARK i. 15.—*Repent ye, and believe the gospel.*

DIVINE dispensations to the church, whether of mercy or of judgment, should excite her members to the exercise of godliness. As this should be the fruit of all those private and personal providences, by which we receive good or evil at the hand of the Lord; so his public providences to the church, of either kind, should produce on us the same effect. As the saints are called to live by faith, the sure prospect of the church's trials and deliverances, on the warrant of the word of God, ought to lead them to religious exercises. Without this, Christians will be unprepared for those sad or joyful events when they occur; but, in this frame of mind, they will be enabled, under the former, to be patient in tribulation, and under the latter, to praise the Lord for his goodness, and for his wonderful works to the children of men. In our text, the Lord Jesus informed men of that change which he would effect, by his coming into the world. He would put an end to that season of imperfection, darkness, and spiritual bondage; and would introduce among men a time of light, liberty, and reformation. The time is fulfilled, and the kingdom of God is at hand. That the generation might be prepared for that important alteration, he calls them to such religious duties as would be a mean of making them ready for those Divine providences, by which this change should be accomplished. Repent ye, and believe the gospel. As our circumstances are very similar to those of the Jews, when Christ began his public ministry among them; the exhortation which he addressed to them, must be peculiarly suited to us. At all times, and in every condition, Christ's exhortation is adapted to the situation of his followers; but when the church is approaching to that crisis, when Antichrist's reign shall be fulfilled, and when the millennial kingdom of God is at hand, the Christians of this generation should apply to themselves, the Redeemer's warning call, Repent ye, and believe the gospel. The duties which are comprehended in this command are very many; but their number does not exceed their necessity and importance. It is usual in the Scriptures to exhibit many profitable duties in a few particulars, and sometimes in those which are mentioned in the text. In a most solemn and farewell address to the Elders of Ephesus, Paul declares the grand substance of the gospel he had preached; "Testifying both to the Jews, and also to the Greeks, repentance toward God, and faith toward our Lord Jesus Christ," Acts xx. 21. The great Teacher, who came from God, exemplified this in our text, Repent ye, and believe the gospel. Let us now proceed to the

V. General branch of our subject. To state the Christian's duty at the present time, by shewing what is included in Christ's command, Repent ye, and believe the gospel.

1. This command requires of us a proper knowledge of the objects, about which faith and repentance are versant. Repentance has a relation to sin, and faith has a respect to the gospel. A knowledge of sin is necessary to our exercising repentance, and an understanding of the gospel is requisite to our believing it. Repentance, therefore, has a

relation to our transgressions. None of God's rational creatures can be the subjects of repentance, but those who have sinned, and come short of the glory of God. A superficial knowledge of sin cannot be a sufficient foundation for genuine repentance. It is that understanding of it, which is conveyed into the soul, by the light of God's word, and the operation of the Divine Spirit. The precepts and threatenings of the holy law are, by Divine agency, powerfully applied to the sinner's conscience, when the person obtains that knowledge of sin, that is followed by true repentance. They know it in its evil nature, as it is an act of rebellion against the authority and law of the King eternal, as it is hateful in his sight, and as it is infinitely dishonouring to him. They see it in its guilt and demerit as it exposes them to Divine wrath, to the curse of the law, and to everlasting punishment. They discern its pollution as it defiles all the faculties of their souls, the members of their bodies, and all their religious duties. They experience that power which it exercises over them, and from which they cannot deliver themselves. They are convinced of the sin of their nature, of their thoughts, words, and actions. They obtain such discoveries of their sin, as constrain them to say, "Innumerable evils have compassed me about; mine iniquities have taken hold upon me, so that I am not able to look up; they are more than the hairs of mine head; therefore my heart faileth me."—Faith has for its object the glorious gospel, the knowledge of which is necessary to our believing it. True Christians know the gospel, by the light of the Divine word shining into their hearts, by the Spirit of wisdom and revelation in the knowledge of Christ. They know it as a revelation of Divine grace and mercy to sinners through the Lord Jesus. The substance of it is declared in the angelic message, "Behold, I bring you good tidings of great joy, which shall be to all people; For unto you is born this day, in the city of David, a Saviour, which is Christ the Lord." Luke ii. 10, 11. They perceive it to be a display of Divine love to men, in the gift of his only begotten Son, that whosoever believeth in him should not perish, but have everlasting life. They know the gospel as a revelation and offer to them of our Lord Jesus Christ, in his person, as he is God and man; in his office as he is the Mediator between God and man; in his righteousness, which he brought in by his obedience, sufferings and death; in his fulness of Spirit and grace for supplying all his people's wants; and in his everlasting salvation, which he will bestow on those who trust in him. They know the gospel as a revelation of the holy Spirit who quickens, enlightens, sanctifies, and comforts believers in the ways of godliness. Without this knowledge of the gospel, none can believe it to the saving of their souls.

2. The duty which Christ enjoins includes a knowledge of the nature of saving faith, and evangelic repentance. Those who have obtained the precious faith of God's elect, have a scriptural knowledge of it; and those who are blessed with repentance unto life, are enabled to understand it. They know the grace of faith in its nature and actings. In its nature they see it to be a supernatural principle implanted in their heart, and in its actings they find it is a compliance with the whole revelation of Divine grace in Christ, for the salvation of their souls. Christ, and the grace of God in him are the great substance of the gospel. Those who are enabled, with all their hearts, to exercise an holy complacency, in the grace of God reigning through righteousness, unto eternal life, by Jesus Christ our Lord, do believe the gospel. Faith in its actings is a receiving Christ, an embracing him in all his offices, a coming to him by a motion of the soul, a looking to him by the eye of the mind, a resting on him, and a trusting in him with the whole heart, for enjoying all the blessings that are contained in the promises of God. This faith ultimately receives and rests on God the Father for the enjoyment of all salvation, through the mediation of his dear Son. By

him do the saints believe in God who raised him up from the dead, and gave him glory; that their faith and hope might be in God.—They have also a scriptural knowledge of true repentance. They find that the actings of that grace in them, are as various, necessary and important, as are the actings of their faith. Having obtained a sight of the evil nature of their sin, having searched into their transgressions in heart and life, and having seen themselves to be guilty, miserable and lost sinners; they accuse and condemn themselves, they mourn over their sin, they afflict their souls before the Lord on account of their iniquity, they confess it to God in all its aggravation, they acknowledge their desert of everlasting punishment, they hate sin with a perfect hatred, more for what it is in itself than for its consequences to them, they justify the Divine law, both in its precept and penalty, they look to the mercy of God through Christ's atonement for pardon, and they endeavour to fear God and avoid evil. In these spiritual exercises of the heart, believers are assured, that the grace of repentance does consist.

3. The Saviour's command includes an understanding of the way, in which a sinner is enabled to repent, and to believe the gospel. By the grace of God in Christ, provision is made for causing sinners obtain faith and repentance. Christians, who truly repent of their sin, and believe the gospel, are assured that they have not, by their own power, produced in themselves those precious exercises. Convinced that they are by nature children of wrath, and dead in trespasses and sins, they will cheerfully confess, that they have received them from above. Repentance is the gift of God. "And when they heard these things they held their peace, and glorified God, saying, Then hath God also to the Gentiles granted repentance unto life." Acts xi. 18. To all who enjoy this precious grace it is the gift of the Divine Saviour. "Him hath God exalted with his right hand to be a Prince and a Saviour, for to give repentance

to Israel, and forgiveness of sins." Acts v. 31. Faith is also the gift of God. "For by grace are ye saved through faith; and that not of yourselves, it is the gift of God." Eph. ii. 8. It is likewise the gift and purchase of Christ: "For to you it is given in the behalf of Christ, to believe on him." Phil. i. 29. The efficient cause of faith and repentance, and of their exercise in the soul, is stated in that great and precious promise, Zech. xii. 10. "And I will pour upon the house of David, and upon the inhabitants of Jerusalem, the Spirit of grace and of supplications; and they shall look upon me whom they have pierced, and they shall mourn for him, as one mourneth for his only son, and shall be in bitterness for him, as one is in bitterness for his first-born." Faith and repentance are bestowed on sinners as the free gift of God's grace, through the merit and satisfaction of Christ, and by the power of the holy Spirit operating on them, through the instrumentality of the word. Their renewed exercise in the saints is produced in the same way. Faith and repentance are planted in the hearts of men at the same time, when they are blessed with the washing of regeneration, and the renewing of the Holy Ghost. The renovated soul exercises faith in Christ first in the order of nature, and evangelic repentance necessarily follows. When the Spirit of grace is poured on the soul, the person first looks, by an act of faith, on Jesus whom he has pierced by his sins, and then he mourns and is in bitterness for the transgressions which he has committed against him. The exercise of faith on Christ, by receiving and resting on him according to the gospel offer and call, is necessary to interest us in him; and a saving interest in Jesus is necessary to our evangelic repentance. Of whatever nature the repentance of men may be, there is a faith of the same kind which must go before it. A legal repentance cannot exist in any person without a legal faith, or a belief of the law, both in its precept and threatening, with an application of it to the person's own conscience. Nor can there be an evangelic repentance in the hearts of men, till they exercise faith in the gospel, and in him whom it reveals to them, as a Saviour from guilt and punishment.

4. The Saviour's injunction requires of us an earnest concern and endeavour to be possessed of faith and repentance. When we are convinced of the excellency of those spiritual principles, a desire to enjoy them will fill our minds. This desire will excite in us a concern to obtain them; and this concern will constrain us to use every appointed mean, that we may receive power from on high to repent, and to believe the gospel. Sensible of our need of those saving graces, convinced of our inability to produce them in ourselves, and encouraged by the promise of God in Christ Jesus to bestow them on us, we will bow our knees before God's throne, and cry to him, that he may fulfil in us the good pleasure of his goodness, and the work of faith with power. Fixing our attention on the Divine promise to pour on us the Spirit of grace and supplication, that we may look on him, and mourn for sin, we will plead for its accomplishment to us, through the mediation of his dear Son. Reading and meditation on the Divine word belong to those exertions which we should make, that we may obtain faith and repentance. Since the word of God is the mean by which the Spirit implants them in our hearts, searching the Scriptures, and thinking on them, must be adapted to our condition. Hearing the gospel preached to us is another mean for attaining the same end. God has often bestowed on sinners faith and repentance, and has revived the exercise of them in the saints, by this holy ordinance. Faith cometh by hearing, and hearing by the word of God. In Peter's sermon to the multitude on the day of Pentecost, this was exemplified: "Now, when they heard this, they were pricked in their hearts, and said unto Peter and to the rest of the Apostles, "Men and Brethren, what shall we do?" Acts ii. 37. Attending on the ordinance of a preached gospel, they were both filled with conviction of sin, and excited to ask for the way of sal-

vation. Peter directs them to repentance, and to faith in Jesus Christ; the former is expressly mentioned, and the latter is included in their being baptised in his name, for the remission of sin. He also presents to them the gospel encouragement; "For the promise is to you, and to your children, and to all that are afar off, even as many as the Lord our God shall call." Those who comply with Christ's command, are not indifferent to those important concerns; but they endeavour to use every mean, that they may obtain from God saving faith, and repentance unto spiritual and eternal life. Having been stirred up to this diligence in the use of the means, they will endeavour to believe, and to repent, to stretch out the withered hand, to come to Christ, to mourn for their sin, and to express before God their willingness and desire to be debtors to his grace in Christ for salvation. While under this concern, and while using those endeavours, the Spirit comes to the soul, and takes up his abode there, and produces in the heart saving faith, and true repentance. The person is then enabled to believe in the Lord Jesus for eternal life, and to pour out his soul in godly sorrow for sin, which worketh repentance unto salvation, not to be repented of.

5. This command requires of us an habitual desire and endeavour, to live in the exercise of faith and repentance. Divine grace in the heart, being a living and active principle, must have its daily exercise. In its principle, it is in the soul a well of water; and in its exercise, by the Spirit's influence, it springeth up into everlasting life. The command, repent ye, and believe the gospel, expresses, the habitual frame of the Redeemer's children. At no time are Christians exempted from the obligation of this command, to exercise faith and repentance; and at no time should they neglect those exercises. With the being of grace in his soul, no believer will be satisfied; but he will desire also the exercise of grace. The glory of God, the honour of Christ, and the comfort of his own soul are connected with the ex-

ercise of the believer's grace. This exercise consists in that believing and penitent frame, which the saints should habitually endeavour to maintain. To be thus spiritually minded is life and peace. The life that Paul lived in the flesh, was by the faith of the Son of God, who loved him, and gave himself for him. It was Hezekiah's resolution to go softly all his years, in the bitterness of his soul. The whole time of the Believer's sojourning in this world, should be passed in the fear of God. Since sin still dwells in believers, and in thought, word, and action, they are daily transgressing the law of the God of their salvation; repentance, humility, godly sorrow and confession of sin should constitute a part of their habitual exercise. Since the object of faith is still presented to them in the word, and the call to believe is recorded there; a believing improvement of that object should be their daily study. In all religious duties, a believing and penitent frame of Spirit should be exercised. Without this, we will worship God with our mouth, and honour him with our lips, while our hearts, by the want of the exercise of grace in them, will be far removed from him. When the saints are enabled to perform duties in the exercise of grace, they worship God, who is a Spirit, in spirit and in truth; for the Father seeketh such to worship him. It is the will of the Lord Jesus, that his people persevere continually in a penitent and believing frame, and they do not fulfil his will, nor obey his command, when this is not their earnest study.

6. Christ's command extends to that concern which Christians should have, that the evidence of their faith and repentance may be ever clear to their minds. The grace of God, in the souls of his people, has not its exercise only, but it has its evidence also. By this the believer knows that he is possessed of saving faith, and that to him God has granted repentance unto life. This must be a very comfortable attainment. A delight in the word of God, an attachment to religious ordinances, hatred of sin, the study

of true holiness, an earnest concern for the dissemination of the knowledge of God among men, a love to the saints, an inclination to think and converse about religion, and a desire that God may be glorified by themselves and others are some of the evidences of the truth of our faith, and of the sincerity of our repentance. Those who have attained to these things and exercise themselves in them with their whole heart's desire, exhibit satisfactory evidences that they, by Divine grace, have become penitent and believing saints. To have the word of Christ dwelling in us richly, to know in our experience, that it is good for us to draw near to God in the ordinances of Divine worship, to cleanse ourselves from the filthiness of the flesh and spirit, and to perfect holiness in the fear of God are distinguishing characters of penitent believers. To desire that the knowledge of God may fill the earth, to account the saints to be the excellent ones of the earth in whom is all our delight, to take pleasure in thinking and in talking of his doings, and to rejoice when God is glorified among men, will also prove that those, who are the subjects of these exercises, are the children of the living God. To endeavour to cultivate those dispositions, and to apply them as evidences of the truth of our faith and repentance, must be our indispensable duty. By the former we lay up stores of evidences of the truth of our grace, and by the other we bring them forth as proofs of the reality of our personal religion. If we become negligent in the one, we will soon find that we are empoverished as to the other. We must, therefore, exercise ourselves unto godliness, that the evidences of the reality of our faith and repentance may abound in us. It is by self examination that those evidences are brought forth and applied, for ratifying this important matter. For this duty we have a Divine warrant: "Examine yourselves whither ye be in the faith; prove your ownselves; know ye not your ownselves, how that Jesus Christ is in you, except ye be reprobates," or disapproved of God, 2 Cor. xiii. 5. When Christians engage in this duty, and enjoy the Spirit's witnessing with their spirits, that they are the children of God, they will be enabled to discern in themselves those religious exercises, which demonstrate that they are believing penitents. Christ's command, repent ye, and believe the gospel, reaches even unto this; that Christians should diligently study all the parts of religious exercises, and that they apply every one of them, in self-examination, as evidences for confirming and comforting their hearts, in the knowledge of the truth of their faith and repentance.

7. This command also requires, that believers endeavour to reap the fruits, and to enjoy the blessings, which flow from the persevering and spiritual exercise of their faith and repentance. Those gracious principles have not their evidences only; but fruits and blessings accompany them, to the Divine glory and to the saint's benefit. This call, repent ye and believe the gospel, must certainly require the saint's endeavour to enjoy the effects of the principle, and of the exercise of grace, in his own heart. An increase of true holiness in the Christian, is one of those effects. The actings of faith and repentance are special parts of inward holiness. As their exercise in the soul has an influence on love to God, on hope in him, on reverence and Godly fear, and on humility, patience and resignation, all the parts of inward holiness are, in some degree, the fruits of their exercise. The believer's outward holiness, which consists in holy words and actions, flowing from the inward exercises of the soul, are, on this account, the effects of the operation of faith and repentance.—Spiritual joy and comfort belong to those fruits which flow from a believing and penitent frame of soul. "Whom having not seen ye love, in whom though now ye see him not, yet believing, ye rejoice with joy unspeakable and full of glory." Strong consolation is enjoyed by those, who, in a penitential and believing frame, have fled for refuge to lay hold on the hope set before them. We are also assured, that those who sow in the tears of believing peni-

tence, shall reap in joy. Jesus also has said, "Blessed are they that mourn; for they shall be comforted."—Spiritual establishment in the ways of God is a part of that fruit, which the exercise of faith and repentance is instrumental in producing. By the exercise of those graces, believers become more confirmed in their holy principles, practices, and profession. They are rooted and grounded in the faith, and settled, and have their fruit unto holiness, and their end everlasting life. By a believing and penitent frame, believers are more delivered from doubts and fears, from uncertainty and wavering, from unbelief and hardness of heart. By these exercises, also they become more confirmed in the faith and hope of the gospel.—Victory over Satan and the world is also a fruit of their exercise. "Above all, taking the shield of faith, wherewith ye shall be able to quench all the fiery darts of the wicked." With this exhortation of Paul, that of Peter harmoniously agrees; "Whom resist stedfast in the faith." As the believer, by this frame, is enabled to vanquish Satan; so he is made to triumph over the world by the same exercise. This is contained in those words of John; "This is the victory that overcometh the world, even our faith. Who is he that overcometh the world, but he that believeth that Jesus is the Son of God." While those believers who are negligent in the exercise of their faith and repentance, will be overcome by their spiritual enemies; those who live in the daily exercise of them, will be enabled to tread on the lion and adder, the young lion and the dragon shall they trample under their feet.—Spiritual and heavenly mindedness must also be a part of those fruits, which proceed from a believing and repenting frame of soul. The exercise of those graces, under the influence of the Spirit, brings spiritual and heavenly objects into the mind, fixes the heart on them, causes the Christian seek those things which are above, where Christ sitteth at the right hand of God, and enables him to set his affections on things above, and not on the things of the earth.—Of those exercises, holy confidence in God through Christ, when the believer is under trouble, and in the prospect of death, will be the happy fruit. When the believer's faith and repentance are in exercise, he will be joyful in hope, and patient in tribulation. Privileged with the influences of the Spirit, and affected with God's word, the Christian, exercised in a penitent and believing frame, will be enabled to say, "O death! where is thy sting? O grave! where is thy victory?" Christ's command, "Repent ye, and believe the gospel," lays an obligation on his people, to persevere in those exercises, till they have gathered up all those blessed fruits which are instrumentally produced by that faith which is of the operation of God, and by that repentance which is unto everlasting life.

8. Christ's command requires that his people exercise their faith and repentance, concerning that change, which he is accomplishing on the earth. This exhortation is connected with that information which is contained in the preceding part of the text. Christ had assured them that the time was fulfilled, and that the kingdom of God was at hand; and, in consequence of this he exhorts them, to repent, and to believe the gospel, The information has a connexion with the advice, both as a motive to excite them to faith and repentance, and as a rule to guide them in those exercises. He called them to repent and to believe the gospel, because the time was fulfilled, and the kingdom of God was at hand; and they were to exercise those dispositions relative to the operations which they saw, and to the change that they expected. "Repent ye;" Be convinced of your own sins, mourn for them, pray for pardon, confess and forsake them; Be convinced of the imperfection even of those Divine ordinances, under which your fathers have lived, and of the sinfulness of those vain traditions which they have added to those ordinances, and which you have foolishly observed. Be affected with the sin, the idolatry, the darkness, and the misery of those nations who know not God, and call not on his name. "Believe the gospel;" Be ye persuaded that the

times of ignorance and imperfection are now come to an end; and that the New Testament kingdom, which shall be extended to the Gentiles as well as to the Jews, will immediately appear. Believe the gospel which I preach to you, and which my servants shall proclaim among men; and embrace the revelation of mercy to miserable sinners through my death, in which I will give my life a ransom for many. In like manner, we are called to exercise faith and repentance, with respect to the things that are promised, and are coming to pass in our own days, improving them both as a motive to animate, and as a rule to direct us in those exercises. God is now calling us to believe that the day is approaching, when the dark and dreary times of popery and wickedness are coming to an end, and that his millennial kingdom will soon be established. The predicted events which relate both to the fall of the Redeemer's enemies, and to the advancement of his church must be the objects of our faith and hope. The things that are foretold concerning the illumination and conversion of the nations, and the recovery and salvation of Israel, will also be most assuredly believed, by all those who possess this precious faith. As those predictions exhibit objects of faith and hope, so the moral condition of those to whom they relate, furnish us with abundant causes of godly sorrow and repentance. Our own personal transgressions, the sins of God's church, the wickedness of Christ's enemies, the iniquities of the darkened parts of the earth, and the provocations of God's ancient people, as they are dishonouring to God and ruinous to immortal souls, will humble the pious Christian to the dust, will cause him pour out his soul in confession before God, will draw the tear of godly sorrow from his eyes, and will excite him to pray for mercy in Christ to himself, to others, and to the church of God. Since God, in his holy word, has revealed such things as these, without the belief of which the gospel itself cannot be believed, let the consideration both of the joyful and of the awful things that are approaching, animate us to study a penitent and believing exercise of soul, under a conviction that Christ is now saying to us, "The time is fulfilled and the kingdom of God is at hand: repent ye, and believe the gospel."

With some inferences, taken from this part of the method in itself, and in its connexion with the other heads of the doctrine, I shall conclude this subject.

1. From it we may learn the knowledge of those things, in which the exercise of true and undefiled religion does consist. It does not consist in an outward profession of the gospel, in an external observation of Divine ordinances, in a visible circumspection of moral conduct, or in great pretensions to Christian knowledge and piety, by the words of the mouth. Commendable as these things are, they may be found in those who are destitute of true religion, who have the form of godliness, and who know nothing of its power. True religion consists in the exercise of saving faith, and evangelical repentance. Without these, there cannot be any real religion, in fallen man. Christ's own words prove the necessity of those gracious dispositions and exercises, "He that believeth not shall be damned. Except ye repent, ye shall all likewise perish." Salvation is impossible, to an unbelieving and impenitent person. Those who shall be saved, are possessed of true faith, and sincere repentance; and they endeavour to live in the exercise of repentance, toward God, and of faith toward our Lord Jesus Christ. This is the life and exercise of the saints. They have got such discoveries of sin, as constrain then to repent; and such views of the gospel, as induce them to believe it. They have got such a view of the nature and actings of faith and repentance, as makes them desire to possess them, and endeavour to exercise them continually. They are blessed with a scriptural knowledge of him, who is both the bountiful giver, and the glorious object of their faith. They know the means of obtaining and exercising these graces in their

hearts, they know their evidences and their fruits, by all which they are filled with an earnest desire, that, by the exercise of faith and repentance, they may live godly in Christ Jesus. By repenting of sin, they have frequent thoughts of the law, both in its precepts and threatenings; and by believing in Christ, their attention is often directed to the gospel, in its doctrines and promises. In the one they see their ruin by sin, and mourn, and turn from it; and in the other they see their recovery by Christ Jesus, and joyfully trust in him for everlasting life. By the Spirit's influence, and by the exercise of grace in them, they are led to the law that wounds them, and to the gospel that heals them; to sin that is the cause of their misery, and to Christ who of God is made unto them wisdom, righteousness, sanctification and redemption. By all those things do believers live, and in every one of them is the life of their spirits. Seek earnestly a saving acquaintance with faith and repentance, endeavour to exercise them daily, and carefully preserve your minds from a doubting and hardened frame. Frequently meditate on the law, and the gospel; on your sin, and on the Saviour from sin. Inquire daily into the frame of your hearts about those objects. Employ yourselves in mourning and in repenting of sin, and in believing in Christ, in receiving him and walking in him.

2. From what was said we may see the evil and the aggravations of impenitence and unbelief. Christ having said to the people, Repent ye, and believe the gospel, they were laid under special obligations to obey this command. As it was promulgated in his own name, and in the name of him who sent him, the disobedience of any of his hearers was rebellion against Divine and Mediatorial authority. Since the Divine record of this, and of similar precepts, has come down to us, they bind us to perform the same duties, equally with those who heard them pronounced; our unbelief and impenitence, therefore, must be rebellion against the same authority. By the sin of unbelief, we re-

ject the counsel of God against ourselves, we disgrace the glorious Saviour, we vex and grieve the Holy Spirit, we neglect the great salvation, we plunge ourselves into everlasting wo. By the sin of impenitence, we refuse to turn to the way of life, we deliberately choose the path of death, we continue to walk in the broad way that leadeth to destruction, we surrender ourselves the voluntary slaves of sin and Satan, and we rush on the thick bosses of Jehovah's bucklers. O what evil is contained in those sins, and with what aggravations must they be accompanied! Oh, that we were wise, that we understood those things, and that we would consider what shall befal us at our latter end! Let us, therefore, turn from the delusive paths of iniquity, and fly to him who hath said, "I am the way, the truth, and the life; no man cometh unto the Father but by me." When Christ came to finish the times, and to erect on earth his spiritual kingdom, "he preached the gospel of the kingdom of God, saying, "the time is fulfilled, and the kingdom of God is at hand: repent ye, and believe the gospel." When his kingdom was rising up among the nations, his servant the Apostle Paul, proclaimed, in one of the principal cities of Greece, "And the times of this ignorance God winked at, but now commandeth all men every where to repent," Acts xvii. 30. To a less civilized people, he taught the same doctrine. "We preach unto you that ye should turn from these vanities unto the living God, who made heaven, and earth, and the sea, and all things that are therein; who in times past suffered all nations to walk in their own ways," Acts xiv. 15, 16. Such a season is again visiting the nations. The God of the whole earth, by most wonderful dispensations of his providence, is now sending to them the words of eternal life, the preaching of the everlasting gospel, and other means of salvation. The times of that ignorance which he winked at, the times in which he suffered all nations to walk in their own ways are now coming to an end, and the merciful call is now addressed to them, that all men every where should repent, and turn from those vanities unto the living God. Blessed shall all those be who comply with this call; but more dreadfully aggravated shall their condemnation be, who utterly reject it. Let Christians, therefore, be earnest at the throne of grace, praying that the nations, who are thus privileged, may receive from God saving faith in Jesus, and repentance unto life; and that he may speedily visit the other nations, with the same gospel privileges, and special grace. In such a time as this, the unbelief and impenitence of those, who have long enjoyed the gospel, must receive extraordinary aggravation. Since the Lord is sending his word and gospel to the uttermost ends of the earth, since he is calling many, who have not formerly enjoyed that call, to repent and believe the gospel, since some of them appear to comply with that call of Divine love and grace, since we profess to take an interest in it, and since many of us have contributed to carry on this great work, will it not greatly aggravate the iniquity of our unbelief and impenitence, if we ourselves have not truly repented and believed the gospel? Let it be our great concern, to repent of all our sins, and to believe in our Lord Jesus Christ, that we may escape the destruction of the wicked when it cometh, and may obtain the everlasting salvation of our souls.

3. A concern about the public prosperity of Christ's kingdom, is not inconsistent with the exercise of true godliness in the heart. The Saviour directs men's attention to those objects, which are of a public nature, the time is fulfilled, and the kingdom of God is at hand; and yet he requires the inward exercise of religion, Repent ye, and believe the gospel. The exercise of faith and repentance is, therefore, consistent with our attention to the fulfilling of the times of darkness, and with a zealous concern for the coming of Christ's kingdom. It is the same gracious principle which inclines believers to take an interest in the outward prosperity of religion, that influences them to the in-

ward exercises of piety; the same Divine Spirit guides them to both, and the same holy word requires and regulates their duty about each of them. To suppose that those who profess a great concern about personal religion, and are careless about the advancement of Christ's kingdom are rightly performing their duty, is a great mistake; and to imagine that these who discover a zeal for the latter, are indifferent to the former, is very uncharitable. Feeble exertions in either of these are a great defect in Christian conduct; but eminence in both is the very perfection of the Christian character. They have a mutual influence on one another. Strong desires and earnest endeavours that God's way may be known on the earth, and his saving health among all nations, will lead Christians to spiritual exercises, both about the means that are used to accomplish that end, and concerning their success. When the means are employed, Christians will pray for the blessing of God to make them successful; and when any success is granted, they will praise the Lord who giveth the increase. These are exercises by which their personal religion will be enlarged. The exercise of true godliness in the soul, will lead Christians to a concern for the glorifying of God, and for the salvation of men, and to do every thing in their power to promote those glorious objects. Where is the believer, enjoying Divine consolations, and the blessings of salvation, who does not a feel a desire, that others may possess the same privileges? This desire is inseparable from the exercises and enjoyments of true religion; and, therefore, it must determine the subjects of it to exert themselves in promoting the salvation of mankind. We must beware of substituting a zealous concern for promoting the Redeemer's kingdom in the world, in the room of personal religion; and also of satisfying ourselves with what we account practical piety, while we neglect every endeavour to advance the kingdom of grace in the world. Happy shall we be if we practise both, and if we experience the influence of one of them animating us to the diligent study of the other.

4. Our lot seems to have fallen in the most perilous and in the most encouraging time, that has ever passed over the church of Christ. There may have been some times more perilous, and others more encouraging; but few, or none of them, have possessed both those qualities in a degree superior to the present time. The day of the church's low condition, and of antichristian darkness and persecution, has been more perilous, but not so encouraging. The apostolic period, when the church was guided by immediate inspiration, was filled with the extraordinary gifts of the Holy Ghost, was privileged with miracles, was blessed with seasons of extraordinary conversion, and was favoured with times of singular refreshing from the presence of the Lord, was more encouraging, but not so perilous as ours. The time that is now passing over the church is in a high degree, both perilous and encouraging. The abounding of sin against God, and the pouring of Divine judgments on men render our time perilous. By them the world is filled with snares, and believers are exposed to temptation and danger. Existing under the third wo, and living in the world while the judgment is sitting, and the vials are pouring out, our time must be perilous indeed. Times are encouraging, when extraordinary exertions are made to disseminate the knowledge of God, and of his Son Jesus Christ among men, by sending to them the word of God, and the preaching of the gospel. Times are encouraging, when most comfortable success is attending those blessed endeavours. Times are encouraging, when Christians understand by the books of inspired prophecy, that Satan's kingdom in the world is about to fall, and that Christ's kingdom, in its prosperous state, will be speedily introduced. Such are the characters of the times, in which we live; and, therefore, though they be perilous, they are also encouraging. Since our times are perilous, Christ's exhortation must be obeyed, if we would be safe; "watch and pray, that ye enter not into temptation." Since our times are encouraging, let us comply

with his call. "Lift up your heads, for your redemption draweth nigh." And since our time is both perilous and encouraging let us join trembling with our mirth, and sing of mercy and of judgment. These mixed features in our time render Christ's exhortation peculiarly suitable to us, Repent ye, and believe the gospel.

5. Without the exercise of faith and repentance, Christians will not be prepared either to bear their sufferings in the day of trial, or rightly to improve the church's triumphant deliverance. Though the millennial saints will enjoy an uninterrupted calm, those who live in the ages immediately before them, must pass through a violent storm. The great city Babylon is not yet thrown down, the judgment to consume and destroy it, is still sitting, and there have not yet completely passed over us the vials, nor the earthquake, which shall so terribly shake the nations, that man's hearts, that are not balanced with Divine grace, will fail them for fear, and for looking after the things that are coming on the earth, for the powers of heaven shall be shaken. Without saving grace, supported in its exercise by the Holy Spirit, Christians, like Peter in the storm, will begin to sink, when they shall behold on the earth distress of nations with perplexity, the sea and the waves roaring. Those who are strangers to faith and repentance, cannot have any solid comfort, when the Lord doeth this; and those who are not in the exercise of those graces, though they may possess them in the habit, will be deprived of sensible comfort. Christians, in this situation, though they have eyes, they will not clearly see the rock of their salvation; and though they have ears, they will not distinctly hear, with application to themselves, the voice of mercy, in the promises of support and deliverance.—Nor can they be prepared, in this frame, for the contemplation or enjoyment of the church's enlargement and prosperity. This may be enjoyed in the prospect of faith, in the solacing foretaste, or in the actual possession. Without a believing and penitent frame, what comfortable

prospect can we take of the millennial sabbath, that remaineth for the people of God? In this condition of soul, what foretaste of that blessed state can we enjoy? Were we to live till the millennial glory appear, and to continue in an unbelieving and impenitent frame, we could not properly relish the precious enjoyment. If unbelief and hardness of heart prevail in us, darkness, doubts and fears, both about our own state, and the church's deliverance, will take such hold of our minds as will fill us with hurtful fears, instead of joyful anticipations, or the assured hope of promised good.—In this frame of mind, we will be like the heath in the desart, and will not see when good cometh. O then, let us be diligent in the use of the means of grace, that we may receive from God faith and repentance; and that, under the influence of his Spirit, they may grow and flourish in our souls.

6. By the exercise of faith and repentance, we will be prepared both for Divine judgments when they shall be poured out, and for the church's joyful prosperity. Though all believers are freed from the curse in every trouble, have the sanctified benefit of those afflictions secured to them, and will be supported under them all; yet those believers only, who are walking by faith in a penitent frame, can apply to themselves this comfort. To a believing and penitent soul, no calamity can be truly overwhelming. When the judgment shall sit, the saints, in those exercises, will be assured, that the sentence will be pronounced, neither against them, nor the church of God. When the vials are poured out, the exercised Christian will be persuaded, that they are designed for the inhabitants of the symbolical earth, and that the symbolical heavens, in which they dwell, shall be safe. When the voices shall be heard, the thunders roar, and the lightnings flash, the believer can rejoice in the faith of the church's preservation and deliverance. When the earthquake shall shake to pieces, and sink into destruction the Redeemer's enemies, the believer's hope is unshaken, and his refuge shall not be moved. He knows

that the judgments which shall divide into parts the antichristian kingdom shall unite the fearers of God; and that the convulsions which shall overturn the cities of the nations, shall establish the city of the Lord. The penitent and believing soul will be persuaded, that when the great hail, the plague of which is exceeding great, shall fall on its devoted objects, there shall no evil befal the church, neither shall any hurtful plague come near the dwellings of the saints.— In the exercise of faith and repentance, we will also be prepared for the church's salvation. By this holy frame our loins will be girded, and our lights burning, and we will be like to men who wait for their Lord. We will be enabled to appreciate duly this glorious deliverance, and to observe with joy the signs of its approach. Concerning every dispensation of his hand for bringing down his enemies, and every operation of his grace for advancing his church, the exercise of those principles in our hearts will enable us to say; "Lo, this is our God, we have waited for him, and he will save us; this is the Lord, we have waited for him, we will be glad and rejoice in his salvation." As the exercise of grace makes believers ready for communion with God in his ordinances, and for their latter end; so it will make them meet for the church's promised glory, in this world. The nature of it, they will understand; its reality, they will believe; its coming, they will expect; and for the enjoyment of it, they will have some comfortable preparation.

7. It ought to be the Christian's great concern, by the exercise of all grace, and by the performance of every duty, to obtain preparation for that season, when the times shall be fulfilled, and when the kingdom of God shall come. For illustrating this, I may direct your attention to two portions of scripture; the former of which relates to that change, to which our text did primarily refer; and the latter belongs to that promised and expected alteration, to which our text has been accommodated. The former contains a part of the Angel's words to Zacharias, concerning his son John the

Baptist. "And he shall go before him in the spirit and power of Elias—to make ready a people prepared for the Lord," Luke i. 17. It was the design of John's ministry to prepare a people for the manifestation of Christ among them, for the abolition of the mosaic system, and for the erection of the new-testament church. For this purpose, he taught the people the doctrine of repentance, and called them to believe in him, who was immediately to be revealed. The existence and exercise of the same graces in the souls of men, are necessary to prepare them for the fulfilling of the times, and for the coming of the millennial kingdom. The ministry of the gospel should now be so conducted, that it may be a mean, in the hand of the Spirit, for making ready a people prepared for the Lord. The doctrines of faith in Jesus Christ, and of repentance unto life, must now be preached, for making ready a people prepared for the millennial church. Repentance toward God, and faith toward our Lord Jesus Christ, must be testified to Christians and Jews, to Mahometans and Pagans, that many of them may be prepared to compose the innumerable company, to enjoy the millennial glory, and to celebrate her triumphant song. With this view should ministers preach those precious doctrines, and with this view should mankind hear, believe and obey them, that they may be made ready as a people prepared for the Lord. The other text of scripture, to which I must now direct your attention, has a reference to the church's approaching deliverance. "Let us be glad and rejoice, and give honour to him, for the marriage of the Lamb is come, and his wife hath made herself ready," Rev. xix. 7. The words I have in view are these, His wife hath made herself ready. To shew that this preparation is not of herself, it is added ver. 8, "And to her was granted that she should be arrayed in fine linen, clean and white; for the fine linen is the righteousness of saints." The careful use of the means on our part, and the Divine blessing attending them on his part, will make the saints ready even for the marriage supper of the Lamb. In a believing and humble dependence on the God of all grace, on the Spirit of grace, and on him who is full of grace and truth, persevere, O Christians, in the use of the means, endeavouring to exercise grace, and to walk circumspectly, so shall ye be prepared as a bride adorned for her husband. There is a preparation for ordinances and for death. This preparation, both in state and frame, we all need. It is by the exercise of faith and repentance, through the blessing of Christ and the working of the Spirit, that we can obtain it. If we have this preparation, we will be made ready for every revival, which God may give to the church, while we are continued in it. Be concerned that others may be made ready. Pray that the means which God hath sent to Jew and Gentile, to the Barbarian, the Scythian, the bond and the free, may be continued, enlarged, and rendered effectual, for making multitudes ready for the millennial church, and for the marriage supper of the Lamb. As the preparation of the heart is from the Lord, pray ye to him, that by means of the word and ordinances, the love of God may be manifested, the grace of Christ may be communicated, and the Spirit may be poured out from on high, to make ready a people prepared for the Lord, that the bride, the Lamb's wife, may make herself ready.

To conclude, you have heard of some of the times that will be fulfilled when Antichrist shall fall, and when the church shall enter into her millennial state. Endeavour to understand the nature of them. Lament over them, as they dishonour God, oppose the Mediator's kingdom, and hurt the church's purity and peace. Be grieved for those disorders and sufferings which their continuance produce among men. Pray for their removal. Observe every providential occurrence, which tends to bring them to an end. Wait with patience, in faith and hope, for that happy time when they shall be fulfilled, and taken out of the way.

You have also heard of some parts of the church's blessedness, in her millennial state. Carefully consider and meditate upon them, and beware of disregarding or despising those glorious things. Endeavour to satisfy yourselves concerning the import of those Divine promises and predictions, which warrant our expectation of such an happy time. Send up supplications daily, to him who heareth prayer, that he may hasten that blessed day. Endeavour to live in the faith, to imbibe the spirit, and to enjoy the foretaste of that season of Christian felicity.

You have also heard of some of the signs, by which you may know that this blessed summer is near. Meditate on every one of them, consider their tendency, and investigate their truth. Pray for their continuance, their increase, and their perfection. Do what you can to support the means which are now employed to enlighten mankind. Consider those providential and spiritual operations, by which Christ maintains, encreases, and renders effectual the means of gathering the nations to himself. Christ and Antichrist seem now to have taken the field, the former to accomplish, and the latter to prevent, the illumination of the world, the conversion of the Jews, and the revival and purification of Christian churches. Watch ye the progress of this conflict. Be ye on the Lord's side. Wo shall be to them who are against him. A curse shall come on them who are neutral; "Curse ye Meroz, said the angel of the Lord, curse ye bitterly the inhabitants thereof; because they came not to the help of the Lord, to the help of the Lord against the mighty."

You have also heard some remarks concerning the prophetic numbers, which state the time when all these things shall be fulfilled. On several things belonging to them we cannot speak with certainty. The most that can be done, relative to these, is only to give an opinion. The day will particularly declare it. The church must wait and watch, believe and hope, pray and be active, that nothing may be wanting on her part, for promoting this work of the Lord. Searching into those numbers, since God has revealed them, is certainly the Christian's duty; but, till the predicted events are accomplished, they will not be circumstantially known; known in the specific nature or kind of some of them, in the direct way in which they will come to pass, in the precise time at which some of them shall be accomplished, in the particular places which will be the scene of their operation, in the persons who will be principally employed, and in the objects who will be the chief sufferers. Since those numbers are mentioned, we may be assured that the duration of the system of darkness is limited, and that the system itself shall perish at the appointed time. From comparing those numbers with one another, and with Divine providences, there is ground to hope, that the following generation will not pass away, till all those things shall be fulfilled.

You have likewise heard of the Christian's duty, at the present time; Repent ye, and believe the gospel. As the principles of faith and repentance in the heart, are at all times necessary to make us Christians indeed, and the exercise of them in our spiritual frame is needful to make us in every situation, holy and comforted saints; so their being and actings are peculiarly requisite to prepare us for the Lord's coming to enlarge and establish his kingdom in the earth. Seek from God, therefore, saving faith and true repentance. To all those who have not obtained them, Jesus is saying, Repent ye, and believe the gospel. These are spiritual principles, which, by our own power, we cannot acquire, and religious exercises, which, of ourselves, we cannot attain; but they are principles which we must acquire, and exercises to which we must attain, otherwise we shall perish for ever. The Divine injunction in the command is acompanied with a revelation of grace in the promise; and it is by the accomplishment of the latter, that any sinner is enabled to comply with the former. The holy Spirit, who quickeneth those that are dead in trespasses and sins, is graciously promised; "I will put my Spirit within you, and cause you to walk in my statutes, and ye shall keep my judgments and do them;" ye shall repent and believe the gospel, Ezek. xxxiv. 27. O that sinners would consider these things, and cry for the Spirit to enable them to obey the gospel call! O that they would apply the precepts of the holy law to their own hearts and lives, and that the Spirit would convince them of the number, the heinous nature, and manifold aggravations of their transgressions! O that they would apply to their own consciences, the threatenings of the broken law, and that the Spirit would convince them of their misery, of their condemnation, and of that everlasting punishment to which they are exposed! O that they were constrained to cry out, what shall we do to be saved from our sins, and from the wrath to come! O that they would turn their attention to the glorious gospel which reveals what Christ has done and suffered to expiate their sins, and to purchase for them eternal life. O that they would meditate on the promises, on the covenant of grace, on Christ the Mediator of that covenant, and on the Divine warrant that they have to believe in him, that they may be saved! In this way, they shall obtain the Holy Spirit to implant in their hearts the principle of saving grace, that they may repent and believe the gospel. To all those who are true believers and real penitents, Jesus is also saying, Repent ye, and believe the gospel. By the grace of God, they enjoy this blessed principle; how hurtful then, is it to themselves, and how dishonouring to their God and Saviour, if they live without the daily exercise of faith and repentance? All the saints are possessed of that high dignity, which is contained in those words, "For the Spirit of glory and of God resteth upon you," 1 Pet. iv. 14. Let them, therefore, live in the Spirit, and walk in the Spirit, that they may abound in the exercise of faith and repentance. Seek grace from above, by which you will be enabled to live in a believing and penitent frame, all the days of your life. Be diligent in the performance of all the duties of religion, that your faith and repentance may be exercised and increased:

Looking for the fulfilling of the time, and for the coming of the kingdom of God, let us all remember and obey Christ's command, "Watch ye, therefore, and pray always, that ye may be accounted worthy to escape all these things that shall come to pass, and to stand before the Son of man."

THE END.

ERRATA.

Page 23 line 23, for for and ever, read for ever and ever.
—— 51 —— 16, for us, read as.
—— 66 —— 16, for person, read prison.
—— 68 —— 25, for profess, read possess.
—— 88 —— 13, for kingdom, read kingdoms.
—— 108 —— 2, for represents in, read represents it in.

Young, Gallie, & Co. Printers.

APPENDIX

TO

AN INQUIRY

INTO

THE PROPHETIC NUMBERS CONTAINED IN

The 1335 Days:

OCCASIONED BY A PAPER IN THE

EDINBURGH CHRISTIAN INSTRUCTOR,

FOR MARCH 1818,

ON

PROPHETIC CHRONOLOGY.

By ARCHIBALD MASON,

Minister of the Gospel, Wishawtown.

Glasgow:

Printed by Young, Gallie, & Co.

SOLD BY

M. OGLE; AND A. & J. M. DUNCAN, GLASGOW: OGLE, ALLARDICE, & THOMSON; OLIPHANT, WAUGH, & INNES; A. BLACK; D. BROWN; AND T. NELSON, EDINBURGH: G. CUTHBERTSON, PAISLEY: W. SCOTT, GREENOCK: J. MEUROS, KILMARNOCK: AND OGLES, DUNCAN, & COCHRAN, LONDON.

1818.

(*Price Sixpence.*)

APPENDIX

TO AN

INQUIRY

INTO

THE PROPHETIC NUMBERS CONTAINED IN THE 1335 DAYS;

Occasioned by a Paper

IN THE

EDINBURGH CHRISTIAN INSTRUCTOR,

FOR MARCH, 1818,

ON

Prophetic Chronology.

NEAR the end of March last, I published five Discourses, containing an Inquiry into the times that shall be fulfilled at Antichrist's fall—The Church's blessedness in her millennial rest—The signs that this happy season is at hand—The prophetic numbers contained in the 1335 days—And the Christian's duty at this interesting crisis. A few days before their publication, a very accurate and ingenious Paper appeared in the Edinburgh Christian Instructor, on prophetic chronology. In turning our attention to this paper, no hostility is intended to that able, useful, and well-conducted, periodical publication in which this paper has appeared. To all who are employed in that work, I ardently wish the greatest success, in propagating by it, wherever it goes, the knowledge of evangelical truth. This paper was preceded by another, containing eleven observations on the prophetic style. These are wisely conceived, accurately arranged, and illustrated with judgment. It has been followed by another, which contains part of an Analysis of the Book of Revelation. It is not to the first or the last of those papers, nor even to the second, but in so far as it fixes the numbers in the prophecy, to which I mean to state any objections. In doing so, I disclaim every design of opposing any judicious and evangelical writer, as the Author of those papers appears to be;—my only intention is more largely to unfold the views which I have been constrained to entertain concerning the prophetic numbers of Daniel and John.

As the time which this writer fixes for the rise and fall of Antichrist, the conversion of the Jews, and the commencement of the millennium, are different from the periods mentioned for those events, in my fourth discourse; it appeared necessary to publish an Appendix to that discourse, stating more particularly our objections to the supposition of Antichrist's rise in 756, and offering more explicitly our reasons for the opinion that he came into existence in 533, and that he was confirmed in his seat in 606. The dates of the Jews' conversion, and the millennium's commencement, with some of his sentiments, on collateral objects, may also be considered.

The view which this accomplished writer suggests of those dates is the following. He concludes that John received his revelations in A. D. 90. By adding to this number 666 years, the number of the beast, Rev. xiii. 18. we have 756, when the Pope became a temporal prince. He considers this year as the date of Antichrist's rise. The 1260 days during which he is to reign, he, like some other writers, considers to be prophetic years, which, being reduced to civil years, make 1242. This number being added to 756, makes 1998. In this year, he supposes the last persecution of the church in Europe shall cease, the temporal power of the Pope will fall, and the Ottoman empire will be dissolved. The Jews will be converted in 2028. They shall remain under discipline 40 years, till 2068.

Four or five years are then allowed for the battle of Armageddon, the binding of Satan, and the establishment of peace in the world. The millennium will then commence in the year 2072. This is the scheme on which we shall make a few remarks.

When the writer of this paper proceeds, "to consult the chronology, relative to Antichrist, and the church of Christ," he begins by saying, "We conclude, that the Book of Revelation was given to John, A. D. 90. Add to this 666, the number of the beast, and you have 756." On what grounds the Author was led to this conclusion, he does not here inform us; but we know that some writers have been obliged to use considerable pains to come at this conclusion, and also for the same end. It is, however, at variance with the ancient record of ecclesiastic history, with the accounts of more modern historians of the church, and with the statements of commentators. Eusebius, who wrote his History in the fourth century, fixes this date in A. D. 97. Dr. Mosheim fixes the commencement of that persecution, in which John was banished to Patmos, in A. D. 93 or 94. Mr. Brown, late of Haddington, is of opinion that John was banished to Patmos in A. D. 95. Mr. Newton, late of London, in his history of the first century of Christianity, fixes on A. D. 94 for the beginning of that persecution. The statements of commentators are equally hostile to that conclusion. Mr. Durham adopts the date mentioned by Eusebius. The Continuator of Mr. Poole thinks that John received his Revelations in A. D. 94 and 95. Mr. Lowman fixes this date at 95. Dr. Gill states it at 95 or 96. Dr. Guyse says, that the Revelation is most commonly thought to have been written about the year of our Lord, 96 or 97. Dr. Doddridge thinks, that if the ancient records are to be credited, the date of this book may be fixed about the year 96. From these authorities, which might easily be increased, we are warranted in declaring the date which is assumed in this paper to be entirely uncertain, if not completely incorrect. On that account, the calculations which are connected with it, so far as they derive probability of truth from that connexion, must be fictitious and unsatisfactory. There are not 666 years from the time, in which John received his revelations, to the date of the Pope's temporal power; and, therefore, if this "is the epoch from which other calculations shall be computed," uncertainty must attach to them all.

I do not object to the application of the number 666, as it describes a period of years, at the expiration of which, Antichrist should be revealed. Of this number, there are two s : iptural descriptions, to which we should attend. It is rep: esented as "the number of the beast," Rev. xiii. 18. And it is expressed as "the number of his name, Rev. xiii. 17—xv. 2. The latter of those descriptions of this number, "the number of his name," warrants the common use to which it has been applied, in proving the church of Rome to be the grand apostacy, and her Popes to be the great Antichrist, by finding the numeral letters in her name amount to 666. The former description of this number, "the number of the beast," authorizes the application of it, as a statement of a number of years. To direct and encourage us to count the number of the beast, it is added, "For it is the number of a man." It is not the number of a Prophet, but it is the number of a man. Its duration must be calculated by the ordinary rules for computing time among men; and not by those methods that are used for fixing the continuance of prophetic numbers. This number must signify 666 years, and as it is applied to the beast, it is the number of the beast's years. It signifies the number of the years in which the Roman power should exist, as the fourth beast in Daniel's vision. When the Roman government should be 666 years old, in the character of the fourth beast which Daniel saw, the Roman ecclesiastic beast should rise up in the church. The first and the second beasts which were presented to Daniel, in his prophetic vision, the

Babylonian and Medo-Persian powers, were Asiatic governments. The third and fourth beasts, in his vision, the Grecian and Roman powers, were originally European dynastics. The first beast, or the Babylonian monarchy, was in its full vigour, and at the height of its power, when Daniel saw the vision. When the Medes and Persians began their attack upon the Empire of Babylon, the second beast of Daniel appeared. When the Grecian armies, under the command of Alexander, the notable horn between the eyes of the he-goat, crossed over into Asia, and began their rapid and successful conquest of the Persian Empire, Daniel's third beast arose, and began to operate on the scene of prophecy. When the Roman power first got possessions in Asia, and commenced their more slow and difficult, but equally successful conquest of the nations of the east, then the fourth beast in Daniel's vision made its appearance, and Rome entered on the scene of prophecy. This happened in the year in which Attalus, king of Pergamous died. By his testament, he bequeathed his effects to the Roman Senate, and they instantly claimed his kingdom as their own, sent an army to take possession of it, subdued it under their power, and reduced it into a Roman province. The greater part of Asia the less, was contained in this kingdom, by the government of which the Romans became an Asiatic power, and commenced their destructive operations, as the fourth beast that Daniel saw. Attalus, king of Pergamus, died, and the Romans claimed that kingdom as its rightful sovereign, in the 133d* year before Christ. If we add to this number, 533 years, our first date for Antichrist's rise, we have exactly 666 years. The Roman power was 666 years old, in the prophetic character of the fourth beast of Daniel's vision, when the Bishop of Rome, by Justinian's decree, was constituted the head of all the churches, when the little horn sprang up among his

* Prideaux, Con. vol. III. p. 319.

ten horns, and that beast rose up out of the earth, which had two horns like a lamb, and which spake as a dragon.

If we attend to the time at which the Roman power was completely established in the east, and all their enemies were first subdued before them, we will find another remarkable epoch in their history. In the 61st year before Christ, Pompey having returned to Rome from his victorious conquests in the East, obtained a triumph in that city for his great services, and wonderful success. In the 60th year before Christ, the Romans having seen their Empire extended and established in Asia, Pompey, Crassus, and Julius Cæsar entered into a confederacy for supporting each other in their pretensions in the Roman state, engrossed the whole power of it into their hands, and divided it among themselves.* This laid the foundation of those destructive civil wars, which soon terminated in the dissolution of the Roman republic, and in the erection of the Roman monarchy. If we add to the 60 years before Christ, 606 years, our second date for Antichrist's rise, when he triumphed over all his rivals, we will again have 666 years, the number of the beast. By either of those calculations, especially the former, or by both taken together, we have a much more satisfactory explanation of the number of the beast, than by that representation which is given in this paper, both from the nature of the things themselves, and the certainty of the dates. Since it is undeniably evident, that 666 years intervened, from the time when the Roman state began to act as the fourth beast in Daniel's prophecy, till the time when the Emperor Justinian constituted the Bishop of Rome the head of all the churches; and since there are also 666 years betwixt the time when the Romans triumphed over their enemies in Asia, and the time when the Pope, by the decree of Phocas, silenced his rivals, and consolidated his ecclesiastic supremacy, there must be good reason to conclude,

* Prideaux, Con. vol. IV. p. 81.

that, in those transactions, the words of John were fulfilled. "Here is wisdom. Let him that hath understanding count the number of the beast; for it is the number of a man, and his number is six hundred three score and six."

When the Author speaks of the time when Antichrist rose, after mentioning some of the dates which expositors have fixed for it, he says; "We are, however inclined to the opinion of those, who date the rise of Antichrist from A. D. 756, when Pepin, king of France, raised Pope Stephen II. to the rank of a temporal prince; for it is in that character that the head of the Roman hierarchy may be considered as the beast." Blame should be imputed to no man, for being inclined to the opinion of those, who date the rise of Antichrist from 756, though our opinion may be different, and we may believe and hope he is mistaken; but it is not so easy to pass over the reason he assigns for it; "For it is in that character that the head of the Roman hierarchy may be considered as the beast." In opposition to this, I am still of opinion, that the Pope's possession of temporal power is not essential to his scriptural character, as the Man of Sin, the Antichrist, and the false Prophet; and, therefore, there is no valid reason for considering the 756th year of the Christian era, as the date of his rise. In that capacity, in which inspired predictions describe Antichrist's characters and actions, to him, in that same capacity, must the prophetic numbers be applied, for fixing the time of his rise and fall. It must be unreasonable to suppose, that the prophecies should delineate his characters and deportment, under one denomination of him, and that the numbers, which are contained in the same prophecies, should measure his duration under another denomination of him. In order to ascertain the precise idea, in which the numbers in prophecy exhibit the beginning and ending of this Antichristian beast, we shall now take a view of the descriptions which are given of this object, in those predictions.

As the man of sin, he is described by the apostle Paul; 2 Thes. ii. 4. "Who opposeth and exalteth himself above all that is called God, or that is worshipped." On account of their office, emperors, kings, and temporal princes are called gods, and are entitled to honour from men. In the fulfilment of this prediction, the head of the Roman hierarchy has assumed sovereign authority over them, and has claimed, and sometimes exercised a power to excommunicate and dethrone them, and to absolve their subjects from their allegiance to them Did he arrogate and exert this power in his civil, or in his ecclesiastic capacity? Certainly not as the temporal potentate of Rome, but as the vicar of Christ, and as the supreme head of the church on earth. The apóstle adds, "so that he as God, sitteth in the temple of God, shewing himself that he is God." These words represent his blasphemous conduct, relative to the great Jehovah. In the apostate church, he has set himself as God, and as being above God, by dispensing with Divine laws, by commanding the worship of creatures and images, in opposition to that law, by making the meaning and obligation of the Divine Word depend on his authority, and by placing himself on the throne of God in the church below, in giving laws to it, appointing ordinances in it, exercising unlimited power over it, and receiving blasphemous titles and worship from its members. Whether do these things apply to him in his civil, or in his ecclesiastic capacity? As he is raised to the rank of a temporal prince, he has no connexion with any one of them; but as he is the spiritual and supreme head of the church, every one of them belongs to him. Whether was it his coming as a temporal prince, or as the blasphemous head of the apostate church, that Paul describes in those affecting words, ver. 9, 10. "Whose coming is after the working of Satan, with all power, and signs, and lying wonders, and with all deceivableness of unrighteousness in them that perish, because they received not the love of the truth that they might be saved?" Whether was it by his temporal or spiritual authority, that the head of the Roman hierarchy forbade to marry, and commanded to abstain from meats? These questions must be answered in the same way, that those things belong to him, and are performed by him, as the head of the church, in his ecclesiastic capacity. The prophetic numbers must also determine his duration, in the same capacity.

The apostle John, in his first epistle, describes this head of the Roman hierarchy, several times, by the name of Antichrist: "Little children, it is the last time; and as ye have heard that Antichrist shall come, even now are there many Antichrists; whereby we know that it is the last time." chap. ii. 18. This emphatic designation represents him as the peculiar enemy and opposer of our Lord and Saviour Jesus Christ. By opposing all the Redeemer's offices, the Pope of Rome carries on a wicked opposition, to the one Mediator between God and man. He states himself as an enemy to Jesus, in his prophetic office, by corrupting the Divine word, by denying the doctrines which it reveals, by propagating those errors which it condemns, and by withholding from the people, that word, concerning which Jesus says to all who profess his name, "Search the scriptures; for in them ye think ye have eternal life; and they are they which testify of me." He is the enemy of Jesus in his priestly office, by maintaining the merit of good works, by the blasphemous sacrifice of the mass, and by employing and depending upon the intercession of saints and angels, as well as on the intercession of the great Advocate with the Father, Jesus Christ the righteous. In Christ's kingly office, he also opposes our Redeemer, by suspending his laws, altering the form of worship, the office-bearers, and the administrations that he hath appointed, and by claiming and exercising that absolute power over the church, which belongs to him who hath said, "All power in heaven and in earth is given unto me." In all this opposition to Christ, whether do we recognize the head of the Roman hierarchy in his temporal, or spiritual capacity? As a temporal prince, he is incapable of it; but it is congenial and essential to him as vested with his spiritual supremacy. The numbers in prophecy must be applied to him in his ecclesiastic, which is his antichristian, character.

In the Revelation of John, there are many things said of this object, by the consideration of which we shall be brought to the same conclusion. The things contained in chap. xvii. only are to be considered. "So he carried me away in the Spirit into the wilderness; and I saw a woman sit on a scarlet coloured beast, full of names of blasphemy, having seven heads and ten horns," ver. 3. The Roman Pope is here exhibited as a woman, which cannot symbolize him as a temporal prince, but is a most appropriate symbol of him, as the head of the apostate church. The same thing is evident from the inscription on her forehead. "And upon her forehead was a name written, Mystery, Babylon the great, the Mother of harlots and abominations of the earth," ver. 5. What mystery is found about him as a temporal prince? Is not this attached to him only in his ecclesiastic character and government? What resemblance is there between the Pope's temporal power, and the extensive sway of the rulers of ancient Babylon? None at all. But there is a very striking likeness in the Pope's spiritual supremacy over all popish christendom, to the universal dominion of the Babylonian monarchs. Was the Pope the mother of harlots and the abominations of the earth, as a temporal prince? Was this the effect of his temporal rule over his small state in Italy? This is impossible. It was as the corrupt and blasphemous head of an apostate and adulterous church, that every species of profanity went forth from him throughout all the earth. John saw this "woman drunken with the blood of the saints, and with the blood of the martyrs of Jesus." ver. 6. It was not by the exercise of his temporal power, which was very limited, but by the influence of his spiritual supremacy over the kings of the earth, that the head of the antichristian church stirred up cruel, bloody, and exterminating wars against the saints; and excited perecution unto death, and execrable, faithless, and indiscriminate massacres against the martyrs of Jesus. "And when I saw her," says John, "I wondered with great admiration." What objects of wonder and great admiration could John see in the head of the Roman hierarchy, as a temporal prince, who reigned over a small part of Italy? But if we consider him in his characters and actions as the blasphemous rival of Christ, the enemy to the doctrines and ordinances of the Christian religion, the persecuting foe of the saints, and as the monstrous head of the antichristian apostasy, all of which belong to him in his ecclesiastic capacity, we will see a terrific and extraordinary figure, which was better calculated to produce wonder and great admiration in such a mind as John's, than any other earthly object, that was ever presented to the observation of man.

In this vision, the subjection of the Rulers and the people on the Roman earth, to this antichristian beast, constitutes two other particulars, which will establish the same truth. Concerning the subjection of the rulers to this beast, John declares, ver. 3, "I saw a woman sit on a scarlet-coloured beast, full of names of blasphemy, having seven heads and ten horns." The angel said to John, ver. 7, "I will shew thee the mystery of the woman, and of the beast that carrieth her, which hath seven heads and ten horns." It is afterwards said in explanation, ver. 12, 13, "And the ten horns which thou sawest are ten kings—These have one mind, and shall give their power and strength unto the beast." The beast that carrieth the woman is the same with that beast that was to continue 42 months, Rev. xiii. 5. It does not signify the Pope's temporal power; but it represents the whole secular power which should exist in that part of the ancient Roman empire, to which the Pope's spiritual jurisdiction extended. The secular Roman beast, having existed 666 years, from the time at which it began its operations as the fourth beast in Daniel's vision, did then identify itself with the antichristian power, and voluntarily became the beast that carrieth the mother of harlots. As the prophecy informs us that they shall perish together, Rev. xix. 20, so the duration of the secular power in the Roman empire, in its new character and connexion, must be the same with the time in which the woman who sits on it must exist. As a rider has the direction of the beast that carries him, and as its power and strength are exerted for his benefit; so the secular power in the Roman empire, existing either in the secular beast or in the ten horns, has been subjected to the Roman Antichrist, and exercised for his support and aggrandizement. Did these kings subject themselves to the Pope as a temporal prince? Was it not to him, as the pretended vicegerent of Christ, that they yielded obedience? Did the Pope rest his claim to subjection to himself from the kings of the earth, on his temporal dominion over them? Did he not rest it entirely on his spiritual supremacy over them? It must be perfectly evident that the kings of the earth were subject to the Pope, not as the man who sat on the throne of the Cesar's; but as the dignified Ecclesiastic who occupied the chair of St. Peter.—The inhabitants of the Roman earth, as well as its rulers, have also yielded subjection to the Pope of Rome. "Come hither," says the Angel to John, ver. 1, "Come hither; I will shew unto thee the judgment of the great whore, that sitteth upon many waters." This symbol is explained, ver. 15, "And he said unto me, the waters which thou sawest, where the whore sitteth, are peoples, and multitudes, and nations, and tongues." This prediction assures us, that multitudes of people, belonging to various nations, and speaking different languages, should submit to the power of the antichristian beast; and we all know that this prophecy has been fully accomplished. In what character were they obedient to his will? Was it in his civil character as a temporal prince? By no means. This kind of subjection to him is peculiar to the few miserable inhabitants of the small state, over which his temporal power is exercised. It is to him in his antichristian character as the head of the church, that the peoples, and multitudes, and nations, and tongues, are subjected.

The characters and operations of this beast, as delineated in prophecy, apply to him in his spiritual, or ecclesiastic capacity; but, from his temporal power, it does not appear, that he is at all described, in those visions of God. His temporal power must, therefore, be adventitious, and not essential to him as the beast of Rome. What concern can his possession of a small part of Italy, or his temporal power over it, have with his essential and comprehensive characters, as the man of sin sitting in the temple of God, as the Antichrist who is the principal enemy of Jesus, and as the false prophet who has deceived the nations? The Pope's enjoyment of his small territory, part of which has been called St. Peter's Patrimony, is not more essential to his establishment as the head of the Roman hierarchy, and of the antichristian church, than the actual possession of the glebe-land, which is bestowed on some gospel ministers, is necessary to constitute their pastoral relation to the people of their ministerial charge. In this opinion we are the more confirmed, because, after the Pope's elevation to temporal power, many of his bishops, from motives of policy or superstition, were constituted temporal princes. We may now ask, How shall we distinguish between the Roman beast, and the secular bishops? Not by his possessing temporal power, for this belonged to them as well as to him; but it is in his spiritual supremacy, and antichristian headship over the church, by which he is distinguished from them, and from every other man in the world. It is, therefore, in that character that the Pope of Rome may, and ought to be considered as the beast.

It has also been insinuated, that the Pope's temporal power is essential to him as the Antichrist, because, in the visions of Daniel he receives the denomination of an horn.

If we attend to Daniel's account of this horn, we will find it to be very different from the rest. To this horn are ascribed peculiar properties, which corresponds not to the temporal, but to the ecclesiastic character and conduct of the Pope. Of him the prophet says, "And, behold, in this horn were eyes like the eyes of a man, and a mouth speaking great things." Dan. vii. 8. The words of the Prophet are of the same import with those of the Apostle. "And I beheld another beast coming up out of the earth, and he had two horns like a lamb, and he spake as a dragon." Rev. xiii. 11. In these two verses, the Pope of Rome is described by three most significant tokens: "In this horn were eyes like the eyes of a man." These eyes import that this horn should possess wisdom, knowledge, discernment, and counsel in a degree superior to the other horns. When these things belong to an unprincipled and immoral power, they enable it, by exercising cunning, deceit, dissimulation, and falsehood, more effectually to accomplish its designs. In every age, this has been notoriously fulfilled, in the conduct of the Pope of Rome, and his council, acting in their ecclesiastic capacity; but, in their temporal rule, they have never evidenced, that they were possessed of the eyes of a man. This beast "had two horns like a lamb." Claiming a relation to the lamb of God, who taketh away the sin of the world, he pretended to meekness, humility, innocence and purity; while he was more cruel, proud, injurious, and polluted, than any of the horns of the beast. This description cannot be applied to him with so much propriety in his temporal rule, as it accords with him in his spiritual characters and administrations. He is represented also, as speaking great things, and speaking like a dragon. In him as a temporal prince this prediction cannot be verified; but, in his ecclesiastic character, it has received an exact accomplishment. By his blasphemous decrees, edicts, bulls, anathemas, excommunications, and commands, as St. Peter's successor, and Christ's vicar, he hath spoken great things against God, against Christ, against gospel doctrines and ordinances, against the true church and her members, against his own vassals when they dared to dispute his will, and against the temporal, spiritual, and eternal welfare of men. In him, therefore, as an ecclesiastic head, exercising a spiritual supremacy over emperors, kings, princes, ecclesiastics, and the laity, all those representations are most minutely fulfilled.

From all these considerations, we are forced to conclude, that it is not in his temporal power, but in his spiritual jurisdiction and operations, that the Roman beast is the object of prophecy—that his temporal power is not essential to his scriptural characters, as the man of sin, the Antichrist, or the false prophet—that it is not in the character of a temporal prince that he may be considered as the beast—that his rise should be dated from the time in which he, being constituted the head of all the churches, as God, took his seat in the temple of God, shewing himself that he is God—and that the year 756 cannot be the date of Antichrist's rise. In his antichristian character, which is his true one, the world had seen him more than 200 years, before that period. From the days of Justinian, they had seen him, in 533, constituted, by an imperial decree, the head of all the churches. During the reign of Phocas they had seen, in 606, his antichristian headship over the church recognised and solemnly established by another imperial decree. They had seen him, during all this period, grasping at this power, and actually exercising it, by sending out swarms of monks, like locusts out of the bottomless pit, to convert, as he called it, the nations to Christianity; by investing the Leader of those who were sent to Britain, with power over all the British bishops, and Saxon prelates, constituting him the first archbishop of Canterbury; by conferring similar dignities on others whom he sent to other countries; by encouraging and employing the different orders of monks, as his most faithful auxiliaries, in extending his power over the rulers of the church; by maintaining and propagating the doctrines concerning the worship of saints and images, the purifying fire of purgatory, the necessity of observing human rites and institutions in order to obtain salvation, and the efficacy of relicts for curing the diseases of soul and body; by adding continually new ceremonies to the ordinances of worship, changing the Lord's supper into the sacrifice of the mass, appointing litanies, or prayers, to be said to the saints, and erecting temples, and instituting public religious festivals to their honour; by pleading for the authority of the church, claiming it to himself, and pretending to work miracles; by resisting the edicts of emperors, and condemning the decrees of councils; by excommunicating emperors, and liberating their subjects from obedience to them; and by encouraging appeals to his tribunal, deciding in them by his own authority, and punishing, as far as he could, those who refused to submit to his sentence. Since all those things, and many more, were done by the Bishop of Rome, long before he became a temporal prince, we are warranted to conclude that the foundation of his beastly power and blasphemous supremacy was laid by the decree of Justinian, and that the ghostly fabric was finished by that of Phocas.

The observations that are contained in this paper concerning "the chronology of numbers and the chronology of events," are very judicious. But, alas! while men are as ready to err in applying "the eventful chronology," as they are in calculating "the numerical chronology," no infallibility can attach to our speculations in any "path." It is necessary, therefore, to consider the reasons he assigns, for fixing the other numbers.

Concerning the Jews conversion, he says, "We conclude that the Jews shall be converted, A. D. 2028." His proof of this is the following: "Our Lord said; 'Jerusalem shall be trodden down of the Gentiles, until the times of the Gentiles be fulfilled.' And Paul said; 'Blindness in part is happened to Israel, until the fulness of the Gentiles be come in.' Luke xxi. 24. Rom. xi. 25, 30—38. The Jews, from the call of Abraham until their unbelief during our Lord's ministry, enjoyed the benefits of revealed religion, to the exclusion of the Gentiles, for 2000 years. As the common era is four years later than his nativity, their unbelief may be dated from the 28th year of his age, according to the common era; adding these to the 2000, it makes 2028, when the equity of the Divine government between them and the Gentiles shall be balanced, and when they shall be converted." In a note, he also says; "Until the time of the Gentiles be fulfilled, that is, until the Gentiles shall possess Jerusalem as long as did the Jews; or, until Christianity should be enjoyed by the Gentiles, as long as the benefits of Divine revelation were enjoyed by the Jews, prior to the incarnation, which was about 2000 years; and in this last sense the contrast is stated by Paul (Rom. xi. 25—30) and to his conclusion we ought to accede."

In the first sense, the contrast will not hold; because from the days of Joshua the son of Nun, till the days of Titus the son of Vespasian, the Jews possessed Jerusalem, including the time of their captivity in Babylon, only about 1520 years; and by his own showing, "the Romans, Saracens, and Turks, have, in succession, possessed it for nearly 1800 years."

The whole of this statement may be invalidated on two grounds; the arbitrary and uncertain manner, in which the dates are fixed—and the entire silence both of our Lord and Paul, concerning the duration of the times of the Gentiles, or of the length of the time, until the fulness of the Gentiles be come in.

The date assigned for the commencement of this period, at the call of Abraham is very unsatisfactory. May it not, with more propriety, be supposed, that the time when the Jews began to enjoy the benefits of Divine revelation, to the exclusion of the Gentiles, should be fixed from the date of their complete organization as a church, at the giving of the law, and at the erection of the tabernacle among them, in the second year after they came out of the land of Egypt; or, from the era of their peaceful settlement in the promised land, a few years after they had passed over Jordan. We cannot consider them, as a people, in the possession of the benefits of Divine revelation, or placed under their peculiar economy, till the former or the latter of those periods. Besides, we must not conclude, that the Jews, from the call of Abraham, enjoyed the benefits of revealed religion, to the exclusion of the Gentiles. The saving knowledge of God and his worship, by traditional revelation, in the light of which the saints, during the patriarchal ages, were guided in the ways of faith and holiness, was not at that time removed from the Gentile nations. Of this truth, the knowledge and piety of Melchizedek, Jethro, Job, his three friends, and Elihu, are most satisfactory demonstrations.

As the date which is mentioned for the commencement of this period is uncertain; so also is the time which is assigned for its termination. The date of the Jews' unbelief, or their rejection of Christ and his gospel, is arbitrarily assumed and improperly fixed. It does not appear that the compassionate Redeemer considered the Jews as fixed in their unbelief at his death; when he, after his resurrection, said to his apostles, "Thus it is written, and thus it behoved Christ to suffer, and to rise from the dead the third day; And that repentance and remission of sins should be preached in his name, among all nations, beginning at Jerusalem." Luke xxiv. 46, 47. Immediately before his ascension, he again declared to them, "But ye shall receive power, after that the Holy Ghost is come upon you; and ye shall be witnesses unto me, both in Jerusalem, and in all Judea, and in Samaria, and unto the uttermost part of the earth." Acts i. 8. Though the fixing of this date is of no avail, in calculating the time of the Jews' conversion; yet it may be affirmed, that the time of the burning of their city and temple, of the miserable destruction of many of themselves, and of their banishment from their own land, is the more eligible date of the two. We have, therefore, abundant cause to conclude, that those calculations and conclusions, to the support of which, such uncertain dates as these are essential, must be a visionary fabric.

But the uncertainty of the dates of this season is not our only, nor indeed our principal objection to this scheme of calculation. We are obliged also to deny that either our Lord or his apostle says one word, in the texts quoted, concerning the duration, either of the Jews enjoying the benefits of revealed religion, to the exclusion of the Gentiles, or of the Gentiles enjoying the gospel, to the exclusion of the Jews. In Luke xxi. 24, our Saviour predicts the uncommon slaughter of the Jews by the edge of the sword, and the total dispersion of the remainder of them into all nations; adding, " And Jerusalem shall be trodden down of the Gentiles, until the times of the Gentiles be fulfilled." In these words, our Lord utters a plain and singular prediction, which has been accomplished for about 1750 years. That idolatrous and unbelieving Gentiles should occupy Jerusalem, and possess the land of Canaan, until the times, in which the Christian and enlightened Gentiles should enjoy the gospel exclusively, shall be fulfilled. Not one hint is given concerning the duration of those times. To assert, therefore, that they shall be of the same duration with the time, in which the Jews enjoyed their peculiar privileges, is without any authority from the words of Christ. Nor does Paul, in Rom. xi. 25—30, say any thing concerning the duration of this time. He compares the holy and sovereign procedure of God with the Jews and Gentiles, in the nature of his dispensations to them both; but says nothing concerning the continuance either of the one or the other. Let the reader examine this important prediction, and judge for himself; if this is the conclusion of the apostle, in those verses, " that Christianity shall be enjoyed by the Gentiles exclusively, as long as the benefits of Divine revelation were enjoyed by the Jews, prior to the incarnation, which was about 2000 years." For my part, I cannot find in it any such thing. Instead, therefore, of feeling any obligation to accede to it, as an apostolic conclusion, there is sufficient cause to reject it, as an invention of men. Since this groundless conjecture is necessary to uphold this scheme of calculation, the whole system, which is built on it, must fall to the ground.

Will the blessed Millennium commence when the Jews shall be converted? No. "The Jews," says he, "shall be converted, A. D. 2028. They shall be under discipline 40 years, Mic. vii. 14, 15, which make 2068." Micah's words, which are here referred to, are the following: "Feed thy people with thy rod, the flock of thine heritage, which dwell solitarily in the wood in the midst of Carmel; let them feed in Bashan and Gilead as in the days of old. According to the days of thy coming out of the land of Egypt will I shew unto him marvellous things." For two reasons, I am obliged to say, that these verses contain no proof of this opinion. The immediate context seems to prove that they do not refer to the millennial deliverance; and though they should predict the final restoration of Israel, they neither countenance nor support the supposition of a forty years' discipline.

In the two following verses, the Prophet says; "The nations shall see, and be confounded at all their might; they shall lay their hand upon their mouth, their ears shall be deaf. They shall lick the dust like a serpent, they shall move out of their holes like worms of the earth; they shall be afraid of the Lord our God, and shall fear because of thee." At Israel's deliverance, which is here predicted, the nations are represented as filled with malignant astonishment and confusion, as desiring neither to speak nor to hear of it, as seized with great grief and perplexity, and as overwhelmed with terror at the Divine operations, and at his people's salvation. That the Jews may have some enemies, who may have such emotions excited in them, at Israel's glorious deliverance, there is no reason to doubt; but that the nations shall be so affected may justly be questioned. By this time, the nations will be enlightened with the holy scriptures; will understand the nature of those dispensations of providence and grace; will see in them a display of the Divine glory, the fulfilment of scripture predictions, and the approach of blessedness to the church; and will be disposed to hail the happy day, by singing songs of praise to the Lord for this wonderful deliverance. We all know, however, that this is a true description of the dispositions and conduct of the nations when the Jews returned from their Babylonian captivity, to which event this prediction may be more properly applied.

As I am not inclined to restrict the application of Old-testament predictions; let it be granted that the Jews' final return to their own land, is the event which is here foretold. Upon this admission, this prophecy will not prove that the Jews, after their conversion, will be under discipline forty years. By the "days of their coming out of the land of Egypt," we certainly should understand the period immediately before and after their triumphant march from the house of bondage. These days include the season of the plagues; of their keeping the first Passover; of the preservation of their first-born; of their solemn departure from Egypt loaded with the spoils of their oppressors; of their miraculous passage with their little ones and cattle through the Red Sea, while the Egyptians, who wickedly pursued them, sank like lead in the mighty waters; of their religious observation of this deliverance by songs of praise to the Lord; and of the blessings which the Lord bestowed on them in the wilderness, till the day when the people rebelled against him, and believed the false report of the unfaithful spies concerning the land of Canaan. It was in those operations of Divine grace and power, that the Lord had shewn to his people marvellous things, in the days of their coming out of the land of Egypt. In all their generations they were taught to sing; "Marvellous things did he in the sight of their Fathers, in the land of Egypt, in the field of Zoan. He divided the sea, and caused them to pass through; and he made the waters to stand as an heap," &c. Psal. lxxviii. 12—16.—On the fifteenth day of the first month of their sacred year, the children of Israel came out of the land of Egypt. As soon as they began their march, "The Lord went before them by day in a pillar of cloud, to lead them in the way; and by night in a pillar of fire, to give them light."—On the fifteenth day of the second month, they came to the wilderness of Sin, where the Lord gave them manna, bread from heaven to eat. At Rephidim, immediately after, he brought forth water to them out of the rock.—On the third month after they had come out of the land of Egypt, they came into the wilderness of Sinai, and Israel encamped before that mount. At this place, the God of Jacob, in the most solemn manner, delivered to his people his most holy law, and gave them many other statutes and judgments.—In the first month of the second year, on the first day of the month, the tabernacle, according to God's command to Moses, was reared in the wilderness. The house of Aaron was then concecrated to the priesthood, and the tribe of Levi to the service of the tabernacle. At this time, the days of their coming out of the land of Egypt were terminated. These are the marvelleus things which the Lord shewed his people, in those days.—The forty years, during which that rebellious generation were doomed to bear their iniquities in the wilderness, and to perish there, commenced immediately after this, and continued till they arrived at Canaan. Micah's prediction assures the Jews, that when the Lord shall deliver them from their unbelief and dispersion, he will accomplish for them all those marvellous works, which their difficult and dangerous situation may require, as he did to their Fathers coming out of the land of Egypt, by feeding them as the flock of his heritage with his Pastoral staff, while they may be in distress as in the midst of Carmel, till he bring them to their own land, and cause them feed in Bashan and Gilead, as in the days of old. There is a great difference between these two expressions, " The days of thy coming out of the land of Egypt;" and, " ye shall bear your iniquities forty years." The former were fulfilled before the latter commenced. The days of their coming out of Egypt, and the forty years bearing their iniquities, are two different periods of time, not coeval with one another; but the latter immediately succeeds the former. Their bearing their inquities forty years, must not be mistaken and substituted for the days of their coming out of the land of Egypt. This is using a liberty in explanation, that no text can bear. This opinion also supposes, that the Jews, after their conversion, shall, like their Fathers in the wilderness, commit against God, some heinous and aggravated transgressions, which will provoke him to prevent their entering into their own land for the space of forty years, after they have found the Messiah. With all deference to those great men, who have adopted this sentiment, and built it on this prediction, I am obliged to declare, that it gives no authority for believing any such thing. There is the more reason for this averment, because no other prediction, that I can recollect, bears a clearer reference, or indeed any reference at all, to this opinion. On these accounts, it must be considered as an unwarranted conjecture, and that system of calculation, of which it is a necessary part, may be considered as falacious.

Will the Millennium begin at the expiration of these forty years' discipline? No. " Allowing," says he, " four or five years for the battle of Armageddon, binding of Satan, and establishing peace in the world, we have 2072, Rev. xx. 1—8." A short enough allowance of time, surely, for accomplishing transactions, which are so solemn in their nature, and important in their consequences.

Besides those opinions which have been considered, there are several other sentiments which are objectionable; but as they do not properly belong to my design, I shall not investigate them particularly. They are the following: That the temporal power of the Pope is the tenth part of the city;—That the seventh trumpet will not sound, and none of the vials will be poured out, till the Pope's temporal power shall be destroyed, and the Ottoman empire be dissolved;—That the death of the witnesses shall take place immediately before 1998;—That the battle of Armageddom shall be fought near Jerusalem;—And that John's 1260 years do not include the period of the vials.

On the first of those opinions, it may be said, that the tenth part of a city is a strange symbol for the Pope's temporal power, and that the falling of the tenth part of a city is a very unsuitable representation of the destruction of that power. Of this great city we read, that it is spiritually called Sodom and Egypt, where also our Lord was crucified, that it was divided into three parts, and came up in remembrance before God, when the seventh vial was poured out. It is not easy to conceive, how the Pope's temporal power can be the tenth part of a city, which is thus described. The falling of the tenth part of the city has been understood to symbolize the defection of a conspicuous part of his adherents, from their subjection to him. This is easy to be understood; but the other is not so As this opinion obliges the Author to place the removal of this power, under the sixth trumpet, it may be considered as one of his fundamental errors. But at the battle of Armageddon, which, according to him, is seventyfour years after the destruction his temporal power, the head of the Roman hierarchy will be all that ever he was, in any period of his existence, Rev. xix. 19, 20. The second and third of those opinions are the necessary consequences of the first. Having adopted the one, the other two, strange and singular as they are, must also be maintained.

The fourth opinion is founded in Dan xi. 45. This prediction seems to have had its accomplishment in the cruel and impious conduct of Antiochus Epiphanes, and in his miserable end. Though he was a type of the great Antichrist, it cannot be perfectly satisfactory to apply to the anti-type, every circumstance in the prediction, which was accomplished in the type. It is a pity that judicious writers should have, with so much confidence, built such a mighty fabric as this, and the things connected with it, on so slender a foundation as the detached part of an Old Testament prediction, which in the events of former times, has had a most unequivocal accomplishment. The destruction of the Antichristian beast, in any place, must sufficiently verify the prophecy, without bringing him to the very spot, where the object which prefigured him, came to his miserable end.

The last of those opinions deserves a more particular consideration. If John's number of 1260 years comes no farther than 1998, according to his view of the times, there is a period of 74 years left out of his prophetic chronology; while he gives most minutely, in chap. xv. xvi. and in some other parts of his book, a prophetic account of the events of that period. How can this be accounted for? That John should exclude from his numerical chronology that season, of which, above all others, he distinctly foretels the transactions, is really not to be believed. It will appear to be still more difficult to embrace this opinion, if we consider, that at the expiration of the 74 years, the period to which his number is supposed not to extend, he begins a new chronology of the events, in two particulars, the one numerical, the other descriptive. The account which is numerical, is the 1000 years for the duration of the church's prevalence, purity, and peace; and that which is descriptive is the "little season," during which Satan shall be loosed out of his prison, when the 1000 years are expired. Can we suppose, that John would give prophetic numbers, which begin at the rise of Antichrist and terminate at the day of judgment, and exclude 74 years about the middle of that period, out of his chronology? It must be very irrational to suppose, that John's numbers are not successive. As Daniel's 1260 days, his 30 days and his 45 days exactly succeed one another; so John's 1260 days, his 1000 years and his "little season" are equally successive, and closely follow each other. As John's little season will begin when his 1000 years are expired; so his 1000 years must commence when his 1260 days run out. It is not, therefore, reasonable to suppose, that the prophetic chronology of John for that period, the events of which he largely predicts, must be supplied from that of Daniel. There is no defect in either of these schemes of prophetic numbers to be supplied from the other; but each of them is a distinct and perfect scheme by itself. We will introduce confusion into our views of the word and works of the God of order, if we blend them together, and do not keep them entirely distinct. Those calculations which are formed, by using, at one time, the numbers of John, and, at another time, the numbers of Daniel, building one prophetic number upon another, till we erect a fabric of many stories, and stretch out the time to its greatest conceivable extent, may justly be suspected of error. By this scheme, the Pope of Rome was in possession of his blasphemous supremacy over the church 223 years, before he became a temporal prince, and will continue in the enjoyment and exercise of that antichristian headship for 74 years after his temporal power has been destroyed; and yet it is as he is possessed of temporal power that he may be considered as the beast, whose existence, in that character, is 1260 prophetic, or 1242 civil years. From this scheme it must also follow, that the time of his existence in his ecclesiastic supremacy, that denomination of him under which prophecy describes his characters and conduct, will be 1539 years. Such are the conclusions, to which our mingling the numbers of Daniel with those of John, necessarily conduct us.

In opposition to the scheme which has been examined, I shall bring into view what I have now said, concerning the prophetic numbers, in connexion with what I have formerly said, in that discourse, to which this is a supplement. From the year 133 before Christ, when the Roman state became an Asiatic power, to the time when the Emperor Justinian, by an imperial decree, constituted the Bishop of Rome the head over all the churches, in A. D. 533, there are 666 years, the age of the Roman secular beast, from the time when he began to devour in Asia, to break in pieces, and to stamp the residue with his feet, till the time when he identified himself with Antichrist, and became the beast that carried the mother of harlots, and abominations of the earth. From 533 to 1792 inclusive, we have Daniel's number of 1260 years, when the judgment began to sit, and the seven vials to be poured out. From 1792 to 1822 we have Daniel's 30 years, at the expiration of which the Jews' conversion is expected to commence, or a new scene of judgments may begin, or perhaps both of them together, Dan. xii. 1. From 1822 we have Daniel's 45 years, the last of which, as belonging to the millennium, being subtracted from that number, gives us the 1866th year, as the time when the judgment shall be finished, and the vials completely poured out.

From the 60th year before Christ, when the Romans had conquered Asia, had made the eastern nations Roman provinces or tributary states, and had triumphed over their enemies, there are 666 years till 606, when the Emperor Phocas, by another imperial decree, ratified to the Bishop of Rome his Antichristian supremacy, caused him triumph over his rivals, and enabled him to overcome his competitors for the chair of St. Peter. When John's 1260 years are added to 606, we are brought to the very same year, 1866: after which the blessed millennium will commence, in the year 1867, which will be the 1335th year of Daniel's numbers, and the first year of John's number of one thousand years. Dan. xii. 12. Rev. xx. 6.

These two remarkable epochs of the Roman secular beast, 133, and 60, before Christ, by the addition of 666, the number of the beast, to each of them, answering so exactly to 533 and 606, the dates of the imperial decrees concerning the Antichristian power, may fill us with wonder, and engage our serious attention. The addition of Daniel's 1334 years to the former of those numbers, and of John's 1260 years to the latter of them, terminating as they do, in the same year, 1866, may also fill us with astonishment, and command our careful consideration. Thus I have given some of the reasons for disagreeing with the statement of dates contained in this paper; and some of the grounds, by which our belief in the calculations I have opposed to it, is encouraged and strengthened.

If any are disposed to object to those calculations, because there is a twofold date mentioned in them for the rise of Antichrist; it may be observed, for their satisfaction, that this is not contrary to the analogy of similar predictions. The captivity to Babylon had a commencement and a perfection; the same may be the case with the rise of the Antichristian beast, and the subjection of the Church to his power and oppression. The principal reason, however, that can be assigned for this twofold date is, the double scheme of numbers representing this period, with which the Spirit, who indicted prophecy, has furnished us; and the double system of providential operations, by which both of them appear to be fulfilled. We are led to this view of the dates, not by choice, but from necessity. Since Daniel, the prophetic statesman, the man greatly beloved, has given us a series of numbers, from the first appearance of Antichrist, till the first year of the millennium, which answers exactly to one chain of the providences; since John, the prophetic divine, the disciple whom Jesus loved, has given us a prophetic number, which agrees to the other operations of providence, and both terminate at the same year; and since John has given us another number, descriptive of the secular beast's age at Antichrist's rise, and Providence has furnished us with two conspicuous eras of the secular beast, when he entered on the scene of prophecy, and when his power was established in the east, between each of which, and the times when Antichrist was placed in his seat, and was afterwards confirmed in it, there are precisely 666 years; we are encouraged to make this application of the numbers to the events, and to look and hope for their consummation, in 1867.

The judicious writer of this paper candidly says; "But be it remembered, that in all the calculations, it is not intended to assert any thing dogmatically." It becomes us all, in treating subjects of this kind, to say the same thing. Those Old and New Testament predictions, relative to Antichrist, consisting of so many parts, referring to such numerous and important transactions, and extending to so long a time; predictions to which so much attention has been given, on which so many have written, and concerning which so many different opinions have been entertained, must present themselves to the mind of an inquirer into their meaning, as a subject of difficult investigation. A strong desire of the happy time which their accomplishment will introduce, may insensibly dispose us to antedate the period of their fulfilment. A sense of the number of the events, which it may be supposed are yet to take place before this desirable day can dawn, may have a secret and powerful influence in determining us to postpone the date of this glorious season. The present dispensations of providence, being mixed with indications of its speedy approach, and with visible obstructions to its coming, may either excite in us too sanguine expectations, or fill our minds with too much despondency. The same person may be at one time under the influence of the former, and at another time he may be affected with the latter. On this momentous concern, Christians should think soberly, should live by the faith of the Son of God, should wait on him for the accomplishment of his word, should pray earnestly for the prosperity of the church, should commit to

God the accomplishment of his own word, and should live under the daily impressions of death, judgment, and eternity.

There is reason to believe, that the Church will not be kept long in suspense, concerning those important matters. If nothing of a singular nature take place, either among the Jews, or among the European nations, in, or about the year 1822; and if all things continue in their present situation, after that time, Christians may conclude that there is some mistake in the above calculations. But if a visible shaking among the dry bones of the scattered nation of the seed of Israel shall take place about that time; or, if the tranquillity of Europe shall then be disturbed, and nation shall again rise up against nation, and kingdom against kingdom, this may be considered as a presage of the last sorrows, and the church may lift up her head and rejoice, for the day of her redemption will appear to be drawing nigh.

The church will never be able to attain, with perfect certainty, the knowledge of the termination of those times, till the predictions themselves are fulfilled. We ought to enquire into these things, we should also form an opinion concerning them, we are warranted, with humility, even to make this known to others; but we should carefully avoid presumptuous and dogmatical assertions. This partial uncertainty, under which the Lord is pleased to place his church, has not, in itself, any tendency to darken our knowledge of the church's happiness, to weaken our faith in it, or to discourage our hope of its coming. From the revelation of those things to us in the Divine word, we are furnished with as ample means for knowing its nature, for believing its truth, and for hoping for it at the Lord's time, as if we knew the day and the hour, when all those things shall be fulfilled. Neither can this uncertainty have any tendency, in itself to damp our spiritual concern, about the coming of this season; or to paralyze our active endeavours for promoting the interests of our Redeemer's kingdom. It has, however, a blessed tendency to increase our humility and dependence on God; to enlarge our hearts in waiting on him, and watching for his coming; to excite us to search the Scriptures, to meditate, to pray, and to talk to one another concerning his doings; and to obey the command, to improve the information, and to believe the promises, which are contained in the Apostle's words, with respect both to our own salvation, and the church's enlargement: "Cast not away, therefore, your confidence, which hath great recompense of reward. For ye have need of patience; that, after ye have done the will of God, ye might receive the promise. For yet a little while, and he that shall come will come, and will not tarry. Now the just shall live by faith."

From the things that are coming to pass in our times, it is the Divine call to the followers of Jesus; "Prepare to meet thy God, O Israel." The saints, who exercise aright their spiritual wisdom, will be making constant preparation for ordinances and providences, for death and a future state. The church may look for a season of public calamities, and a day of glorious deliverance. Since the cessation of bloody wars, the nations, especially our own, have suffered, in different ways, unparalleled distress. There is reason to fear, that at one time or another, the storm will increase. For this we should make preparation. The exercise of faith in Jesus as our Saviour, and in God as our Father and Portion in him, should be our study; saying, "Yea, in the shadow of thy wings will I make my refuge, until these calamities be overpast." Freedom from immoderate attachment to worldly enjoyments should also be our concern; hearkening to the Divine call, "Seekest thou great things for thyself? seek them not; for, behold, I will bring evil upon all flesh, saith the Lord." A scriptural view of God's design in all the judgments of his hand constitutes a part of this preparation; "The Lord's voice crieth unto the city, and the man of wisdom shall see thy name." Cleaving to the truths of the gospel in our profession, and to the precepts of the holy law in our practice, make an important part of this preparation which is required of us. We should also seek preparation for the church's deliverance. When the mind is deeply affected with a conviction of the glory that shall be given to God, the honour that shall redound to Christ, and the felicity that shall be brought to men, by the church's enlargement; when the heart is filled with desire that Satan's kingdom, in all its forms, may fall like lightning from heaven; and when these impressions constrain to prayer, expectation, and zealous concern that the Sun of righteousness may arise upon the nations with healing under his wings, the Christian has some comfortable preparation for that happy day, "When the light of the moon shall be as the light of the sun, and the light of the sun shall be sevenfold, as the light of seven days, in the day that the Lord bindeth up the breach of his people, and healeth the stroke of their wound."

THE END.

Young, Gallie, & Co. Printers, Glasgow.

www.ingramcontent.com/pod-product-compliance
Lightning Source LLC
Chambersburg PA
CBHW030558300426
44111CB00009B/1021

* 9 7 8 3 3 3 7 1 4 8 5 2 2 *